HEALTH CARE ISSUES, COSTS AND ACCESS

MEDICARE, HEALTH CARE DELIVERY AND PAYMENT REFORM RECOMMENDATIONS

Health Care Issues, Costs and Access

Additional books in this series can be found on Nova's website under the Series tab.

Additional E-books in this series can be found on Nova's website under the E-books tab.

HEALTH CARE ISSUES, COSTS AND ACCESS

MEDICARE, HEALTH CARE DELIVERY AND PAYMENT REFORM RECOMMENDATIONS

LEONORE GATI
AND
TRAVIS PADILLA
EDITORS

Nova Science Publishers, Inc.
New York

For permission to use material from this book please contact us:
Telephone 631-231-7269; Fax 631-231-8175
Web Site: http://www.novapublishers.com

Additional color graphics may be available in the e-book version of this book.

Library of Congress Cataloging-in-Publication Data

ISBN 978-1-62100-050-1

Published by Nova Science Publishers, Inc. † New York

CONTENTS

PREFACE

As part of its mandate from Congress, each June the Medicare Payment Advisory Commission reports on Medicare payment systems and on issues affecting the Medicare program, including changes in health care delivery and the market for health care services. In this book, several issues are examined, including payments for physician services, the design of Medicare's traditional fee-for-service (FFS) benefit package and its impact on beneficiaries; Medicare's technical assistance to health care providers for quality improvement; improving coordination of the care of beneficiaries dually eligible for Medicare and Medicaid and the variation in private-sector payment rates for services across and within markets.

Chapter 1 - As part of its mandate from the Congress, each June the Commission reports on Medicare payment systems and on issues affecting the Medicare program, including changes in health care delivery and the market for health care services. In this report, authors examine several issues within Medicare itself, including: payments for physician services, with one chapter that considers alternatives to the sustainable growth rate (SGR) system and another on ways to improve payment accuracy and promote appropriate use of ancillary services; the design of Medicare's traditional fee-for-service (FFS) benefit package and its impact on beneficiaries and the program overall; and Medicare's technical assistance to health care providers for quality improvement.

Chapter 2 - Each year since 2002, the statutory method for determining the annual updates to the Medicare physician fee schedule, known as the sustainable growth rate (SGR) system, has resulted in a reduction in the reimbursement rates (or a "negative update"). With the exception of 2002, when a 4.8% decrease was applied, Congress has passed a series of bills to override the reductions. The SGR system was established because of the concern that the Medicare fee schedule itself would not adequately constrain overall increases in spending for physicians' services. While the fee schedule limits the amount that Medicare will pay for each service, there are no limits on the volume or mix of services. The SGR system was intended to serve as a restraint on aggregate spending. If expenditures over a period are less than the cumulative spending target for the period, the update is increased. However, if spending exceeds the cumulative spending target over a certain period, future updates are reduced to bring spending back in line with the target.

In: Medicare, Health Care Delivery and Payment Reform ... ISBN: 978-1-62100-050-1
Editors: Leonore Gati and Travis Padilla

Chapter 1

MEDICARE AND THE HEALTH CARE DELIVERY SYSTEM: REPORT TO THE CONGRESS*

Medicare Payment Advisory Commission

The Medicare Payment Advisory Commission (MedPAC) is an independent congressional agency established by the Balanced Budget Act of 1997 (P.L. 105–33) to advise the U.S. Congress on issues affecting the Medicare program. In addition to advising the Congress on payments to health plans participating in the Medicare Advantage program and providers in Medicare's traditional fee-for-service program, MedPAC is also tasked with analyzing access to care, quality of care, and other issues affecting Medicare.

The Commission's 17 members bring diverse expertise in the financing and delivery of health care services. Commissioners are appointed to three-year terms (subject to renewal) by the Comptroller General and serve part time. Appointments are staggered; the terms of five or six Commissioners expire each year. The Commission is supported by an executive director and a staff of analysts, who typically have backgrounds in economics, health policy, and public health.

MedPAC meets publicly to discuss policy issues and formulate its recommendations to the Congress. In the course of these meetings, Commissioners consider the results of staff research, presentations by policy experts, and comments from interested parties. (Meeting transcripts are available at www.medpac.gov.) Commission members and staff also seek input on Medicare issues through frequent meetings with individuals interested in the program, including staff from congressional committees and the Centers for Medicare & Medicaid Services (CMS), health care researchers, health care providers, and beneficiary advocates.

Two reports—issued in March and June each year—are the primary outlets for Commission recommendations. In addition to annual reports and occasional reports on subjects requested by the Congress, MedPAC advises the Congress through other avenues, including comments on reports and proposed regulations issued by the Secretary of the Department of Health and Human Services, testimony, and briefings for congressional staff.

---

* This is an edited, reformatted and augmented version of a Medicare Payment Advisory Commission publication, dated June 2011.

June 15, 2011

The Honorable Joseph R. Biden
President of the Senate
U.S. Capitol
Washington, DC 20510

The Honorable John A. Boehner
Speaker of the House
U.S. House of Representatives
U.S. Capitol
Room H-232
Washington, DC 20515

Dear Mr. Vice President and Mr. Speaker:

I am pleased to submit the Medicare Payment Advisory Commission's June 2011 *Report to the Congress: Medicare and the Health Care Delivery System*. This report fulfills the Commission's legislative mandate to evaluate Medicare payment issues and to make recommendations to the Congress.

The report contains seven chapters. Four chapters examine issues within Medicare itself:

- One chapter considers alternatives to the sustainable growth rate system, which has known flaws and currently requires rates for physician and other health professional services to be cut about 30 percent in the 2012 fee schedule.
- One chapter makes recommendations to improve payment accuracy and promote appropriate use of in-office ancillary services such as diagnostic imaging that have seen significant growth in recent years and reached high, and possibly inappropriate, levels of utilization.
- One chapter makes recommendations to fundamentally change Medicare's technical assistance to health care providers for quality improvement to better complement recent payment policy innovations and improve the quality of care beneficiaries receive.
- One chapter describes the design of Medicare's traditional fee-for-service benefit package and its impact on beneficiaries and the program overall.

Three chapters examine aspects of the broader health care system. They include a chapter on improving care coordination for beneficiaries dually eligible for Medicare and Medicaid, a chapter on the function of federally qualified health centers and how these entities intersect with the Medicare program, and a chapter on variation in private-sector payment rates for services across and within markets.

In an appendix, as required by law, we review the Centers for Medicare & Medicaid Services' preliminary estimate of the update to payments under the physician fee schedule for 2012.

I hope you find this report useful as the Congress continues to grapple with the difficult task of controlling the growth of Medicare spending while preserving beneficiaries' access to high-quality care.

Sincerely,

Glenn M. Hackbarth, J.D.

Enclosure

ACKNOWLEDGMENTS

This report was prepared with the assistance of many people. Their support was key as the Commission considered policy issues and worked toward consensus on its recommendations.

Despite a heavy workload, staff members of the Centers for Medicare & Medicaid Services were particularly helpful during preparation of the report. We thank Melanie Bella, Kent Clemens, Jennifer Coleman, Thomas Hamilton, Marc Hartstein, Paul McGann, George Mills, Danielle Moon, Jerry Mulcahy, and Liz Richter.

The Commission also received valuable insights and assistance from others in government, industry, and the research community who generously offered their time and knowledge. They include Shawn Bloom, Monica Brenner, Rich Bringewatt, Christine Brudevold, Pam Curtis, Maurine Dennis, Iola D'Souza, Jessica Farb, Nancy Foster, Mark Gibson, Kurt Gillis, Paul Ginsburg, Lisa Goldstein, Daniel Hawkins, Bob Houchens, Lori Housman, Rebecca Kelly, Todd Ketch, Leighton Ku, Jim Macrae, Sandy Marks, Sharon McIlrath, Colleen Meiman, Cynthia Moran, Tom Morris, Walter Ochinko, Christie Peters, Chris Queram, Randy Ricktor, Sue Rohan, Sherry Smith, Gerry Smolka, Bruce Steinwald, Jane Sung, Curt Thorne, Margaret Vanamringe, Jim Verdier, Robert Wachter, and Brian Whitman.

Once again, the programmers at Social and Scientific Systems provided highly capable assistance to Commission staff. In particular, we appreciate the hard work of Aaron Aamodt, Valerie Aschenbach, Po-Lun Chou, Daksha Damera, Weiwei Han, Ed Hock, Deborah Johnson, Sanee Maphungphong, Cindy Martinez-Saiontz, John May, Shelly Mullins, Leon Roberts, Bryan Sayer, Mary Beth Spittel, Charles Thomson, Susan Tian, and Beny Wu.

Finally, the Commission wishes to thank Cay Butler and Hannah Fein for their help in editing and producing this report.

EXECUTIVE SUMMARY

As part of its mandate from the Congress, each June the Commission reports on Medicare payment systems and on issues affecting the Medicare program, including changes in health care delivery and the market for health care services. In this report, we examine several issues within Medicare itself, including:

- payments for physician services, with one chapter that considers alternatives to the sustainable growth rate (SGR) system and another on ways to improve payment accuracy and promote appropriate use of ancillary services;
- the design of Medicare's traditional fee-for-service (FFS) benefit package and its impact on beneficiaries and the program overall; and
- Medicare's technical assistance to health care providers for quality improvement.

We also examine aspects of the broader health care system, including:

- improving coordination of the care of beneficiaries dually eligible for Medicare and Medicaid,
- the function of federally qualified health centers (FQHCs) and how they intersect with the Medicare program, and
- variation in private-sector payment rates for services across and within markets.

In an appendix, as required by law, we review CMS's preliminary estimate of the update to payments under the physician fee schedule for 2012.

The Commission continues to be concerned with the sustainability of the Medicare program and continues to explore every avenue for protecting the access of Medicare beneficiaries to high-quality care while reducing the rate of growth in Medicare expenditures. Some efficiency can be derived from stronger incentives to better coordinate care and to use high-value versus low-value services. This report identifies opportunities to better coordinate care by increasing the emphasis on primary care in the physician fee schedule (discussed in Chapter 1 on the SGR), by coordinating services for beneficiaries dually eligible for Medicare and Medicaid, by changing the quality infrastructure, and through the use of FQHCs. It also considers changing incentives for the use of high-value versus low-value care by changing the benefit structure in traditional Medicare and by making payment for in-office ancillary services more accurate. We will continue to examine Medicare's payment systems and to reevaluate them in light of changes in the broader health care system. We will also look for opportunities to get good value for the program's expenditures and to move away from FFS payment systems that pay providers more when they deliver more services without regard to the quality or value of those services.

The Sustainable Growth Rate System: Policy Considerations for Adjustments and Alternatives

In current law, a formulaic system—the SGR system— requires rates for physician and other health professional services to be cut about 30 percent in 2012. Although the Congress has repeatedly taken legislative action in recent years to override most of the SGR's fee schedule reductions, these "fixes" have been temporary and the frequent need to override increasingly steeper cuts is undermining provider and patient confidence in Medicare, potentially jeopardizing beneficiaries' future access to care.

As discussed in Chapter 1, there are two fundamental problems with the current SGR system. First, the formula aggregates spending across all physicians and practitioners who furnish services to Medicare beneficiaries and, therefore, does not provide incentives at a more granular level (e.g., individual physicians, group practices) to control volume growth or improve care quality. Accordingly, the current construct does little to counter the volume incentives that are inherent in FFS payments. Second, the budget cost of replacing or restructuring the SGR is very high. According to the Congressional Budget Office, eliminating the SGR fee cuts and replacing them with a 10-year freeze in fee schedule rates would cost $300 billion or more. The Commission is committed to helping the Congress continue to find budgetary offsets within Medicare. For example, some Medicare policy changes—such as lower updates in other sectors, as recommended in our March 2011 report—could partially offset this amount. It is unlikely, however, that the full offset needed to eliminate the SGR cuts can be found easily in Medicare within the applicable budget window.

In considering replacement of the SGR system, a fundamental issue is whether to maintain an expenditure target—either narrowly (i.e., in the physician fee schedule) or more broadly throughout all of Medicare. Commissioners have expressed a concern that SGR targets currently are borne solely by physicians and clinical practitioners and have discussed how broader targets would spread cost restraints across sectors. However, a broader expenditure target could have the same flaws as the SGR system: little incentive at the individual provider level to control the volume of services and, if volume trends are not restrained, a need for large-scale, formulaic rate reductions.

Replacing the SGR and expenditure targets with a different payment structure—without the current scheduled cuts— presents an opportunity to introduce needed payment reforms. That is, in exchange for eliminating the future fee cuts, reforms could be made in FFS Medicare to improve the accuracy of payments under the physician fee schedule, to increase payments for cognitive (or nonprocedural) services relative to procedural services, and to give the Secretary discretion to adjust payments. For example, research shows that at least some of the fee schedule's payment rates are likely too high, perhaps by a wide margin. The Congress could require that the Secretary identify and reduce payments for overpriced services. More precisely, the update for all physicians could be made contingent on the Secretary identifying and reducing the relative values for overpriced services. The amount of the reduction necessary for a full update would be set in law. Reforms could also include steps toward delivery system reform and alternative payment models such as accountable care organizations, medical homes, and bundling.

While the prospect of replacing the SGR could serve as a vehicle for hastening at least some elements of reform, it may not be necessary to delay an SGR replacement until all the elements of reform are fully implemented. Reform is not a single event. It is a multipart process that unfolds gradually. In the meantime, last-minute SGR "fixes" are taking a toll. Considering the time and effort that will be involved in determining how to structure future payments for physician and other health professional services, interim fee schedule updates should apply for a minimum of one year—ideally at least two years—to provide stability for CMS, claims-processing contractors, and the practitioners who bill Medicare.

Improving Payment Accuracy and Appropriate Use of Ancillary Services

An exception to the Ethics in Patient Referrals Act allows physicians to provide imaging, clinical laboratory tests, physical therapy, and radiation therapy in their offices. This provision is known as the in-office ancillary services exception.

In Chapter 2, we find that physician investments in diagnostic testing equipment have contributed to rapid growth of these services under the physician fee schedule and resulted in levels of utilization that are likely to include unnecessary services. On the one hand, the Commission recognizes that many of these services enable physicians to diagnose and treat illness with greater speed and precision and, in some cases, with greater convenience for patients. On the other hand, there is strong evidence that physicians who own imaging equipment generate more service volume. In addition, several types of imaging are usually not provided on the same day as an office visit, which raises questions about patient convenience. Rapid volume growth contributes to Medicare's growing financial burden on taxpayers and beneficiaries, leads to concerns about the accuracy of physician fee schedule payment rates, and raises questions about inappropriate use.

But physician self-referral in and of itself is not the problem. Rather, physician self-referral of ancillary services leads to higher volume when combined with FFS payment systems, which reward higher volume, and mispricing, which makes some services more profitable than others. The preferred long-term approach to address self-referral is to develop payment systems under which providers are rewarded for constraining volume growth while improving the quality of care. Because it will take several years to develop new payment systems, we recommend the following policies that could be adopted sooner:

- The Secretary should accelerate and expand efforts to combine into a single payment rate multiple discrete services often furnished together during the same encounter by the same provider. The payment rates for these comprehensive codes should reflect efficiencies in physician work and practice expense that occur when two or more services are provided together.
- The Congress should direct the Secretary to account for efficiencies that occur in an imaging study's professional component when multiple imaging services are provided to the same patient by a single practitioner. This policy would reduce the payment rate for the second and subsequent services performed in the same session.
- • The Congress should direct the Secretary to reduce the physician work component of imaging and other diagnostic tests that are ordered and performed by the same practitioner. This policy would account for efficiencies that occur in those cases (e.g., reviewing the patient's history). This recommendation would apply in all settings, including physicians' offices and hospitals.

The savings from these three recommendations should be redistributed to other physician fee schedule services.

We also recommend that the Congress direct the Secretary to establish a prior notification and prior authorization program for practitioners who order substantially more advanced diagnostic imaging services than their peers.

In the first stage, prior notification, CMS would compare outlier physicians' use of imaging to evidence-based clinical guidelines and educate physicians about the appropriate use of imaging. It is possible that providers could use clinical decision support systems (DSS) instead of participating in a prior notification program as long as the DSS uses the same guidelines as CMS and providers transmit data to CMS. In the second stage, outlier physicians who order imaging inappropriately would be required to participate in a prior authorization program, in which CMS or a contractor would review and approve their requests to order imaging services before they are provided. Outlier physicians who order imaging appropriately would not be subject to prior authorization. This flexibility would help ensure appropriate use of imaging by both self-referring and non-self-referring practitioners without subjecting all providers to prior authorization.

The Commission remains concerned about the potential for self-referral in an FFS context to lead to higher volume. Therefore, if these recommendations and delivery system reforms are not successful at stemming the growth of ancillary services and their inappropriate use, we may revisit options to narrow the in-office ancillary services exception.

Medicare's Fee-for-Service Benefit Design

The Commission has been examining reform of the traditional benefit package for several years, and we present our current findings in Chapter 3. Our objective is to give beneficiaries better protection against high out-of pocket (OOP) spending but at the same time promote incentives for them to weigh their use of discretionary care without discouraging needed care. A further objective is to slow the growth of Medicare spending so that the program will be sustainable, recognizing that cost-sharing changes alone will not fully accomplish this objective.

The current FFS benefit design includes a relatively high deductible for inpatient stays, a relatively low deductible for physician and outpatient care, and a cost-sharing requirement of 20 percent for most physician care and outpatient services. Under this design, no upper limit exists on the amount of Medicare cost-sharing expenses a beneficiary can incur. If not supplemented with additional coverage, the FFS benefit design makes Medicare beneficiaries face substantial financial risk and may discourage the use of valuable care.

To guard against the risk of high OOP expenses, more than 90 percent of beneficiaries take up supplemental coverage or have Medicaid, which mute the effect of OOP costs. However, researchers agree that Medicare beneficiaries with supplemental coverage tend to have higher use of services and spending than those with no supplemental coverage. As currently structured, many supplemental plans cover all or nearly all of Medicare's cost sharing, which removes any price sensitivity beneficiaries might have and leads to higher spending. Most costs of increased utilization are borne by the Medicare program.

In the short term, incremental changes to the FFS benefit, such as adding a cap to beneficiaries' OOP costs, could reduce financial risk for beneficiaries. At the same time, requiring supplemental policies to have fixed-dollar copayments for services such as office visits and emergency room use, could lead to reductions in use of Medicare services sufficient to help finance the addition of an OOP cap. These changes could be coupled with exceptions that waive cost sharing for services in certain circumstances—for example, if evidence identified them as leading to better health outcomes. The changes could also include cost-sharing protections for low-income beneficiaries so that they would not forgo needed care. In total, these changes would be costly unless specifically designed to be budget neutral.

However, incremental changes may not be sufficient to create a modern benefit design. For the longer term, the goal would be to design a benefit that supports innovations in provider payments and changes in health care delivery. Some payers have initiated innovative benefit designs to steer enrollees toward high-value care. We interviewed public and private payers and identified four strategies they use to achieve this goal: lowering cost sharing for high-value services, raising cost sharing for low-value services, creating financial incentives for enrollees to see high-performing or low-cost providers, and providing incentives for enrollees to adopt healthier behaviors. The Commission will continue to consider the need to move toward benefit designs that give individuals incentives to use higher value care and discourage them from using lower value care.

Enhancing Medicare's Technical Assistance to and Oversight of Providers

In recent years, the Commission has recommended numerous payment policy changes to encourage quality improvement, including pay for performance, medical homes, penalties for high rates of hospital readmissions, and bundled payment. In Chapter 4, the Commission concludes that additional policy levers—technical assistance and conditions of participation—could be redesigned to better complement and support the intent of recent changes in payment policy and contribute to quality improvement.

The record of Medicare's primary vehicle for improving quality, the quality improvement organizations (QIOs), has been uneven. The Commission recommends fundamental changes to the current QIO program to:

- give providers and communities the choice of who assists them and flexibility in how they use quality improvement resources,
- increase the number and variety of technical assistance entities that can assist providers and communities to introduce a greater range of choices for assistance in quality improvement, and
- make technical assistance to low-performing providers and community initiatives a high priority as a strategy to complement payment policy and address persistent health care disparities.

We recognize that these recommendations are substantial and will require considerable effort on the part of CMS to implement. However, given the pronounced need for quality improvement, Medicare must try a new approach. Instead of a standing organization in every state financed by the federal government to ask providers to participate in quality improvement activities, funding would be made available directly to providers and communities to be used by them to purchase technical assistance in the market. Recently enacted payment incentives and increasing transparency of performance on quality measures should motivate providers to seek the most effective technical assistance for quality improvement.

In addition, we recommend:

- updating the conditions of participation so that the requirements incorporate and emphasize evidence-based measures of quality care,

- increasing accountability of providers by expanding CMS's use of interventions that promote system-wide remediation of quality problems among persistently low-performing providers, and
- increasing public recognition of high-performing providers that participate in learning networks to assist low-performing providers.

This package of recommendations should complement recent payment policy innovations and lead to substantial improvement in the quality of care beneficiaries receive.

Coordinating Care for Dual-Eligible Beneficiaries

Beneficiaries who qualify for Medicare and Medicaid often have complex care needs that result in high program spending, yet the care furnished to them is typically uncoordinated. In June 2010, the Commission reported that combined program spending on dual-eligible beneficiaries varied considerably by number of chronic conditions, whether the beneficiary had dementia, and whether the beneficiary received care in a nursing home. It noted that care for dual-eligible beneficiaries could be improved by integrating care financing across Medicare and Medicaid and coordinating care delivery across sectors.

In Chapter 5, we report on programs with the potential to integrate and coordinate services provided to their enrollees. Commission staff conducted interviews and site visits to understand how integrated programs coordinate care and what lessons can be learned. Under integrated programs, either a managed care organization or a provider receives capitated payments from the Medicare and Medicaid programs and assumes risk for the full spectrum of the dual-eligible beneficiaries' care. Some care coordination programs retain the FFS system and pay providers a small monthly care coordination fee. While these programs do not align the financial and care management incentives as the capitated programs do, they represent a step toward integration of Medicare and Medicaid benefits.

We found that these programs vary considerably in their design and in the scope of services they manage. No single approach seems likely to fit in every state, and the lack of comparable outcomes research on most approaches leaves open the question of which models are more effective. Nevertheless, we found two constants. First, administrators of integrated programs told us that the flexibility of capitated payments allowed them to deliver the mix of medical and social services each patient needed. Second, all the programs were similar in a number of key care coordination activities, including care transitions, medication reconciliation, patient education, and patient assessment with respect to risk for hospitalization or nursing home placement.

Expanding enrollment was a challenge for many of the programs. Program officials had ideas about how to grow enrollment but acknowledged that these ideas were likely to result in only incremental expansion. Many interviewees told us that requirements to recruit on a person-by-person basis were a key limitation to expansion of these programs. State officials also consistently commented on the lack of financial incentives for states to pursue integrated programs, most notably that states cannot share in Medicare savings.

Another avenue for coordination is dual-eligible special needs plans (D–SNPs), which are Medicare Advantage (MA) plans that target their enrollment to dual-eligible beneficiaries. D–SNPs have the potential to integrate and coordinate the services covered by both Medicare and Medicaid, but to evaluate whether they are doing so CMS may want to revise its reporting requirements. First, D– SNPs report "models of care" but the information submitted is too general to evaluate the plans' care coordination activities or whether the D–SNPs integrate Medicare and Medicaid services; also, SNPs already report about those activities in their MA applications and in quality reporting. CMS should target and streamline its model-of-care requirements to those key elements that are not available elsewhere. Second, it is not possible to evaluate the quality of care furnished by most D–SNPs. The star rating information for most SNPs is included in the overall reporting under a larger MA contract. In addition, many measures are not publicly reported. Finally, the Commission encourages CMS to shift its quality focus to publicly reported outcome measures, which would allow for comparisons across MA plans, SNPs, and FFS Medicare.

Federally Qualified Health Centers

FQHCs provide access to primary care in areas where primary care resources are otherwise constrained (designated health care shortage areas). FQHCs are required to be community-centered, not-for-profit organizations that emphasize coordination of care. FQHCs also make use of physician assistants, advanced practice nurses, and clinical nurse midwives where appropriate. Patients at FQHCs are predominantly low income and largely either uninsured or covered by Medicaid.

Chapter 6 focuses on FQHCs for three reasons. First, FQHCs are illustrative of a team-based approach to primary care, relying on advanced practice nurses, physician assistants, and other nonphysician practitioners as well as physicians. Second, FQHCs are required to provide care in medically underserved areas and play a role in meeting primary care capacity challenges in low-density rural areas. Third, Medicare's payment system for FQHCs is changing from a per visit cost-based reimbursement to a prospective payment system (PPS), which will likely result in higher payments, potentially altering their role. We plan to follow the PPS for FQHCs as it develops.

Variation in Private-Sector Payment Rates

In Chapter 7, we examine how payment rates in the private sector vary across and within geographic areas. A better understanding of the dynamics of private health care markets can inform the development of Medicare payment policies. Questions of particular interest are: to what extent are factors such as the market power of providers or insurers affecting the variation in private-payment rates and, if they are major factors that explain the variation, what does that mean for Medicare payment policy and policies that are intended to promote greater integration among providers?

In a preliminary analysis of private-sector payment rates for hospital and physician services, we find wide variation in payment rates geographically for both types of services, with greater differences for hospital services. Payment rates for some physician services—certain imaging services, for example—vary more across areas than others, such as payment rates for office visits and obstetric care. Within a given area, payment rates can vary markedly as well. We found no strong pattern of correlation between rates for physician services and those for hospital services; that is, areas with relatively high rates for physician services do not necessarily have high rates for hospital services, and vice versa.

In future work, we will explore the reasons for variation in payment rates. Factors such as the market structure and relative market power of providers and insurers are likely to affect the payment negotiation process and the resulting payment rates. The exact nature of the relationship between market characteristics and variation in rates is likely to be complex. We plan to continue our data analysis and undertake a more in-depth look at specific markets. We will also seek alternative ways to measure provider and insurer market power and market concentration to examine their effect on variation in private-payment rates.

Review of CMS's Preliminary Estimate of the 2012 Update for Physician and Other Professional Services

In CMS's annual letter to the Commission on the 2012 update to payments for physician and other professional services, the agency's preliminary estimate is –29.5 percent. Most of the prescribed reduction would result from the expiration of a series of temporary payment increases to override negative updates under the SGR formula—which would otherwise update Medicare's payment rates for physician and other professional services. Under current law, the temporary increases expire at the end of 2011, requiring the SGR formula to produce a negative update for 2012.

The appendix provides the Commission's mandated technical review of CMS's estimate. We find that CMS's calculations are correct and that—absent a change in law—expiration of the temporary increases and the formula's update for 2012 are very unlikely to produce an update that differs substantially from –29.5 percent. Some components of the SGR update for 2012 could change between now and when CMS would implement the update in January, but any such changes are likely to be small compared with the total reduction prescribed. While the appendix is limited to technical issues, the Commission has concerns about the SGR as a payment policy. Those concerns are discussed in Chapter 1 of this report.

The Sustainable Growth Rate System: Policy Considerations for Adjustments and Alternatives

Summary

Medicare's payment system for physician and other health professional services is flawed in many ways: It continues to call for unrealistically steep fee cuts, it inherently rewards volume over quality and efficiency, and it favors procedural services over primary care, which has serious implications for the nation's future primary care workforce. The Commission is concerned about these issues, particularly because physicians and other health professionals are often the most important link between beneficiaries and the health care delivery system.

Sustainable Growth Rate System Raises Policy and Budget Concerns

In current law, a formulaic expenditure target system—known as the sustainable growth rate (SGR) system—requires Medicare payment rates for physician and other health professional services to be cut by about 30 percent in 2012. As the size of this cut has grown over much of the last decade, Medicare is confronting mounting frustration in the provider community that could jeopardize beneficiaries' future access to care. Although the Congress has repeatedly taken action to override most of the SGR's prescribed fee schedule reductions, these "fixes" have been temporary, accounting for relatively small periods of time. As a consequence, the frequent need to override increasingly steeper cuts is undermining confidence in the Medicare program.

Beyond the issue of looming payment cuts are two fundamental problems with the current SGR system. The first set of problems relates to its design as a strict budgetary tool, with no mechanism for influencing provider performance toward improved care and prudent use of resources. In comparing total spending with a calculated target, the SGR formula aggregates spending across all physicians furnishing services to Medicare beneficiaries and, therefore, does not provide incentives for individual physician practices to control health care spending or improve care quality. Moreover, the SGR system does little to counter the volume incentives that are inherent in fee-for-service payments.

The second problem policymakers face with respect to the SGR is the cost of replacing or restructuring it. According to the Congressional Budget Office, eliminating the SGR fee cuts and replacing them with a 10-year freeze in fee schedule rates would cost about $300 billion—at a minimum. The Commission is committed to helping the Congress continue to find budgetary offsets within Medicare. For example, some Medicare policy changes—such as smaller updates in other provider sectors, as recommended in our March 2011 report—could partially offset this amount. It is unlikely, however, that the full offset needed to eliminate the SGR cuts can be found easily in Medicare within the applicable budget window.

Expenditure Target Formulas Present Several Issues

In considering replacement of the SGR system, a fundamental issue is whether to maintain an expenditure target—either narrowly (i.e., in the physician fee schedule) or more broadly throughout all of Medicare. Some contend that expenditure target policies offer no method for improving how providers deliver services. Rather, their restraint on payment rates may encourage providers to engage in activities that ultimately result in higher volume and Medicare costs. Others contend that pressure from the SGR has at least resulted in smaller updates and, considering Medicare's fiscal sustainability problems, it is prudent to retain an expenditure target system to have some limit on spending growth and to regularly alert policymakers about growth in Medicare spending. As indicated below, the Commission is discussing whether spending can be constrained by using a more discretionary, targeted approach.

Many Commissioners have expressed a concern that expenditure targets should not be borne solely by physicians and clinical practitioners. The Commission has also discussed how broader targets would spread cost restraints across sectors. Broader expenditure target systems, however, carry many of the same risks as the SGR system. That is, if volume trends are not restrained, a broader expenditure target system could require larger scale rate reductions, depending on the construction of the system's formula. As an alternative to expenditure targets, we may consider a policy that would link payment updates for all physicians to progress in improving the accuracy of payments for selected services. Research discussed in this chapter has shown that at least some of the fee schedule's payment rates are likely too high, perhaps by a wide margin.

SGR Termination Could Be Contingent on a Set of Trade-offs to Improve the Payment System

An alternative to expenditure target systems is to pursue a multipronged strategy with several components, each addressing aspects of Medicare's payment approach for physicians and other health professionals. Aspects to address within the fee-for-service system include the accuracy of fee schedule payments, the Secretary's option to adjust these fees, and the level of payments for cognitive (or nonprocedural) services relative to procedures. Outside the fee-for-service system, additional approaches could include steps toward delivery system reform and alternative payment models such as accountable care organizations, medical homes, and bundling.

Replacing the SGR with a different payment structure—devoid of the scheduled cuts—presents an opportunity to introduce needed payment changes for fee schedule services. That is, in exchange for eliminating future fee cuts, new policies could be implemented that improve and stabilize the fee schedule, restrain cost growth, and promote primary care and better coordination across sectors. The Commission is considering a range of policy ideas for reform:

- Set limited future updates in law, across all fee schedule services.
- Make the above updates contingent on the Secretary identifying and reducing the relative values for overpriced fee schedule services. The net savings the Secretary would achieve from these service-specific reductions would also be defined in law.
- Enhance efforts to continuously improve the accuracy of fee schedule payments, with particular attention to estimates of the time required to provide services.
- Realign payments for physician and other health professionals to help ensure an adequate supply of practitioners in cognitive (nonprocedural) specialties who focus on managing patients with chronic conditions.
- Reform delivery systems to shift payment away from the fee schedule's disproportionate emphasis on procedures and tests and toward payment models focused more on care coordination and population health.

The above is not an exhaustive list of policies that could be considered in replacing the SGR. We will consider other policies as well. However, this set of policies, even if implemented on a staggered basis, represents a path to move away from the SGR and its negative effects. While the prospect of replacing the SGR could serve as a vehicle for hastening at least some elements of reform, a potential SGR replacement need not await full implementation of all reform elements. Reform is not a single event but a multipart process that unfolds over time.

Interim Updates Should Apply for a Minimum of One Year

Considering the time and effort that will be involved in determining how to structure future payments for physician and other health professional services, interim fee schedule updates should apply for a minimum of one year—ideally at least two years—to provide stability for CMS, claims-processing contractors, and practitioners who bill Medicare. Furthermore, these updates should be scheduled well in advance of their applicable time periods to provide certainty about the level of payment. Significant problems arose in 2010 when updates applied to shorter time periods and were so delayed that they had to be applied retroactively. In addition to added administrative costs for CMS's claims processing and cash flow problems for some clinical practices, the most disturbing outcome resulting from the short-term fixes was damage to patients' and providers' confidence in Medicare.

Medicare's payment system for physician and other health professional services is flawed in many ways: It continues to call for unrealistically steep fee cuts (i.e., about 30 percent in 2012), it inherently rewards volume over quality and efficiency, and it favors procedural services over primary care, which has serious implications for the nation's future primary care workforce.

Given the continual threat of fee cuts during much of the past decade, the Commission is concerned that Medicare is facing mounting frustration from the provider community that could jeopardize beneficiaries' future access to physicians and other health professionals. Although the Congress has repeatedly taken legislative action to override most of these fee schedule reductions, these "fixes" have been temporary, accounting for relatively small periods of time. As a consequence, the frequent need to override increasingly steeper cuts is undermining patient and provider confidence in the Medicare program.

Background: What Is the Sustainable growth rate system?

The sustainable growth rate (SGR) system is the formulaic method for annually updating fees for physician and other health professional services. Established by the Balanced Budget Act of 1997, the SGR system was designed to keep aggregate Medicare expenditures for these services on an affordable ("sustainable") trajectory, through an expenditure target approach.

The SGR system sets an expenditure target for growth in Medicare spending on fee schedule services. This target allows for annual Medicare spending to grow at a rate consistent with the sum of four factors—namely, changes in:

- the nation's per capita gross domestic product (GDP),
- the number of beneficiaries enrolled in fee-for-service (FFS) Medicare,
- inflation in practice costs for physicians and other health professionals, and
- spending due to law and regulation.

With respect to the first factor—per capita GDP—the SGR formula essentially allows the volume of fee schedule services to grow at the same rate as per capita GDP. Volume is tightly linked to spending because Medicare pays providers on an FFS basis. Therefore, when the SGR spending target allows for growth in the nation's per capita GDP, the formula allows for the volume of fee schedule services to grow at the same rate. Additionally, the SGR expenditure target is adjusted to account for three other factors: changes in the number of Medicare beneficiaries, changes in physician practice costs, and changes in covered services due to law and regulation. When these rates increase, so does the expenditure target, essentially allowing higher aggregate spending.

To determine fee schedule updates under the SGR, CMS is required, annually, to compare actual cumulative Medicare spending (starting in April 1996) on fee schedule services with the target amount over the same period. If cumulative expenditures equal the cumulative target, the SGR formula sets physician fee updates to the Medicare Economic Index (MEI). However, if expenditures exceed the spending target, the update for the subsequent year is reduced, with the goal of bringing cumulative spending back in line with the target. (The reverse is also true; if cumulative expenditures are less than the target amount, then the subsequent year's update is higher.)

In the first several years of the SGR system, actual expenditures did not exceed spending targets because volume did not grow faster than per capita GDP. Therefore, updates to the physician fee schedule in the early years of the SGR system were at or above the MEI. However, beginning in 2001, actual cumulative expenditures exceeded allowed targets and the discrepancy has grown each year, resulting in a series of ever-larger cuts prescribed under the formula. With the exception of 2002, the Congress has passed a series of bills to override these reductions. The resulting updates have been fairly modest. Overrides that were implemented before 2007 contributed to the amount of dollars that need to be recouped under the SGR formula.

The primary rationale for each override of the SGR cuts has been to preserve beneficiary access to physician services. The reason why the overrides have been short term is that longer term adjustments have higher estimated costs ("scores") and thus require the Congress to find proportionately larger spending offsets. (The text box, p. 8, explains the budgetary costs in further detail.) The most recent override expires on December 31, 2011, after which payments are set to decline under current law by 29.5 percent. Although official estimates have not been released, further prescribed cuts in 2013 and 2014 are also expected. Nevertheless, even the Medicare Trustees refer to the SGR cuts in current law as "unrealistic" (Boards of Trustees 2010).

Why does it cost so much to "fix" the sustainable growth rate system?

Despite general acceptance that multiple consecutive years of large negative updates for physician and other health professional services would be detrimental to beneficiary access to care, longer term proposals to fix the sustainable growth rate (SGR) system face a major hurdle: They carry high budgetary costs ("scores") compared with current law, which assumes that steep payment reductions will occur in the coming years. The estimated scores for some long-term proposals are more than 10 times greater than the cumulated difference between actual and target spending amounts. For instance, although the current cumulated overage in spending compared with the target differs by about $20 billion, the Congressional Budget Office scores a freeze (i.e., a 0 percent update) from 2012 through 2021 at $298 billion.

Why does it cost so much to eliminate the SGR cuts? And more specifically, why is there such a large difference between the cumulated overage and the price of eliminating negative updates through 2021? Two main factors are at play:

- The cumulated overage between actual and target spending compounds every year that the fee reductions are postponed—retrospectively and prospectively. Also, the spending attributable to the 2003–2006 overrides was added to the total amount of dollars that must be recouped in accordance with the SGR formula. Thus, these overrides resulted in increasing the deficit between actual cumulative spending and the SGR cumulative target.

- Under current law, the reduced future fees would become the base for payment levels in all subsequent years. So, while cumulative spending would equal the SGR target after the 30 percent cut, the updates would be based on much lower fees. In other words, a fee that is $100 today is scheduled to drop to $70 in 2012, and subsequent updates would start from the $70 level. Proposals that restore future fees to today's levels or higher have to account for the aggregate cost of each and every year in which fees are above $70—or even less, assuming further cuts in 2013 and 2014. This circumstance highlights that the bulk of the SGR costs stems from averting future cuts rather than making up for past spending above the target.

Recognizing these two factors, we see that the gap between projected spending under current law and projected spending under long-term SGR-modification proposals grows increasingly larger every year. In one administrative action, however, CMS reduced the amount that was needed to be recouped by retroactively removing Part B drugs (generally those administered in a physician's office) from all SGR calculations.

Eliminating the SGR cuts has budgetary ramifications beyond Medicare's payments for physician services. For example, expenditures under the Medicare Advantage (MA) program would increase because the MA capitation payments are tied to fee-for-service benchmark spending. The military's TRICARE expenditures would also rise because its physician reimbursements are based on Medicare's physician fee schedule. Furthermore, since Medicare Part B premiums are required to cover 25 percent of total Part B expenditures, increases in physician reimbursement levels would likewise raise future Part B premiums. Alternatively, if these premiums were not increased, the budgetary score for eliminating the SGR cuts would be significantly higher.

SGR Policy Issues

In previous reports, congressional testimonies, and public deliberations, the Commission has reiterated several widely held criticisms and flaws of the SGR system (Medicare Payment Advisory Commission 2007, Medicare Payment Advisory Commission 2011). A main flaw of the current SGR system is its inability to differentiate among providers; it neither rewards individual practitioners who restrain unnecessary volume growth nor penalizes those who contribute most to inappropriate volume increases.

The SGR also results in a so-called "passive devaluation" problem for specialties that are highly dependent on evaluation and management (E&M) services (such as primary care). That is, procedural specialties can more readily compensate for fee restrictions by generating greater service volume. Under the SGR, this higher volume will likely lead to restraints on fees, further disadvantaging E&M-dependent specialties that are less able to increase volume. Moreover, the SGR does little to counter the volume incentives that are inherent in FFS payments. While some contend that the existence of the SGR system exerted pressure to restrain fee updates in recent years, it is not clear that it lowered total spending.

Perhaps an even greater problem with the SGR system is its toxic effect on Medicare's reputation. Providers have expressed deep frustration and stress attributed to uncertain future Medicare payments, short-term "fixes," and looming payment cuts in the balance. Often referred to as temporary fixes, legislative SGR overrides have accounted for relatively small periods of time. For 2011, the Congress passed a 1-year override; for 2010, two 1-month overrides, two 2-month overrides, and one 6-month override. While these stopgap measures successfully averted payment cuts, their short-term nature was problematic. Moreover, the threat of steep payment cuts continues to loom in the near future.

Therefore, in addition to systemic flaws with the formulaic nature of the SGR system, there is widespread agreement that the updates it has prescribed are unrealistic and untenable. Consequently, the existence of the SGR system, which continues to call for large payment cuts and requires congressional action to override, could jeopardize provider willingness to serve Medicare beneficiaries in the future. The temporary fixes implemented in recent years have created uncertainty, frustration, and financial problems for clinical practices. Furthermore, they add significant administrative costs to CMS's claims-processing activities.

Additional complications arise from the unrealistic updates that remain in current law under the SGR system. Specifically, Medicare's physician fee schedule is used as a benchmark for rate setting in other health programs, such as Medicare Advantage and the military's TRICARE program, as a basis for private payers' fee schedules, and as a tool for provider organizations to measure physician productivity. On a larger scale, regarding future Medicare reforms (such as accountable care organizations (ACOs) and other shared savings initiatives that seek to improve the quality and efficiency of care delivery), it will be important for the Congress and the Secretary to use actual and realistic fee schedule updates when analyzing the potential for these reforms to be effective. If unrealistic updates (i.e., those in current law under the SGR) are used in these analyses, the budget baseline will be artificially low, making it difficult to determine whether payment innovations reduce total spending.

Solving the SGR problem must be considered in light of two fundamental issues, each requiring different policy tools and actions:

- ***Replacement update and payment method***—To address some of the SGR flaws, Medicare needs to structure a stable payment system for physicians and health professionals that rewards practitioners' quality and efficiency to the extent possible. Changes would involve reforming Medicare's payment systems to motivate coordination and collaboration among practitioners rather than volume. At the same time, ongoing efforts should be made to balance compensation among providers and to improve payment accuracy within the fee schedule.
- ***Budgetary ("scoring") issues***—Positive updates for fee schedule services in future years carry high budgetary scores. For an across-the-board freeze (no increase) in updates from 2012 through 2021, the Congressional Budget Office estimates the cost at $298 billion. Estimated costs for an update equal to the MEI over the same time period are higher. Higher still are estimates that include policies in which beneficiaries' Part B premiums are held harmless from this spending increase. Under current law, replacing or changing the SGR to achieve positive updates in the coming years requires offsets in federal spending.[1]

In consideration of these two categories of issues, we briefly discuss several policy opportunities for future updates and for setting Medicare payments on the path to improved care delivery. Then, we examine some issues surrounding the high budget score involved with eliminating the SGR cuts.

Expenditure Target Formulas Raise Several Issues

In considering replacement of the SGR system, a fundamental issue is whether to maintain a formulaic expenditure target component—either as a target covering the fee schedule system or more broadly covering all of FFS Medicare or the entire Medicare program. In general, disagreement about the utility of formulaic expenditure targets exists among policy analysts and experts. Some contend that expenditure target policies offer no method for improving how providers deliver services. Rather, their restraint on payment rates may encourage providers to engage in activities that ultimately result in higher Medicare costs—for example, furnishing services of marginal value or prioritizing services by their profitability, which raises patient access concerns for services that generally have lower profitability, such as nonprocedural services.

Other experts contend that, considering Medicare's fiscal sustainability problems, it is prudent to retain an expenditure target to limit payment rate increases and regularly alert policymakers about growth in Medicare spending. With respect to the SGR, its expenditure target mechanism was likely an influential factor in constraining updates in the past several years. Nevertheless, spending per beneficiary grew much faster than the updates.

In 2001, the Commission recommended that the Congress replace the SGR system and require that the Secretary update physician payments for the coming year based on factors influencing the unit costs of efficiently providing physician services. Under this recommendation, the Commission would examine payment adequacy indicators annually and advise the Congress accordingly—with no expenditure target framework. When the Commission made this recommendation, it would have had little budgetary effect on Medicare spending.

In our 2007 SGR report, the Commission explored alternatives that would eliminate the SGR, restructure its formula, or broaden the expenditure target approach to include all of FFS Medicare (Medicare Payment Advisory Commission 2007). For instance, discussions about restructuring the SGR's formula examined many of the design elements of expenditure target systems, including the following parameters (discussed in detail in our 2007 report cited above):

- the scope of services affected by the expenditure target system;
- the spending growth targets;
- potential variation in spending targets by selected characteristics (e.g., type of service);
- corresponding updates when spending is above, below, or on target;
- the degree of a cumulative aspect in spending calculations; and
- possible exemptions for selected entities such as participants in medical homes.

Many Commissioners have expressed a concern that expenditure targets should not be borne solely by physicians and clinical practitioners. The Commission has also discussed how broader targets would spread cost restraints across sectors. However, they carry many of the same risks as the SGR system. That is, if volume trends are not restrained, a broader expenditure target system could call for larger scale rate reductions, depending on the construction of the system's formula.

Another expenditure target option would link payment updates to progress in improving the accuracy of payments under the physician fee schedule. Research discussed later in this chapter has shown that at least some of the fee schedule payment rates are likely too high, perhaps by a wide margin. To create an action-forcing mechanism, the Congress could require that the Secretary identify and reduce payments for overpriced services. More precisely, the update for all physicians could be contingent on the Secretary identifying and reducing the relative values for overpriced services. The amount of the reduction necessary for a full update would be set in law.

Sgr Termination Could Be Contingent on a Set of Trade-offs to Improve the Payment System

Replacing the SGR with a different payment structure— devoid of the scheduled cuts— presents an opportunity to introduce needed payment changes for fee schedule services. That is, in exchange for eliminating the future fee cuts, new policies that improve and stabilize the fee schedule, restrain cost growth, and promote primary care and better coordination across sectors could be implemented. Such policies could create incentives for high-quality, patient-centric care that would replace current incentives to increase volume and thus could significantly change the status quo.

The Commission is considering a range of policy ideas for reform (Figure 1-1):

- For a specified number of years, Medicare's physician fee schedule updates could be set at modest levels— established in law—to replace the SGR's future fee cuts. Such a statutory series of updates would achieve the same restraint in price growth as has been legislated through SGR overrides in the last several years but with fewer deleterious effects. For instance, it would provide security and stability to providers regarding their payments and would reduce uncertainty about their willingness to accept Medicare patients.

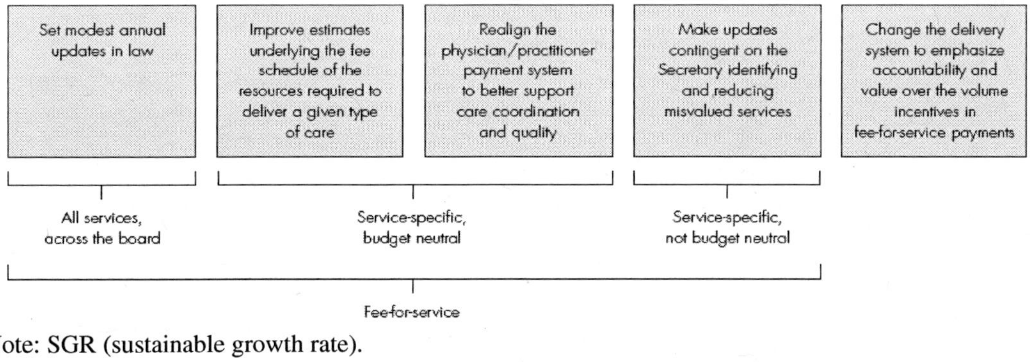

Note: SGR (sustainable growth rate).

Figure 1-1. Typology of policies that could link to replacing the SGR system.

- A comprehensive physician payment policy could include a concerted effort to improve the accuracy of the estimates embedded in the physician fee schedule, specifically those that pertain to the time and intensity required to provide given services. One set of ideas for improving payment accuracy— collecting data from a cohort of practices and other settings where practitioners work—is discussed later in this chapter. Previously, the Commission made recommendations to improve the accuracy of payments for costly imaging services by incorporating more realistic assumptions about equipment use rate in the calculation of payments. Chapter 2 of this report includes specific recommendations on improving the accuracy of payments for ancillary services.
- Appropriate evaluation, management, and coordination of patients' care (among providers and across sectors) are especially crucial for elderly and disabled patients with chronic conditions. Future changes to the payment system for physicians and other health professionals should recognize the importance of these activities in ensuring comprehensive, population-based care for Medicare beneficiaries. Toward that end, we envision some shift of resources from procedural to cognitive services—particularly for physicians and health professionals who focus on managing patients with chronic conditions. This shift would help overcome the relatively lower reimbursements for primary care and ensure a workforce with greater emphasis on generalists. Although payment rates for primary care services (and E&M services, in particular) have increased over the last several years, a concentrated realignment of the payment system is still needed.
- The Commission's longstanding position is that unnecessary growth in the volume of services furnished by physicians and other professionals is driven in part by the overpricing of a number of services in the physician fee schedule. The Congress could require that the Secretary identify and reduce payments for overpriced services, in a non-budget-neutral manner. More specifically, the Congress could make future, across-the-board fee schedule updates contingent on the Secretary identifying and reducing relative values for overpriced services. The amount of net savings needed from such reductions could be set in law.
- Future payment policies should be designed to move toward alternative payment models that focus on population health and coordination of care—such as ACOs, medical homes, bundling, and similar payment models. With existing payment methods, volume growth has remained high—even under the SGR—because of the underlying incentives in FFS reimbursement. New payment models can change those incentives in fundamental ways by establishing accountability for quality and efficient use of resources.

The above list is not an exhaustive list of policies that could be considered in replacing the SGR. We will consider others as well. However, this set of policies, even if implemented on a staggered basis, represents a path to move away from the SGR and its negative effects. Payment reform is not a single event but a multipart process that unfolds over time. Pursuing an SGR replacement policy that incorporates all five or more of these reforms need not await resolution of all policy issues.

While pressure from the SGR may have resulted in smaller annual updates than would have occurred in the absence of the SGR, it has taken a significant toll on providers and beneficiaries in terms of their confidence in the Medicare program. These effects only worsen as the SGR deficit grows and the temporary fixes cover shorter periods of time. Last-minute rescues impose burdens on practitioners, beneficiaries, and CMS administration. Given that the budget score for these rescues will continue to increase, resulting in greater difficulty finding offsets within the budget window to pay for eliminating the SGR, we fear a downward spiral. One option the Commission is considering is to repeal the SGR and pursue a range of policies such as those discussed above.

Budget Issues

Given the cost of replacing the SGR, the Commission is committed to helping the Congress find budgetary offsets within Medicare. The Commission has made numerous recommendations that would produce significant savings, many of which the Congress has embraced. It is unlikely, however, that the full offset needed to eliminate the SGR cuts can be found easily in Medicare within the necessary budget window of time—particularly considering that $575 billion in Medicare savings is already slated for implementation, in accordance with the Patient Protection and Affordable Care Act of 2010 (PPACA) (Foster 2010).

In its March 2011 report, the Commission made recommendations that would produce federal savings to the Medicare program (Medicare Payment Advisory Commission 2011). For example, for 2012 we recommended either payment reductions or payment freezes for home health agencies, skilled nursing facilities, and inpatient rehabilitation facilities. The Commission based these recommendations on careful analysis of several factors, including beneficiaries' access to care, changes in quality over time, and the relationship between practitioners' costs and their Medicare payments. These analyses are described in more detail in the report. In upcoming work, the Commission will continue to analyze other options within Medicare that could help offset the additional spending that would result from eliminating the SGR cuts.

Interim Future Updates Should Apply for a Minimum of One Year

While determining a new way to set updates for fee schedule services, interim payment rates for these services should apply for a minimum of one year—ideally at least two years. Furthermore, these updates should be scheduled well in advance of their applicable time periods. Significant problems arose in 2010 when updates applied to shorter time periods and were so delayed that they had to be applied retroactively. It caused cash flow problems for some clinical practices and added administrative costs for CMS's claims processing. Overall, the most disturbing outcome of multiple short-term fixes could be damage to patients' and providers' confidence in the Medicare program.

Improving the Accuracy of Payments to Physicians and Other Health Professionals

Improving the accuracy of prices in Medicare's payment systems is an urgent concern. Overpriced services are subject to being overprovided when they become more profitable than other services. In the case of services furnished by physicians and other professionals, overpricing can skew compensation levels—favoring some practitioners at the expense of others. Distorted compensation can discourage new practitioners from entering certain specialties, such as primary care, and may induce some physicians to retire when they might otherwise remain in practice.

Improving payment accuracy is also a step in the evolution of Medicare's payment systems. Medical homes, bundled payments, ACOs, and other innovations would move payment systems away from FFS payment, with its incentives to provide services based solely on volume, and toward systems of providers who accept some level of financial risk for the services they provide. In the meantime, accurate prices under Medicare's current FFS system—together with comparative effectiveness information, measures that link payment to quality, and measurement of resource use—are needed to ensure that providers have incentives to furnish low-cost, high-quality care for Medicare beneficiaries. Accurate FFS prices could serve as building blocks for units of payment—such as bundled payments—that are a composite of payments for discrete services (Berenson 2010). By overcoming current distortions, accurate prices may affect the willingness of some physicians to participate in ACOs and other innovative payment arrangements.

For services furnished by physicians and other professionals, Medicare's FFS payment system is the program's physician fee schedule. The fee schedule is designed to account for differences among services in resource costs classified into three categories: the work of the practitioner, practice expense, and professional liability insurance. This chapter focuses primarily on the accuracy of the payments for practitioner work, which account for about 48 percent of fee schedule payments, and considers the accuracy of payments for practice expense, which account for another 47 percent of fee schedule payments.[2]

Research for CMS and the Assistant Secretary for Planning and Evaluation of the Department of Health and Human Services has shown that the time estimates (an important factor in the practitioner work category) are likely too high for some services (Cromwell et al. 2010, Cromwell et al. 2007, McCall et al. 2006). Overstated time estimates can cause a service to be overvalued and—because changes in fee schedule payment rates are budget neutral—other services to be undervalued. In addition, as discussed in Chapter 2 of this report, research by the Government Accountability Office has found that Medicare's physician fee schedule does not adequately account for efficiencies that occur when a physician furnishes multiple services for the same patient on the same day (Government Accountability Office 2009). Taken together, these research findings lead the Commission to have a deep concern about the accuracy of the time estimates and to conclude that the time data are flawed.

Pricing accuracy has taken on greater importance under the PPACA requirement that the Secretary establish a process to validate the fee schedule's relative value units (RVUs). The validation process is to include a sampling of services that meet criteria such as rapid growth, use of new technologies, and substantial changes in practice expenses or that meet other criteria for identifying services that may be misvalued. The process is to consider work elements such as time, mental effort, and other factors. As part of the process, the law gives the Secretary the authority to make appropriate adjustments to the RVUs for practitioner work. CMS sees validation of RVUs as a new requirement and one that would complement the ongoing efforts of the Relative Value Scale Update Committee (RUC) to provide recommendations on valuation of fee schedule services.[3]

The Commission is concerned that the process for developing time estimates relies on surveys conducted by physician specialty societies and that those societies and their members have a financial stake in the process. To address the issue, the Commission is examining a specific alternative to the time estimates.

After working with a contractor to consider alternatives, we find that CMS could replace the current time estimates with data collected from physician offices and other settings where practitioners provide care. The data will not be collected easily, however, if the methodologic decision is made to collect data on the time practitioners spend on each discrete billable service. Nonetheless, there may be approaches to collecting data that reduce the burden for CMS and practitioners and that make the effort feasible.

While collecting objective time data has evident challenges, we do not consider it reasonable and prudent to base more than $60 billion in annual Medicare spending on the current process of collecting time data by specialty societies. While the RUC does attempt to adjudicate the time estimates and the resulting RVUs, the process lacks an objective basis for modifying the time estimates. Both the RUC's and CMS's responsibilities would be furthered with timely provision of objective data, with the limitations of these data understood.

Ensuring the accuracy of estimates for the practice expense component of a fee is also important. There are two data problems in developing these estimates. First, the estimates rely in part on information about the prices practitioners pay for equipment and supplies, and CMS does not have a data source that allows for regular updating of these prices. Second, the estimates also rely on data obtained from a survey on total practice costs incurred by practitioners, and CMS has not articulated a strategy for keeping the survey data up to date. Our conclusion is that it is feasible to collect practice expense data while collecting data to replace the time estimates for practitioner work.

Aassigning Relative Values to Services Furnished by Physicians and Other Health Professionals

The fee schedule's RVUs account for the relative costliness of the resources used to provide services: the work of physicians and other health professionals, practice expenses, and professional liability insurance (PLI) expenses. The RVUs for practitioner work are a scale rating the time, mental effort and judgment, technical skill and physical effort, and stress associated with providing each service relative to other services. The RVUs for practice expense are measures of the expenses practitioners incur for office space, supplies and equipment, and nonphysician clinical and administrative staff. The PLI RVUs are based on the premiums physicians pay for professional liability insurance, also known as medical malpractice insurance.

Resource-based payments for practitioner services began with a research project at the Harvard School of Public Health conducted in the 1980s under a cooperative agreement with the Health Care Financing Administration, now CMS. The Harvard investigators surveyed approximately 4,000 physicians using vignettes describing typical clinical scenarios for each service considered. The resulting resource-based work RVUs were first used for payment in 1992. Depending on the service, the current work RVUs are from one of two sources:

- the Harvard research, or
- CMS, based on recommendations from the RUC.

For practice expenses, CMS established resource-based payments starting in 1999 with RVUs determined according to a methodology developed by the agency. Resource-based payments for PLI started in 2000 based on a CMS-developed methodology.

Medicare adopted the fee schedule to remedy problems inherent in the prior charge-based payment system. That system was criticized as being inflationary and administratively complex. Further, in part because E&M services as a group were believed to be undervalued and procedures overvalued relative to the resource costs needed to provide them, many believe that the charge-based payment system created inappropriate incentives for the use of medical services and may have influenced physicians' decisions on where to locate and what to specialize in (Physician Payment Review Commission 1987).

The resource-based payment system has three limitations. First, it is vulnerable to mispricing. As an example, the assigned RVUs for a service may become too high over time when practitioners and staff gain the ability to furnish the service more quickly and routinely than when it was first introduced into medical or surgical practice. Consequently, practitioners can increase their service volume—and payments received from Medicare—with little change in the number of hours they work.

Second, resource-based payments generally ascribe higher values to performing procedures than to conducting E&M services. The higher relative values and the greater ability to generate volume result in significantly higher cumulative reimbursements for specialties that perform more procedures than for those that do not, such as primary care. This differential raises concerns about future career choices for physicians.

Third, resource-based payments do not adequately account for the relative effects of different services on clinical outcomes. In other words, a resource-based payment system values all services on an equal footing, regardless of their clinical efficacy. The Commission has contracted with the University of Minnesota to examine whether the private sector has developed innovative approaches to valuing practitioner services (see text box, pp. 16–17).

Using Time Estimates to Value Services Furnished by Physicians and Other Health Professionals

According to the Medicare statute, the fee schedule's payments for the work of a practitioner— physician, nurse practitioner, physician assistant, or other practitioner—eligible to bill Medicare work can account for two factors: time and intensity. Time (measured in minutes) is the time a practitioner typically spends furnishing a service. An estimate of such time has been developed for each service listed in the fee schedule.

Intensity, by contrast, is less intuitive both as a concept and in its measurement. Early in their research, the Harvard investigators found that when physicians were asked to give estimates of time and explicit ratings of intensity, their ratings of intensity were confounded with time (Hsiao et al. 1988). Multiplying time and these ratings of intensity resulted in ratings of work that increased exponentially with time, a finding that did not have face validity when presented to physicians. Consequently, the researchers decided that they should not ask physicians for explicit ratings of service intensity. Instead, they used the method of magnitude estimation whereby physicians gave ratings of work defined as an overall rating that takes into consideration the time required to furnish the service, mental effort and judgment, technical skill and physical effort, and stress due to potential risk for the patient. All these factors are considered relative to a standard reference service in the physicians' specialty. Such ratings of work were found to have face validity with clinicians and to meet statistical tests of internal and external validity. In addition, when the work value for a service is divided by its time estimate (work per unit of time), we get a measure of intensity that is implicit in the measures of work and time.

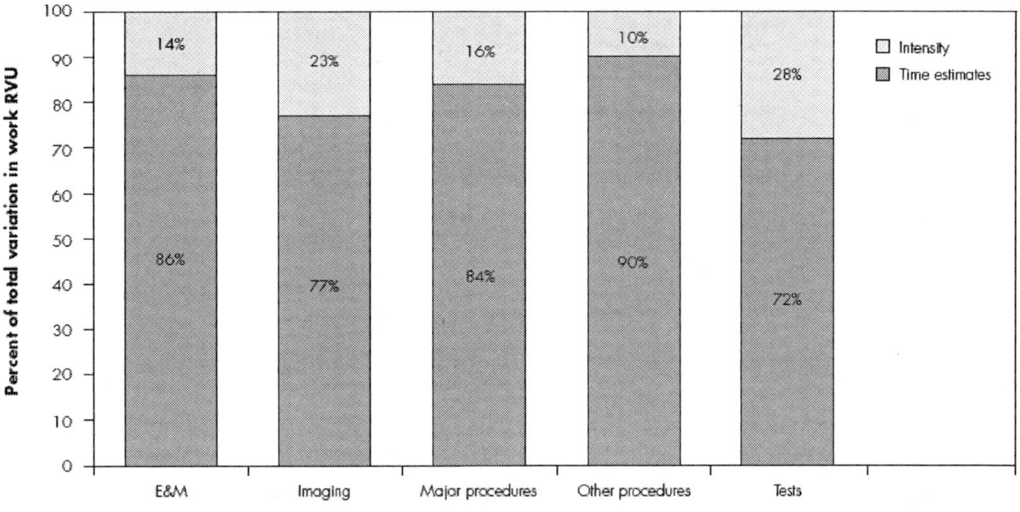

Note: RVU (relative value unit), E&M (evaluation and management). The percentages for physician time estimates are from five regression analyses: one for each service type. In these analyses, the log of estimated physician time was the explanatory variable, and the log of work RVU was the dependent variable. The percentages for intensity are the differences between the time percentages and 100 percent.

Source: MedPAC analysis of 2010 time data and work RVUs from CMS.

Figure 1-2. Fee schedule's time estimates explain much variation in the relative values for physician work.

We find that time explains most of the variation in the work RVUs (Figure 1-2) in each of the broad service categories.4 Depending on the type of service, the fee schedule's time estimates explain from 72 percent to 90 percent of the variation in the fee schedule's RVUs for practitioner work. Given the strength of this relationship, the time estimates are an important determinant of the accuracy of the work RVUs.

The time estimates are important also in determining the RVUs for practice expense. For example, when a procedure requires the presence of nonphysician clinical staff (a practice expense input) for 100 percent of the time a physician or other practitioner performs the procedure, the time estimate for nonphysician clinical staff is set equal to the practitioner time. Alternatively, if nonphysician clinical staff are required for only a portion of the time that the practitioner is performing a service, the time estimate for nonphysician clinical staff is set as a percentage of practitioner time.[5]

How might the time estimates become inaccurate? Efficiency gains are one possibility. Many services have never been reexamined to determine whether the average time and intensity of effort necessary to perform them has changed as a result of advances in technology, technique, or other factors. When efficiency gains are achieved, the work value for the affected services should decline accordingly, and—through application of budget-neutrality requirements—the values for all other services should increase (assuming all else equal). But because reviews of services are not always timely, categories of services without new procedures—such as primary care—become undervalued over time and thus risk being underprovided. The converse—that overvalued services may be overprovided—is also a concern.

The process for developing time estimates can be another source of inaccuracy. For the most part, the estimates are based on surveys conducted by physician specialty societies.[6] According to RUC requirements, a survey must include the participation of at least 30 practicing physicians (American Medical Association 2010). After conducting a survey, a specialty society uses the results to recommend a time estimate (and RVU) and defend its recommendation to the RUC. In turn, the RUC may adopt a specialty society's recommendation, but the RUC may also decide to refer a recommendation back to the society or may modify the recommendation before submitting it to CMS. Despite the deliberative nature of the process, however, the question is whether the survey data coming from the specialty societies—the starting point for the process—are objective given the specialty societies' financial stake in the process (Medicare Payment Advisory Commission 2006). Progress has been made in identifying and correcting misvalued services. As an example, changes in the RVUs for primary care services have increased payments for these services by 19.6 percent since 2006 (Medicare Payment Advisory Commission 2011). Nonetheless, the process for identifying and correcting misvalued services is occurring over several years and with inherent conflicts.

Alternative approaches to valuing services furnished by physicians and other health professionals

Stakeholders and researchers have raised concerns about how Medicare's physician fee schedule values services provided by physicians and other health professionals. To help inform the Commission's work in evaluating and improving the physician fee schedule, the Commission contracted with the University of Minnesota to examine alternative approaches used in the private sector to value physician services. The researchers evaluated methods used by health plans to pay for physician services as well as approaches used by integrated delivery systems (which can include hospitals, physician practices, and health plans) and physician groups to compensate employed physicians. We use the term provider organization to refer to both integrated delivery systems and physician groups.

The contractor, with participation by Commission staff, conducted structured interviews with leaders at 24 health plans and provider organizations. Fifteen plans and provider organizations were selected from across the United States and nine were chosen from the Minneapolis–St. Paul market. The researchers focused on the Minneapolis–St. Paul market because of the area's significant experimentation with new payment mechanisms. Because the organizations in the study were not randomly selected, their payment methods do not necessarily reflect the prevalence of similar approaches nationally. The key findings from the interviews include:

- Most health plans purchase physician services from provider organizations on a fee-for-service basis. This model leads provider organizations to compensate physicians based (in large part) on the number of services they provide to patients. If health plans shifted from fee-for-service payment to risk sharing, physician compensation models within provider organizations would need to change.

- The most common physician compensation model within provider organizations is based on the number of Medicare work relative value units provided by physicians combined with a target compensation amount. The target compensation is based on compensation for physicians in the same market and specialty. There is often a small adjustment based on quality and patient satisfaction metrics.
- We did not find evidence that plans or provider organizations have developed alternative approaches to valuing individual physician services, such as basing the relative weight of a service on its clinical value for patients.
- Collaborative efforts exist between plans and provider organizations to test innovative payment arrangements such as shared-savings models, medical homes, and bundled payments. Some of these efforts have been in existence for several years, whereas others are still in the discussion phase or are in the process of being implemented. Many of the arrangements identified by this study are concentrated in the Minneapolis–St. Paul market. The motivation for these experiments is dissatisfaction with the behavioral incentives in feefor-service payment systems and a desire by health care providers to gain experience with accountable care organization models that may become prevalent in the future.
- All the plans and most of the integrated delivery systems in the Minneapolis–St. Paul market have negotiated arrangements in which the delivery systems share in the overall savings they can achieve for their patients if total spending (including physician and hospital spending) falls below a negotiated target amount and the systems meet quality goals. In some contracts, delivery systems share in the risk that spending will exceed the target, but this approach is not typical. The interview respondents identified patient attribution—linking patients to the individual providers who serve them—and data sharing between plans and providers as key issues. The high level of patient loyalty to specific delivery systems made it easier to attribute patients. For one delivery system, these new financial arrangements constitute the majority of revenue from private plans.
- Factors that contribute to this high level of innovation in the Minneapolis–St. Paul market include a history of collaboration among plans and providers in quality measurement and improvement, the presence of large integrated delivery systems, and encouragement and support from the public sector and an organized employer group.
- Because shared-savings contracts are in their infancy, most of the organizations were not able to provide empirical evidence of their effectiveness. However, one health plan respondent reported that delivery systems had received significant shared savings in the first two years of the contract. Other respondents have observed behavioral changes among primary care physicians (such as seeking information on the most efficient specialists).

Alternative Approaches to Collecting Objective Time Data

To consider options for collecting objective time data, the Commission has contracted with RTI International for a study that has two objectives:

- identify and evaluate data currently available on the time that physicians and nonphysician clinical personnel spend in furnishing services billable under Medicare's physician fee schedule.

- assess the feasibility of primary data collection that would provide time estimates from a cohort of physician offices and other settings where physicians and nonphysician clinical practitioners work.

The project is ongoing, but progress to date suggests that time data to replace the fee schedule's current time estimates will not be collected easily. Much work will be necessary to establish an approach to collecting the data, develop data collection methods, carry out data collection activities, and analyze the data collected.

On the question of whether time data are already available from secondary sources, the contractor has found that, with some limitations, sources may be available for services such as E&M and surgical services. Those sources include the National Surgical Quality Improvement Program (NSQIP) and the National Ambulatory Medical Care Survey. However, while procedures in the NSQIP database are identified with billing codes from the Healthcare Common Procedure Coding System (HCPCS), services in other databases (such as the National Ambulatory Medicare Care Survey) are not so identified. The contractor is continuing work to identify whether these databases can be used to produce objective time estimates.

As to primary data collection, the contractor is conducting telephone interviews with managed care organizations and integrated delivery systems. After interviews with representatives of five organizations, the contractor has not found an organization that is collecting clinical service time by HCPCS code. Depending on the organization, there is the possibility of linking time data from electronic health records (EHRs) or patient scheduling systems to billing or encounter data that contain HCPCS codes. Alternatively, it may be possible to add HCPCS codes to time data collected as part of a prospective data collection activity. For the organizations contacted, some assembly of data—perhaps from disparate sources—would be necessary before they could submit time data.

The contractor has developed preliminary findings specific to certain types of services:

- For E&M services, electronically capturing clinical time presents a number of challenges. Face-to-face (intraservice) time may be available using time stamps in EHR systems. One caveat, however, is that it is difficult to know if interruptions occurred during a visit. In addition, some clinicians complete their documentation during the time with the patient while others wait until after the encounter. Either way, it appears that preservice and postservice activities—such as reviewing the medical history before seeing the patient and completing medical record documentation afterward—would be difficult to capture as distinct activities.
- For procedures performed outside an operating room (e.g., endoscopy, cardiac catheterization, removal of skin lesions), time data are generally not collected. It may be possible to estimate the duration of these procedures with information from patient scheduling systems.
- Time data are most likely to be available for the component of major surgical procedures that requires time in a hospital operating room, as recorded in operating room logs. However, it appears that HCPCS codes are not usually attached to such data.

The contractor has also asked interviewees about the acceptance and use of direct observation or time and motion studies. Some thought their clinicians would not welcome direct observation studies. Others may view direct observation differently. For instance, organizations that have adopted "lean" production methods make direct observation a part of their culture (Chalice 2007).

Collecting Time Data from a Cohort of Practices

If time data are not sufficiently available from secondary sources, primary data collection will be necessary. The Commission's June 2006 report discussed two alternatives for collecting primary data. One is to conduct voluntary surveys of practitioners, such as those that have been conducted by the American Medical Association (AMA) and physician specialty societies. The difficulty with this approach is that response rates are usually low; response rates of 20 percent or less are not uncommon (Medicare Payment Advisory Commission 2006). Low response rates raise questions about the representativeness of the practitioners participating and, therefore, the data collected.

Another alternative is to make data reporting mandatory for all, similar to the requirement that institutional providers must submit cost reports. While mandatory reporting would overcome the problem of low response, it would require a change in regulation. In addition, the administrative burden on practitioners could be a problem, depending on the level of detail of reporting requirements.

To avoid the difficulties of voluntary surveys and mandatory cost reports, CMS could collect data on a recurring basis from a cohort of physician offices and other settings where physicians and other health professionals work. These entities would be recruited through a process that would require participation in data reporting among those selected. The cohort would consist of practices with a range of specialties, practitioner types, and services and would be large enough to ensure that estimates derived from the cohort are reliable. CMS could develop a cohort that consisted of practices that were more efficient than others. If necessary, practices could be paid to participate.

This approach to collecting time data could be broadened to also give CMS the opportunity to collect accurate and current data for determining practice expense RVUs (see text box, pp. 20–21). Similar to data for work RVUs, practice expense RVUs are partly a function of estimates of the time that nonphysician clinical staff spend in furnishing services in nonfacility settings such as practitioner offices. Practice expense RVUs also rely on information about the prices that practitioners pay for equipment and supplies, and CMS's methodology for determining practice expense RVUs requires data on practitioners' total practice costs.

Collection of data from a cohort of practices would raise a number of methodologic and administrative questions:

- What data are needed to validate the fee schedule's time estimates?
- If it is necessary to collect time data for discrete HCPCS-coded services furnished in a practice, would the data be needed for all services or a subset? If a subset, what statistical methods could be used to extrapolate to a broader set of services?
- How many practices should participate to ensure that estimates are reliable?
- Would Medicare need to compensate practices for participating in the data collection effort? If so, how would rates be determined?

- Would the cohort of practices remain constant from year to year or is there an advantage to rotating practices into and out of the cohort?
- Are measures of practitioner time affected by factors such as practice patterns that vary geographically, the mix of services furnished by a practice, or a practice's payer mix? If so, how should the sample design account for such variation?
- Who would collect the data? Would practices submit data according to a standard format or would fieldwork by a CMS contractor be necessary?
- If practices submit the data, would CMS need an audit capability—similar to that for the cost reports submitted by facility-based providers—to ensure data accuracy? How would reported results be verified?
- Such data collection would be costly for CMS. What level of resources would the agency need?

Except for the first two questions—what time data to collect and whether to collect time data for all services or for a subset—these questions are of a type that is typically encountered in research design.

What Time Data Are Needed?

The purpose of collecting time data from a cohort of practices is to validate the fee schedule's time estimates and, as necessary, to replace those estimates with objective data. The data must include an HCPCS code for each service represented. The data must also include the three components of each service: preservice, intraservice, and postservice.

As our contractor has discovered, assembling time data at this level of detail is difficult. For instance, it may be necessary to draw the data from more than one system in a practice—EHR, patient scheduling, billing, etc.—and link data based on data elements such as a patient identifier and date of service that are common to each system, which raises the question of whether there is a way to collect time data but minimize the administrative burden for practices.

There are options that could reduce or eliminate the need for a practice to merge data from multiple systems. For example, CMS could specify a template for data collection. With this template, practices could: (1) tabulate all the services (by HCPCS code) that a given practitioner furnished to his or her patients in a given week of work, and (2) record the total hours worked by the practitioner in the week.

With such data, validation of the fee schedule's time estimates would be straightforward, as a time estimate for each HCPCS-coded service exists in the fee schedule. Multiplying a practitioner's units of service by these estimates and summing across all services billed by the practitioner would give an estimate of total hours worked. Estimated hours worked could then be compared with actual hours worked. Any differences found would suggest that there are errors in the time estimates. Statistical analysis of these results for all (or a subset of) practitioners would show which services are most likely to be sources of the errors and, therefore, most in need of new time estimates.

In validating the fee schedule's existing time estimates, it may be possible to use the data collected from the cohort of practices to develop new time estimates. If sufficient data are collected, time per unit of service could be estimated with statistical analysis of actual hours worked as a function of units of service by HCPCS code. The estimates would show the effect that a one-unit change in services has on hours worked.[8]

CMS needs accurate and current data for determining practice expense relative value units

In addition to the time estimates for practitioner work, another set of estimates addresses the time typically spent by nonphysician clinical employees who work in practitioners' offices. These estimates are used in CMS's methodology for determining the practice expense relative value units (RVUs).7 The time estimates for practice expense are based on specialty society surveys and have the same vulnerabilities as the time estimates for practitioner work.

CMS's practice expense methodology also requires data on prices for equipment and supplies used in practitioners' offices. On this issue, the Commission has a longstanding concern that CMS has yet to adopt a schedule for updating these prices (Medicare Payment Advisory Commission 2006). The Commission's view is that it is important for the agency to regularly (e.g., every two years) update these prices. Inaccurate prices, particularly of high-cost medical equipment and supplies, can result in distortions in practice expense RVUs for different services over time. Prices for new supplies and equipment are likely to drop over time as they diffuse into the market and as other companies begin to produce them.

Most recently, in the proposed rule for the 2011 physician fee schedule, CMS outlined a process to update the prices of high-cost supplies (items with a price of $150 or more) every two years, relying on the General Services Administration medical supply schedule. However, in the final rule, CMS did not adopt the method. Instead, the agency stated that it would continue to study the issue over the coming months.

Separately, CMS's practice expense methodology accounts for the cost of indirect inputs with data on total practice costs for each physician specialty. Beginning in 2007, CMS determined the cost of indirect inputs by using practice cost data submitted by seven specialties (allergy/immunology, cardiology, dermatology, gastroenterology, urology, radiology, radiation oncology) and independent diagnostic testing facilities. Use of these data was a response to a requirement in the Balanced Budget Refinement Act of 1999, which mandated that the agency establish a process to consider more current practice cost data submitted by specialties when updating the physician fee schedule.

For most other specialties, CMS used practice cost data that the American Medical Association (AMA) collected between 1995 and 1999. Using more current data for the eight specialties increased estimates of their practice costs relative to all other specialties. The concern was that selective updating of the practice cost information had distorted relative practice expense payments across services. The AMA and specialty societies then fielded a new, privately sponsored, voluntary survey—the Physician Practice Information Survey (PPIS) to collect more current practice cost data from nearly all specialty groups. CMS supported the effort.

Beginning with the 2010 fee schedule, CMS used the more current data obtained from the PPIS. Although concerns have been raised about the PPIS's representativeness and low response rate, this survey is a step forward compared with the multiple data sources CMS previously relied on. The advantages of the PPIS are that it: (1) reflects current practice patterns and costs, (2) measures costs of nearly all physician and nonphysician specialties, and (3) uses a standard protocol for all specialty groups that was designed to derive practice expense RVUs. The concern is that CMS has not articulated a strategy for keeping the practice cost data up to date via a survey or other method.

Is It Necessary to Collect Time Data for All Services?

If it is necessary to collect service-specific data on the time practitioners spend furnishing discrete, HCPCS-coded services, the administrative burden on practices could be limited by focusing the data collection on selected services. Some services account for a relatively large share of spending. Some may be good candidates for other reasons.

- Medicare claims data show that 460 services account for 90 percent of spending under the physician fee schedule. While validation of time data for all of the more than 7,000 services may be perceived as prohibitive, any collection of service-specific data should be feasible for 5 percent to 10 percent of the services. In turn, it should be possible to consider similarities among services and use statistical techniques to validate the time estimates for other services.
- Depending on the year, a subset of services exhibits rapid growth compared with other services. For instance, in 2009, the volume per beneficiary of certain types of spine surgery went up by more than 10 percent compared with 3 percent growth in per beneficiary volume for all practitioner services (Medicare Payment Advisory Commission 2011). Rapid volume growth may be a sign that a service's time estimate is too high and that it is mispriced.
- Some services require relatively little practitioner time. For instance, the 10th percentile of the time estimates for services in the diagnostic tests category is 11 minutes. The 10th percentile of the time estimates for imaging services is 6 minutes. Despite their time estimates, however, short-duration services can account for relatively large shares of spending because of their volume or because they have high intensity (high RVUs per unit of time). Thus, a small error in the time estimate for a short-duration service can represent a large proportion of the total. A 2-minute error in the time estimate for a 20-minute service (the 10th percentile of the time estimates for E&M services) is an error of 10 percent. But a 2-minute error in the estimate for an 11-minute service is an error of 18 percent, and a 2-minute error in the estimate for a 6-minute service is an error of 33 percent. High-volume, short-duration services could be considered in any collection of service-specific time data.
- CMS's estimate is that in 2008 about 2,900 services had work RVUs that dated back to the 1980s and the Harvard project on the fee schedule (Centers for Medicare & Medicaid Services 2010). These services accounted for $5 billion in spending, or about 8 percent of the total. According to a RUC analysis, 296 of the services have an annual volume of 10,000 services or more. These services could be considered as candidates for collection of time data.
- The RUC has established a list of 316 services, known as multispecialty points of comparison (MPC), which are reference services used in the valuation of new, revised, or newly reviewed services. Recently, the RUC has undertaken a review of some MPC services. In addition, CMS has ranked services on the MPC list according to the volume of services and allowed charges and has requested that the RUC review 33 high-priority services. Given their importance, MPC services might be another category of services to consider.

Endnotes

[1] In February 2010, the Congress passed a provision in law that allows a limited exception to rules of the Statutory Pay-As- You-Go Act of 2010 (S–PAYGO) when overriding the SGR formula. Since passage of this S–PAYGO exception, only two of the temporary SGR overrides have invoked it. The Congressional Budget Office estimated that these S–PAYGO exceptions incurred about $3 billion dollars in spending that did not require an offset, which amounts to less than 5 percent of the total amount allowed to be excepted under the SGR S– PAYGO exception.

[2] Payments for professional liability insurance account for the remainder of payments under the physician fee schedule.

[3] PPACA did not include additional resources for CMS to accomplish these activities.

[4] The method is regression analysis. We conducted five analyses, one for each type of service: E&M, imaging, major procedures, other procedures, and tests. The log of each service's work RVU was the dependent variable and the log of the service's time estimate was the explanatory variable. The proportion of variation in work RVUs explained by the regression model is the model's coefficient of determination, R^2.

[5] In addition to influencing the estimates of nonphysician clinical staff time for some services, time estimates for practitioner work influence the allocation of indirect practice costs. Indirect practice costs are among the practice costs considered in CMS's methodology for determining practice expense RVUs. Indirect practice costs include administrative labor and office expense.

[6] RUC-valued services—based on specialty society surveys— account for more than 90 percent of spending under the fee schedule. The remainder consists of services valued during the fee schedule research at Harvard (Centers for Medicare & Medicaid Services 2010).

[7] In the fee schedule's method for valuing practice expense, nonphysician clinical staff are valued with time estimates (and wage rates). Administrative staff are classified as an indirect expense and are valued separately, without time estimates.

[8] The analysis would be a regression analysis with the practitioner as the unit of observation. Hours worked would be the dependent variable. Units of service by HCPCS code would be the explanatory variables. The parameter estimates for each HCPCS code would be the change in hours worked associated with a one-unit change in the number of services. That is, the parameter estimate for each code would be a time estimate—the time spent furnishing one unit of the service.

References

American Medical Association. 2010. *AMA/Specialty Society RVS update process*. Chicago, IL: AMA. http://www.ama-assn.org/ resources/doc/rbrvs/ruc-update-booklet.pdf.

Berenson, R. A. 2010. *Out of whack: Pricing distortions in the Medicare physician fee schedule*. NIHCM expert voices.

Boards of Trustees, Federal Hospital Insurance and Federal Supplementary Medical Insurance Trust Funds. 2010. *2010 annual report of the Boards of Trustees of the Federal Hospital Insurance and Federal Supplementary Insurance Trust Funds.* Washington, DC: Boards of Trustees.

Centers for Medicare & Medicaid Services, Department of Health and Human Services. 2010. Medicare program; payment policies under the physician fee schedule and other revisions to Part B for CY 2011. Final rule. *Federal Register* 75, no. 228 (November 29): 73169–73860.

Chalice, R. 2007. *Improving healthcare using Toyota lean production methods: 46 steps for improvement.* Milwaukee, WI: American Society for Quality Press.

Cromwell, J., N. McCall, K. Dalton, et al. 2010. Missing productivity gains in the Medicare physician fee schedule: Where are they? *Medical Care Research and Review* 67, no. 6 (December): 676–693.

Cromwell, J., N. T. McCall, S. Hoover, et al. 2007. *Assessment of the potential impact of productivity changes on Medicare RVUs.* Report for Assistant Secretary for Planning and Evaluation. Research Triangle Park, NC: RTI International. December.

Foster, R. 2010. Estimated financial effects of the "Patient Protection and Affordable Care Act," as amended. Memo from the Centers for Medicare & Medicaid Services, Office of the Actuary. April 22.

Government Accountability Office. 2009. *Medicare physician payments: Fees could better reflect efficiencies achieved when services are provided together.* GAO–09–647. Washington, DC: GAO.

Hsiao, W. C., D. B. Yntema, P. Braun, et al. 1988. Measurement and analysis of intraservice work. *Journal of the American Medical Association* 260, no. 16 (October 28): 2361–2370.

McCall, N., J. Cromwell, and P. Braun. 2006. Validation of physician survey estimates of surgical time using operating room logs. *Medical Care Research and Review* 63, no. 6 (December): 764–777.

Medicare Payment Advisory Commission. 2006. *Report to the Congress: Increasing the value of Medicare*. Washington, DC: MedPAC.

Medicare Payment Advisory Commission. 2007. *Report to the Congress: Assessing alternatives to the sustainable growth rate system.* Washington, DC: MedPAC.

Medicare Payment Advisory Commission. 2011. *Report to the Congress: Medicare payment policy*. Washington, DC: MedPAC.

Physician Payment Review Commission. 1987. *Medicare physician payment: An agenda for reform.* Washington, DC: PPRC.

Washington, DC: National Institute for Health Care Management. http://nihcm.org/pdf/NIHCM-EV-Berenson_FINAL.pdf.

RECOMMENDATIONS

2-1 The Secretary should accelerate and expand efforts to package discrete services in the physician fee schedule into larger units for payment.

COMMISSIONER VOTES: YES 16 • NO 0 • NOT VOTING 0 • ABSENT 1

2-2 The Congress should direct the Secretary to apply a multiple procedure payment reduction to the professional component of diagnostic imaging services provided by the same practitioner in the same session.

COMMISSIONER VOTES: YES 16 • NO 0 • NOT VOTING 0 • ABSENT 1

2-3 The Congress should direct the Secretary to reduce the physician work component of imaging and other diagnostic tests that are ordered and performed by the same practitioner.

COMMISSIONER VOTES: YES 16 • NO 0 • NOT VOTING 0 • ABSENT 1

2-4 The Congress should direct the Secretary to establish a prior authorization program for practitioners who order substantially more advanced diagnostic imaging services than their peers.

COMMISSIONER VOTES: YES 15 • NO 1 • NOT VOTING 0 • ABSENT 1

Improving Payment Accuracy and Appropriate Use of Ancillary Services

Summary

Many physicians have expanded their practices in recent years to provide diagnostic imaging, clinical laboratory testing, physical therapy, and radiation therapy. Ancillary services—particularly diagnostic imaging—account for a significant share of Part B revenue for certain specialties. In addition, a survey of physicians conducted in 2008 by the Center for Studying Health System Change found that 29 percent of physicians were in practices that owned or leased equipment for noninvasive testing procedures (e.g., echocardiograms and nuclear medicine studies), 25 percent were in practices that owned or leased clinical lab testing equipment, 23 percent owned or leased X-ray equipment, and 17 percent owned or leased MRI or computed tomography machines. An exception to the Ethics in Patient Referrals Act, also known as the Stark law, allows physicians to provide ancillary services such as diagnostic imaging, radiation therapy, clinical laboratory tests, and physical therapy to patients in their offices. This provision is known as the in-office ancillary services (IOAS) exception.

Physician investment in diagnostic testing equipment has contributed to rapid growth of imaging and other tests under the physician fee schedule and has resulted in a high level of utilization that likely includes unnecessary services. The Commission recognizes that many of these services enable physicians to diagnose and treat illness with greater speed and precision and, in some cases, with greater convenience for patients. On the other hand, physician ownership is associated with higher volume; studies by the Commission and other researchers have found that physicians who furnish imaging services in their offices order more imaging than other physicians (Baker 2010, Hughes et al. 2010, Medicare Payment Advisory Commission 2009a). In addition, several types of imaging are usually not provided on the same day as an office visit, which raises questions about patient convenience. Rapid volume growth contributes to Medicare's growing financial burden on taxpayers and beneficiaries, leads to concerns about the accuracy of physician fee schedule payment rates, and raises questions about inappropriate use.

Physician self-referral of ancillary services leads to higher volume when combined with fee-for-service payment systems, which reward higher volume, and the mispricing of individual services, which makes some services more profitable than others. However, under an alternative payment structure in which providers are rewarded for constraining volume growth while improving the quality of care, the volume-increasing effects of self-referral would be mitigated. Therefore, the preferred long-term approach to address self-referral is to develop new payment systems. Because it will take several years to establish new payment models and delivery systems, we have explored a range of interim approaches to address concerns raised about self-referral. One such option is to narrow the types of services or physician groups covered by the IOAS exception. However, the Commission is concerned that limiting the IOAS exception could have unintended consequences, such as inhibiting the development of organizations that integrate and coordinate care within a physician practice. In addition, it could be difficult to craft a more limited IOAS exception that distinguishes between group practices that improve quality and coordination and those that use additional services of marginal clinical value. Therefore, we do not currently recommend that the exception be changed.

Instead, our recommendations are designed to improve payment accuracy for imaging and other diagnostic tests and ensure the appropriate use of advanced imaging studies. These recommendations recognize that mispricing and inappropriate use are problems that go beyond self-referral. The first three recommendations, which address mispricing, would improve the overall accuracy and equity of the physician fee schedule and reduce the financial incentives for physicians to invest in ancillary services. The savings from these three recommendations should be redistributed to other physician fee schedule services. However, pricing accuracy is not sufficient to ensure the optimal use of imaging. Therefore, the fourth recommendation is to create a prior authorization program for practitioners who order a substantially larger number of advanced imaging services than other physicians who treat similar patients. Although our recommendations do not directly address self-referral of physical therapy, radiation therapy, and anatomic pathology tests, we will continue to track the growth of these services and may consider policy options to specifically address them in the future.

The Commission remains concerned about the expansion of physician investment in imaging, other diagnostic tests, and therapeutic services (e.g., physical therapy and radiation therapy) and the potential for self-referral to lead to higher volume. Therefore, if the recommendations in this chapter are adopted and—together with delivery system reform—are not successful at stemming the growth of ancillary services and their inappropriate use, we may revisit options to narrow the IOAS exception. CMS has proposed criteria for an accountable care organization (ACO) model that include financial penalties for rapid growth in spending. One option would be to have a broader IOAS exception for physicians in ACOs that are at risk for expenditure growth and a narrower exception for physicians outside such ACOs.

BACKGROUND

Many physicians have expanded their practices in recent years to provide diagnostic imaging, clinical laboratory testing, physical therapy, and radiation therapy (Anscher et al. 2010, Armstrong 2005, Carreyrou and Tamman 2010, Centers for Medicare & Medicaid Services 2007, Medicare Payment Advisory Commission 2006a, Pham et al. 2004, Pham and Ginsburg 2007, Saul 2006, Stein 2011). Ancillary services—particularly diagnostic imaging—account for a significant share of Part B revenue for certain specialties (Medicare Payment Advisory Commission 2010a). For example, imaging accounted for 38 percent of cardiology's Part B revenue in 2008, up from 35 percent in 2003, and it represented 23 percent of vascular surgery's Part B payments in 2008, compared with 20 percent in 2003.

According to a survey of physicians conducted in 2008 by the Center for Studying Health System Change, 29 percent of physicians were in practices that owned or leased equipment for noninvasive testing procedures (e.g., echocardiograms and nuclear medicine studies) (Reschovsky et al. 2010). In addition, 25 percent were in practices that owned or leased clinical lab testing equipment, 23 percent owned or leased X-ray equipment, and 17 percent owned or leased MRI or computed tomography (CT) machines.

Physician investment in diagnostic testing equipment has contributed to rapid growth of imaging and other diagnostic tests under the physician fee schedule (see p. 35 for more information on volume growth). The Commission recognizes that many of these services enable physicians to diagnose and treat illness with greater speed and precision and, in some cases, with greater convenience for patients. On the other hand, physician ownership is associated with higher volume; studies by the Commission and other researchers have found that physicians who furnish imaging services in their offices order more imaging than other physicians (Baker 2010, Gazelle et al. 2007, Government Accountability Office 1994, Hillman et al. 1990, Hillman et al. 1992, Hughes et al. 2010, Kouri et al. 2002, Litt et al. 2005, Medicare Payment Advisory Commission 2009a). (See text box, p. 32, for further detail on two of these studies.) In addition, several types of imaging are usually not provided on the same day as an office visit, which raises questions about the link between self-referral and patient convenience (Medicare Payment Advisory Commission 2010a). Rapid volume growth contributes to Medicare's rising financial burden on taxpayers and beneficiaries, leads to concerns about the accuracy of physician fee schedule payment rates, and raises questions about inappropriate use.

Factors other than physician investment in equipment have also played a role in the growth of ancillary services:

- technological innovation and new clinical applications,
- mispricing of services in Medicare's fee-for-service (FFS) payment systems,
- defensive medicine,
- consumer demand for diagnostic tests,
- lack of research on the impact of imaging on clinical decision making and patient outcomes,
- inconsistent adherence to clinical guidelines, and
- collaborative relationships between hospitals and physicians, such as joint ventures and hospital employment of physicians (Medicare Payment Advisory Commission 2008b).[1]

The Ethics in Patient Referrals Act, also known as the Stark law, prohibits physicians from referring Medicare patients for designated health services (DHS)—such as imaging, radiation therapy, home health care, durable medical equipment, clinical laboratory tests, and physical therapy—to entities with which they have a financial relationship, unless the relationship fits within an exception. The in-office ancillary services (IOAS) exception allows physicians to provide most DHS to patients in their offices (see text box, p. 33).

Physician self-referral of ancillary services leads to higher volume when combined with FFS payment systems, which reward higher volume, and the mispricing of individual services, which makes some services more profitable than others. However, under an alternative payment structure in which providers are rewarded for constraining volume growth while improving the quality of care, the volume-increasing effects of self-referral would be mitigated. Therefore, the preferred long-term approach to address self-referral is to develop new payment systems.

Because it will take several years to establish new payment models and delivery systems, we have explored a range of interim approaches to address concerns raised by self-referral (Medicare Payment Advisory Commission 2010a). One such option is to narrow the types of services or physician groups covered by the IOAS exception. However, the Commission is concerned that limiting the IOAS exception could have unintended consequences, such as inhibiting the development of organizations that integrate and coordinate care within a physician practice. In addition, it could be difficult to craft a more limited IOAS exception that distinguishes between group practices that improve quality and coordination and those that create incentives to use additional services of marginal clinical value. Therefore, we do not currently recommend that the exception be changed. In the future, however, the scope of the exception could be narrowed for physicians who are not part of an accountable care organization (ACO) that has financial incentives to improve quality and reduce the volume of unnecessary care.

Recent studies show that physician self-referral is associated with additional use of imaging services

Two recent studies show that physician self-referral is associated with additional use of imaging services. In one study, the Commission used 2005 Medicare claims for beneficiaries in six markets to analyze whether physician self-referral affected the use of imaging within an episode of care, adjusting for differences in patients' clinical conditions and the type of imaging (Medicare Payment Advisory Commission 2009a). We examined 22 combinations of different types, or modalities, of imaging (e.g., computed tomography and MRI) and conditions (e.g., migraine headache, ischemic heart disease, and joint degeneration of the back).

Our methodology allowed us to compare the observed cost of a given episode with the average cost of similar types of episodes (adjusting for severity of illness, physician specialty, and market area). There were two key results:

- Compared with episodes with no self-referring physician, a higher proportion of episodes with a self-referring physician received at least one imaging service. The magnitude of the variation ranged from 2 to 23 percentage points depending on the condition and modality; in all but one comparison, the differences were statistically significant. The magnitude of the variation was 10 percentage points or more for 14 of the 22 condition–modality pairs.
- Episodes with a self-referring physician had a higher mean ratio of observed-to-expected spending for an imaging modality than episodes with no self-referring physician. The differences between the ratios ranged from 5 percent to 104 percent, depending on the condition and modality. (For all the comparisons, the differences were statistically significant.) For example, the mean spending ratio for nuclear medicine for ischemic heart disease was twice as high for episodes with a self-referring physician as for episodes with no self-referring physician. Across all condition–modality pairs, the mean difference between ratios was 68 percent (weighted by the number of episodes

in each pair).

In addition, we found that greater use of imaging is associated with greater overall resource use for the types of episodes we examined, adjusting for patient severity and other factors. This finding supports other research suggesting that results from imaging may initiate a cascade of diagnostic tests and interventions, thereby increasing total episode costs (Deyo 2002).

In another recent study, Laurence Baker found that orthopedists and neurologists who acquired MRI machines during the early 2000s ordered substantially more MRI scans after they began billing for MRI services (Baker 2010). For example, after orthopedists began billing for MRI studies, the number of scans ordered within 30 days of the patient's first visit increased by 38 percent. Much of the increased MRI use did not take place on the day of the patient's initial visit, which undermines the argument that the convenience of having an MRI machine in the physician's office was the main driver of higher volume. In addition to higher spending on MRI services, acquisition of an MRI machine was also associated with increased spending on other services such as procedures.

Instead, our recommendations are designed to improve payment accuracy for imaging and other diagnostic tests and ensure the appropriate use of advanced imaging studies. These recommendations recognize that mispricing and inappropriate use are problems that go beyond self-referral. The first three recommendations, which address mispricing, would improve the overall accuracy and equity of the physician fee schedule and reduce the financial incentives for physicians to invest in ancillary services. Although the Congress and CMS have made several changes to improve payment accuracy, there remain inaccuracies that should be addressed. (See text box for a description of recent changes to payments for imaging services.)

The in-office ancillary services exception

The in-office ancillary services (IOAS) exception to the Ethics in Patient Referrals Act, also known as the Stark law, applies to diagnostic imaging, radiation therapy, clinical laboratory tests, and physical therapy.2 The exception has three key criteria known as the supervision, building (or location), and billing requirements: (1) The services must be personally furnished by the referring physician, a physician who is a member of the group practice, or an individual who is supervised by the referring physician or another physician in the group (the supervision requirement). (2) The services must be furnished in the same building where the referring physician provides non-designated health services (non-DHS); alternatively, groups may furnish services in a centralized facility used by the group for ancillary services (the building requirement). (3) The services must be billed by the physician performing or supervising the service, the group practice, an entity that is wholly owned by the performing or supervising physician or by that physician's group practice, or a third-party billing company acting as an agent of the physician or group (the billing requirement) (42 CFR § 411.355 (b)).

The definition of a group practice is important because it allows physicians greater flexibility to provide ancillary services in their offices. Physicians who are in a group may order services that are furnished or supervised by other physicians in the group, and groups may also provide services in a centralized facility. The Stark law defines a group practice as one in which substantially all of the services provided by members of the group are furnished through the group and billed by the group. The Stark regulations interpreted "substantially all" as requiring that at least 75 percent of the patient care services provided by members of the group be provided and billed by the group (42 CFR § 411.352 (d)). Members include owners and employees of the group. The 75 percent rule applies to all the services collectively provided by physicians who are group members; individual members do not have to meet the 75 percent threshold. This rule can make it difficult for groups to qualify as a group practice under the Stark law if they have many part-time physician members who also work for other groups. However, the Stark regulations created a new category called "physicians in the group" that applies to physicians who independently contract with the group. These physicians are not counted toward the 75 percent rule. Thus, groups can contract with physicians on a parttime basis to provide or supervise ancillary services without affecting their ability to comply with the 75 percent test.

In addition to group practices that provide imaging in their offices, arrangements exist in which a practice shares a facility with another practice or leases a block of time from a separate imaging provider. Under a block-of-time lease arrangement, a physician practice sends its patients to another provider for imaging and bills Medicare for the services, profiting from the difference between Medicare's payment rate and the fee paid by the practice to the provider that performs the services.

According to data from a California health plan, more than 60 percent of physicians who billed the plan for MRI or computed tomography (CT) scans engaged in a block lease or similar arrangement (Mitchell 2007). Shared facility or block lease arrangements may comply with the IOAS exception as long as the supervision, building, and billing requirements are met (e.g., the imaging study is performed in the same building where the referring physician furnishes non-DHS services).3 Under a CMS rule, however, imaging providers that are enrolled in Medicare as fixed-site independent diagnostic testing facilities (IDTFs) may not lease their operations to or share testing equipment with other organizations (42 CFR § 410.33). This rule does not apply to mobile IDTFs. Although this rule prohibits leasing arrangements between group practices and fixed-site IDTFs, groups may still engage in block-of-time leases with each other.

The Patient Protection and Affordable Care Act of 2010 requires physicians who provide MRI, CT, or positron emission tomography services under the IOAS exception to inform their patients that they may obtain these services from another provider and to provide patients with a list of alternative providers in their area (Centers for Medicare & Medicaid Services 2010b).

Recent changes to physician fee schedule payment rates for imaging services

Between 2005 and 2010, the Congress and CMS made several changes to payment rates for diagnostic imaging services. Nevertheless, the Commission believes there are still opportunities to improve payment accuracy.

The Deficit Reduction Act of 2005 required that physician fee schedule payment rates for the technical component of imaging services could not exceed hospital outpatient rates for the same services. This provision, which became effective in 2007, reduced the fee schedule amounts for many imaging services.

In 2005, CMS adopted a policy to reduce the payment rate for the technical component of second and subsequent imaging studies by 25 percent when multiple services are performed on contiguous body parts during the same session (Centers for Medicare &

Medicaid Services 2005). For example, when a patient received an MRI of the pelvis and an MRI of the abdomen in the same session, the technical component payment for the lower paid study—MRI of the pelvis—was reduced by 25 percent. This policy—which became effective in 2006—is based on a Commission recommendation and is designed to account for efficiencies in clinical labor, supplies, equipment, and indirect practice costs when multiple studies are performed in the same session (Medicare Payment Advisory Commission 2005b). The Patient Protection and Affordable Care Act of 2010 (PPACA) expanded the payment reduction for multiple technical component services from 25 percent to 50 percent, effective July 1, 2010.

In 2007, CMS made major changes to the method for calculating practice expense relative value units (RVUs) under the physician fee schedule. These changes— which were phased in over four years—shifted practice expense RVUs from imaging services and major procedures to evaluation and management services and nonmajor procedures (Medicare Payment Advisory Commission 2007b).

For 2010, CMS began using more current practice expense data from a new, privately sponsored, voluntary survey of physician and nonphysician specialties (Centers for Medicare & Medicaid Services 2009). This change is redistributing practice expense RVUs among specialties and services over a four-year period. Several of the provider groups experiencing a decline in RVUs (e.g., radiology, cardiology, and independent diagnostic testing facilities) perform many imaging services.

The Commission recommended that Medicare increase the equipment use rate assumption for expensive diagnostic imaging equipment from 25 hours to 45 hours per week, or 90 percent of the time that providers are assumed to be open for business (Medicare Payment Advisory Commission 2009b). CMS implemented this policy in 2010 with a four-year phase-in. It reduced practice expense payments for MRI, computed tomography, and positron emission tomography services. PPACA superseded this policy by setting the equipment use assumption for these types of imaging equipment at 75 percent beginning in 2011.

Some imaging services that are frequently performed together by the same practitioner on the same date have been combined into comprehensive codes under a process developed by the American Medical Association/Specialty Society Relative Value Scale Update Committee and the Current Procedural Terminology Editorial Panel. Comprehensive codes have been created for computed tomography of the abdomen and pelvis, myocardial perfusion imaging (a type of nuclear medicine study), and echocardiography (Centers for Medicare & Medicaid Services 2009, Centers for Medicare & Medicaid Services 2010b). To account for efficiencies when services are furnished at the same time, the RVUs of the new comprehensive codes are generally lower than the sum of the RVUs for the component codes they replaced.

However, pricing accuracy is not sufficient to ensure optimal use of imaging. Therefore, the fourth recommendation is to create a prior authorization program for practitioners (whether or not they are self-referring) who order substantially more advanced imaging services than other physicians who treat similar patients. Although our recommendations do not directly address self-referral of physical therapy, radiation therapy, and anatomic pathology tests, we will continue to track the growth of these services and may consider policy options to specifically address them in the future.

Volume of Ancillary Services under Physician Fee Schedule Has Grown Rapidly

Many physician fee schedule services covered under the IOAS exception experienced rapid volume growth from 2004 to 2009.4 The volume of diagnostic imaging services increased from 2004 to 2008 by 6.3 percent per FFS beneficiary per year and from 2008 to 2009 by 2.0 percent (Medicare Payment Advisory Commission 2011). The volume of outpatient therapy services (which include physical therapy, occupational therapy, and speech–language pathology services) rose from 2004 to 2008 by an average of 7.5 percent per FFS beneficiary per year; from 2008 to 2009, growth was even higher (11.2 percent). Radiation therapy services increased from 2004 to 2008 by 7.1 percent per FFS beneficiary per year and from 2008 to 2009 by 1.9 percent. By comparison, all physician services grew from 2004 to 2008 by 4.1 percent per FFS beneficiary per year and from 2008 to 2009 by 3.3 percent.

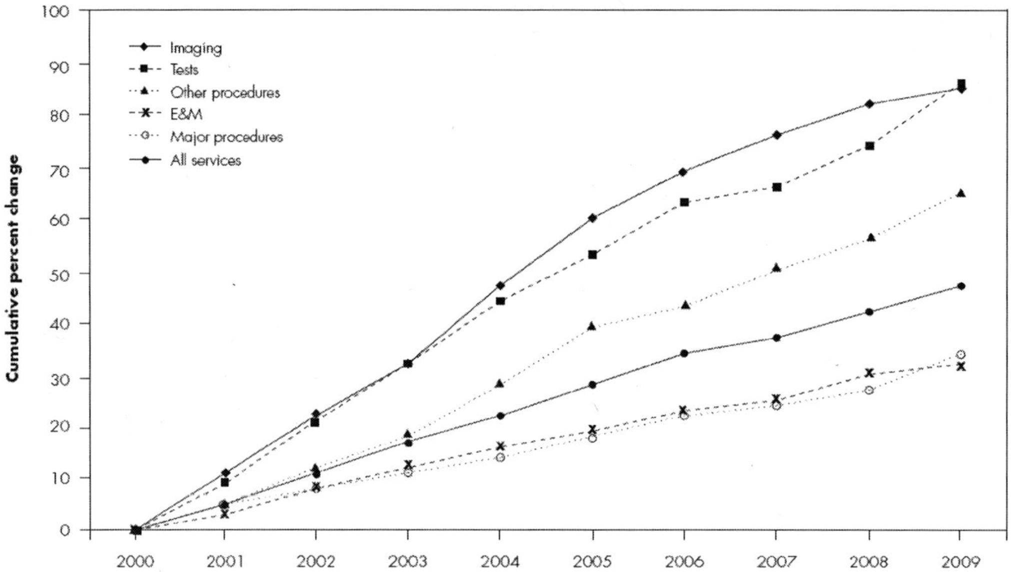

Note: FFS (fee-for-service), E&M (evaluation and management). Volume is measured as units of service multiplied by each service's relative weight (relative value unit) from the physician fee schedule.

Source: MedPAC analysis of carrier claims data for 100 percent of Medicare beneficiaries.

Figure 2-1. Growth in the volume of physician services per FFS beneficiary, 2000–2009.

Although the volume growth of imaging services has decelerated in recent years, the growth rate has remained positive and was preceded by many years of rapid increases. As shown in Figure 2-1, cumulative volume growth of imaging per FFS beneficiary from 2000 to 2009 outpaced all other categories of physician services except tests (the category of tests includes electrocardiograms, cardiovascular stress tests, and nerve conduction tests).

Imaging rose by 85 percent during this period compared with 47 percent growth in all physician services. As described below, there are reasons to be concerned that some of these additional imaging studies may not be appropriate. This rapid growth has also raised concerns about the long-term impact of radiation exposure. Certain types of imaging (e.g., CT and nuclear medicine) expose beneficiaries to ionizing radiation, which is associated with an increased risk of developing cancer (Brenner and Hall 2007, Center for Devices and Radiological Health 2010, Smith-Bindman et al. 2009).

Imaging Services Are Migrating from Inpatient to Ambulatory Settings

Some of the volume growth of imaging services in the physician fee schedule is related to the shift of imaging from inpatient hospital settings to ambulatory settings (physicians' offices, independent diagnostic testing facilities (IDTFs), and hospital outpatient departments) from 2004 to 2009. On the basis of changes in the site of care for the professional component of imaging services (the professional component covers the physician's work involved in interpreting the study and is paid under the physician fee schedule regardless of where an imaging service is performed), we found that inpatient settings accounted for 32 percent of all imaging studies in 2004, dropping to 28 percent in 2009. By comparison, physicians' offices and IDTFs accounted for 27 percent of imaging studies in 2004, increasing to 28 percent in 2009. Hospital outpatient departments' share of imaging grew from 38 percent in 2004 to 40 percent in 2009 (outpatient departments include emergency rooms). When imaging studies shift from inpatient settings to physicians' offices and IDTFs, the technical component portion of the service (which covers the cost of the nonphysician clinical staff who perform the test, medical equipment, medical supplies, and overhead expenses) is paid under the physician fee schedule, which generates additional fee schedule spending. Some of the growth of imaging in outpatient departments could be related to the trend of hospitals purchasing physician practices and converting those practices to outpatient hospital settings. It is difficult to test this hypothesis because Medicare claims data do not identify whether physicians are employed by hospitals.

Questions About the Clinical Appropriateness of Imaging Services

There is evidence that some diagnostic imaging services ordered by physicians are not clinically appropriate and that inappropriate use occurs in both physicians' offices and hospitals. The American College of Cardiology Foundation (ACCF) and United Healthcare assessed the appropriateness of nuclear cardiology procedures performed by six nonhospital practices using criteria developed by the ACCF and the American Society of Nuclear Cardiology (Hendel et al. 2010). The researchers found that 14 percent of the studies performed at these sites were inappropriate and 15 percent were of uncertain appropriateness. Using the same criteria, an analysis of nuclear cardiology procedures provided at the University of Chicago found that 13 percent were inappropriate and 7 percent were of uncertain appropriateness (Mehta et al. 2008). Similarly, another study examined the appropriateness of cardiac imaging stress tests conducted at the Mayo Clinic and found that between 14 percent and 18 percent of the tests were inappropriate (Gibbons et al. 2008).[5]

A significant proportion of noncardiac imaging studies may also be inappropriate. For example, one study found that nearly 30 percent of Medicare beneficiaries with uncomplicated low back pain received an imaging service within 28 days, even though imaging is rarely indicated for this condition in the absence of specific complications or comorbidities (Pham et al. 2009). According to data on CMS's Hospital Compare website, one-third of Medicare beneficiaries with low back pain who were given an MRI of the lumbar spine in hospital outpatient departments in 2008 did not receive more conservative therapy first, as is recommended by the American College of Radiology and the Agency for Healthcare Research and Quality (Centers for Medicare & Medicaid Services 2011c).

Overuse of MRI scans for low back pain carries the risk of false-positive findings, increased costs for the Medicare program and beneficiaries, and the potential to induce a cascade of additional procedures, such as surgery (Baras and Baker 2009, Centers for Medicare & Medicaid Services 2011c). A recent analysis of orders from primary care physicians for outpatient, nonemergency CT and MRI scans at a large urban hospital found that 26 percent did not meet appropriateness criteria developed by a radiology benefit management program (Lehnert and Bree 2010). Inappropriate orders included CT for chronic headache, spine MRI for acute back pain, and knee and shoulder MRI for osteoarthritis.

Improving Payment Accuracy for Imaging and Other Diagnostic Tests

The Commission makes three recommendations to improve the accuracy of physician fee schedule payments for imaging and other diagnostic tests (e.g., electrocardiograms and cardiovascular stress tests).

- The first recommendation is that CMS should work with the American Medical Association/Specialty Society Relative Value Scale Update Committee (RUC) to accelerate and expand ongoing efforts to combine into a single payment rate multiple discrete services often furnished together during the same encounter by the same provider. The payment rates for these comprehensive codes should reflect efficiencies in physician work and practice expense that occur when two or more services are provided together.
- Because the process of creating comprehensive codes for services commonly furnished together takes several years, CMS should also implement policies to improve payment accuracy sooner. Under the second recommendation, Medicare would account for efficiencies that occur during an imaging study's professional component—the physician's work involved in interpreting the study's results and writing a report—when multiple imaging services are provided during the same session to the same patient by a single practitioner. This policy would reduce the payment rate for the second and subsequent services performed in the same session. It would be similar to an existing Medicare policy that reduces the payment rate for an imaging study's technical component—the cost of the nonphysician clinical staff who perform the test, medical equipment, medical supplies, and overhead expenses—when multiple imaging studies are performed in the same session. The goal of this recommendation is to pay more accurately for imaging services in all settings (e.g., physicians' offices, hospital outpatient departments, and IDTFs) whether or not self-referral is involved.
- The third recommendation would account for efficiencies in physician work that occur when the same practitioner orders and performs imaging and other diagnostic tests. This recommendation would apply in all settings, including physicians' offices and hospitals.

The Commission has previously expressed concerns about mispricing of services in the physician fee schedule and the inequity of a payment system that allows some physicians to generate volume and revenue more easily than others (Medicare Payment Advisory

Commission 2010b). We have made several other recommendations to address mispricing of physician fee schedule services. For example, the Commission has recommended ways to improve the process through which CMS reviews the fee schedule's relative values for accuracy (Medicare Payment Advisory Commission 2006b). Although CMS—with advice from the RUC—has improved the review process since our recommendations, certain areas remain to be addressed.

Combining Discrete Services into Larger Units of Payment

CMS and the RUC should accelerate and expand efforts to combine multiple discrete services often furnished together during the same encounter into a single payment rate. The payment rate for a comprehensive bundle of services should account for duplications in physician work and practice expense that occur when multiple services are provided at the same time. This approach would improve payment accuracy and help reduce financial incentives to provide additional imaging studies, other diagnostic tests, and procedures. The Commission has expressed concern that the relatively small units of payment for many physician fee schedule services give physicians a financial incentive to increase volume (Medicare Payment Advisory Commission 2005a). The Commission has also noted that time savings are likely when services are furnished together instead of independently, and it may be appropriate to change payments to reflect these efficiencies (Medicare Payment Advisory Commission 2006b). For example, when a physician performs the professional component of two MRI studies during the same encounter, certain activities (such as reviewing the patient's records and discussing the findings with the referring physician) are likely to occur only once. However, the current valuation of physician work for each service assumes that these services are provided independently and that each activity is performed twice.

Since 2007, a RUC workgroup has been reviewing services that are frequently performed together by the same practitioner on the same date to determine whether such services should be bundled to account for efficiencies in physician work (Centers for Medicare & Medicaid Services 2010b, Government Accountability Office 2009). Under this process, the workgroup reviews pairs of services performed together more than 75 percent of the time (initially the threshold was 95 percent of the time) (American Medical Association 2010).[6] The RUC refers some of these codes to the Current Procedural Terminology (CPT) Editorial Panel for the development of bundled, or comprehensive, codes. Once the comprehensive codes have been created, the RUC works with the relevant specialty societies to develop work RVUs and practice expense inputs for the new codes to recommend to CMS. These values should account for efficiencies that occur when multiple services are performed together. CMS then reviews and approves the new values through its rulemaking process. Based on the review of services furnished together 95 percent of the time, the RUC referred 53 codes to CMS (American Medical Association 2011). The RUC has also identified 89 codes that are performed together more than 75 percent of the time for further examination.[7] According to the AMA, the RUC has focused on reviewing the codes with the highest share of expenditures.

This process of creating comprehensive codes has led to the packaging of imaging guidance codes with their associated procedures as well as the development of bundled codes for several imaging and procedural services, such as CT of the abdomen and pelvis, myocardial perfusion imaging (a type of nuclear medicine study), diagnostic cardiac catheterization, endovascular revascularization, and echocardiography. Between 2009 and

2011, CMS adopted RVUs for the new comprehensive codes that reflect efficiencies associated with performing multiple services during the same encounter (Centers for Medicare & Medicaid Services 2009, Centers for Medicare & Medicaid Services 2010b). For 2011, for example, the RUC recommended—and CMS adopted— values for new comprehensive codes that include two component codes: CT of the abdomen and CT of the pelvis (Centers for Medicare & Medicaid Services 2010b).[8] The RUC recommended using 100 percent of the work RVU for the component code with the highest RVU and reducing the work RVU for the second code by 50 percent to account for efficiencies. Consequently, the total work RVUs for the new comprehensive codes are about 25 percent less than the sum of the work RVUs for the component codes. The practice expense RVUs of the comprehensive codes are also lower than the sum of the practice expense RVUs of the component codes. For 2010, CMS adopted new values for comprehensive codes for myocardial perfusion imaging; the work RVUs for the comprehensive codes are between 29 percent and 40 percent lower than the sum of the work RVUs for the component codes.

Although this process is an important step forward in accounting for efficiencies in physician work and practice expense, we are concerned that it takes several years to develop and value comprehensive codes and that a relatively small number of comprehensive codes have been adopted to date. CMS recognizes that additional imaging and other diagnostic tests that are frequently furnished together likely involve efficiencies and plans to review them (Centers for Medicare & Medicaid Services 2010b). CMS should also encourage the RUC and CPT Editorial Panel to expand their efforts to create comprehensive codes. For example, these entities should consider:

- reviewing and bundling codes that are provided together less than 75 percent of time but more than 50 percent of the time;
- creating bundled codes that include different types of services that are frequently performed at the same time, such as nuclear medicine studies and cardiovascular stress tests or evaluation and management services and certain diagnostic tests; and
- combining radiopharmaceuticals with their associated imaging services (e.g., packaging myocardial perfusion studies with their related radiopharmaceuticals), as is done in the outpatient prospective payment system.

In addition, for imaging services that have not yet been bundled into comprehensive codes, CMS should reduce payment rates for the professional component of these services when multiple studies are provided during the same session. This policy—which would account for efficiencies in physician work—is described in the following section.

In future work, we plan to explore opportunities for combining into a single payment those services furnished during multiple encounters by a single provider—such as diagnostic tests, office visits, and procedures. There are precedents for this type of approach in the physician fee schedule. Under the global surgical policy, for example, physicians receive a global payment rate for many surgical procedures that includes some preoperative care, the surgery, and postoperative visits in the hospital and office (for 10 days or 90 days after the surgery, depending on the type of surgery). In addition, Medicare pays physicians a monthly capitation payment for all routine outpatient dialysis care furnished to dialysis patients. For patients treated in dialysis centers, the monthly capitation payment varies according to the number of face-to-face visits the physician has with the patient during the month and the patient's age. The monthly payment increases with the number of visits and decreases with increasing age.[9]

Recomendation 2 – 1

The Secretary should accelerate and expand efforts to package discrete services in the physician fee schedule into larger units for payment.

Rationale 2 – 1

To account for efficiencies in physician work and practice expense that occur when multiple services are provided at the same time, CMS and the RUC should accelerate and expand efforts to combine multiple services often furnished together during the same encounter by the same provider into a single payment rate. This approach would improve payment accuracy and help reduce financial incentives to provide additional imaging studies, other diagnostic tests, and procedures. The RUC and CPT Editorial Panel have created several comprehensive codes that encompass services frequently provided together.

The payment rates for these new codes reflect efficiencies associated with performing multiple services during the same encounter. CMS should work with the RUC and CPT Editorial Panel to build on these efforts.

Implications 2 – 1

Spending

- We estimate that this recommendation would not affect federal program spending because it would be implemented in a budget-neutral manner; savings from packaging discrete services into larger units of payment would be redistributed to other physician fee schedule services.

Beneficiary and Provider

- We do not expect this recommendation to affect beneficiaries' access to care or providers' willingness or ability to furnish services.

Reducing Payment Rates for the Professional Component of Multiple Imaging Studies

Because the process of creating comprehensive codes for services commonly furnished together takes several years and a relatively small number of comprehensive codes have been adopted to date, CMS should also develop policies to improve payment accuracy that can be implemented more rapidly. The Government Accountability Office (GAO) has noted that relying solely on the RUC to account for efficiencies that occur when services are provided together would limit CMS's ability to quickly identify opportunities for addressing mispricing (Government Accountability Office 2009). Therefore, Medicare should account for efficiencies in physician work by reducing payment rates for the professional component of multiple imaging studies that are performed on the same patient in the same session by the same practitioner. This policy should apply across settings (e.g., physicians' offices, IDTFs, and hospitals) because there are likely to be efficiencies in physician work regardless of the setting.

GAO found that there are efficiencies in physician time when two or more imaging services are furnished together because certain activities are not done twice, such as reviewing the patient's medical history and reviewing the final report and following up with the referring physician after the service (Government Accountability Office 2009).[10] With the help of medical directors from Medicare contractors and other experts, GAO examined 118 pairs of imaging studies and estimated that Medicare could save over $175 million annually if the program accounted for efficiencies in physician work that occur when these tests are furnished together.[11]

GAO also identified 149 pairs of other services commonly performed together—such as physical therapy, interventional radiology procedures, pulmonary tests, and pathology tests—that contain efficiencies in practice expense. GAO recommended that CMS account for these efficiencies. In 2010, CMS adopted a policy that reduces payments for multiple outpatient therapy services (physical therapy, occupational therapy, and speech– language pathology services) that are provided to the same patient on the same day (Centers for Medicare & Medicaid Services 2010b). Under this policy, Medicare reduces the practice expense portion of the payment rate for the second and subsequent outpatient therapy service by 25 percent.[12] The Physician Payment and Therapy Relief Act of 2010 changed the reduction from 25 percent to 20 percent.

Reducing payment rates for the professional component of multiple studies would align the policy for the professional component of an imaging service with the current policy for the technical component. Under Medicare's multiple procedure payment reduction (MPPR), CMS reduces the payment rate for the technical component of second and subsequent imaging studies by 50 percent when multiple services are performed in the same session. This policy is based on a previous Commission recommendation and is designed to account for efficiencies in clinical labor, supplies, equipment, and indirect practice costs when multiple studies are performed in the same session (Medicare Payment Advisory Commission 2005b). It includes CT, MRI, certain ultrasound, and certain nuclear medicine services. CMS defined the same session to be one encounter in which a patient received one or more imaging studies (Centers for Medicare & Medicaid Services 2005). If a patient receives two imaging services during two separate encounters on the same day for a medically necessary reason, the provider would receive the full payment amount for each service.

How CMS maintains budget neutrality in the physician fee schedule

By law, increases or decreases in the physician fee schedule's relative value units (RVUs) must be budget neutral. If the changes would cause expenditures for the year to increase or decrease by more than $20 million, CMS must make adjustments to preserve budget neutrality. When calculating the impact of changes to RVUs on total spending, CMS uses recent volume data; the agency does not project future volume changes. For example, when estimating the impact of RVU changes for 2011, CMS used volume data from 2009 (Centers for Medicare & Medicaid Services 2010b). CMS uses slightly different methods to account for changes in physician work RVUs and practice expense RVUs.

In the case of payments for physician work RVUs, CMS adjusts the fee schedule's conversion factor (average payment amount) to account for changes in work RVUs. For example, a budget-neutrality adjustment was applied to the conversion factor for 2011, increasing it by 0.4 percent (Centers for Medicare & Medicaid Services 2010b). Changes in the work RVUs for 2011 would have decreased overall expenditures by 0.4 percent, which would have exceeded the statute's threshold of $20 million. Therefore, the conversion factor was increased by 0.4 percent to offset this change.

In the case of payments for practice expense RVUs, CMS adjusts all practice expense RVUs to offset changes in some practice expense RVUs.

For 2011, for example, CMS expanded the multiple procedure payment reduction policy for the technical component of certain imaging studies by applying it to multiple imaging services that are performed on noncontiguous parts of the body during the same session (Centers for Medicare & Medicaid Services 2010b). To offset these reduced payments, CMS increased practice expense RVUs for all fee schedule services by about 0.1 percent.

The MPPR policy for the technical component originally applied to services performed on contiguous body parts within the same type of imaging (such as CT scans of the abdomen and pelvis). For 2011, however, CMS expanded this policy by applying it to multiple imaging services that are performed on noncontiguous parts of the body during the same session, even if the services use different types of imaging (Centers for Medicare & Medicaid Services 2010b). For example, if CT of the head and CT of the abdomen are performed during the same session, the payment rate for the less costly service is reduced by 50 percent. CMS has also said that it plans to review possible expansions of this policy to the professional component of multiple imaging studies (Centers for Medicare & Medicaid Services 2010b).

Comprehensive codes that include multiple related imaging studies (e.g., the codes for CT of the abdomen and pelvis discussed on p. 38) are not subject to the MPPR for the technical component because they already account for efficiencies in practice expense associated with multiple services (Centers for Medicare & Medicaid Services 2010b). Similarly, an expansion of the MPPR to the professional component should not apply to comprehensive codes that reflect efficiencies in physician work. Thus, as the RUC, CPT Editorial Panel, and CMS create and value additional comprehensive codes for multiple imaging services, these new codes should not be subject to the MPPR.

This recommendation would apply to physicians and other health professionals (e.g., nurse practitioners and physician assistants) who interpret imaging studies and bill for the professional component. According to a recent report, several states permit nurse practitioners to order and interpret diagnostic tests (Institute of Medicine 2010).

CMS should calculate the payment reduction for the second and subsequent professional component services performed in the same session by analyzing the efficiencies in physician work associated with multiple services. These efficiencies may vary by type of imaging. This policy change should be implemented in a budget-neutral manner. In other words, CMS should redistribute savings from payment reductions to the professional component of multiple imaging studies to other services in the physician fee schedule. (The text box explains how CMS maintains budget neutrality in the physician fee schedule.) CMS applies an MPPR to surgical procedures that also is budget neutral (Centers for Medicare & Medicaid Services 2010b). By contrast, the Congress required that the MPPR that applies to the technical component of imaging studies be exempt from budget neutrality; in other words, the savings from this policy reduce aggregate Medicare spending.[13]

Recommendation 2 - 2

The Congress should direct the Secretary to apply a multiple procedure payment reduction to the professional component of diagnostic imaging services provided by the same practitioner in the same session.

Rationale 2 - 2

To account for efficiencies in physician work, CMS should expand the MPPR to the professional component of multiple imaging studies that are performed in the same session by the same practitioner. When two or more imaging services are furnished together, certain physician activities are probably not done twice, such as reviewing the patient's medical history and reviewing the final report and following up with the referring physician after the test. This recommendation would align the MPPR policy for the two portions of an imaging service: the technical component and the professional component. This policy should apply across settings because there are likely to be efficiencies in physician work regardless of the setting.

Implications 2 – 2

Spending

- We estimate that this recommendation would not affect federal program spending because it would be implemented in a budget-neutral manner; savings from reducing payments for the professional component of multiple imaging studies that are performed in the same session would be redistributed to other physician fee schedule services.

Beneficiary and Provider

- The recommendation would reduce Medicare payments for providers who perform the professional component of multiple imaging studies in the same session to account for efficiencies in physician work.

However, we do not expect this recommendation to affect beneficiaries' access to care or to reduce providers' willingness or ability to furnish appropriate care. There is no evidence that the MPPR for the technical component of imaging studies reduced access to care.

Reducing Payment Rates for Imaging and Other Diagnostic Tests Ordered and Performed by the Same Practitioner

We recommend that Medicare reduce payment rates for imaging and other diagnostic tests paid under the physician fee schedule when the same practitioner orders and performs the test because some efficiencies occur in these cases. Some of the physician work involved in interpreting a test likely duplicates activities that have already been performed by the referring physician. For example, the work RVUs for a test often include activities that occur during the preservice phase of the service, such as reviewing the patient's history, medical records, symptoms, and medications as well as reviewing the indications for the test (the preservice phase describes the work involved before a specific procedure). If the physician who performs the test also ordered it, the physician should have already obtained and reviewed much of this information during an evaluation and management (E&M) service (the

E&M service may have occurred on the same day as the test or before the day of the test). The payment for a test also includes postservice activities, such as discussing the findings with the referring physician; this activity is unnecessary when the referring and interpreting physician are the same (the postservice phase includes activities performed after a procedure). Therefore, it would be appropriate to remove these duplicate activities from the payment rate for tests that are ordered and performed by the same practitioner. Currently, the work RVUs for these services do not account for these efficiencies, which makes them more profitable than other services and could contribute to the increase in self-referral of imaging and other tests.

This recommendation applies to all diagnostic imaging studies (e.g., MRI, CT, nuclear medicine, and ultrasound) as well as other diagnostic tests that are paid under the physician fee schedule (e.g., electrocardiograms, cardiovascular stress tests, and anatomic pathology tests). It does not apply to tests paid under the clinical laboratory fee schedule, such as urinalysis and blood tests, because these tests do not involve physician work. This policy should apply to all settings where imaging and other diagnostic tests are provided (e.g., physicians' offices, IDTFs, and hospitals) because there are likely to be similar efficiencies in physician work across settings. It should apply whether the physician who ordered and performed the test provided an E&M service on the day of the test or before the day of the test; regardless, the practitioner should be familiar with the patient's history and prior test results.

Table 2-1. Share of imaging services ordered and performed by same practitioner, by setting and type of imaging, 2009

		type of setting	
type of imaging	**Nonhospital**	**hospital**	**all**
Standard imaging	40%	3%	15%
Nuclear medicine	31	9	22
Computed tomography	8	2	3
MRI	7	2	4
PET	9	1	5
Echography (ultrasound)	40	11	25
Imaging procedures	29	32	31
all imaging	**35**	**6**	**16**

Note: PET (positron emission tomography). The numbers represent the percent of diagnostic imaging services, by type of imaging, in which the ordering and performing practitioner have the same National Provider Identifier. Nonhospital settings include physicians' offices and independent diagnostic testing facilities. Hospital settings include inpatient settings and outpatient departments. To avoid double-counting the number of services, the data exclude claims that are only for the technical component of a study. Standard imaging includes chest, musculoskeletal, and breast X-rays. Imaging procedures include stereoscopic X-ray guidance for delivery of radiation therapy, fluoroguide for spinal injections, and other interventional radiology procedures.

Source: MedPAC analysis of 5 percent carrier Standard Analytic File from CMS, 2009.

Savings from this policy should be redistributed to other physician fee schedule services. In other words, it should be implemented in a budget-neutral manner. As with Recommendation 2-2, this recommendation would apply to physicians and other health professionals (e.g., nurse practitioners and physician assistants) who order and perform diagnostic tests.

A key issue is identifying duplicate activities and estimating their share of the total work RVUs for a service. CMS, with assistance from the RUC, could identify duplicate activities associated with tests that are ordered and performed by the same practitioner and use this information to develop a uniform percent reduction for the work RVUs of such tests. CMS could also apply different percent reductions to different types of tests (e.g., advanced imaging, all other imaging, and nonimaging tests). The Medicare administrative contractors, which pay Medicare claims, could implement this policy by matching the National Provider Identifier (NPI) of the ordering practitioner to the NPI of the performing practitioner on claims for imaging and other diagnostic tests.

Table 2-2. Illustration of the impact of Recommendations 2-2 and 2-3 on professional component payments for multiple imaging services provided during the same session

		payment for:	
Study ordered and performed by:	First imaging study during session (reduced by 25% if same practitioner orders and performs study)	Second imaging study during session (reduced by 50%)	third imaging study during session (reduced by 50%)
Different practitioners	$100	$50	$50
Same practitioner	75	50	50

Note: In this illustration, the normal payment amount for the professional component of each imaging study performed during the session is $100. Under Recommendation 2-2, Medicare would reduce the payment rate for the professional component of the second and subsequent services performed in the same session (for illustrative purposes only, we have assumed a 50 percent reduction). This policy would apply whether or not the study was performed by the same practitioner who ordered it. Under Recommendation 2-3, Medicare would reduce the payment rate for the professional component of the first imaging service that is ordered and performed by the same practitioner during a session but not subsequent services during the same session (for illustrative purposes only, we have assumed a 25 percent reduction in this case).

Another important policy question is whether to apply a payment reduction when the practitioner who performs the test is different from the ordering practitioner but shares the same practice as the ordering practitioner. If the policy does not apply when the ordering and performing practitioners share a practice, an incentive would exist to bill for the test in the name of a different practitioner from the one who ordered it, even if the same practitioner both ordered and performed it. If this were to occur, the bill would be considered a false claim and the provider who submitted it could be subject to repayment and penalties. On the other hand, applying this policy to practitioners who share a practice could be unfair to the practitioner who performs the test, who would need to review the patient's history, medical records, symptoms, and medications. In addition, because practitioners who share a practice may not always share the same tax number, it could be difficult for CMS to identify whether practitioners are part of the same practice. Thus, this policy should be limited to individual practitioners who order and perform imaging and other diagnostic tests. CMS should educate practitioners that they need to accurately report the name of the ordering and performing provider on claims for imaging and other diagnostic tests to avoid filing a false claim.

We examined the potential scope of this recommendation by identifying the share of imaging services in 2009 in which the professional component of the study was performed by the same practitioner who ordered it (we did not examine the share of other diagnostic tests that were ordered and performed by the same practitioner). We separately examined imaging studies performed in nonhospital settings (physicians' offices and IDTFs) and hospitals (inpatient settings and outpatient departments). We found that 35 percent of studies provided in nonhospital settings were ordered and performed by the same practitioner (as indicated by the NPI) (Table 2-1). This proportion varied by type of service, ranging from 7 percent of MRI scans to 40 percent of standard imaging (e.g., chest X-rays) and echography. By contrast, only 6 percent of studies provided in hospital settings were ordered and performed by the same practitioner, ranging from 1 percent of positron emission tomography scans to 32 percent of imaging procedures (such as interventional radiology) (Table 2-1). The lower share in hospital settings is probably related to two factors:

- hospital privileging policies that often limit the right to interpret imaging studies to radiologists and certain other specialties, and
- referrals by community-based physicians to hospital radiology departments.

Across all settings (hospital and nonhospital), 16 percent of imaging studies were ordered and performed by the same practitioner.

Recommendation 2-3 would reduce the payment rate for the professional component of the first imaging service ordered and performed by the same practitioner during a session. If multiple imaging services were ordered and performed by the same practitioner in the same session, the payment rate for the professional component of the second and subsequent services would be reduced under the MPPR policy (Recommendation 2-2). It would not make sense to apply both policies to the same service, as they account for similar efficiencies (e.g., reviewing the patient's medical history before the test and following up with the referring physician after the service).

Table 2-2 illustrates the interaction between Recommendations 2-2 and 2-3. For illustrative purposes, we have assumed that, under Recommendation 2-2, Medicare would reduce the payment rate for the professional component of the second and subsequent services performed in the same session by 50 percent. We have also assumed for illustrative purposes that, under Recommendation 2-3, Medicare would reduce the payment rate by 25 percent for the professional component of the first imaging service ordered and performed by the same practitioner during a session.

Under both recommendations, CMS should determine the actual payment reductions based on an analysis of the efficiencies that occur. These reductions may vary from the illustrative reductions shown in Table 2-2.

Recommendation 2 - 3

The Congress should direct the Secretary to reduce the physician work component of imaging and other diagnostic tests that are ordered and performed by the same practitioner.

Rationale 2 - 3

Medicare should reduce payment rates for imaging and other diagnostic tests paid under the physician fee schedule when the same practitioner orders and performs the test because some efficiencies occur in these cases. The work involved in interpreting a test likely duplicates activities that have already been performed by the referring practitioner, such as reviewing the patient's history, medical records, symptoms, medications, and the indications for the test. If the practitioner who performs the test is the same provider who ordered it, the practitioner should have already obtained and reviewed much of this information during an E&M service. Accounting for these efficiencies should reduce the financial incentive for practitioners to self-refer for imaging and other tests. This policy should apply in all settings where imaging and other diagnostic tests are provided (e.g., physicians' offices, IDTFs, and hospitals) because there are likely to be similar efficiencies in physician work across settings.

Implications 2 – 3

Spending

- We estimate that this recommendation would not affect federal program spending because it would be implemented in a budget-neutral manner; savings from reducing payments to providers who both order and perform imaging and other diagnostic tests would be redistributed to other physician fee schedule services.

Beneficiary and Provider

- We do not expect this recommendation to affect beneficiaries' access to care. Although the recommendation would reduce Medicare payments for providers who both order and perform imaging and other diagnostic tests to account for efficiencies that occur in these cases, we do not anticipate a decline in providers' willingness or ability to furnish appropriate care.

Require High-Use Practitioners to Participate in a Prior Authorization Program for Advanced Diagnostic Imaging

In addition to policies that aim to improve payment accuracy, we also recommend that Medicare adopt a tool called prior authorization to foster more appropriate use of advanced imaging (MRI, CT, and nuclear medicine). Advanced imaging services have been growing rapidly over the last decade and there is evidence that they are sometimes used inappropriately (see pp. 35–36). Prior authorization is used widely by private payers for advanced imaging but has not been adopted by Medicare.

Under this approach, Medicare would require physician outliers—those who order a significantly greater number of advanced imaging services than other physicians who treat similar patients—to participate in a prior authorization process for advanced imaging. Such an approach would help ensure that outlier physicians use advanced imaging services appropriately without subjecting all physicians to prior authorization. It would also encourage all physicians to be more prudent in their use of imaging to avoid being subject to this requirement. The focus on outlier physicians—rather than all physicians—would reduce CMS's administrative costs and limit the burden on practitioners and beneficiaries. Because of CMS's limited resources, this program should target imaging services that account for a significant share of spending and volume, have evidence-based guidelines for appropriate use, and exhibit variations in utilization among physicians and geographic areas. Although we have tried to minimize the administrative costs for CMS, the agency would still need additional resources to develop and operate a prior authorization program. Eventually, policymakers may want to consider expanding such a program to other services that are experiencing rapid spending growth, such as physical therapy and radiation therapy. This recommendation would apply to physicians and other health professionals (e.g., nurse practitioners and physician assistants) who order advanced imaging studies.

CMS has tried to manage inappropriate use of imaging and other services primarily through retrospective claims review and other postpayment approaches, although the agency is testing whether decision support systems (DSS) can promote appropriate ordering of imaging services at the time of service (see text box, pp. 50–51) (Centers for Medicare & Medicaid Services 2010a, Government Accountability Office 2008). In 2008, GAO recommended that CMS examine the feasibility of adopting front-end methods to managing imaging services, such as prior authorization programs used by private plans (Government Accountability Office 2008).

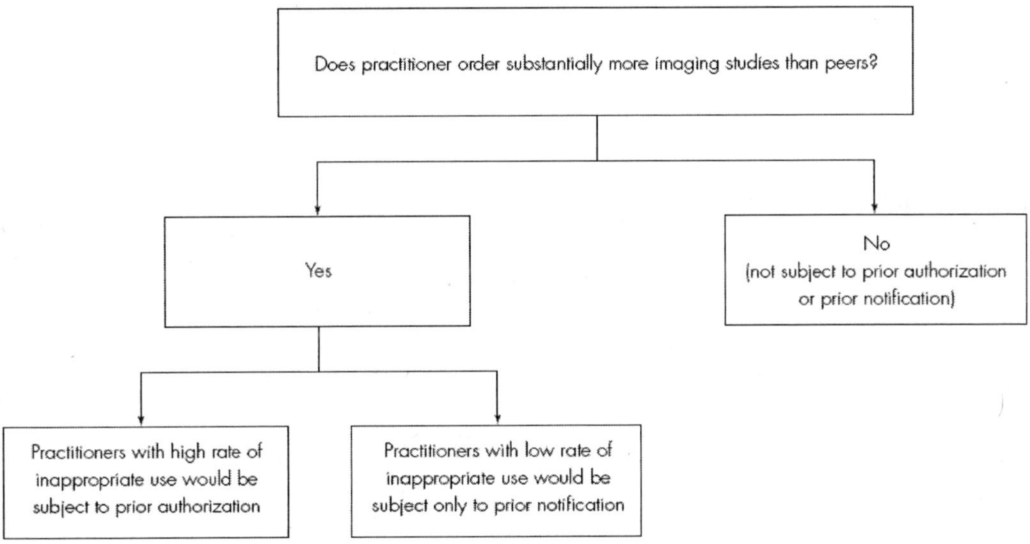

Figure 2-2. Illustration of prior authorization program for advanced imaging in Medicare.

A prior authorization policy in Medicare would likely involve three steps (Figure 2-2). First, CMS would identify physicians and other health professionals who are outliers in terms of the number of advanced imaging studies they order, compared with practitioners in the same specialty who treat patients with similar conditions. Second, these outlier physicians would submit clinical information to CMS when they order advanced imaging, which would enable the agency to compare their use of imaging to evidence-based clinical guidelines and provide them with confidential feedback. CMS would develop these guidelines in consultation with physician specialty societies and other stakeholders. The main purpose of this stage—called prior notification—is to educate physicians about the appropriate use of imaging. It is possible that providers could use clinical DSS instead of participating in a prior notification program as long as the DSS uses the same guidelines as the prior notification process and the providers transmit data from the DSS to CMS so that CMS could track their use of imaging (see text box on pp. 50–51 for more information on DSS).[14] Allowing providers to use DSS instead of prior notification would reduce the burden on them but still allow CMS to monitor their ordering patterns. Under a pilot program conducted in Minnesota, five medical groups used DSS instead of prior notification (Institute for Clinical Systems Improvement 2010).

If some practitioners persist in ordering imaging inappropriately, despite the information they receive during prior notification or from a DSS, they would be required to participate in a prior authorization program, in which CMS or a contractor would review and approve their requests to order imaging services before they are provided. Outlier physicians with relatively low rates of inappropriate ordering would not be subject to prior authorization; they would remain in the prior notification program. They would still submit clinical data to CMS so that CMS could track their ordering patterns and provide them with feedback, but they would not be required to have their imaging requests approved. Outlier physicians whose rates of inappropriate use changed over time could switch from prior authorization to prior notification, and vice versa.

A prior authorization policy could exclude physicians and other health professionals who are part of an accountable care organization (ACO) that participates in the Medicare program under section 3021 or 3022 of the Patient Protection and Affordable Care Act of 2010 (PPACA), as long as the ACO shares risk with Medicare for the cost growth for its patients. The rationale for excluding ACO physicians is that they would have financial incentives to control the volume of imaging and other services they provide to beneficiaries.

A prior authorization approach builds on the Commission's recommendation that Medicare measure physicians' resource use over time and share the results with physicians on a confidential basis (Medicare Payment Advisory Commission 2005b, Medicare Payment Advisory Commission 2008a). These resource use reports would allow physicians to assess their practice styles, evaluate whether they tend to use more resources than their peers or what evidence-based research recommends, and revise practice styles as appropriate. In particular, such reports could encourage physicians who refer patients for more imaging services than their peers to reconsider their ordering behavior (Medicare Payment Advisory Commission 2005b). The Medicare Improvements for Patients and Providers Act of 2008 established a Medicare Physician Feedback Program and directed the Secretary to use Medicare claims data to provide physicians with confidential reports that measure the total amount of resources involved in furnishing care to beneficiaries.[15] PPACA directed the Secretary to expand and make significant changes to the Physician Feedback Program, including a requirement to provide reports to individual physicians that compare their resource use patterns with patterns of other physicians. Although resource use reports are an important step in reducing unwarranted practice variation, we do not believe that they alone are sufficient to ensure that high-use physicians order imaging appropriately. Thus, Medicare should also develop a targeted prior authorization program for advanced imaging.

Many Private Plans Use Prior Authorization Programs for Advanced Imaging

Many private plans have been using prior authorization programs for several years to control the growth of advanced imaging services and improve the appropriate use of these studies (Government Accountability Office 2008, Levin et al. 2010, Mitchell and Lagalia 2009, Tynan et al. 2008).[16]

In addition, some state Medicaid programs use prior authorization for advanced imaging (Smith et al. 2010). Adapting this approach to Medicare raises certain concerns, however, including the administrative burden on physicians, the strength of guidelines used to review imaging requests, and the administrative implications for CMS.

In private plans' prior authorization programs, physicians who wish to order certain studies must first obtain approval from the plan; plans will not pay for tests that are not approved. Some plans use prior notification programs in which physicians submit requests for imaging services to the plan for review but requests are not denied.

In researching these programs, we examined information from:

- studies published by GAO, the Center for Studying Health System Change, and other researchers (Government Accountability Office 2008, Levin et al. 2010, Mitchell and Lagalia 2009, Tynan et al. 2008);
- interviews and meetings with plans and radiology benefit managers (RBMs), the vendors who operate these programs; and
- presentations by physicians from two health plans at a public Commission meeting in 2007 (Medicare Payment Advisory Commission 2007a).

We have also met with representatives from physician specialty societies and imaging providers to discuss their concerns about prior authorization programs.

Prior Authorization Programs Use Clinical Guidelines to Review Imaging Requests

According to plans and RBMs, prior authorization programs are based on clinical guidelines developed by physician specialty groups, such as the American College of Radiology and American College of Cardiology, and supplemented by literature reviews and clinician panels.[17] If appropriateness criteria do not exist for new technologies or new indications for an existing technology, the plan or RBM may convene an expert panel to develop guidelines. Plans and RBMs use these clinical guidelines to develop algorithms, or decision trees, that they use to approve or deny requests for tests. The algorithms are usually based on modality, body part, and indication. For example, the rules for MRI of the lumbar spine for low back pain would contain a list of indications for which this test is considered appropriate, such as suspicion of cancer.

Prior authorization programs vary in the types of tests they cover, their approval criteria, and their administrative processes. However, there are several similarities. These programs generally exclude tests provided in inpatient hospital settings and emergency rooms. Their processes for reviewing imaging requests, outlined in Figure 2-3, are also similar. In step 1, the ordering physician submits a request to the plan or RBM that includes clinical information, such as the patient's diagnosis, signs and symptoms, prior treatments, and prior test results. The initial request may be made by phone, fax, or through a web-based interface. In step 2, the plan or RBM checks whether the request is consistent with its clinical criteria. For example, if a physician requests an MRI of the lumbar spine for a patient with symptoms of low back pain, a web-based program will guide the physician through a list of questions to determine whether the request meets the plan's clinical guidelines. If so, the plan approves the test (step 3a, Figure 2-3). Plans and RBMs told us that 60 percent to 85 percent of requests are approved at the first stage of the process, which usually takes less than 10 minutes. We were not able to independently verify this information.

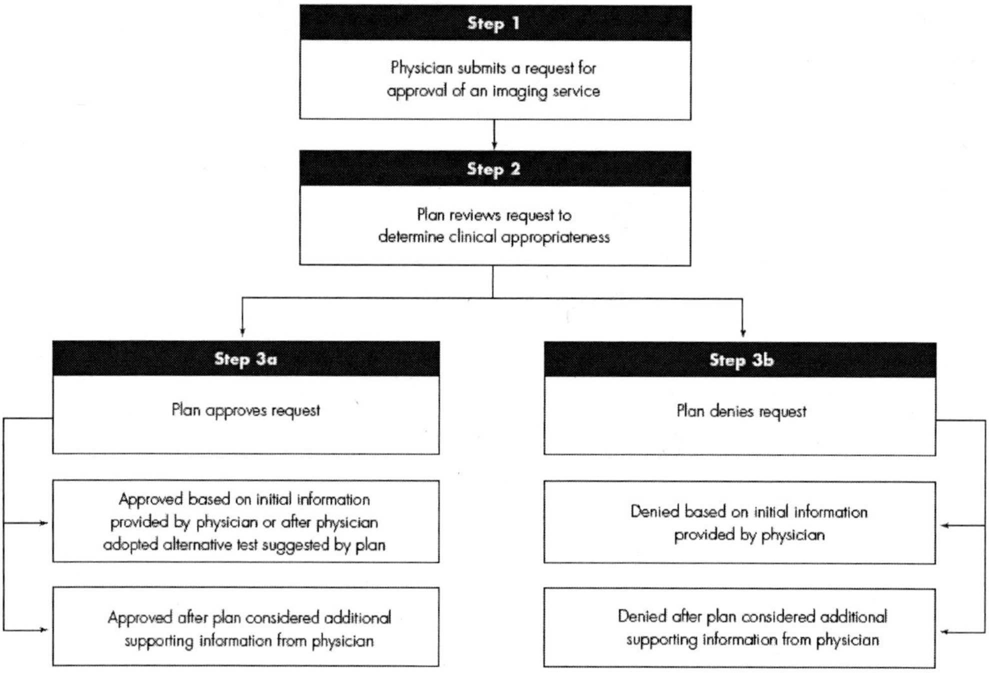

Source: Government Accountability Office analysis of information from radiology benefit management companies and private plans (Government Accountability Office 2008).

Figure 2-3. Steps that typically occur in prior authorization programs used by private plans.

If the plan does not approve the request at the first stage, the request usually goes to a nurse reviewer, who may suggest a more appropriate alternative test or ask for additional clinical information. If the request is not approved at the second stage, the physician can discuss the case with a physician reviewer employed by the plan, such as a radiologist. Sometimes, the ordering physician agrees to change the request to a more appropriate test. If the request is ultimately denied (step 3b, Figure 2-3), the physician can use the plan's formal appeals process to appeal the decision. Although 15 percent to 40 percent of requests go through additional levels of review, plans and RBMs told us that about 95 percent of all requests are resolved within 24 hours of the initial request (we were not able to independently verify these figures).

Variations of Prior Authorization Programs

Some plans and RBMs use a variation of prior authorization called prior notification (Government Accountability Office 2008, Levin et al. 2010, Tynan et al. 2008). In these programs, ordering physicians provide clinical information to plans about studies they wish to order and receive feedback on whether the studies are appropriate. If the request does not meet guidelines set by the plan, the plan suggests an alternative approach but does not deny payment if physicians decide to order the originally requested study. The plan may use this information to create profiles of physicians' ordering patterns.

In another variation of prior authorization, some RBMs and plans have a "gold card" program in which ordering physicians who have high approval rates receive automatic approval when they order studies. These physicians must still notify the RBM or plan when they order a test and provide clinical information about the studies they order, but they do not have to receive formal approval. Although some plans and RBMs claim that gold card programs are successful because they reduce the administrative burden on physicians with high approval rates, others argue that these programs have downsides, such as the risk that physicians who are exempt from receiving prior approval will be less motivated to order imaging appropriately.

Impact of Prior Authorization on Volume of Imaging

Several plans report that prior authorization programs have significantly reduced the volume growth of expensive imaging studies, but there are no independent studies that measure the impact of these programs using a control group (Government Accountability Office 2008, Levin et al. 2010, Mitchell and Lagalia 2009, Tynan et al. 2008). Plans interviewed by GAO reported that the annual growth of imaging services declined to less than 5 percent after prior authorization was implemented; before these programs were adopted, growth rates ranged from 10 percent to 20 percent (Government Accountability Office 2008). The largest reductions in use occurred immediately after the programs were implemented. According to our interviews with plans and RBMs, the savings from prior authorization programs more than offset the administrative costs (most RBMs charge plans a per member per month fee to operate the program).

A case study of three health plans that adopted prior authorization programs in 2004 or 2005 also found that the most significant impacts occurred during the first year after the programs were established (Mitchell and Lagalia 2009). In the year preceding the programs' implementation, all three plans experienced double-digit growth in the use of advanced imaging services. One year after the programs were adopted, the number of CT scans per capita declined significantly (declines ranged from 9 percent to 14 percent) and the number of MRI scans per capita also dropped (declines ranged from 8 percent to 15 percent). However, results for the second year of the programs were mixed: The number of CT and MRI studies per capita continued to decline in one of the plans but increased in the other two plans. The authors of this study speculate that the two plans' volumes increased in the second year for several reasons: The plans began to exempt certain physicians from obtaining prior approval (e.g., conducted a gold card program), physicians increased their approval rate by learning which diagnoses lead to approval, clinical applications for advanced imaging expanded, the supply of imaging equipment continued to increase, and physician self-referral was not restricted. A weakness of this study is that it did not control for time trends and other factors that might have influenced the changes in imaging use. In addition, the study examined changes in use for only two years after the programs were implemented, and the study included only three plans.

Prior authorization programs reduce the growth of imaging by influencing physicians to withdraw or change their requests for tests, denying requests, and discouraging physicians from ordering inappropriate tests in the future. According to our interviews with plans and

RBMs, a small proportion of imaging requests (less than 10 percent) are withdrawn or changed to a different test. Similarly, a published study found that 4 percent of requests submitted to a single RBM were either canceled or changed (Levin et al. 2010). Findings from our interviews and other evidence suggest that denial rates vary widely by RBM, from 1 percent to about 20 percent. This variation may be related to geographic differences in practice patterns or differences in approval criteria. Common reasons for denial include ordering multiple studies of contiguous body parts (e.g., CT of the abdomen and pelvis) when a single study is sufficient, ordering an inappropriate modality for an indication (e.g., MRI instead of CT), and not providing sufficient clinical information. According to data from an RBM that contracted with a Medicare Advantage plan, 12 percent of requests for advanced imaging were denied in a single month (Iglehart 2009). The most frequently denied requests were for nuclear cardiology studies to detect coronary artery disease and positron emission tomography scans ordered by nononcologists to monitor cancer treatment. An investigation by the Senate Commerce Committee found that one RBM denied 22 percent of requests for nuclear cardiology studies submitted by providers in Delaware (Committee on Commerce, Science, and Transportation 2011). Plans interviewed by GAO reported that denial rates were low, primarily because requesting physicians agreed to order a more clinically appropriate test or to forgo the test (Government Accountability Office 2008). These plans also found that physicians are less likely to request inappropriate tests in the future as a result of their interaction with the program.

Developing a Prior Authorization Program for Medicare

Several issues would be involved in developing a prior notification and prior authorization program for Medicare that would apply to physicians and other health professionals who order substantially more advanced imaging studies than their peers. Some of these challenges are also faced by prior authorization programs used by private plans. Key issues include:

- limiting the administrative burden on practitioners who are required to submit requests for prior approval;
- minimizing the additional waiting time for patients to receive imaging;
- developing transparent, high-quality clinical guidelines for approving imaging studies; and
- identifying physician outliers.

We also address the administrative implications of establishing and managing a prior authorization program and CMS's statutory authority to require prior authorization.

Issues Related to Practitioners and Patients

According to plans, RBMs, and a Senate Commerce Committee report, physicians often view prior authorization as creating new administrative burdens and challenging their clinical autonomy (Committee on Commerce, Science, and Transportation 2011, Iglehart 2009). There is also a concern that these programs delay important tests for patients. Plans and RBMs we interviewed said that they address these concerns by using web-based interfaces to streamline and shorten the approval process. A prior authorization program developed by Medicare would also need to use web-based interfaces and other tools to speed the review process. In addition, CMS would need to disseminate the approval criteria to physicians and beneficiaries. Limiting prior authorization to the minority of physicians who use substantially more advanced imaging than their peers would reduce the administrative burden on all physicians and wait times for beneficiaries.

Transparency and Quality of Guidelines Used for Prior Authorization

Providers and others have raised concerns about the quality and transparency of the clinical criteria that plans and RBMs use to review and approve imaging requests. Although these criteria are usually based on clinical guidelines developed by physician specialty societies, they may differ in some respects. For example, an investigation by the Delaware Department of Insurance found that an RBM's guidelines for cardiac stress tests agreed with criteria developed by the American College of Cardiology Foundation (ACCF) in many but not all areas; there were important differences with regard to the appropriate first test for intermediate-risk and high-risk patients (Delaware Department of Insurance 2011). If a specific request is not addressed by an RBM's protocols, a physician reviewer may have discretion to approve the study. CMS has also raised concerns that RBMs use potentially proprietary information in their clinical review protocols, which may be inconsistent with the public nature of Medicare (Government Accountability Office 2008).

Because guidelines developed by specialty societies are very important for prior authorization programs, we describe how two societies—the American College of Radiology (ACR) and the ACCF—create guidelines. Both groups have assembled expert panels composed of multiple specialties to develop appropriateness criteria for different organ systems or imaging modalities (American College of Radiology 2011, Patel et al. 2005). The panels collect evidence from the medical literature, but because there is often a lack of empirical information about the benefits of imaging for clinical decision making and patient outcomes, the panels use clinical judgment to reach consensus about whether a given study is appropriate for a specific condition (Douglas et al. 2006). Imaging studies are rated on a scoring system from one to nine, indicating the least to most appropriate examination. ACR panels have established criteria for the use of imaging for over 175 conditions, such as low back pain, acute chest pain, and acute pancreatitis. ACCF panels have developed criteria for cardiac CT, cardiac MRI, echocardiography, and myocardial perfusion imaging (a type of nuclear medicine study). One area in which the evidence is relatively strong is the use of imaging studies for patients with low back pain: A meta-analysis of six randomized trials found no difference between imaging and usual care without imaging in terms of pain, functional ability, quality of life, and overall improvement (Chou et al. 2011).

Using decision support systems to improve appropriate ordering of imaging

Some health systems have adopted clinical decision support systems (DSS) to improve the appropriate use of imaging, an approach that is now being tested in a Medicare demonstration program. DSS are decision aids that provide real-time feedback to ordering physicians on the appropriateness of imaging studies based on clinical guidelines. Two providers—Virginia Mason Medical Center and Massachusetts General Hospital—have reported that implementation of DSS for imaging was followed by a decline in the rate of growth of imaging or an absolute drop in the number of studies (Blackmore et al. 2011, Sistrom et al. 2009). However, because of the unique characteristics of these organizations and the circumstances in which they adopted DSS, these results may not be generalizable to the broader health care system.

Virginia Mason—an integrated, multidisciplinary health system in the Pacific Northwest—adopted a DSS linked to a system for ordering imaging studies (Blackmore et al. 2011). The system focused on three high-cost procedures with high variability in use: lumbar MRI for low back pain, head MRI for headache, and sinus computed tomography (CT) for suspected sinus disease. Virginia Mason providers developed decision rules for these types of imaging based on evidence-based guidelines and a review of the literature. Physicians who wished to order one of the targeted studies had to first document that the imaging request was consistent with an approved indication. If the request was not considered appropriate, the DSS would prevent the test from being ordered and suggest alternatives to imaging (such as physical therapy for lumbar back pain). Subspecialists (e.g., neurologists and spine specialists) could override the DSS if they considered the imaging test clinically indicated. Researchers compared the rate of imaging for specific conditions before and after adoption of the DSS for imaging and found a statistically significant decline in the number of targeted imaging procedures after the DSS was implemented. For example, the rate of imaging for lumbar MRI for low back pain dropped by 23 percent after implementation.

The unique characteristics of Virginia Mason likely influenced these results. Because all providers at Virginia Mason are salaried employees, they do not have a financial incentive to generate additional imaging studies. Also, the institutional culture at Virginia Mason has a strong focus on efficiency and evidence-based medicine. Another important factor is that most referrals for imaging come from within the health system, which makes it easier to influence physician ordering behavior.

Massachusetts General—an academic medical center— adopted a DSS for a broad range of MRI and CT procedures. The DSS provided feedback to physicians on the appropriateness of these imaging tests when they were ordered. The appropriateness scores were based on criteria developed by the American College of Radiology and criteria established by consensus panels of physicians. The DSS applied to physicians who ordered outpatient studies at Massachusetts General. Researchers found a significant decline in the growth rate of CT and MRI studies after implementation of the DSS in 2004. They attributed the results to a gatekeeper effect (the requirement to follow a new set of steps to order a test) and an educational effect (providing feedback to ordering physicians on the appropriateness of imaging requests). Because the study lacked a control group, it is possible that external factors such as changes in payment rates and greater awareness of the risks of radiation may have influenced the reduction in the growth of CT and MRI scans. In addition, the faculty practice group at Massachusetts General had an incentive to reduce the use of less appropriate imaging studies because it had contractual agreements with payers to reduce the use of high-cost imaging. This factor may have led to greater physician compliance with the feedback provided by the DSS.

A two-year demonstration program recently launched by CMS—called the Medicare Imaging Demonstration—will test whether the use of DSS can promote appropriate ordering of advanced imaging services (Centers for Medicare & Medicaid Services 2010a).

This program was authorized by the Medicare Improvements for Patients and Providers Act of 2008, which prohibited the demonstration from testing the use of prior authorization. CMS selected 11 advanced imaging procedures for the demonstration based on their high spending and use and the availability of appropriateness guidelines for these services.[18] For these 11 procedures, CMS identified published guidelines developed by specialty societies, such as the American College of Radiology, American College of Cardiology, American Academy of Neurology, and American College of Physicians. The agency selected five organizations—Brigham & Women's Hospital, Henry Ford Health System, Maine Medical Center–Physician Hospital Organization, the University of Wisconsin– Madison, and National Imaging Associates (a radiology benefit manager)—to recruit physicians to participate in the demonstration (Centers for Medicare & Medicaid Services 2011a). Each organization will select and use a DSS that incorporates appropriateness guidelines, collect data from the participating physicians, and distribute payments to physicians for reporting the data.

In developing criteria for prior notification and prior authorization, CMS should review existing clinical guidelines developed by specialty societies and providers such as Virginia Mason Medical Center and Massachusetts General Hospital (see text box). CMS should also consult with professional societies, RBMs, and other stakeholders. CMS could form an advisory committee to assist in developing criteria. The agency should also solicit public comments on the criteria before they are finalized. Medicare's criteria should be transparent and available to providers, beneficiaries, and the general public. In addition, CMS should:

- ensure that the criteria are kept up to date to reflect changes in practice and technology;
- use the same criteria for both prior notification and prior authorization; and
- require that its contractors use the same uniform criteria to review imaging requests, provide feedback, and approve requests.

Under an imaging demonstration program recently launched by CMS, the agency identified guidelines for 11 advanced imaging procedures (e.g., MRI of the lumbar spine and CT of the brain) developed by several specialty societies (see text box). CMS has also adopted seven outpatient imaging efficiency measures for hospital outpatient departments, such as the use of MRI of the lumbar spine for low back pain (Centers for Medicare & Medicaid Services 2011c). The purpose of these measures is to reduce unnecessary exposure to contrast materials and radiation, improve adherence to evidence-based medicine and practice guidelines, and promote efficient use of imaging.

Identifying Practitioners Who Order Substantially More Advanced Imaging than Their Peers

In adopting a prior authorization approach for Medicare, a key issue is how CMS would define outlier physicians who order significantly more advanced imaging than their peers. The ideal approach would probably measure physicians' use of advanced imaging on both a per episode and a per capita basis. Episode measurement would examine imaging use for specific episodes of care (e.g., ischemic heart disease or low back pain). Although measuring the use of imaging per episode would allow CMS to control for variations in the types of conditions treated, physicians who order many imaging studies across multiple episodes may not be identified as outliers if their per episode average is low. Thus, CMS should also use a per capita approach that calculates the average number of advanced imaging studies ordered by each physician per patient. Under a per capita approach, CMS would have to develop a method to attribute patients to an individual physician. For example, patients could be attributed to the physician who provided the plurality of their E&M services during the year.

Physicians who are identified as outliers with regard to overall resource use under a per episode approach also tend to be identified as outliers under a per capita approach. Using both per episode and per capita methodologies, we found that approximately two-thirds of physicians in the top decile of resource use according to episode-based measurement were also in the top decile of resource use based on per capita measurement.

Based on an analysis of physician fee schedule claims data from 2009, we found that physicians who order substantially more advanced imaging services account for a disproportionate share of all advanced imaging studies (Table 2-3). We included advanced imaging studies performed in one of three settings: physicians' offices, IDTFs, and hospital outpatient departments; we excluded studies performed in emergency rooms and inpatient settings because they are usually not covered by prior authorization programs.[19] We ranked all physicians who ordered at least one advanced imaging service in 2009 by the number of studies they ordered within each modality (CT, MRI, and nuclear medicine are separate modalities). Physicians in the top quartile of imaging ordering for each modality accounted for three-quarters or more of all the studies ordered for that modality (Table 2-3). Physicians in the top decile of imaging ordering for each modality accounted for more than half of all the studies ordered for that modality. These results suggest that targeting prior authorization to outlier physicians would likely cover the majority of advanced imaging studies without creating a burden for most physicians who order these services. Notably, however, our analysis had certain limitations: It did not adjust for the number of patients treated by each physician, the number and type of episodes furnished by each physician, physician specialty, or geographic region. We recognize that CMS would have to consider adjusting for these factors when identifying physician outliers. These adjustments could affect whether physicians are identified as outliers and the number of studies that would be subject to prior approval.

Using the same data set, we found that a significant share of physicians in the top decile of imaging ordering are also self-referring physicians (Table 2-4). We used two definitions of self-referral for this analysis: the expansive definition includes physicians who referred at least 1 percent of the imaging studies they ordered within each modality to physicians in their practice during 2009, and the restrictive definition includes physicians who referred more than 50 percent of the imaging studies they ordered within each modality to their practice. Using the expansive definition of self-referral, more than one-quarter of the physicians in the top decile of CT and MRI ordering and more than one-half of the physicians in the top decile of nuclear medicine ordering were self-referring physicians for those modalities (Table 2-4). Using the more restrictive definition, 16.6 percent of the physicians in the top decile of CT ordering, 13.7 percent of the physicians in the top decile of MRI ordering, and almost half of the physicians in the top decile of nuclear medicine ordering were self-referring physicians for those modalities (Table 2-4). Our analysis did not adjust for important factors such as the number of patients treated by each physician and the number and type of episodes furnished by each physician. These and other factors would likely influence whether a self-referring physician is classified as an outlier physician.

Table 2-3. Physicians who ordered substantially more advanced imaging accounted for a disproportionate share of total volume and spending for advanced imaging, 2009

percent of all imaging studies that were ordered by:		
type of imaging	physicians in the top quartile of imaging ordering	physicians in the top decile of imaging ordering
CT Share of volume	77.7%	55.6%
Share of spending	75.3	52.5
MRI Share of volume	75.9	52.1
Share of spending	75.6	52.3
Nuclear medicine Share of volume	81.4	60.2
Share of spending	83.7	63.7

Note: CT (computed tomography). The data include advanced imaging studies paid under the physician fee schedule that were performed in physicians' offices, independent diagnostic testing facilities, and hospital outpatient departments; we excluded tests performed in emergency rooms and inpatient settings. The data include global and professional component services. To avoid double-counting, the data exclude claims for technical component services. Physicians in the top quartile of CT ordering accounted for 27 or more CT scans during 2009; physicians in the top decile ordered 61 or more scans. Physicians in the top quartile of MRI ordering accounted for 15 or more MRI scans; physicians in the top decile ordered 34 or more scans. Physicians in the top quartile of nuclear medicine ordering accounted for 11 or more nuclear medicine studies; physicians in the top decile ordered 28 or more studies.

Source: MedPAC analysis of carrier claims data for 100 percent of Medicare beneficiaries.

Administrative Implications of a Prior Authorization Program for CMS

CMS has indicated that a prior authorization approach would require significant administrative resources (Government Accountability Office 2008). CMS or its contractors would have to select or develop appropriateness criteria, identify outlier physicians, establish systems for these physicians to transmit requests for imaging, and employ staff to review and approve the requests. However, the focus on outlier physicians—rather than all physicians—would reduce CMS's administrative costs. CMS could also leverage its limited resources by focusing on imaging services that account for a significant share of spending and volume, have high-quality guidelines for appropriate use, and exhibit variations in utilization among physicians and geographic areas.

In addition, a prior authorization program would interact with beneficiaries' rights to appeal claims that are not paid by Medicare (Government Accountability Office 2008). If a high proportion of imaging requests denied under prior authorization were later appealed, more cases would be added to the appeals process, thereby increasing the costs of this process. If a high proportion of imaging requests denied during the prior authorization process were later overturned during the appeals process, aggregate savings would be reduced (Government Accountability Office 2008).

Table 2-4. Share of physicians in the top decile of imaging ordering who are self-referring physicians, 2009

percent of physicians in the top decile of imaging ordering who:		
type of imaging	referred at least 1 percent of the studies they ordered to their practice	referred more than 50 percent of the studies they ordered to their practice
CT	29.8%	16.6%
MRI	27.3	13.7
Nuclear medicine	56.6	49.1

Note: CT (computed tomography). The data include advanced imaging studies paid under the physician fee schedule that were performed in physicians' offices, independent diagnostic testing facilities, and hospital outpatient departments; we excluded tests performed in emergency rooms and inpatient settings. The data include global and professional component services. To avoid double-counting, the data exclude technical component services. Physicians in the top decile of CT use ordered 61 or more scans during 2009. Physicians in the top decile of MRI use ordered 34 or more scans. Physicians in the top decile of nuclear medicine use ordered 28 or more studies.

Source: MedPAC analysis of carrier claims data for 100 percent of Medicare beneficiaries.

Impact of a Prior Authorization Program on Medicare Spending for Advanced Imaging

It is difficult to quantify the savings from a prior authorization program in Medicare, net of the administrative costs. Although our interviews with plans and RBMs indicated that the savings from prior authorization programs more than offset their administrative costs, there are no independent studies that measure the impact of these programs on spending using a control group, which is a concern expressed by CMS (Government Accountability Office 2008).

In 2008, the Congressional Budget Office (CBO) estimated that a prior authorization program for advanced imaging services would reduce spending by $220 million over 5 years and by about $1 billion over 10 years (Congressional Budget Office 2008). CBO assumed that such a program would apply to all physicians who order advanced imaging rather than a targeted subset of physicians. Although the administrative costs would be less for a program that applied to a smaller group of physicians, the potential savings would also be less.

The President's budget request for 2010 projected that a program in which RBMs would ensure appropriate use of imaging services would reduce spending by $70 million over 5 years and by $250 million over 10 years (Office of Management and Budget 2009). The scope of the program envisioned in the budget request is unclear.

Does CMS Need Statutory Authority to Require Prior Authorization?

It is unclear whether CMS currently has statutory authority to establish a prior authorization program. According to GAO's report on imaging services in Medicare, CMS stated that it was not aware of any statutory provision that authorized or prohibited the use of approaches such as prior authorization (Government Accountability Office 2008). GAO recommended that CMS further assess whether it has the authority to adopt strategies such as privileging and prior authorization and determine if legislation is necessary (Government Accountability Office 2008). Because of this uncertainty, we recommend that the Congress enact legislation directing CMS to implement prior authorization for advanced imaging and clarify that the agency has the authority to do so. The legislation should also allow CMS to expand prior authorization to other services that experience rapid spending growth, such as physical therapy and radiation therapy.

Recommendation 2 – 4

The Congress should direct the Secretary to establish a prior authorization program for practitioners who order substantially more advanced diagnostic imaging services than their peers.

Rationale 2 - 4

The rapid volume growth of advanced imaging services (MRI, CT, and nuclear medicine) over the past decade and questions about appropriate use justify the development of a prior authorization program in Medicare for physicians and other health professionals who order a significantly greater number of advanced imaging services than other practitioners who treat similar patients. Such an approach would ensure that outlier practitioners are using advanced imaging services appropriately without subjecting all providers to prior authorization. The focus on outlier practitioners—rather than all providers—would reduce CMS's administrative costs and the burden on practitioners and beneficiaries. Because of CMS's limited resources, a prior authorization program should target advanced imaging services that account for a significant share of spending and volume, have evidence-based standards for appropriate use, and exhibit variations in utilization among providers and geographic areas. Although we have tried to minimize the administrative costs for CMS, the agency would still need additional resources to develop and operate a prior authorization program.

Implications 2 - 4

Spending

- We estimate that this recommendation would reduce federal program spending relative to current law by less than $50 million in the first year and by less than $1 billion over 5 years. This estimate accounts for CMS's administrative costs to develop and manage a prior authorization process.

Beneficiary and Provider

- We do not expect this recommendation to affect beneficiaries' access to clinically appropriate advanced imaging services. This recommendation would reduce beneficiaries' unnecessary exposure to contrast materials and radiation from inappropriate CT and nuclear medicine studies. It would also reduce beneficiaries' Part B premiums and cost sharing. Practitioners who are not subject to prior authorization would not be affected. Practitioners who are subject to prior authorization would incur some administrative costs to obtain prior approval.

Conclusion

Physician self-referral of ancillary services leads to higher volume when combined with FFS payment systems, which reward higher volume, and the mispricing of individual services, which makes some services more profitable than others. However, under an alternative payment structure in which providers were rewarded for constraining volume growth while improving the quality of care, the volume-increasing effects of self-referral would be mitigated. Therefore, the preferred long-term approach to address self-referral is to develop new payment systems. Because it will take several years to establish new payment models and delivery systems, we have explored a range of interim approaches to address concerns raised by self-referral (Medicare Payment Advisory Commission 2010a). Although the Commission examined options to narrow the types of services or physician groups covered by the IOAS exception, we are concerned that limiting the IOAS exception could have unintended consequences, such as inhibiting the development of organizations that integrate and coordinate care within the practice. Therefore, we do not currently recommend that the exception be changed. Instead, our recommendations are designed to improve payment accuracy for imaging and other diagnostic tests and ensure the appropriate use of advanced imaging studies. These recommendations recognize that mispricing and inappropriate use are problems that go beyond self-referral. Although our recommendations do not directly address self-referral of physical therapy, radiation therapy, and anatomic pathology tests, we will continue to track the growth of these services and may consider policy options to specifically address them in the future.

The Commission remains concerned about the expansion of physician investment in imaging, other diagnostic tests, and therapeutic services (e.g., physical therapy and radiation therapy) and the potential for self-referral to lead to higher volume. We will continue to monitor the growth of these services and evidence of inappropriate use. If the recommendations in this chapter are adopted and—together with delivery system reform—are not successful at stemming the growth of ancillary services and their inappropriate use, we may revisit options to narrow the IOAS exception. CMS has proposed criteria for an ACO model that include financial penalties for rapid growth in spending (Centers for Medicare & Medicaid Services 2011b). Therefore, one option would be to have a broader IOAS exception for physicians in ACOs that are at risk for expenditure growth and a narrower exception for physicians outside of such ACOs.

Endnotes

[1] In a prior report, we describe the proliferation of a variety of relationships between hospitals and physicians and their contribution to volume growth (Medicare Payment Advisory Commission 2008b).

[2] The IOAS exception does not apply to most types of durable medical equipment or parenteral and enteral nutrients, equipment, and supplies because there is no clear justification for referring physicians to offer these services.

[3] Such arrangements would have to comply with at least two other federal requirements: (1) the anti-kickback statute, which prohibits the offer, payment, or receipt of anything of value to induce the referral of patients for services reimbursed by federal health programs; and (2) the anti-markup rules, which apply to a physician who bills Medicare for diagnostic tests that are performed (or supervised) by a physician who does not share a practice with the billing physician. In such cases, Medicare will not pay more than the performing provider's

net charge to the billing physician. The anti-markup rules do not apply to tests performed or supervised by a physician in the same building where the billing physician regularly furnishes patient care (42 CFR § 414.50).

[4] Volume is measured as the units of service multiplied by each service's relative weight (relative value units) from the physician fee schedule. Thus, volume growth accounts for changes in both the number of services and the complexity, or intensity, of those services.

[5] Between 9 percent and 11 percent of the tests were of uncertain appropriateness.

[6] The workgroup has also begun considering groups of related codes rather than simply pairs of related codes.

[7] The CPT Editorial Panel deleted 5 of these codes and will consider 49 during the 2013 cycle. The RUC will submit recommendations on the work and practice expense RVUs for 32 codes to CMS for the 2012 physician fee schedule and will review 3 codes for the 2013 physician fee schedule (American Medical Association 2011).

[8] The new comprehensive codes are 74176 (CT, abdomen and pelvis, without contrast), 74177 (CT, abdomen and pelvis, with contrast), and 74178 (CT, abdomen and pelvis, with and without contrast).

[9] The payment for physicians who treat patients receiving home dialysis varies only by the patients' age.

[10] The RUC estimates the amount of physician time spent on activities before, during, and after the interpretation of an imaging study. For example, the RUC estimates that the total physician time for CT of the pelvis with contrast (72193) is 18 minutes. Prior to the interpretation, the physician spends 3 minutes reviewing the reason for the study, the clinical history, and prior imaging studies, and determining the appropriate protocol for the study. The physician spends 10 minutes interpreting the images and writing the report. After the interpretation, the physician spends 5 minutes reviewing and signing the final report and discussing the findings with the referring physician.

[11] GAO found that the extent of the efficiencies in physician work varied by service pairs. Because some imaging codes have been packaged and revalued since 2009, the level of savings (or redistribution of dollars from imaging to other services) would probably be less than $175 million.

[12] This 25 percent payment reduction was based on CMS's analysis of the efficiencies associated with five high-volume pairs of therapy codes.

[13] However, CMS's recent expansion of the MPPR to the technical component of multiple imaging services (regardless of modality) that are performed on noncontiguous body parts in the same session was implemented in a budget-neutral manner. According to CMS, the statute exempts only payment reductions for multiple imaging services performed on "consecutive body parts" from budget neutrality (Centers for Medicare & Medicaid Services 2010b).

[14] DSS may be embedded in a provider's electronic medical record system or accessed through the Internet.

[15] In response, CMS in 2009 implemented the first phase of the Physician Feedback Program, sending approximately 310 reports to randomly selected physicians in 12 metropolitan areas across the United States. Phase two of the Physician Feedback Program was initiated in late 2010 and is expected to continue through 2011.

[16] GAO interviewed 17 plans with a total of about 72 million covered lives that used a prior authorization or prior notification program for imaging services (Government Accountability Office 2008).

[17] For purposes of this discussion, the terms plan and RBM are used interchangeably.

[18] The 11 imaging procedures are myocardial perfusion imaging, MRI of the lumbar spine, CT of the lumbar spine, MRI of the brain, CT of the brain, CT of the sinus, CT of the thorax, CT of the abdomen, CT of the pelvis, MRI of the knee, and MRI of the shoulder.

[19] Our data came from the 100 percent carrier claims file from CMS. The data include global and professional component imaging services. To avoid double-counting, the data exclude technical component services.

References

American College of Radiology. 2011. *ACR Appropriateness Criteria: Overview.* Reston, VA: ACR. http://www.acr.org/SecondaryMainMenuCategories/quality_safety/ app_criteria/overview.aspx.

American Medical Association. 2010. The RUC Relativity Assessment Workgroup and CPT. Presentation at the CPT Annual Advisors Meeting. October. http://www.ama-assn.org/ama1/pub/ upload/mm/362/relativity-assessment-workgroup.pdf.

American Medical Association. 2011. *The RUC Relativity Assessment Workgroup progress report*. Chicago, IL: AMA.

Anscher, M. S., B. M. Anscher, and C. J. Bradley. 2010. The negative impact of Stark law exemptions on graduate medical education and health care costs: the example of radiation oncology. *International Journal of Radiation Oncology Biology Physics* 76, no. 5 (April): 1289–1294.

Armstrong, D. 2005. Lucrative operation: How some doctors turn a $79 profit from a $30 test. *Wall Street Journal*, September 30.

Baker, L. C. 2010. Acquisition of MRI equipment by doctors drives up imaging use and spending. *Health Affairs* 29, no. 12 (December): 2252–2259.

Baras, J. D., and L. C. Baker. 2009. Magnetic resonance imaging and low back pain care for Medicare patients. *Health Affairs* 28, no. 6 (November–December): w1133–1140.

Blackmore, C. C., R. S. Mecklenburg, and G. S. Kaplan. 2011. Effectiveness of clinical decision support in controlling inappropriate imaging. *Journal of the American College of Radiology* 8, no. 1 (January): 19–25.

Brenner, D. J., and E. J. Hall. 2007. Computed tomography—An increasing source of radiation exposure. *New England Journal of Medicine* 357, no. 22 (November 29): 2277–2284.

Carreyrou, J., and M. Tamman. 2010. A device to kill cancer, lift revenue. *Wall Street Journal,* December 7.

Center for Devices and Radiological Health, Food and Drug Administration. 2010. *Initiative to reduce unnecessary radiation exposure from medical imaging*. Silver Spring, MD: CDRH.

Centers for Medicare & Medicaid Services, Department of Health and Human Services. 2005. Medicare program; revisions to payment policies under the physician fee schedule for calendar year 2006 and certain provisions related to the competitive acquisition program of outpatient drugs and biologicals under Part B. Final rule. *Federal Register* 70, no. 223 (November 21): 70116–70150.

Centers for Medicare & Medicaid Services, Department of Health and Human Services. 2007. Medicare program; proposed revisions to payment policies under the physician fee schedule, and other Part B payment policies for CY 2008; proposed revisions to the payment policies of ambulance services under the ambulance fee schedule for CY 2008; and the proposed elimination of the e-prescribing exemption for computer-generated facsimile transmissions. Proposed rule. *Federal Register* 72, no. 133 (July 12): 38122–38395.

Centers for Medicare & Medicaid Services, Department of Health and Human Services. 2009. Medicare program; payment policies under the physician fee schedule and other revisions to Part B for CY 2010. Final rule. *Federal Register* 74, no. 226 (November 25): 61737–62206.

Centers for Medicare & Medicaid Services, Department of Health and Human Services. 2010a. Medicare announces demonstration testing decision support systems for advanced medical imaging services. Press release. July 22.

Centers for Medicare & Medicaid Services, Department of Health and Human Services. 2010b. Medicare program; payment policies under the physician fee schedule and other revisions to Part B for CY 2011. Final rule. *Federal Register* 75, no. 228 (November 29): 73169–73860.

Centers for Medicare & Medicaid Services, Department of Health and Human Services. 2011a. CMS announces selection of demonstration participants in Medicare Imaging Demonstration Project. Press release. February 2.

Centers for Medicare & Medicaid Services, Department of Health and Human Services. 2011b. Medicare program; Medicare Shared Savings Program: Accountable care organizations and Medicare program: Waiver designs in connection with the Medicare Shared Savings Program and the Innovation Center. Proposed rule and notice. *Federal Register* 76, no. 67 (April 7): 19527–19654.

Centers for Medicare & Medicaid Services, Department of Health and Human Services. 2011c. *Outpatient imaging efficiency (OIE) measures*. Listening session background paper. Baltimore, MD: CMS.

Chou, R., A. Qaseem, D. K. Owens, et al. 2011. Diagnostic imaging for low back pain: Advice for high-value health care from the American College of Physicians. *Annals of Internal Medicine* 154, no. 3 (February 1): 181–189.

Committee on Commerce, Science, and Transportation. 2011. *Consumers' access to diagnostic heart tests in Delaware.* Staff report for Chairman Rockefeller. Prepared by Office of Oversight and Investigations majority staff. Washington, DC: U. S. Senate.

Deyo, R. A. 2002. Cascade effects of medical technology. *Annual Review of Public Health* 23: 23–44.

Douglas, P., A. E. Iskandrian, H. M. Krumholz, et al. 2006. Achieving quality in cardiovascular imaging: Proceedings from the American College of Cardiology–Duke University Medical Center Think Tank on Quality in Cardiovascular Imaging. *Journal of the American College of Cardiology* 48, no. 10 (November 21): 2141–2151.

Gazelle, G. S., E. F. Halpern, H. S. Ryan, et al. 2007. Utilization of diagnostic medical imaging: Comparison of radiologist referral versus same-specialty referral. *Radiology* 245, no. 2 (November): 517–522.

Gibbons, R. J., T. D. Miller, D. Hodge, et al. 2008. Application of appropriateness criteria to stress single-photon emission computed tomography sestamibi studies and stress echocardiograms in an academic medical center. *Journal of the American College of Cardiology* 51, no. 13 (April 1): 1283–1289.

Government Accountability Office. 1994. *Medicare: Referrals to physician-owned imaging facilities warrant HCFA's scrutiny*. GAO/HES–95–2. Washington, DC: GAO.

Government Accountability Office. 2008. *Medicare Part B imaging services: Rapid spending growth and shift to physician offices indicate need for CMS to consider additional management practices*. GAO–08–452. Washington, DC: GAO.

Government Accountability Office. 2009. *Medicare physician payments: Fees could better reflect efficiencies achieved when services are provided together.* GAO–09–647. Washington, DC: GAO.

Hendel, R. C., M. Cerqueira, P. S. Douglas, et al. 2010. A multicenter assessment of the use of single-photon emission computed tomography myocardial perfusion imaging with appropriateness criteria. *Journal of the American College of Cardiology* 55, no. 2 (January 12): 156–162.

Hillman, B. J., C. A. Joseph, M. R. Mabry, et al. 1990. Frequency and costs of diagnostic imaging in office practice—A comparison of self-referring and radiologist-referring physicians. *New England Journal of Medicine* 323, no. 23 (December 6): 1604– 1608.

Hughes, D. R., M. Bhargavan, and J. H. Sunshine. 2010. Imaging self-referral associated with higher costs and limited impact on duration of illness. *Health Affairs* 29, no. 12 (December): 2244– 2251.

Iglehart, J. K. 2009. Health insurers and medical-imaging policy—A work in progress. *New England Journal of Medicine* 360, no. 10 (March 5): 1030–1037.

Institute for Clinical Systems Improvement. 2010. *Decision support for ordering appropriate high-tech diagnostic imaging scans at the point-of-order.* Bloomington, MN: ICSI.

Institute of Medicine. 2010. *The future of nursing: Leading change, advancing health.* Washington, DC: The National Academies Press.

Kouri, B. E., R. G. Parsons, and H. R. Alpert. 2002. Physician self-referral for diagnostic imaging: Review of the empiric literature. *American Journal of Roentgenology* 179, no. 4 (October): 843–850.

Lehnert, B. E., and R. L. Bree. 2010. Analysis of appropriateness of outpatient CT and MRI referred from primary care clinics at an academic medical center: How critical is the need for improved decision support? *Journal of the American College of Radiology* 7, no. 3 (March): 192–197.

Levin, D. C., R. L. Bree, V. M. Rao, et al. 2010. A prior authorization program of a radiology benefits management company and how it has affected utilization of advanced diagnostic imaging. *Journal of the American College of Radiology* 7, no. 1 (January): 33–38.

Litt, A. W., D. R. Ryan, D. Batista, et al. 2005. Relative procedure intensity with self-referral and radiologist referral: Extremity radiography. *Radiology* 235, no. 1 (April): 142–147.

Medicare Payment Advisory Commission. 2005a. *Report to the Congress: Issues in a modernized Medicare program.* Washington, DC: MedPAC.

Medicare Payment Advisory Commission. 2005b. *Report to the Congress: Medicare payment policy.* Washington, DC: MedPAC.

Medicare Payment Advisory Commission. 2006a. *Report to the Congress: Increasing the value of Medicare.* Washington, DC: MedPAC.

Medicare Payment Advisory Commission. 2006b. *Report to the Congress: Medicare payment policy.* Washington, DC: MedPAC.

Medicare Payment Advisory Commission. 2007a. Public meeting of the Medicare Payment Advisory Commission. Washington, DC. September 6–7.

Medicare Payment Advisory Commission. 2007b. *Report to the Congress: Promoting greater efficiency in Medicare.* Washington, DC: MedPAC.

Medicare Payment Advisory Commission. 2008a. *Report to the Congress: Medicare payment policy.* Washington, DC: MedPAC.

Medicare Payment Advisory Commission. 2008b. *Report to the Congress: Reforming the delivery system.* Washington, DC: MedPAC.

Medicare Payment Advisory Commission. 2009a. *Report to the Congress: Improving incentives in the Medicare program.* Washington, DC: MedPAC.

Medicare Payment Advisory Commission. 2009b. *Report to the Congress: Medicare payment policy.* Washington, DC: MedPAC.

Medicare Payment Advisory Commission. 2010a. *Report to the Congress: Aligning incentives in Medicare.* Washington, DC: MedPAC.

Medicare Payment Advisory Commission. 2010b. *Report to the Congress: Medicare payment policy.* Washington, DC: MedPAC.

Medicare Payment Advisory Commission. 2011. *Report to the Congress: Medicare payment policy*. Washington, DC: MedPAC.

Mehta, R., R. P. Ward, S. Chandra, et al. 2008. Evaluation of the American College of Cardiology Foundation/American Society of Nuclear Cardiology appropriateness criteria for SPECT myocardial perfusion imaging. *Journal of Nuclear Cardiology* 15, no. 3 (May–June): 337–344.

Mitchell, J. M. 2007. The prevalence of physician self-referral arrangements after Stark II: Evidence from advanced diagnostic imaging. *Health Affairs Web Exclusives* (April 17): w415–424.

Mitchell, J. M., and R. R. Lagalia. 2009. Controlling the escalating use of advanced imaging: The role of radiology benefit management programs. *Medical Care Research and Review* 66, no. 3 (June): 339–351.

Office of Management and Budget, Executive Office of the President. 2009. *Budget of the United States government for fiscal year 2010*. Washington, DC: OMB.

Pham, H. H., K. J. Devers, J. H. May, et al. 2004. Financial pressures spur physician entrepreneurialism. *Health Affairs* 23, no. 2 (March–April): 70–81.

Pham, H. H., and P. B. Ginsburg. 2007. Unhealthy trends: The future of physician services. *Health Affairs* 26, no. 6 (November– December): 1586–1598.

Pham, H. H., B. E. Landon, J. D. Reschovsky, et al. 2009. Rapidity and modality of imaging for acute low back pain in elderly patients. *Archives of Internal Medicine* 169, no. 10 (May 25): 972–981.

Reschovsky, J. D., A. Cassil, and H. H. Pham. 2010. *Physician ownership of medical equipment*. Data bulletin no. 36. Washington, DC: Center for Studying Health System Change.

Saul, S. 2006. Profit and questions on prostate cancer therapy. *New York Times*, December 1.

Sistrom, C. L., P. A. Dang, J. B. Weilburg, et al. 2009. Effect of computerized order entry with integrated decision support on the growth of outpatient procedure volumes: Seven-year time series analysis. *Radiology* 251, no. 1 (April): 147–155.

Smith-Bindman, R., J. Lipson, R. Marcus, et al. 2009.

Radiation dose associated with common computed tomography examinations and the associated lifetime attributable risk of cancer. *Archives of Internal Medicine* 169, no. 22 (December 14): 2078–2086.

Smith, V. K., K. Gifford, E. Ellis, et al. 2010. *Hoping for economic recovery, preparing for health reform: A look at Medicaid spending, coverage and policy trends. Results from a 50-state Medicaid budget survey for state fiscal years 2010 and 2011.* Prepared by staff from Health Management Associates and the Kaiser Commission on Medicaid and the Uninsured/Kaiser Family Foundation. Washington, DC: KCMU.

Stein, R. 2011. Doctor-owned centers spark criticism, scrutiny. *Washington Post,* February 28.

Tynan, A., R. A. Berenson, and J. B. Christianson. 2008. *Health plans target advanced imaging services: Cost, quality and safety concerns prompt renewed oversight.* Issue brief no. 118. Washington, DC: Center for Studying Health System Change. February.

Patel, M. R., J. A. Spertus, R. G. Brindis, et al. 2005. ACCF proposed method for evaluating the appropriateness of cardiovascular imaging. *Journal of the American College of Cardiology* 46, no. 8 (October 18): 1606–1613.

MEDICARE'S FEE-FOR-SERVICE BENEFIT DESIGN

Summary

The Commission has been considering reform of the traditional benefit package for several years to complement our ongoing work on improving the payment system. Our aims have been to give beneficiaries better protection against high out-of-pocket (OOP) spending and to promote innovation in benefit design that will create incentives for beneficiaries to use high-value services and weigh their use of discretionary care without discouraging needed care. A further aim is to slow the growth of Medicare spending so that the program will be sustainable for future generations, although we recognize that cost-sharing changes alone are not sufficient to slow spending.

The current fee-for-service (FFS) benefit design includes a relatively high deductible for inpatient stays, a relatively low deductible for physician and outpatient care, and a cost-sharing requirement of 20 percent of allowable charges for most physician care and outpatient services. Under this design, no upper limit exists on the amount of Medicare cost-sharing expenses a beneficiary can incur. If not supplemented with additional coverage, the FFS benefit design exposes Medicare beneficiaries to substantial financial risk and may discourage the use of high-value care.

The lack of comprehensiveness in the FFS benefit design leads more than 90 percent of beneficiaries to take up supplemental coverage or have Medicaid, which mutes the effect of high OOP costs. Researchers agree that Medicare beneficiaries with supplemental coverage tend to have higher use of services and spending than those with no supplemental coverage. As currently structured, many supplemental plans cover all or nearly all of Medicare's cost-sharing requirements regardless of whether there is evidence that the service is ineffective or, conversely, whether it might prevent a hospitalization. Supplemental coverage addresses beneficiaries' concerns about the uncertainty of OOP spending under the FFS benefit, but it also dampens financial incentives to control utilization. Most of the costs of increased utilization are borne by the Medicare program.

There are short-term and long-term approaches to reforming benefits. In the short term, incremental changes to the FFS benefit and to supplemental coverage could begin changing beneficiaries' incentives. The aim of these improvements would be to reduce financial risk for beneficiaries with the highest levels of cost sharing. Potential improvements could include, for example, adding a cap to beneficiaries'

OOP costs in the FFS benefit and, at the same time, requiring supplemental policies to have fixed-dollar copayments for services such as office visits and emergency room use. Such restrictions on supplemental coverage could lead to reductions in use of Medicare services sufficient to help finance the addition of an OOP cap. These strategies could be coupled with exceptions that waive cost sharing for services in certain circumstances—for example, if evidence identified them as leading to better health outcomes. The strategies could also include cost-sharing protections for low-income beneficiaries so that they would not forgo needed care. In total, these changes would be costly, unless specifically designed to be budget neutral.

However, incremental changes may not be sufficient to create a modern benefit design. For the longer term, the goal would be to design a benefit that supports innovations in provider payments and changes in health care delivery. The Medicare program will need to move toward benefit designs that give individuals incentives to use higher value care and discourage them from using lower value care.

Some payers have initiated innovative benefit designs to steer enrollees toward high-value care. We interviewed public and private payers and identified four strategies they use to achieve this goal: lowering cost sharing for high-value services, raising cost sharing for low-value services, creating financial incentives for enrollees to see high-performing or low-cost providers, and providing incentives for enrollees to adopt healthier behaviors.

Much of the Commission's work focuses on changing Medicare's payment systems to give providers incentives to maintain adequate access to care, improve quality, and use fewer resources. Complementary to this work is research on improving the design of Medicare's traditional fee-for-service (FFS) benefit, along with that of supplemental coverage. Reforming the FFS benefit offers an opportunity to align beneficiary incentives and program goals to obtain high-quality care for the best value. Of particular importance, reforms could improve financial protection for individuals who have the greatest need for services and who currently have very high cost sharing.

The current FFS benefit design includes a relatively high deductible for inpatient stays, a relatively low deductible for physician and outpatient care, and a cost-sharing requirement of 20 percent of allowable charges for most physician care and outpatient services. Under this design, no upper limit exists on the amount of Medicare cost-sharing expenses a beneficiary can incur. If not supplemented with additional coverage, the FFS benefit design makes Medicare beneficiaries face substantial financial risk and may discourage the use of valuable care.

Neither the FFS payment system nor its benefit design is built around incentives that reward delivery and use of high-quality, high-value care. The status quo encourages growth in the volume and intensity of services and has led to care that is often not coordinated, sometimes inappropriate, and occasionally risky to patients. It has also left beneficiaries with rising Part B premiums and out-of-pocket (OOP) costs and has left taxpayers with the unsustainable burden of financing the program.

The Commission has been considering reform of the traditional benefit package. Our aim has been to give beneficiaries better protection against high OOP spending and to promote incentives for them to weigh their use of discretionary care without discouraging needed care. A further aim is to slow the growth of Medicare spending so that the program will be sustainable for future generations.

There are both short-term and long-term approaches to reforming benefits. In the short term, incremental changes in benefit design can be implemented more quickly and can provide better financial protection and give better price signals to beneficiaries seeking care. However, incremental changes are not sufficient to create a modern benefit design. A longer term goal would be to design a benefit that promotes a patient-centric Medicare program and supports innovations in provider payments and changes in health care delivery. Changes in beneficiary incentives should mirror changes in provider payments. Ideally, these changes could encourage use of lower cost, high-quality providers.

Our analysis of the current FFS benefit package examines Medicare benefits, sources of supplemental coverage, and variation in OOP spending. We also describe programs designed to protect low-income beneficiaries from high OOP costs. We discuss recent statutory changes to benefits and supplemental coverage policies and illustrate the effects of some short-term approaches to benefit reform. Last, we examine private payers' experiences with innovative benefit designs.

Background

Today, about 75 percent of beneficiaries receive health benefits through traditional FFS Medicare.[1] FFS Medicare's benefit design is uniform, with the same Part B premium nationwide despite large regional differences in average use of services and program expenditures.[2] Beneficiaries can use any provider willing to accept Medicare's conditions of participation and payment rates. To cover gaps in the FFS benefit, most beneficiaries have supplemental coverage through former employers or individually purchased medigap policies, or they have additional coverage through Medicaid or other sources. Despite Medicare's lower average payment rates to providers compared with private payers' rates, the FFS program has certain desirable characteristics for providers, including little or no utilization management (American Medical Association 2009).[3] Under this arrangement, there are few restrictions on the services providers and beneficiaries decide to use, and Medicare bears full insurance risk for beneficiaries' health spending.

For insured individuals outside the Medicare program, premiums act as a signal of the breadth of coverage and available providers. Premiums also reflect the relative health status and average use of services of the insured population. For example, plans with relatively tight networks of providers are expected to have lower premiums—the trade-off for less choice of providers is a lower price. In the Medicare program, however, the various premiums a beneficiary can face are not good signals of cost differences. Despite geographic differences in average use of services, FFS Medicare's Part B premium does not vary (except by income). In addition, many beneficiaries (or their former employers) pay premiums for supplemental insurance that covers much of Medicare's cost sharing. While premiums for medigap policies vary widely, that variation reflects the health status of a particular pool of insured individuals and each insurer's ratings method more than breadth of coverage. Premiums for medigap policies can also be expensive because of high administrative costs, largely due to the need for medigap insurers to market directly to individuals (Moon 2006).

Beneficiaries' use of care is strongly affected by the recommendations of medical providers. Still, the amount patients must pay for health care at the point of service can affect whether they seek care, the type of provider they see, and which treatment they receive. Ideally, the benefit design would encourage beneficiaries at the point of service to use care only when it is of high value. The challenge is to create such a design while also providing beneficiaries with clear information about the potential risks and benefits of treatment options.

Under Medicare's FFS benefit, which has changed very little since 1965, the cost-sharing structure has considerable requirements and provides no OOP cap. For Part A services, it includes a relatively high deductible for inpatient stays ($1,132 in 2011) and daily copayments for long stays at hospitals and skilled nursing facilities.[4] Patients with more than one hospital stay can owe more than one hospital deductible for the year. For Part B services, the FFS benefit has a relatively low deductible ($162 in 2011) and requires beneficiaries to pay 20 percent of allowable charges for most services, except for home health and clinical laboratory services. Increases in the deductibles and copayments under Part A and Part B are linked to average annual increases in Medicare spending for those services. There is no upper limit on how much cost sharing a beneficiary could owe under the FFS benefit. (Tables 3-1 and 3-2 show Part A and Part B premiums and cost sharing.) Analyses suggest that the actuarial value—the percent of medical spending for a standard population paid by an insurer—of the traditional Medicare benefit is significantly lower than typical employer-sponsored health coverage (Peterson 2009, Yamamoto et al. 2008).

More recent changes to the FFS benefit design include greater coverage of and incentives for preventive care. The benefit now covers a "welcome to Medicare" physical within each beneficiary's first 12 months of enrollment in Part B and annual wellness exams thereafter. It also waives the Part B cost sharing for certain preventive services, including those that are recommended by the U.S. Preventive Services Task Force with a grade A or B.

Table 3-1. Premiums and cost-sharing requirements for Part A services in 2011

Category	amount
Premiums	$0 if entitled to Social Security retirement or survivor benefits, railroad retirement benefits, Social Security or railroad retirement disability benefits, or end-stage renal disease benefits. $248 per month for individuals who are not eligible for premium-free Part A and have 30–39 quarters of Medicare-covered employment. $450 per month for individuals who are not eligible for premium-free Part A and have fewer than 30 quarters of Medicare-covered employment.
Hospital stay	$1,132 deductible for days 1–60 each benefit period. $283 per day for days 61–90 each benefit period. $566 per "lifetime reserve day" after day 90 each benefit period (up to 60 days over lifetime).
Skilled nursing facility stay	$0 for the first 20 days each benefit period. $141.50 per day for days 21–100 each benefit period. All costs for each day after day 100 in the benefit period.
Home health care	$0 for home health care services.
Hospice care	$0 for hospice visits. Up to a $5 copay for outpatient prescription drugs. 5% of the Medicare-approved amount for inpatient respite care.
Blood	All costs for the first 3 pints (unless donated to replace what is used).

Note: A benefit period begins the day a beneficiary is admitted to a hospital or skilled nursing facility and ends when the beneficiary has not received hospital or skilled nursing care for 60 days in a row. If the beneficiary is admitted to the hospital after one benefit period has ended, a new benefit period begins and the beneficiary must again pay the inpatient hospital deductible. There is no limit to the number of benefit periods. Part A cost sharing increases over time by the same percentage update applied to payments to inpatient hospitals and adjusted to reflect real change in case mix.

Source: Centers for Medicare & Medicaid Services 2011b.

Table 3-2. Premiums and cost-sharing requirements for Part B services in 2011

Category	amount
Premiums	$96.40 per month: Same premium as in 2009 applies if beneficiaries had the SSA withhold Part B premium payments from their Social Security check in 2009 and if income is below the following: Single beneficiaries with incomes of $85,000 or less. Couples with incomes of $170,000 or less.
	$110.50 per month: Same premium as in 2010 applies if beneficiaries had the SSA withhold Part B premium payments from their Social Security check in 2010 and if income is below the following: Single beneficiaries with incomes of $85,000 or less. Couples with incomes of $170,000 or less.
	$115.40 per month: All beneficiaries with incomes below the thresholds shown above and who are new to Part B for 2011 or have premiums paid by state Medicaid programs or Medicare Savings Plans.
	$161.50 per month: Single beneficiaries with incomes between $85,001 and $107,000. Couples with incomes between $170,001 and $214,000.
	$230.70 per month: Single beneficiaries with incomes between $107,001 and $160,000. Couples with incomes between $214,001 and $320,000.
	$299.90 per month: Single beneficiaries with incomes between $160,001 and $214,000. Couples with incomes between $320,001 and $428,000.
	$369.10 per month: Single beneficiaries with incomes above $214,000. Couples with incomes above $428,000.
Deductible	The first $162 of Part B-covered services or items.
Physician and other medical services	20% of the Medicare-approved amount for physician services, outpatient therapy (subject to limits), and durable medical equipment.
Outpatient hospital services	A coinsurance or copayment amount that varies by service, projected to average 22% in 2011. These rates are scheduled to phase down to 20% over time. No copayment for a single service can be more than the Part A hospital deductible ($1,132 in 2011).
Mental health services	45% of the Medicare-approved amount for outpatient mental health care. This coinsurance rate is scheduled to phase down to 20% by 2014.
Clinical laboratory services	$0 for Medicare-approved services.
Home health care	$0 for home health care services.
Durable medical equipment	20% of the Medicare-approved amount.
Blood	All costs for the first 3 pints, then 20% of the Medicare-approved amount of additional pints (unless donated to replace what is used).

Note: SSA (Social Security Administration). Medicare began phasing in income-related premiums over a three-year period beginning in 2007. As of 2011, higher income individuals pay monthly premiums equal to 35 percent, 50 percent, 65 percent, or 80 percent of Medicare's average Part B costs for aged beneficiaries, depending on income. Normally, all other individuals pay premiums equal to 25 percent of average costs for aged beneficiaries. In 2011, however, most beneficiaries pay the same premium as in 2009 or 2010 because of a provision in law that does not permit the Part B premium to increase by a larger dollar amount than beneficiaries' Social Security checks. CMS estimates that about 6 percent of Medicare beneficiaries pay the higher premiums. The Part B deductible increases over time by the rate of growth in per capita spending for Part B services.

Source: Centers for Medicare & Medicaid Services 2011b.

Table 3-3. Medicare cost-sharing liability in 2008

range of cost-sharing liability per person	percent of FFS beneficiaries	average amount of cost sharing per beneficiary
$1 to $499	42%	$250
$500 to $1,999	36	$1,071
$2,000 to $4,999	16	$3,036
$5,000 to $9,999	4	$6,879
$10,000 or more	2	$15,402

Note: FFS (fee-for-service). Amounts reflect cost sharing under FFS Medicare—not what beneficiaries paid out of pocket. Most beneficiaries have secondary insurance that covers some or all of their Medicare cost sharing.

Source: MedPAC based on data from CMS.

Shortcomings of the FFS Benefit and the Role of Supplemental Plans

The Commission and its predecessor commissions have explored problems with traditional Medicare's benefit design for many years (Medicare Payment Advisory Commission 2009, Medicare Payment Advisory Commission 2010, Physician Payment Review Commission 1997). The FFS benefit alone does not provide true insurance—financial protection against very high levels of OOP spending. Compared with other types of coverage, Medicare's benefit has a high inpatient deductible and a low outpatient deductible. These features lead to a small percentage of Medicare beneficiaries incurring very high levels of cost sharing (Table 3-3).

Types of Supplemental Coverage

Since the FFS benefit provides indemnity insurance, cost sharing is one of the few means by which the Medicare program can provide incentives to affect beneficiaries' behavior regarding use of medical services. But about 90 percent of FFS beneficiaries have supplemental coverage that fills in some or all of Medicare's cost sharing, effectively nullifying the program's tool for influencing beneficiary behavior. Supplemental plans include medigap plans, employer-sponsored retiree plans, and Medicaid and other plans for beneficiaries with limited incomes. Most beneficiaries can also choose Medicare Advantage (MA) plans that include some supplemental benefits and variations on cost sharing (see text box, pp. 70–71).

Medigap Plans

The one form of supplemental insurance available to all elderly Medicare beneficiaries (as well as to disabled Medicare beneficiaries under age 65 in most states)— medigap coverage—is popular among beneficiaries.

A 2009 survey found that 88 percent of medigap policyholders are satisfied with their secondary coverage, and 77 percent believe these policies are a good value (America's Health Insurance Plans/Blue Cross Blue Shield Association 2009). The most popular types of medigap policies, standard Plan C and Plan F, fill in nearly all of Medicare's cost-sharing requirements, including both the Part A and Part B deductibles (Table 3-4 and Table 3-5

Table 3-4. Benefits offered under standard medigap policies in 2011

Category	plan type										
	A	B	C	D	F	F (high deductible)	G	K	L	M	N
Part A hospital costs up to an additional 365 days after Medicare benefits are used up	✓	✓	✓	✓	✓	* ✓ ($2,000)	✓	✓	✓	✓	✓
Part B cost sharing for other than preventive services	✓	✓	✓	✓	✓	✓	✓	✓** (50%)	✓** (75%)	✓	✓** ($20/$50)
Blood (first 3 pints)	✓	✓	✓	✓	✓	✓	✓	✓** (50%)	✓** (75%)	✓	✓
Hospice care cost sharing	✓	✓	✓	✓	✓	✓	✓	✓ (50%)	✓ (75%)	✓	✓
SNF coinsurance			✓	✓	✓	✓	✓	✓ (50%)	✓ (75%)	✓	✓
Part A deductible		✓	✓	✓	✓	✓	✓	✓ (50%)	✓ (75%)	✓ (50%)	✓
Part B deductible			✓		✓	✓					
Part B excess charges					✓	✓	✓				
Foreign travel emergency (up to plan limits)			✓	✓	✓	✓	✓			✓	✓

Note: SNF (skilled nursing facility). Insurers began offering standard Plan M and Plan N in June 2010.

*High-deductible Plan F pays the same benefits as Plan F after one has paid a calendar year deductible of $2,000 in 2010. Out-of-pocket expenses for this deductible are expenses that would ordinarily be paid by the policy. These expenses include the Medicare deductible for Part A and Part B but do not include the plan's separate foreign travel emergency deductible.

**Plan K and Plan L require the insured to pay 50 percent and 75 percent, respectively, of cost-sharing payments other than cost sharing for extended hospital stays. After meeting an out-of-pocket limit of $4,620 in Plan K or $2,310 in Plan L, the plan pays 100 percent of Medicare cost sharing for covered services for the rest of the calendar year. Plan N has set dollar amounts that beneficiaries pay in lieu of certain Part B coinsurance payments ($20 for office visits and $50 for emergency room visits).

Source: Centers for Medicare & Medicaid Services 2011a. Additional information from the National Association of Insurance Commissioners.

(p. 72)). By effectively eliminating any of FFS Medicare's price signals at the point of service, supplemental coverage generally masks the financial consequences of beneficiaries' choices about whether to seek care and which types of providers and therapies to use.

Medigap policies can be expensive because they are sold to beneficiaries individually and thus tend to cover people with higher health spending and have administrative costs of 20 percent or more (Scanlon 2002).[5] Premiums for medigap policies also vary widely, even in the same market. This variation is due in part to different approaches that states allow insurers to use for setting premium rates.[6] But considerable variation in medigap premiums also exists in states that allow only community rating—that is, premiums cannot vary by an individual's age, gender, or health status. For example, in 2009 in Albany, New York, premiums for a medigap Plan F policy (the most popular plan type) varied between $1,940 and $4,130 (Table 3-5, p. 72). Much of this variation likely reflects the average health status and utilization trends of each medigap insurer's covered population.[7]

Policymakers, insurers, and regulators have taken several steps to develop more affordable types of medigap policies, but so far those products have not attracted much enrollment. Medicare SELECT® plans have the same standard designs as other medigap policies but require beneficiaries to use a provider network in return for lower premiums.[8] A 1997 evaluation found that SELECT plans provide a weak form of managed care in that they recruit hospitals willing to provide a discount for their networks but generally do not form physician networks (Lee et al. 1997). In 2006, insurers had 1.1 million Medicare SELECT plans in force—11 percent of all medigap policies (America's Health Insurance Plans 2008). In addition, after 1997 insurers were allowed to sell high-deductible versions of Plan F and Plan J in return for lower premiums.[9]

The Medicare Prescription Drug, Modernization, and Improvement Act of 2003 created two other types of standard products—Plan K and Plan L—that fill in less of Medicare's cost sharing in return for lower premiums. Plan K and Plan L require policyholders to pay 50 percent and 75 percent, respectively, of cost-sharing payments other than cost sharing for extended hospital stays. Although they have lower premiums than other types of medigap policies, as of 2009, Plan K and Plan L combined made up only 0.6 percent of all medigap enrollment.

Cost sharing in Medicare Advantage plans

The Medicare Advantage (MA) program allows Medicare beneficiaries to receive their Part A and Part B benefits through a private MA plan rather than through the traditional Medicare fee-forservice (FFS) program. While the plans must cover all Medicare benefits, they can limit the choice of providers through networks and can establish different cost-sharing requirements from those in FFS Medicare. Plans can also provide extra benefits, including lower cost sharing. On the other hand, CMS can require that plans provide certain additional benefits.

In practice, cost sharing under MA plans tends to be very different than under FFS Medicare. Few MA plans use FFS Medicare's cost-sharing structure. Only 1 percent of MA enrollees are in plans that charge the Part A deductible of $1,132 per spell of illness. In contrast to FFS Medicare's coinsurance for physician services (Part B), almost all MA enrollees are in plans that charge flat copayments for physician services. Under FFS Medicare, there is no cost sharing for home health services, but about 5 percent of MA enrollees are in plans that charge some cost sharing for home health services.

On an actuarial basis, cost sharing is substantially lower in MA plans than in FFS Medicare, because plans can lower cost sharing through efficiency savings, supplemental premiums, or the use of Medicare payment subsidies. (For 2011, the Commission estimates that Medicare will pay plans on average 10 percent more than the program would have spent on similar beneficiaries under FFS Medicare.) However, in some MA plans cost sharing for particular services can be higher. For example, MA plans tend to use per diem copayments for inpatient hospital care. The per diem copayments can be as high as $400 per day but are often charged on only the first few days in the hospital.

For a five-day stay in a hospital (the average Medicare hospital length of stay), the average cost sharing for MA enrollees is expected to be around $1,025 in 2011, with 25 percent of enrollees being charged more than $1,250 and 25 percent being charged less than $500. The MA average cost sharing for a five-day hospital stay is typically comparable to FFS Medicare cost sharing, but FFS Medicare's $1,132 deductible would seem high compared with MA cost sharing for a 2-day or 3-day stay and would be low compared with typical MA cost sharing for a 10-day stay.

Although MA plans usually have flat copayments for physician office visits rather than 20 percent coinsurance, plans often differentiate between primary care visits and specialty care visits. For primary care visits, copayments average about $12.50 (with a median of $15.00) and can range up to $40. Copayments for specialty care visits are higher, averaging about $28.50 (with a median of $30) and can be as high as $50.

MA plans tend to follow FFS Medicare's 20 percent coinsurance structure for durable medical equipment (DME) and Part B drugs. About 95 percent of MA enrollees are in plans that charge coinsurance for DME: Nine of 10 enrollees are in plans that charge 20 percent coinsurance, and almost all enrollees face between 10 percent and 30 percent coinsurance. For Part B drugs, which include chemotherapy drugs, about four of five enrollees are in MA plans that charge 20 percent coinsurance. In previous years, some plans had coinsurance higher than 20 percent, but recently CMS limited the allowable coinsurance to 20 percent in response to complaints that higher levels were discriminatory against some of the sickest beneficiaries most likely to require Part B drugs.

While CMS has used various incentives to encourage MA plans to include an out-of-pocket (OOP) cap on beneficiary cost-sharing liability over the last several years, for 2011 CMS required that plans have a cap of no more than $6,700 for in-network and out-of-network Medicare-covered services. Plans can have lower caps and can also have a separate lower cap on in-network cost sharing. For 2011, the average OOP cap for an MA enrollee who obtains Medicare-covered services from providers in the plan's network is $4,300. Half of MA enrollees have a cap of $3,400 or less. In addition to the OOP cap, most plans enhance the Medicare-covered services by waiving the three-day hospital stay requirement that FFS Medicare applies before qualifying beneficiaries for skilled nursing facility care. Ninety-five percent of MA enrollees are in plans that waive the three-day stay requirement.

In addition to the use of cost sharing and provider networks to influence beneficiaries' use of services, plans use other utilization management techniques. Using descriptions of plan benefit packages as a crude tool to determine the extent to which plans use prior authorization and utilization review techniques, we found that 60 percent of enrollees are in plans that require the plan's medical director to approve the use of home health services.

This text box looks at common characteristics of MA plan benefit designs. However, there is variation. Some plans mimic FFS Medicare's benefit package, while others have no in-network cost sharing but charge a substantial premium. Also of note, beneficiaries in FFS

Medicare may buy a supplemental policy (medigap) that covers some or all Medicare cost sharing, but MA enrollees may not be sold medigap policies.

In June 2010, medigap insurers introduced two new types of policies—Plan M and Plan N—that do not fill in all Medicare cost sharing. Plan M covers 50 percent of the Part A deductible but none of the Part B deductible. Plan N covers all of the Part A deductible but none of the Part B deductible, and it requires copayments of up to $20 for office visits and up to $50 for emergency room visits (National Association of Insurance Commissioners 2010).[10] Both Plan M and Plan N are expected to have lower premiums than other medigap policies. While official data are not yet available, insurers report that Plan N is popular among new policyholders (National Association of Insurance Commissioners 2011). Its popularity is attributed to lower premiums and a relatively simple benefit design that beneficiaries can readily understand.

The Patient Protection and Affordable Care Act of 2010 (PPACA) directs the National Association of Insurance Commissioners (NAIC) to revise standards for medigap policies Plan C and Plan F. These standard types are the only ones that cover all Medicare Part B cost sharing. The new law requests the NAIC to revise Plan C and Plan F standards to include requirements for nominal cost sharing to encourage the appropriate use of physicians' services under Part B. New standards are to be based on evidence published in peer-reviewed journals or current examples used in integrated delivery systems. NAIC's revised standards are, to the extent practicable, to be in place as of January 1, 2015.

Employer-Sponsored Retiree Plans

Employer-sponsored insurance typically provides beneficiaries with broader coverage for lower premiums than medigap policies. However, employer-sponsored coverage may not fill in all cost sharing and is not available to everyone. Retiree policies through large employers typically include a lower deductible for hospitalizations than Medicare's deductible; a cap on OOP spending; and sometimes benefits that FFS Medicare does not cover, such as dental care (Yamamoto et al. 2008). Employers who offer retiree plans often pay much of the premium for supplemental coverage. One 2007 survey found that, on average, large employers subsidized 60 percent of the total premium for single coverage; retirees paid 40 percent (Gabel et al. 2008).

Many employer plans require retirees enrolled in Medicare to pay deductibles and cost sharing just as active workers and younger retirees do. But it is unclear whether these cost-sharing arrangements apply to all retirees or primarily those who are in younger cohorts. In 2007, Actuarial Research Corporation analyzed 2005 data from the Medical Expenditure Panel Survey for the Commission. At that time, about 20 percent of Medicare beneficiaries with supplemental coverage through an employer had no OOP spending other than their premiums—their retiree plans paid for their Medicare cost sharing. In 2009, Direct Research used 2005 data from the Medicare Current Beneficiary Survey to estimate that 50 percent of FFS beneficiaries with employer-sponsored coverage paid 5 percent or less of their Part B spending OOP.

These estimates suggest that today a sizable portion of beneficiaries with employer-sponsored coverage have most of their Medicare cost sharing filled in by secondary insurance.

Although the percentage of Medicare beneficiaries with employer-sponsored retiree coverage has remained fairly constant since the early 1990s (Merlis 2006), the number of large employers offering such coverage to new retirees has been declining, which will affect future cohorts of Medicare beneficiaries (Employee Benefit Research Institute 2008). As those cohorts replace older ones in Medicare, employer-sponsored supplemental coverage will play less of a role than it does today.

Table 3-5. Distribution of medigap policies and average premiums nationally and range of premiums for Albany, NY

	National values for 2009			
plan type	Number of policyholders (in thousands)	percent of policyholders	average annual premium	range of premiums in albany, New York, February 2009*
All	9,454	100%	$2,100	N/A
A	260	3	1,400	$1,230–$2,420
B	474	5	1,800	$1,670–$3,240
C	1,469	16	2,000	$1,830–$3,750
D	378	4	2,100	$1,800–$2,920
E, H, I, J	1,260	13	2,000	$1,810–$2,720
F	3,827	41	2,000	$1,940–$4,130
F (high deductible)	36	0	500	$850–$1,190
G	329	3	1,900	$1,810–$2,720
K	21	0	900	$890–$1,340
L	38	0	1,500	$1,240–$1,900
Waiver-state policies	590	6	2,300	N/A
Pre-1991 policies	724	8	2,700	N/A

Note: N/A (not applicable). Plans E, H, I, and J closed to further enrollment in 2010. Insurers began offering standard Plan M and Plan N in June 2010. Waiver states include Massachusetts, Minnesota, and Wisconsin. Percentages may not sum to 100 due to rounding.

*New York state uses community rating, meaning that premiums cannot vary by age, gender, or health status of the insured individual.

Source: MedPAC analysis of 2009 data from the National Association of Insurance Commissioners. Data for premiums from Albany, New York, from New York State Insurance Department website.

Supplemental Benefits for Beneficiaries with Low Incomes

Medicare and Medicaid provide supplemental coverage for low-income Medicare beneficiaries but the eligibility criteria vary by state. Beneficiaries with incomes below 75 percent of the federal poverty level with assets no greater than $2,000 for individuals ($3,000 for couples) are entitled to full Medicaid benefits as well as coverage for the Medicare Part B premium and Medicare cost sharing. These criteria are tied to eligibility for the Supplemental Security Income program. States have flexibility to raise the income level and disregard certain forms of income. In 2009, 24 states set Medicaid eligibility at or below these Supplemental Security Income requirements (Kaiser Family Foundation 2010). Some states provide full Medicaid benefits to additional categories of the elderly and disabled population. For example, 33 states plus the District of Columbia have a medically needy program that allows individuals with higher incomes or resources to qualify for Medicaid coverage if they have high medical expenditures (Jacobson et al. 2011).

The Congress has created a number of additional programs, called Medicare Savings Programs (MSPs) to help beneficiaries with limited incomes pay for Medicare premiums and cost sharing (Table 3-6). Medicare beneficiaries with incomes below 100 percent of the federal poverty level who meet their state's resource limits can enroll in the Qualified Medicare Beneficiary (QMB) program with Medicaid covering their Part B premium and cost sharing. Beneficiaries with incomes below 135 percent of the poverty level can have their Part B premium covered under either the Specified Low Income Beneficiary (SLMB) or Qualified Individual (QI) program.

Table 3-6. Federal eligibility criteria for Medicare Savings Programs

Medicare Savings program	Income	asset limit	Covered costs and services
Qualified Medicare beneficiary (QMB)	<100% of poverty	$6,880 individual, $10,020 couple	Medicare premiums and cost sharing
Specified low-income beneficiary (SLMB)	100%–120% of poverty	$6,880 individual, $10,020 couple	Medicare premiums
Qualifying individual (QI) block grant funded by federal government	120%–135% of poverty	$6,880 individual, $10,020 couple	Medicare premiums

Note: States have the flexibility to adjust countable income and assets.
Source: Jacobson et al. 2011.

About 8.8 million individuals are dually eligible for and enrolled in both Medicare and Medicaid. Most receive full Medicaid coverage, with enrollment in the programs declining as income rises (Kaiser Family Foundation 2010). Medicaid provides supplemental coverage to 62 percent of beneficiaries with incomes below 100 percent of poverty and 34 percent of beneficiaries with incomes between 100 percent and 150 percent of poverty (Jacobson et al. 2011). Those beneficiaries eligible but not enrolled in MSPs are more likely to report that they did not receive needed health care because of cost.

In addition, the Congress designed a low-income drug subsidy (LIS) to supplement the Medicare Part D drug benefit for individuals with limited incomes. Beneficiaries who meet resource limits and have incomes below 135 percent of poverty receive full coverage of Part D premiums and nominal cost sharing. In addition, beneficiaries with incomes between 135 percent and 150 percent of poverty who meet resource limits can apply for a partial subsidy with sliding scale premiums and reduced cost sharing.

At present, about 10 million beneficiaries (36 percent of Part D enrollees) receive the LIS, and 6.4 million of them are dually eligible beneficiaries. Another 3.5 million qualify for the LIS either because they receive benefits through the MSP or the Supplemental Security Income program or because the Social Security Administration determined that they were eligible after they applied directly to that agency (Medicare Payment Advisory Commission 2011).

In 2008, the Commission made three recommendations to increase beneficiary participation in MSPs (Medicare Payment Advisory Commission 2008). These recommendations included linking the resource limit for MSP eligibility to the limits set for the Part D LIS, increasing funding for the state health insurance assistance programs that counsel beneficiaries about their choices, and allowing Social Security offices to screen beneficiaries for MSP eligibility when they apply for the LIS. These recommendations were largely enacted in the Medicare Improvements for Patients and Providers Act of 2008.

The Role of Supplemental Plans

The lack of comprehensive coverage in the FFS benefit design leads more than 90 percent of beneficiaries to take up supplemental coverage (Figure 3-1, p. 74). In 2007, employer-sponsored retiree policies that wrap around the Medicare FFS benefit covered the most beneficiaries, followed by individually purchased medigap policies, private Medicare plans, and Medicaid.[11] Only 9 percent of beneficiaries relied solely on Medicare's benefit.

The RAND Health Insurance Experiment

There is an extensive literature about the effects of cost sharing on the use of health care services. The RAND Health Insurance Experiment (HIE) remains the gold standard on this subject (RAND Corporation 2006).The HIE was a large-scale randomized experiment conducted between 1971 and 1982. More than 7,750 individuals (all under age 65) participated. It concluded that:

- Participants who paid a share of their health care used fewer health services than a comparison group given free care.
- Cost sharing reduced the use of both highly effective and less effective services in roughly equal proportions. Cost sharing did not significantly affect the quality of care participants received.
- In general, cost sharing had no adverse effect on participant health but there were exceptions: Free care led to improvements in hypertension, dental health, vision, and selected serious symptoms. These improvements were concentrated among the sickest and poorest patients.
- Reduced use of services was attributed mainly to participants declining to initiate care. Once patients entered the health care system, cost sharing only modestly affected the intensity or cost of an episode of care.

Additional research continues to show that lower cost sharing can lead to higher utilization and higher spending on health care. More controversial, however, is the effect of increases in cost sharing on health outcomes. Much of the literature is consistent with the notion that cost sharing can have both beneficial and detrimental effects on beneficiaries' health. (For an in-depth look at the literature see Medicare Payment Advisory Commission (2010).) The HIE found no short-term ill effects on the health of the average person.

A recent meta-analysis of the literature on cost sharing found that these results stand (Swartz 2010). However, consistent with the HIE findings, low-income individuals in poorer health may be more likely to forgo needed care as cost sharing increases. For example, one analysis involved retired California public employees who faced increased copayments for physician visits and prescription drugs (Chandra et al. 2010). The study found that increases in copayments for ambulatory care modestly increased hospital use for the average elderly person, but hospital spending increased significantly for chronically ill patients as physician and drug use decreased. Another line of research suggests that the responsiveness of beneficiaries to cost sharing is varied and the effects of supplemental coverage are more modest for individuals in poorer health (Remler and Atherly 2003).

Researchers agree that Medicare beneficiaries with medigap or retiree health coverage tend to have higher use of services and spending than those with no supplemental coverage (Table 3-7). Many supplemental plans cover all or nearly all of Medicare's cost-sharing requirements, regardless of whether there is evidence that the service is ineffective or, conversely, whether it might prevent a hospitalization. (Insurers providing supplemental coverage make no determinations about medical necessity.) Thus, some portion of the higher spending of these beneficiaries is arguably due to an insurance effect. Studies that attribute at least a portion of higher spending to an insurance effect find a spending increase of about 25 percent, with estimates ranging from 6 percent to 44 percent (Atherly 2001).[12] Estimates for the effects of medigap policies are generally higher than for employer-sponsored retiree coverage, and they tend to show larger effects for outpatient than for inpatient services.

Table 3-7. Average cost-sharing liability and out-of-pocket spending by type of supplemental coverage in 2007

	All FFS beneficiaries	Medicare only	employer sponsored	Medigap	Medicaid
Average per capita spending					
Medicare services	$8,335	$5,005	$7,351	$9,591	$11,180
Medicare payment	7,139	4,268	6,168	8,127	10,111
Medicare cost-sharing liability	1,196	738	1,184	1,464	1,068
Beneficiary out of pocket	262	606	229	219	167
As percent of total spending for Medicare services					
Medicare payment	86%	85%	84%	85%	90%
Medicare cost-sharing liability	14	15	16	15	10
Beneficiary out of pocket	3	12	3	2	2
Premiums					
Health insurance	$1,029	$37	$951	$2,082	$31
Medicare and health insurance	1,864	939	1,890	3,116	141

Note: FFS (fee-for-service). Excludes long-term institutionalized beneficiaries and those for whom Medicare is the secondary payer. Beneficiaries' secondary coverage is based on their monthly coverage status. Therefore, beneficiaries in one coverage category can have some months of enrollment in other coverage categories. Differences in spending also reflect differences in beneficiary characteristics not related to their supplemental insurance.

Source: MedPAC analysis of preliminary 2007 Medicare Current Beneficiary Survey Cost and Use files.

Commission-Sponsored Study

A recent Commission-sponsored study showed evidence that when elderly beneficiaries are insured against Medicare's cost sharing, they use more care, and Medicare spends more on them (Hogan 2009). That analysis found that the effects of supplemental coverage differed depending on the service. For example, having secondary insurance was not associated with higher spending for emergency hospitalizations, but it was associated with higher Part B spending that ranged from 30 percent to over 50 percent more. Overall, beneficiaries with private supplemental insurance spent more on elective hospital admissions, preventive care, office-based physician care, medical specialists, and services such as minor procedures, imaging, and endoscopy.

Paying little OOP seemed to be an influential factor associated with higher Medicare spending. Analyses comparing OOP limits for beneficiaries with retiree coverage and for beneficiaries with medigap policies suggest that if supplemental coverage did not fill in as much of Medicare's cost sharing, cost sharing could be structured in ways to encourage beneficiaries to choose high-value care. For example, differential copayments between primary and specialty care could be used to encourage more of the former.

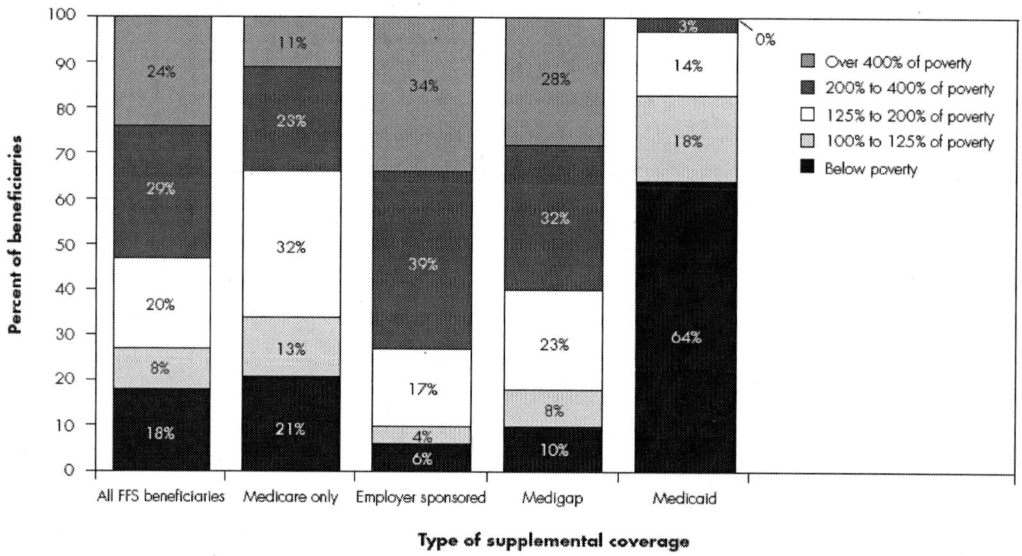

Note: FFS (fee-for-service). Excludes long-term institutionalized beneficiaries and those for whom Medicare is the secondary payer. Beneficiaries' secondary coverage is based on their monthly coverage status. Therefore, beneficiaries in one coverage category can have some months of enrollment in other coverage categories. Categories may not sum to 100 percent due to rounding.

Source: MedPAC analysis of preliminary 2007 Medicare Current Beneficiary Survey Cost and Use files.

Figure 3-2. Distribution of FFS beneficiaries' income by type of supplemental coverage in 2007.

The Commission's analysis also found that lower income beneficiaries were somewhat more sensitive to cost sharing than higher income individuals. In general, when either lower income or higher income beneficiaries had supplemental insurance, their Medicare spending was higher than that of individuals without supplemental coverage but with similar incomes. However, the presence of secondary insurance had a somewhat stronger effect on spending for lower income beneficiaries. This finding is consistent with other research that suggests the difference in price sensitivity to rising copayments for prescription drugs may account for some of the observed disparities in health across socioeconomic groups (Chernew and Gibson 2008).

Supplemental Insurance and Beneficiary Income

The economic circumstances of beneficiaries differ significantly across categories of supplemental insurance. Among all FFS beneficiaries, in 2007, about 46 percent had incomes of 200 percent of the poverty threshold or less (Figure 3-2).[13] On average, beneficiaries with employer-sponsored retiree coverage or medigap policies had higher incomes than individuals with no supplemental insurance or with both Medicare and Medicaid benefits. At the median, Medicare beneficiaries spent about 16 percent of their income on premiums and other OOP health spending in 2005 (Neuman et al. 2009). However, that figure masks considerable variation across individuals. Generally, beneficiaries with higher Medicare spending pay a larger proportion of their income than those with lower Medicare spending, but the relative burden of financial liability depends on the beneficiary's type of supplemental coverage. Two groups tend to pay comparatively more than others: (1) beneficiaries with medigap policies and (2) those with no supplemental coverage and high use of Medicare services (Medicare Payment Advisory Commission 2009).

Shorter Term Potential Improvements to FFS Medicare

For the near term, incremental steps can be taken to begin changing beneficiaries' incentives. The aims of these measures include:

- reducing financial risk for beneficiaries who currently have very high cost sharing,
- redefining the role of supplemental coverage to avoid encouraging beneficiaries' use of lower value services, and
- encouraging beneficiaries to use high-quality, low-cost providers.

Providing beneficiaries with clear information about the potential risks and benefits of their treatment options through shared decision making with their medical providers could also be complementary to changes in benefit design.

Reducing Financial Risk for Beneficiaries with High Spending

While most individuals have at least one outpatient physician visit in a year, only about one in five has a hospital stay. Beneficiaries who have a hospitalization during a year can accumulate considerably more cost-sharing expenses than those who are not hospitalized. (Over several years, the odds of having one or more hospital stays go up considerably. For example, among beneficiaries who were in Medicare in 2004 and were alive in 2008, about half had a hospital stay at some point over that five-year period.) Although unlikely, beneficiaries with multiple hospitalizations may need to pay the inpatient deductible repeatedly, and those who require longer stays also pay sizable daily copayments. In addition, patients who are hospitalized have little control over care associated with their stay—for example, the professional services of physicians, imaging, and physical therapy—and pay 20 percent coinsurance for those services. They may also require considerable post-acute care services. Although much of Medicare beneficiaries' cost sharing is triggered by a hospitalization, most of the cost sharing they incur stems from coinsurance on their use of Part B services (Medicare Payment Advisory Commission 2009).

The Commission believes that protecting beneficiaries against the economic impact of catastrophic illness is very important. Providing a budget-neutral OOP cap on spending would reduce the financial risk for beneficiaries with high spending and may mitigate the need to purchase supplemental insurance, a significant expense for many beneficiaries.

Including an OOP cap in the FFS benefit without other design changes would generally lower spending for beneficiaries and raise spending for the government. Such a policy would benefit individuals who currently pay very high Medicare cost sharing, particularly those with no supplemental coverage, and would tend to lower supplemental premiums for many other beneficiaries. However, Medicare would begin paying for some of the costs now covered by secondary insurers. Because beneficiaries who have medigap policies pay the full premium for the supplemental benefits of everyone in their insurance pool (including some beneficiaries with high Medicare cost sharing), all beneficiaries with medigap policies would see lower premiums, but Medicare spending would grow. An OOP cap would also lead to somewhat higher Part B premiums since these premiums are set as a percentage of Medicare's spending for Part B services.

One way to reduce Medicare's program costs under an OOP cap would be to combine the FFS deductibles for Part A and Part B services. To remain budget neutral, a combined deductible would need to be high. To illustrate, using conservative assumptions about beneficiaries' behavioral responses, Table 3-8 (p. 78) shows the combinations of the OOP cap and combined deductible under which Medicare spending would break even and the new benefit would not worsen the program's financial sustainability. (Table 3-8 assumes no changes in current coinsurance rules.) For example, if today's separate deductibles were replaced in 2011 with a combined deductible under a policy that capped OOP expenses at $5,000, all enrollees in FFS Medicare would need to pay for the first $1,170 of Part A or Part B services. At this amount, about 34 percent of beneficiaries would have higher OOP spending by about $300 on average compared with current law. In contrast, about 7 percent of beneficiaries would have lower OOP spending by more than $1,050 on average. Although only a small proportion of beneficiaries would actually have OOP spending high enough to benefit from the cap in a given year, other beneficiaries would also benefit from the reduced uncertainty of incurring very high OOP spending. Furthermore, a much higher proportion of beneficiaries would benefit from the OOP cap over time, as about half of beneficiaries have a hospital stay over a five-year period. At a lower OOP cap, the combined deductible would be higher and more beneficiaries would face higher OOP spending. If supplemental policies were permitted to fill in this combined deductible, the majority of beneficiaries would likely see little change or a net lowering of their combined OOP spending, Part B premiums, and premiums for supplemental coverage.

Redefining the Role of Supplemental Coverage

Instead of replacing the current Part A and Part B deductibles with a combined deductible, policymakers could focus on redefining the amount of Medicare cost sharing that supplemental insurance could fill in. For example, the Congressional Budget Office (CBO) estimates that if medigap insurers were barred from paying any of the first $550 of a policyholder's cost sharing and medigap coverage was limited to 50 percent of the next $4,950 in Medicare cost sharing with all further cost sharing covered by the policy, the option would lower federal spending by over $5 billion per year beginning in 2014 (Congressional Budget Office 2011).[14] This option would apply only to medigap policies—it would not affect beneficiaries with employer-sponsored retiree coverage.

Table 3-8. Level of combined FFS deductible required to hold constant Medicare program spending in 2011

		How FFS beneficiaries' OOP spending would differ			
Catastrophic limit on OOP spending	Combined deductible required to break even	Nonspenders	No appreciable change*	Higher	Lower
None — current law	$595	5%	61%	28%	6%
$7,000	960	5	56	33	6
$5,000	1,170	5	54	34	7
$4,000	1,328	5	53	35	6
$3,000	1,635	5	52	36	7

Note : FFS (fee-for-service), OOP (out of pocket). Percents may not sum to 100 due to rounding. This analysis excludes Part D. OOP spending includes only cost-sharing amounts paid by the beneficiary—it excludes any cost sharing paid through supplemental coverage. OOP also excludes any premiums for Part A, Part B, and supplemental coverage.

*Change of $50 or less.

Source: Actuarial Research Corporation, based on 2004–2006 Medical Expenditure Panel Survey data calibrated to 2011 spending and utilization statistics for Medicare's FFS population from the 2009 Medicare Trustees Report.

Another approach to prohibit first-dollar coverage in supplemental insurance would be to require beneficiaries to pay some fixed-dollar copayment for services such as office visits and use of hospital emergency rooms. Copayments could be set to change beneficiaries' incentives toward certain types of care—for example, by setting lower copayments for office visits to primary care providers. This approach is used by medigap Plan N and commonly by MA plans and commercial insurers.

Estimates of the effects of such copayments can vary substantially depending on the groups of services to which copayments apply. For example, MA plans often apply copayments to face-to-face visits with providers for evaluation and management services as well as X-rays and other imaging services, chiropractic care, and physical therapy. By comparison, recent guidance developed by NAIC in conjunction with CMS suggests that insurers offering medigap Plan N will use a narrow interpretation of office visits. The guidance states that Plan N will apply copayments of up to $20 only for services under specific billing codes for evaluation and management of new and established patients (National Association of Insurance Commissioners 2010). Such an interpretation may not achieve the degree of reduction in use of Part B services that was envisioned with changes to medigap Plan C and Plan F called for in PPACA. For Medicare FFS to adopt this approach of limiting or calibrating supplemental insurance coverage to types of services provided, other details would need to be evaluated carefully, such as the level of copayment that would apply when a beneficiary receives primary care from a medical specialist.

The copayment approach could be coupled with other changes to the FFS benefit to encourage appropriate use of services and allow a lower OOP cap. Cost sharing could be made more uniform across services and could be applied to services for which none is required today, such as laboratory tests and home health care. A separate approach involves an excise tax on insurers that offer the most complete coverage—supplemental policies that fill in most of Medicare's cost sharing. This approach uses a different philosophy in that it does not prohibit supplemental policies from filling in all of Medicare's cost sharing but instead charges the insurer for at least some of the added costs imposed on Medicare because of such comprehensive coverage. Applying a tax only to supplemental policies that fill in nearly all of Medicare's cost sharing could serve several purposes. First, the tax would help to recoup some of the additional Medicare spending associated with that more complete coverage.[15] Medigap insurers would pay taxes directly to the Medicare trust funds through the same Medicare administrative contractors that process Medicare claims.[16] Presumably, insurers would pass the excise tax along by raising premiums for their more complete plans. In turn, this increase would provide an incentive for beneficiaries in those plans to voluntarily consider newer medigap policies that cover less of Medicare's cost sharing.

A potential consequence of higher premiums is that some beneficiaries, rather than switching to a different supplemental plan, could choose to drop coverage altogether. If dropping all supplemental coverage led some beneficiaries to forgo necessary care, it could worsen their health outcomes and potentially result in higher Medicare spending for those beneficiaries. To encourage individuals to move into newer medigap policies or other sources of additional benefits, policymakers may want to consider reducing hurdles that prevent switching. For example, an option to change to medigap policies without first-dollar coverage that are not subject to the excise tax on a guaranteed-issue basis might limit the number of beneficiaries who choose to drop supplemental coverage.

As an example, CBO has estimated that if a 5 percent excise tax were levied on medigap plans, revenues would increase on the order of $1 billion per year, and Medicare spending would decrease by $100 million to $200 million per year (Congressional Budget Office 2008). The tax would, in all likelihood, need to be significantly greater than 5 percent to recoup the induced demand attributable to medigap coverage. However, because of the difficulty in disentangling the effects of a pure insurance effect from selection bias, the exact percentage is uncertain. If the excise tax encouraged beneficiaries to change to the newer medigap policies that require paying more of Medicare's cost sharing at the point of service, that change could lead to slower growth in Medicare spending.

Encouraging Beneficiaries to Use High-Quality, Low-Cost Providers

Another option would be to create incentives for beneficiaries to use providers designated as high quality for specific services or procedures. Medicare FFS has had some experience using innovative methods to designate certain hospitals as providers of high-quality, low-cost services. Beneficiaries who chose these providers faced lower OOP costs. Two Medicare demonstration projects feature identification of high-quality, low-cost providers and reduced cost sharing for beneficiaries who use the designated facilities.

Coronary Artery Bypass Graft Demonstration

Using its existing demonstration authority, CMS (known as the Health Care Financing Administration at the time of the demonstration) conducted the coronary artery bypass graft (CABG) demonstration between 1991 and 1996. It examined the effect of selecting facilities based on discounted price, quality of care, and geographic dispersion to receive a bundled payment for hospital and physician services related to cardiac bypass surgery. It selected seven sites, each of which could market itself as a Medicare Participating Heart Bypass Center to increase market share.

The evaluation found that the demonstration generated considerable interest among providers, reduced the costs to Medicare and the majority of participants, and increased quality of care. It did not, however, increase market share for the majority of participating sites as many expected.

Defining the Market

As a first step in defining the competitive marketplace, CMS selected services surrounding two procedures that were high cost and growing in volume. CMS defined the product as all inpatient hospital and physician services that apply to the two diagnosis related groups associated with bypass surgery: with catheterization and without catheterization.

Payment for hospital services included an estimated outlier amount based on each hospital's previous experience, any related readmissions, and standard Medicare hospital pass-through payments. Physician services included not only those by thoracic surgeons, cardiologists, anesthesiologists, and radiologists (all of whom were assumed to be involved in every bypass surgery) but also any other consulting physicians. For example, if a bypass patient was also depressed, the consulting psychiatrist would be paid under the bundled payment. However, the bundle excluded preadmission and postdischarge physician services, except for the standard inclusions in the surgeon's global fee.

All 734 hospitals nationwide that performed CABG surgery on Medicare patients in 1986 were eligible to participate. Participation was national, but local pressures largely motivated the competition.

The Bidding Process

CMS invited applicants to submit their best price for the bundled payment. Hospitals calculated separate cost estimates for Part A hospital and Part B physician services, decided on a set discount rate for each, and then offered Medicare an overall global payment rate. Applicants were judged on price (50 percent), quality (25 percent), service (e.g., coverage of unrelated procedures) (10 percent), financial incentives offered to patients (e.g., reduced cost sharing), information systems, and bypass volume (5 percent each). After negotiations with CMS, seven hospitals eventually enrolled in the demonstration.

The participating institutions wanted to protect or expand their current market (Medicare Payment Advisory Commission 2003). First, they believed it was to their advantage to participate at the beginning of the program if it became the basis for selective contracting or a permanent part of the program. Second, other payers were interested in the bundled CABG payments and hospitals were concerned that failure to participate could affect their standing in the private market. Third, they worried that another hospital in the local market would be designated a Heart Bypass Center.

Results

Overall, the demonstration had a positive impact by reducing providers' costs, improving quality, and reducing Medicare spending. Medicare saved about $42.3 million on bypass patients treated in the demonstration hospitals, a savings of roughly 10 percent of the expected $438 million spending on bypass patients, which included a 90-day postdischarge period. Eighty-six percent of the savings came from CMS-negotiated discounts, 5 percent from lower than expected spending on postdischarge care, and 9 percent from a shift in market share toward lower cost demonstration facilities. In addition, beneficiaries saved $7.9 million in cost sharing based on the discounted Medicare charges for both hospital and physician services for a total estimated savings of $50.3 million over 5 years.

Participating sites were largely successful in reducing their internal costs per episode. For example, several hospitals had statistically significant declines in intensive care unit and direct nursing expenses. They also achieved savings in pharmacy and laboratory costs. However, one site saw its costs per case increase.

Beneficiaries experienced improved quality and lower costs. The evaluators found that demonstration hospitals reduced inpatient mortality rates, which was notable considering their lower than average baseline mortality rates. Compared with beneficiaries at competitors' facilities, beneficiaries who received care through the demonstration sites were more satisfied with the nursing care, shorter length of stay, and reduced paperwork.

Despite these positive results, the majority of participating sites did not see as great an increase in market share or volume as expected. Several factors may account for this finding. First, many sites did not widely advertise their participation in the demonstration. A second factor was changing local market conditions and technology, as more competing hospitals developed bypass surgery capabilities and catheterization labs. Finally, the failure to increase market share may be partly attributed to beneficiaries' and physicians' reluctance to change their site of care in response to quality information.

Acute Care Episode Demonstration

Building on lessons learned from the CABG demonstration, in 2009 CMS began implementing the acute care episode demonstration of bundled payments for physician and hospital services treating patients who need specified orthopedic or cardiovascular procedures. The goal of the demonstration is to improve quality for FFS Medicare beneficiaries; produce savings for providers, beneficiaries, and Medicare by using market-based mechanisms; increase price and quality transparency; and encourage collaboration among providers. In this demonstration, physicians receive their full Medicare payment and can share in savings if they improve quality and achieve savings.

Five demonstration sites were chosen from applicants in Texas, Oklahoma, New Mexico, and Colorado on the basis of competitive bids. Medicare provides a single payment to cover all Part A and Part B services, including physician services, related to an inpatient stay for FFS beneficiaries. Sites can reward individual clinicians, interdisciplinary teams, and other hospital staff on the basis of measurable quality and efficiency improvements.

Participating demonstration sites can market themselves to beneficiaries and referring physicians as Value-Based Care Centers. Unlike the CABG demonstration, CMS plans to take an active role in marketing the demonstration.

Beneficiary Incentives

Beneficiaries who receive the designated services at one of the demonstration sites receive payment incentives if the demonstration results in program savings. Medicare shares 50 percent of the savings it gains under the demonstration with beneficiaries up to a maximum of the annual Part B premium. Hillcrest Medical Center, the first demonstration site to begin reporting results, announced that, after nine months, surgical quality has improved and patients have received checks from CMS up to $1,157 (Coughlin 2010). Beneficiaries undergoing joint replacement have received an average payment of $350 from Medicare.

Additional Results

In 2009, Hillcrest Medical Center also saw a 28 percent increase in volume for cardiology procedures and a 31 percent volume increase for orthopedic procedures. Independent evaluation will be necessary to explain the volume increases. Beneficiary surveys done at the demonstration facilities suggest that payment incentives do not drive beneficiaries' choice of providers but that independent validation of the facility as high quality has had an effect on their decision. For cardiology procedures, patients are most influenced by their physicians.

The main source of savings for Hillcrest has come from increased bargaining power for equipment and supplies from vendors. Physicians have agreed on a limited number of devices and supplies after learning the cost of various supplies. The hospital has found that the bargaining power over vendors gained through sufficient market share is a more significant source of savings than increasing the volume of patients (Hund and Joshi 2010).

Similarly, Baptist Health System in San Antonio, Texas, another demonstration site, attained $4 million in device and supply savings over the first 18 months of the demonstration. Participating physicians—about 150 in number—shared gains of $558,000, and 2,000 patients received an average of $300 per beneficiary (Vesely 2011).

Medicare Certification

In addition to the acute care episode demonstration, Medicare has issued several national coverage determinations limiting coverage for certain services and procedures of a complex nature to facilities that meet certain criteria. These criteria require, in part, that the facilities be recognized as providers with the ability and expertise to perform the procedure and ensure patient safety. For example, a facility must be certified as Medicare approved to perform the following procedures: carotid artery stenting, ventricular assist devices for destination therapy, bariatric surgery, and lung volume reduction surgery. In these cases, Medicare certification depends on quality standards and does not have payment implications.

Other Ideas to Explore

The Commission will continue to explore other options that might encourage beneficiaries to seek out high-quality, low-cost providers. Pilot or demonstration programs may provide a way to try out new approaches involving supplemental coverage. NAIC is beginning to catalog states' approval of "new or innovative benefits" offered by medigap insurers. State insurance regulators have had authority to approve the addition of such benefits to standard medigap policies for some time, but so far relatively little information has been shared. This information would allow states and insurance companies to look for best practices.

Longer Term Potential Improvements to Medicare

For the longer term, the Medicare program needs to move toward a redesigned benefit that gives individuals incentives to use higher value care and avoid using lower value care. These determinations must be evidence based. Several years ago the Commission recommended that policymakers establish an independent, public–private entity that would produce information to compare the clinical effectiveness of a health service with its alternatives (Medicare Payment Advisory Commission 2008). Along the same lines, PPACA established the Patient-Centered Outcomes Research Institute to identify national priorities for comparative clinical effectiveness research and to sponsor comparative-effectiveness research efforts. In addition, Medicare could examine the factors that affect beneficiaries' health care decisions and use that information to help transform the structure of health care delivery.

Policymakers have become more aware that not all health care services have the same value, but identifying which services are of higher or lower value can be difficult. The term "value based" is applied to strategies for reimbursing providers (value-based purchasing) and cost-sharing options designed to encourage beneficiaries to use high-value health care services or providers and to discourage use of low-value services or providers (value-based insurance design). Testing these approaches would help policymakers decide which of them could steer beneficiaries more effectively toward the use of high-value health care services or away from services of low value.

Some insurers have begun setting different levels of cost sharing for the same medical intervention based on its clinical benefit to the individual (Chernew et al. 2007, Fendrick et al. 2001). When there is evidence that specific therapies are comparatively more effective and appropriate for certain patients, lowering their cost sharing to help increase their adherence could improve health outcomes. If greater adherence leads to fewer exacerbations of the patient's condition, this approach could also lower spending. At the same time, where evidence suggests that medical therapies are less effective, increasing beneficiaries' cost sharing could deter use of those services. Designs of this kind would lead to overall lower spending only if it helped to reduce medical interventions when the costs outweigh the clinical benefits. However, many services do not save money, although they are cost-effective. In a previous report, we discussed the literature testing key elements of this benefit design (Medicare Payment Advisory Commission 2010). In sum, the extent to which this benefit design could reduce Medicare program spending depends on beneficiaries' underlying health risk, the cost of adverse outcomes, beneficiaries' responsiveness to copayments, and the effectiveness of medical therapies at reducing risk (Chernew et al. 2010).

Although information is limited, surveys of large employers indicate that many use or are considering using innovative benefit designs to align cost sharing with the value of services to promote the efficiency of providers and encourage employees to manage their chronic conditions. For example, in the 2007 Mercer National Survey of employer-sponsored health plans, 15 percent of large employers (500 or more employees) lowered cost sharing for prescription drugs or nondrug treatments, and about 25 percent used enrollee incentives for participation in disease management programs. In addition, 80 percent of the largest employers (10,000 or more employees) expressed interest in implementing this type of program in the next five years, and more than 50 percent were interested in implementing tiered provider networks in the future (Hargrave et al. forthcoming).

To explore the experiences of payers who implemented cost sharing and other benefit design strategies, we organized a panel on identifying high-value and low-value services and conducted interviews and site visits with these payers.

Panel on Identifying High-Value and Low-Value Services

To examine ways of identifying the value of services and the implications for Medicare, we convened a panel of 11 participants, including academics, employers, benefit consultants, health plan representatives, and a consumer advocate. The panel included five physicians, a nurse, and two pharmacists. In this section, we present a summary of their discussion.[17]

Our panelists generally agreed that reforming the Medicare FFS benefit design to encourage the use of high-value services and discourage the use of low-value services was a good idea. They generally said that identifying most specific services as high value or low value for individual beneficiaries was too difficult with current data and information systems. Several panelists stressed that most services provide value to some people. If the determination is too rigid, people may not get the services they need. On the other hand, if the incentive covers all use of a service that is high value for some, cost sharing may be waived for populations for whom the benefit is not proven and costs for the program will increase. In addition, they noted, a design using varied copayments targeting specific subpopulations must address both ethical and technical issues.

However, they thought that other strategies to encourage high-value, high-quality health care were feasible. These strategies include lowering cost sharing for services identified as high value (e.g., preventive care), raising cost sharing for services that can be identified as low value, providing incentives for beneficiaries to see high-quality efficient providers, and encouraging beneficiaries to adopt healthier behaviors.

Some general themes emerged from the panel discussion:

- The value of a service often depends on who gets it. Beneficiary and provider incentives must be aligned.
- Medical management must be a part of benefit design.
- Public acceptance of a benefit design based on value depends on the process used to identify the value of services.
- Beneficiaries will be more open to benefit changes if presented with choices, including choice of plans, programs, and providers.

Several panelists linked clinical effectiveness and cost-effectiveness. One panelist said that "low value is a function of mispricing." For example, two treatments may be equally safe and effective but if one is much more expensive than the other, it becomes low value.

Most agreed that the process of identifying low-value services should be incremental, but each had different starting places. Some suggested identifying low-value services as those that can harm patients—for example, the potential for too much advanced imaging to overexpose a patient to radiation. Another panelist suggested a data-driven approach that looks first at the services that cost the program the most money and uses clinical evidence to determine their value. Another suggested starting with the Part D drug benefit, because beneficiaries are used to copayments varying depending on the tier in which the drugs are placed, and there is more comparative effectiveness evidence for medications. Tiering could be based on value if comparative clinical effectiveness information is available.

Panelists agreed that raising or lowering copayments for a service would have more effect on utilization if the incentive created for beneficiaries is aligned with that for physicians. Attention focused on conflicting incentives in pay-for-performance programs. One physician spoke about his frustration when a health plan rates him on the percentage of his eligible patients who receive colonoscopies at the same time that it raises patient cost sharing for this procedure. Panelists also noted that Medicare supplemental policies must be aligned with benefit changes. They were concerned that first-dollar coverage would blunt any incentives created by variable cost sharing. Panelists mentioned not just medigap but also employer retiree plans. Some panelists suggested that, to the extent that private payer incentives are also aligned, the effect on utilization of high-value and low-value services would be magnified.

Others suggested that medical management needs to be in sync with the identification of services. For example, one plan charges higher copayments for advanced imaging without precertification. Panelists mentioned that medical management is particularly important for lower income beneficiaries because higher cost sharing would be impractical for them.

Another panelist suggested that ranking individual services was too difficult and politically charged. A number of panelists believed that cost sharing based on provider quality and resource use was a more practical way to achieve the goal of promoting the use of high-value care. They said the program would gain traction by tiering copayments to steer beneficiaries toward the most efficient providers. One participant talked about a plan that does both: For certain conditions, the plan uses evidence-based guidelines to define care pathways. The pathways may include referrals to specific providers who use these guidelines. Patients who choose to follow these pathways have lower copayments.

One idea that generated a lot of discussion was the introduction of what one panelist called a graded benefit. It would be a Medicare FFS benefit that would be offered to beneficiaries as an alternative to traditional Medicare. Cost sharing in this benefit design would be based on the value of services and the use of high-quality efficient providers. The option could apply to new Medicare beneficiaries.

Those who chose this option could have a separate Part B premium and opportunities for reduced cost sharing if the plan resulted in savings. Panelists agreed that beneficiaries would be more likely to accept such a benefit if they had choices. Panelists did not fully consider the many design questions raised by this approach.

Panelists also discussed whether people should be encouraged to choose the plan by rewards or face penalties if they do not. A number of panelists suggested that penalties are more effective than rewards. For example, one person noted that the literature was clear that raising copays for drugs decreases utilization but less clear that lowering copayments increases utilization at a comparable rate. Although cost can be a barrier to medication adherence, people also may skip medication because of its side effects or because they do not believe they need it, among other reasons. The result is that lowering copays leads to some increased utilization but mostly to lower costs for the patients who were already adherent. One plan provided incentives for members to fill out risk assessments and got 30 percent participation. After it put a surcharge on premiums for those who did not fill out an assessment, participation increased to more than 70 percent. A number of panelists suggested the need for a combination of rewards and penalties.

Payer Experiences

Working with researchers from NORC, we interviewed more than 70 individuals, including researchers, insurers, and public and private payers. The interviews included individual phone interviews and 10 site visits. We found that differential cost sharing was employed as part of larger strategies that included creating incentives for individuals to see high-quality efficient providers and modify their health behaviors. Strategies were integrated into the benefit design and were generally not evaluated individually. Most interviewees said that the reforms had to be treated as a package. In fact, no interviewee relied on a single technique.

From our interviews, we identified four design strategies:

- lowering cost sharing for high-value services,
- raising cost sharing for low-value services,
- creating incentives for enrollees to see high-performing or low-cost providers, and
- providing incentives for enrollees to adopt healthier behaviors.

Lowering Cost Sharing for High-Value Services

Payers were most likely to lower cost sharing for preventive services and prescription drugs that treat chronic conditions. Many of the plan sponsors with whom we spoke had a long history of waiving the copayments for preventive services or creating an exemption to the deductible for specified preventive services. Some of the services most frequently targeted for variable cost sharing included preventive health or wellness services (e.g., immunizations, primary care visits) and health screenings (e.g., mammograms, Pap smears). Many spoke about it as "the right thing to do" but did not necessarily believe it would save money, even in the long term.

Another preventive care focus for some employers has been to waive cost sharing for participating in weight-management programs. The Oregon benefits boards for public employees cover the cost of participating in a weight-reduction program for those individuals who attend a set number of sessions. While the board acknowledged that evidence for the effectiveness of these programs is lacking, they determined that because many of their members were overweight or obese, it was "a pressing enough issue that we couldn't just not do anything." Thus far, they say that hundreds of individuals have met their weight goals.

Many of the payers interviewed have reduced or eliminated copayments for services related to care for chronic conditions that, if not well controlled, could lead to additional health complications (e.g., prescription drugs for diabetes care). These programs are structured in several different ways:

- Payers reduce or eliminate cost sharing for all drugs in a therapeutic class.
- Payers reduce cost sharing for all tiers of drugs in a therapeutic class while maintaining differences among the tiers. For example, they lower copayments in the targeted class by 100 percent for the lowest tier drugs (generally generics), 50 percent for the second tier, and 25 percent for the third tier.

- Payers reduce cost sharing for specific patient populations with conditions such as diabetes for which medication adherence has a significant effect on patient health over time.

The better a plan is at targeting the individuals who are most likely to increase their medication adherence, the greater is the likelihood the program will be cost neutral or cost saving. However, individual targeting can be challenging to implement and raises equity concerns.

Some plan sponsors indicated that cost-sharing changes were a way to provide an incentive to enrollees to participate in activities aimed at better managing their condition and stressed the importance of pairing the reduced cost sharing with some required action on the part of the enrollees. One employer mentioned that during a brief period of time—when the plan was not providing careful oversight to ensure that beneficiaries were participating in its disease management program— the program was unable to produce cost savings for the employer. Once the disease management program was more firmly reinstated, overall medical costs began to drop again.[18]

At the same time, some employers are hesitant to "attach strings" to reduced cost sharing. One benefit manager was concerned that in his worker population (which includes many hourly workers, some of whom do not speak English as a primary language), the requirement to attend a program in a language they did not understand might prevent some individuals from receiving low-cost medications.

Some payers interviewed have reduced cost sharing for a wide range of services for specific populations. For example, for individuals with diabetes, some plans have developed insurance products that do not have cost sharing for a range of services, including diagnostic procedures, lab tests, medications, dietician visits, and endocrinologist visits as long as these individuals enroll in a special diabetes health plan and follow certain guidelines that are tracked on a score card.

Other payers have varied cost sharing as an incentive to use minimally invasive procedures (MIPs). Some evidence suggests that compared with open surgery, MIPs for hysterectomy, breast biopsy, and colectomy are often associated with shorter hospital stays, reduced infection rates and complications, and faster recovery time and return to work (Center for Health Value Innovation 2010). One employer introduced a lower copayment for individuals opting for MIPs for colectomy, gall bladder removal, hysterectomy, bariatric surgery, and appendectomy. They also required preauthorization for more invasive surgery for individuals who needed those procedures. They educated employees about alternative treatments in these instances. The employer reported increased use of MIPs for all the procedures except appendectomy. One barrier to this strategy mentioned by an interviewee is the limited number of providers with experience in the field in some parts of the country.[19]

Raising Cost Sharing for Low-Value Services

Increasing cost sharing for low-value services can protect individuals from potentially unnecessary and even harmful procedures. It has two potential cost-saving effects: It can deter the use of low-value services as patients seek lower cost options, and it also recoups more of the cost of the low-value services that are provided. Yet this approach has not commonly been implemented, and few of our interviewees had experience identifying low-value services and increasing cost sharing for them. Some plans raise cost sharing for most services and lower cost sharing for a few other services, but generally increases affect high-value and low-value services alike. Options for explicitly instituting higher cost sharing for low-value services range from adding a flat copay for selected services to charging a higher coinsurance rate.

As a form of targeted higher cost sharing, some payers interviewed use reference pricing. One plan, where comparable prescription drugs exist, covers the full cost of the lowest price option, but individuals opting for a higher cost option pay the full price difference. In another example, a company that initially waived cost sharing for colonoscopies discovered large price differences in its area and moved to a reference pricing system. The company now covers the costs of the procedure up to $1,500 and enrollees who need a routine screening are responsible for any expenses above that amount. The company also provides its enrollees with information about which providers charge $1,500 or less so that enrollees can make informed decisions about where they receive care. Other interviewees suggested that they were interested in adopting reference pricing in the future.

A number of initiatives are taking place in Oregon to identify and raise cost sharing for low-value services. These efforts build on the state's history incorporating value into its decisions about health coverage. Oregon began rank ordering services in 1989, with creation of the Oregon Health Plan, a state Medicaid waiver program that sought to cover more people by covering fewer services. Composed of health professionals and consumer representatives and informed by public input (surveys, focus groups, and town hall meetings), scientific evidence, and expert opinion, the Health Services Commission developed a prioritized list of services. The list consists of about 700 condition–treatment pairs rank-ordered by importance. As many services as possible are covered within the constraints of the Medicaid budget, starting with the highest priority services.

In 2006, the Health Services Commission changed the list's ranking methodology. The new system has a population focus and has moved certain preventive services higher on the list. This new methodology serves as the basis for the state's more recent efforts to develop an essential benefits package. While the details of this plan are still in development, the concept is that a set of 20 services with a very strong evidence base would be available to enrollees at no cost. Other services would be ranked in four additional tiers, each with higher coinsurance. Actuarial modeling suggests that the plan may have the potential to produce savings of 3 percent to 5 percent initially. However, the estimate is sensitive to factors such as the initial utilization rates of enrollees. The Oregon Health Authority is presenting this proposed plan to state policymakers and soliciting feedback at public meetings.

A concurrent effort is being led by the Oregon Health Leadership Council (OHLC), an organization of business leaders, health plans, and providers seeking to reduce the rate of increase of health care costs and create a simpler benefit design with three tiers of service. A middle tier—level 2—resembles most traditional plans with a deductible and coinsurance for most services. But the plan alters cost sharing for high-value and low-value services. Benefit level 1 covers prescription drugs and some lab and imaging and other ancillary services related to six chronic conditions—coronary disease, congestive heart failure, chronic obstructive pulmonary disease, diabetes, asthma, and depression—with minimal or no cost sharing. OHLC originally wanted to include primary care visits in the tier without cost sharing; however, administrative barriers may not make it feasible for all insurers. For example, their billing systems may not be able to distinguish primary care visits for a specific chronic condition.

Level 3 focuses on "services that are nationally recognized as overused and driven by provider preference or supply rather than evidence-based need." Level 3 services are subject to higher coinsurance and a separate deductible and OOP maximum. Services included in this tier are outpatient upper endoscopy; outpatient MRI, computed tomography, and positron emission tomography screening; some spine surgery and orthopedic joint procedures; percutaneous transluminal coronary angioplasty; stents; CABG surgery; electron beam computerized tomography; and non-cancer-related hysterectomy. In addition, if individuals have an emergency room visit that does not result in an admission to the hospital or is related to one of these level 3 procedures, they face the higher cost sharing.

OHLC estimates that if insurers implement the benefit design as they have laid it out, it could result in a premium reduction of between 8 percent and 12 percent. (Plans that are already tightly managed would save less.) In those projections, the actuaries assume no net gain or loss on the level 1 services and predict most of the savings from level 3. OHLC acknowledges that the plan has received some criticism as an attempt to shift costs to consumers. OHLC counters that this approach is a more rational way to shift costs than by introducing a $2,000 deductible for all services.

While no plan sponsor has implemented OHLC's benefit design as is, several have adapted it to meet their needs. A workgroup of the Public Employees' Benefit Board (PEBB) and Oregon Educators' Benefit Board (OEBB) recommended making several minor changes to the plan before implementing it for the 2010–2011 plan year. Enrollees in the plan face no cost sharing for 17 preventive services and can receive free tobacco-cessation and weight-management benefits. For level 3 services, individuals face a flat $500 copayment, which is in addition to coinsurance for those services and is not included in the general deductible or OOP maximum. In reviewing the OHLC plan, the PEBB/OEBB workgroup decided to remove cardiac treatments and hysterectomy from level 3, because keeping them in a high cost-sharing tier was considered too contentious. The workgroup also recommended creating an intermediary tier with a $100 copayment for advanced imaging and sleep studies. Representatives of the workgroup noted that in past years, less than 5 percent of their plans' membership use the services designated in the highest cost-sharing tier— roughly the same percentage of enrollees who are affected by the highest tier of their drug formulary.

Evraz Inc., which operates steel mills in Oregon and Delaware, began offering its employees a plan based on the OHLC model as of January 1, 2011. The plan includes cholesterol and blood pressure medications on the nocost-sharing tier. While some workers have the option of staying in their current plan or selecting the value-based plan, the company is waiving the employee premium contribution for individuals who opt for the new offering. A similar plan has been rolled out to the employees of the health insurer ODS.

Insurers have found few employers who are willing to implement this OHLC benefit design. They contend that employers are interested in the concept but want to add services to the tier without cost sharing. In our discussion, an OHLC representative pointed out that to reach the goal of a 10 percent premium reduction, "we can't just add good stuff. We need to take away bad stuff. That's the value." Another potential obstacle is the response of providers who might stand to lose some business if their services appeared on the third tier. In response, the OHLC representative noted that it had received less provider pushback than expected.

A concern that was echoed by nearly all the individuals with whom we spoke in Oregon is enrollees' perception that services on the third tier are not covered. The insurers and plan sponsors emphasize that enrollees can receive those services but are encouraged to think through the alternatives first. PEBB/OEBB explained that they view the new design structure as more about "influencing behavior and plan utilization" than about cost shifting.

To facilitate decision making, plans offer shared decision making about the potential risks and benefits of some procedures and give enrollees access to decision aids where they are available.

A related criticism stated by payers interviewed is that even for services typically of low value, some individuals will benefit. Some employers expressed an interest in making exceptions for level 3 services for cases in which these services are considered medically necessary, but OHLC and insurers are reluctant to establish this precedent. They note that these services are considered covered but with a higher level of cost sharing.

ODS and Providence, who administer the plans for PEBB/OEBB, see the increased cost sharing for lower value services as a complement to prior authorization strategies they have already successfully used. An ODS representative explained that the insurer had previously used prior authorization for some expensive procedures that have less invasive alternatives. However, he explained that "prior authorization doesn't by itself change behavior. Copays are necessary." The interviewee noted that providers often learn how to get around prior authorization requirements. In addition, a Providence representative noted that the new benefit design may be less administratively burdensome because, unlike prior authorization, the benefit design is not subject to debates between physicians and plan administrators and to appeals.

Creating Incentives for Enrollees to See High-Performing or Low-Cost Providers

Efforts to influence the behavior of plan enrollees can also align with initiatives such as value-based purchasing and high-quality provider networks. Purchasers and health plans can identify which physicians provide care consistent with clinical guidelines and select them for these networks, known as top tier networks. Payers can then use incentives to encourage enrollees to see providers in that high-value tier. From our interviews, we learned that plans used a variety of efforts to achieve this aim, including establishing preferred provider networks, encouraging use of the most efficient site of care, and paying for second opinions.

Provider Networks

Starting in 2002, Minnesota implemented a program to give state employees an incentive to see more efficient providers. Each year the state ranks its primary care clinics in order from those whose patients have the overall lowest risk-adjusted claims to those with the highest. The ordered list is then divided into four tiers, with the "lower" tiers representing the most favorable in terms of cost sharing. Patients who enroll with primary care providers in the lower tiers face lower cost sharing than those who enroll with providers in the higher tiers. The state works with providers to explain what they need to do to move into a lower cost tier, including lowering their payment rates, changing their referral patterns, and better managing patients with chronic conditions. Interviewees say the state achieved about 7 percent in savings as enrollees signed up with more efficient providers. Aetna began establishing high-performance networks by identifying specialists who were most efficient in providing care. Enrollees face reduced cost sharing for visits to those providers. Minnesota and Aetna also take into account issues of access to ensure that enrollees in various geographic areas have provider options in the high-performance tier.

One challenge facing plan administrators who are interested in establishing a tiered provider network is making sure they have adequate data to rank providers in tiers. Providers may argue that an individual insurer covers only a small fraction of the patients in their panel and therefore question the validity of the rating system. Confusion arises when a provider is considered a high performer by one insurer and not by another. Purchasers in Oregon note that statewide data-sharing initiatives might solve this problem.

For the provider tiers to have their intended effect, enrollees need to be aware of their plan's cost-sharing differences among providers. General Electric (GE) established a Health Coach program that allows employees to call a telephone hotline to help them decide which providers to see. The coaches provide information about quality ratings of providers, their tier ranking, and their associated cost-sharing requirements. The Health Coach also provides other assistance, including helping to make and prepare for appointments and transferring records if necessary.

Site of Care

In addition to providing assistance and incentives to steer patients to specifically designated, efficient primary care providers and specialists, plan sponsors implement strategies to encourage the use of primary care. On the basis of its "core strategy that everything begins with primary care," QuadMed has lowered cost sharing for primary care visits to a $7 copayment, making them much less expensive than specialist visits. Minnesota also encourages the use of convenience clinics to provide services such as strep tests at the lowest cost possible.

Other programs steer patients in need of complex procedures to facilities that specialize in that type of care. GE pays living and travel expenses and waives cost sharing for enrollees who go to centers of excellence for transplant surgery or for the treatment of some complicated cancers. By designating a particular facility as a center of excellence, the company is often able to negotiate discounted prices as well as see an improvement in quality and reduction in complications.

One supermarket chain sought opportunities for enrollees to receive more efficient care abroad. When the company realized the price differential between joint replacements in their area and those in other countries, it developed a benefit for enrollees to go to Singapore for the procedure, incur no cost sharing, and receive travel expenses for an accompanying spouse. The company never sent a patient to Singapore because local facilities renegotiated a much lower price to perform the procedures.

Second Opinions

GE has established an eSecond Opinion program through which individuals with serious health conditions are able to consult with a specialist at the Cleveland Clinic at no cost to the enrollee. The company provided several examples of cases in which the online program caught potentially serious misdiagnoses. Similarly, Hannaford Brothers, a New England supermarket chain, partnered with the Dana Farber Cancer Institute to provide oncologist-to-oncologist consultations; the program has resulted in many instances in which diagnoses or treatment plans have changed.

Providing Incentives for Enrollees to Adopt Healthier Behaviors

Some interviewees provide incentives to enrollees to engage in activities such as taking a health risk assessment, exercising, and quitting smoking. The employers with whom we spoke took various approaches to wellness programs. Roy O'Martin, a small lumber company in Louisiana, holds annual health fairs where employees can undergo biometric screenings (including measuring weight and height and testing cholesterol level, blood sugar, and prostate-specific antigen) and can review the results with an occupational health nurse. In discussion with the nurse, the employee sets goals for the coming year. Employees are not mandated to meet particular goals but choose their own. If they meet those goals, their portion of their health insurance premium is waived.

Hannaford Brothers phased in its wellness incentives. In the first year, enrollees had to complete a health risk appraisal and abstain from smoking to receive a $20 per week healthy behavior credit. In year two, enrollees had to accept a call from a nurse case manager if something in the risk appraisal triggered the need for outreach.

Starting in the third year, individuals contacted by a case manager needed to negotiate and meet goals related to the risk factor. In addition, all employees need to receive preventive care recommended by guidelines. The program has been well received by primary care providers who noted that increased accountability has prompted patients to talk to providers about their preventive care needs.

While the programs described above emphasize health risk assessments, not all employers with whom we spoke were convinced of their value. One employer explained the company does not see much return from having employees fill out health risk assessments. Another wondered how actionable the information derived from these assessments would be. Most employers and insurers who value health risk assessments believe they must be combined with other outreach activities. One interviewee put it bluntly: "anything that's not integrated is probably a waste of time." For example, Cigna uses the data to engage high-risk individuals in disease management efforts.

In addition to health screenings and risk assessments, some employers create incentives for individuals to stop smoking. At GE, employees who smoke and who do not agree to try to quit are required to pay a premium surcharge. Next year, employees who currently smoke will have to stop smoking for at least 90 days to avoid the surcharge. QuadMed also charges $11 per week more in premiums for individuals who do not sign up to be tobacco free and receive recommended screenings.

Impact of Benefit Design Changes

Although some interviewees reported successful results from their benefit design initiatives, limited research is available to evaluate these programs. In some cases, the programs are too new to be able to assess results. Several of our interviewees noted that even if a strategy is effective, how that translates into costs or savings may vary from one organization to another. Under a cost-sharing program, for example, a company that had a high baseline adherence rate for statins would find itself paying the full cost of statin prescriptions, which employees would take regardless of incentives, and would see fewer returns in preventing additional heart attacks than a company with a lower baseline adherence rate. Of course, the rationale for lowering cost sharing for high-value services does not rest solely on the notion that employers should save money. Wage offsets and risk alleviation could justify lower copays for high-value services even if few employees changed behavior.

Nevertheless, companies with low baseline adherence rates could achieve better results with a cost-sharing incentive program, as it would have further to go to change enrollee behavior and prevent additional heart attacks.

The Commission will consider these and other policy options. We need to assess the relevance of these strategies to Medicare. All the strategies would entail choosing among design options with both technical and policy implications.

Future Work

In the coming year, the Commission will continue looking at ways to improve the Medicare FFS benefit design. One issue is particularly important. Providing a budget-neutral OOP cap on spending would protect beneficiaries against the economic impact of catastrophic illness. Ideally, it could mitigate the need for individuals to purchase supplemental insurance, a significant expense for many beneficiaries.

To add an OOP cap to Medicare, we must examine the program's cost-sharing structure. Commissioners agree that rationalizing cost sharing is an important goal but one that raises complex issues. We will analyze different options and assess their distributional impacts.

The Commission continues to be interested in some of the innovative benefit designs being tested in the private sector. In particular, we will examine ways to provide incentives for beneficiaries to use high-quality, efficient providers. Defining such providers and providing beneficiaries with sufficient educational resources to make informed decisions is a necessity of such an approach.

Thus, improving the Medicare benefit design is an important endeavor that will enhance price signals in the Medicare program and support payment and other health care reforms. An improved benefit package can reduce beneficiary risk, help control program costs, and create incentives to increase the efficiency of the Medicare program.

Endnotes

[1] The other quarter of Medicare beneficiaries are enrolled in private plans, primarily Medicare Advantage (MA) plans. MA plans can vary the benefit structure, within limits, as long as the actuarial value of the benefit is at least as high as the traditional FFS Medicare benefit. For more information on the MA program see our March 2011 report (Medicare Payment Advisory Commission 2011).

[2] Higher income beneficiaries pay a higher income-related Part B premium.

[3] For example, the American Medical Association's 2009 National Health Insurer Report Card shows that Medicare performed similar to or better than private insurers on several claims-processing measures, such as indicators for timeliness, transparency, and accuracy of claims processing (American Medical Association 2009). The report card noted that, although Medicare had higher rates of denied claims (4 percent) than several of the private insurers, Medicare does not require preauthorization for services, as do many private insurers.

[4] In 2007, the Part A deductible was $992 and the Part B deductible was an additional $131. By comparison, in 2007, a typical large employer used a combined deductible for inpatient and outpatient care of $500 per individual ($1,000 per family) for in-network care (Yamamoto et al. 2008). (For out-of-network providers, it was $1,000 per individual ($2,000 per family).) For people younger than age 65 who are not enrolled in Medicare, deductibles can be much higher than Medicare's if they purchase insurance in the individual market—that is, without the benefit of a large risk pool like major employers and Medicare have. In a 2009 survey, the median respondent who purchased a single, individual policy with a preferred provider

organization or an HMO with a point-of-service option faced a deductible between $2,000 and $2,500 (America's Health Insurance Plans 2009).

[5] By comparison, a 2006 survey of Blue Cross Blue Shield plans that covered their own insured business as well as plans run for self-insured employer groups found that administrative costs were typically about 12 percent of premiums (Merlis 2009).

[6] Wide ranges in premiums suggest that the market for supplemental coverage is not very efficient. Different ratings methods are one reason for the wide range, and they include the following:

- *Community rating*—all beneficiaries are charged the same rate for a given plan.
- *Issue age rating*—all beneficiaries in a plan are charged a set rate based on how old they are when they first purchase the plan.
- *Attained age rating*—all beneficiaries of a given age are charged the same within a plan.
- *Individual medical underwriting*—the process that an insurance company uses to decide, based on the applicant's medical history, whether to accept the application for insurance. Except in guaranteed issue situations, beneficiaries in poorer health may be refused coverage entirely and may have fewer choices of plans available to them (sometimes only higher priced options), and preexisting condition exclusions may apply.

[7] While beneficiaries may be confused by the array of premium choices and lose confidence that they can select the plan that is best for them, there is a safeguard against plans providing poor value. Medigap plans must return a minimum level of benefits relative to their premiums, with a medical loss ratio of not less than 65 percent; that is, each medigap plan must pay out in medical benefits at least 65 percent of the premiums collected from the policyholders. Group policies, which are sold through employers, unions, and other groups and tend to have lower administrative costs, must have a minimum loss ratio of 75 percent. The National Association of Insurance Commissioners reports that for 2008, the average medigap loss ratio was 80 percent (81 percent for group policies and 79 percent for individual policies).

[8] Medicare SELECT provider networks are usually just for inpatient care but in some cases include specific physicians. When a policyholder does not use a network provider for nonemergency care, she must pay some or all of Medicare's cost sharing.

[9] Under the terms of the Medicare Prescription Drug, Improvement, and Modernization Act of 2003, insurers cannot issue new Plan J policies because they would compete with Part D by including prescription drugs in their covered benefits. In 2009, enrollees paid the first $2,000 in Medicare cost sharing under the high deductible of Plan F.

[10] Plan N's cost sharing is the lesser of a $20 copayment or Medicare's coinsurance amount for Part B evaluation and management services for specialist or nonspecialist office visits. The lesser of a $50 copayment or Part B coinsurance applies for each covered emergency room visit. However, that cost sharing is waived if the beneficiary is admitted and the emergency visit is covered subsequently by Part A (National Association of Insurance Commissioners 2010).

[11] Some employers offer retiree coverage through MA plans. As of April 2010, about 18 percent of enrollment in MA plans was through employer groups.

[12] One often-cited estimate based on data from the mid-1990s suggests that use of services ranged from 17 percent higher for those with employer coverage to 28 percent higher for those with medigap policies (Christensen and Shinogle 1997).

[13] In 2007, the poverty threshold was $10,210 for single people and about $13,690 for married couples.

[14] CBO prepared estimates for this option beginning in 2013, with the amounts of restrictions on medigap policies indexed each year to the average annual growth in Medicare costs. Because CBO assumes some ramp up of the policy in 2013, we present their steady-state estimates for 2014.

[15] It is similar in nature to the approach used in Part D, in which beneficiaries who enroll in plans with enhanced benefits must pay premiums that incorporate an assumption about their higher use of services stemming from having supplemental benefits.

[16] Insurers are also facing new taxes under the new health reform law. Specifically, the law calls for a general fee on health insurance providers and places an excise tax on high-cost employer-sponsored health coverage.

[17] The Commission did not conduct an independent analysis to evaluate panelists' conclusions.

[18] Note that all discussions of costs in this section are based on interviewees' comments and not on any independent analysis.

[19] Savings with this strategy could be offset by an increase in volume for the procedures. We have no data on whether such a volume offset occurred in this instance.

References

America's Health Insurance Plans. 2008. *Medigap: What you need to know.* Washington, DC: AHIP.

America's Health Insurance Plans. 2009. *Individual health insurance 2009: A comprehensive survey of premiums, availability, and benefits.* Washington, DC: AHIP.

America's Health Insurance Plans/Blue Cross Blue Shield Association. 2009. Medigap policyholder survey. Slideshow of results prepared by Gary A. Ferguson, Senior Vice President, American Viewpoint.

American Medical Association. 2009. *2009 national health insurer report card.* Washington, DC: AMA.

Atherly, A. 2001. Supplemental insurance: Medicare's accidental stepchild. *Medical Care Research and Review* 58, no. 2 (June): 131–161.

Center for Health Value Innovation. 2010. *Minimally invasive procedures: Expanding value-based design for optimal accountability including the outcomes-based contracting framework for breast biopsy, hysterectomy, and colectomy.* St. Louis, MO: Center for Health Value Innovation.

Centers for Medicare & Medicaid Services, Department of Health and Human Services. 2011a. *Choosing a Medigap policy: A guide to health insurance for people with Medicare.* Baltimore, MD: CMS. http://www.medicare.gov/Publications/Pubs/pdf/10050.pdf.

Centers for Medicare & Medicaid Services, Department of Health and Human Services. 2011b. *Medicare & You 2011.* Baltimore, MD: CMS. http://www.medicare.gov/Publications/Pubs/ pdf/10050.pdf.

Chandra, A., J. Gruber, and R. McKnight. 2010. Patient cost-sharing and hospitalization offsets in the elderly. *American Economic Review* 100, no. 1 (March): 193–213.

Chernew, M., and T. B. Gibson. 2008. Cost sharing and HEDIS performance. *Medical Care Research and Review* 65, no. 6 (December): 713–728.

Chernew, M. E., I. A. Juster, M. Shah, et al. 2010. Evidence that value-based insurance can be effective. *Health Affairs* 29, no. 3 (March–April): 530–536.

Chernew, M. E., A. B. Rosen, and A. M. Fendrick. 2007. Value-based insurance design. *Health Affairs* 26, no. 2 (March–April): w195–w203.

Christensen, S., and J. Shinogle. 1997. Effects of supplemental coverage on use of services by Medicare enrollees. *Health Care Financing Review* 19, no. 1 (Fall): 5–17.

Congressional Budget Office. 2008. *Budget options, volume 1: Health care.* Washington, DC: CBO.

Congressional Budget Office. 2011. *Reducing the deficit: Spending and revenue options.* Washington, DC: CBO.

Coughlin, B. 2010. Ardent CEO: ACE Demo improves quality, lowers cost. *InsideHealthPolicy.com*, April 29. http://www. insidehealthpolicy.com.

Employee Benefit Research Institute. 2008. *The future of employer-based health benefits: Have employers reached a tipping point?* EBRI notes 29, no. 2. Washington, DC: EBRI.

Fendrick, A. M., D. G. Smith, M. E. Chernew, et al. 2001. A benefit-based copay for prescription drugs: Patient contribution based on total benefits, not drug acquisition cost. *American Journal of Managed Care* 7, no. 9 (September): 861–867.

Gabel, J., H. Whitmore, and J. Pickreign. 2008. *Survey of retiree health benefits, 2007: A chartbook.* New York, NY: The Commonwealth Fund/NORC.

Hargrave, E., J. Kronstadt, and A. Brown. Forthcoming. *Innovative benefit design: Findings from interviews and site visits with employers, insurers, state health officials, researchers, and consultants.* Report prepared by staff from NORC at the University of Chicago for the Medicare Payment Advisory Commission. Washington, DC: MedPAC.

Hogan, C. 2009. *Exploring the effects of secondary insurance on Medicare spending for the elderly.* A study conducted by staff from Direct Research, LLC, for MedPAC. Washington, DC: MedPAC.

Hund, C., and M. Joshi. 2010. *Early learnings from the Bundled Payment Acute Care Episode Demonstration Project.* Chicago, IL: Health Research & Educational Trust.

Jacobson, G., T. Neuman, A. Damico, et al. 2011. *The role of Medicare for the people dually eligible for Medicare and Medicaid.* Menlo Park, CA: Kaiser Family Foundation.

Kaiser Family Foundation. 2010. *Summary of new health reform law.* Menlo Park, CA: KFF. June 18.

Lee, A. J., S. A. Garfinkel, R. K. Khandker, et al. 1997. Impact of Medicare SELECT on cost and utilization in 11 states. Health Care Financing Review 19, no. 1 (Fall): 19–40.

Medicare Payment Advisory Commission. 2003. Report to the Congress: Variation and innovation in Medicare. Washington, DC: MedPAC.

Medicare Payment Advisory Commission. 2008. *Report to the Congress: Reforming the delivery system.* Washington, DC: MedPAC.

Medicare Payment Advisory Commission. 2009. *Report to the Congress: Improving incentives in the Medicare program.* Washington, DC: MedPAC.

Medicare Payment Advisory Commission. 2010. *Report to the Congress: Medicare payment policy.* Washington, DC: MedPAC.

Medicare Payment Advisory Commission. 2011. *Report to the Congress: Medicare payment policy.* Washington, DC: MedPAC.

Merlis, M. 2006. *Health benefits in retirement: Set for extinction?* National Health Policy Forum background paper. Washington, DC: NHPF.

Merlis, M. 2009. *Simplifying administration of health insurance.* Washington, DC: National Academy of Social Insurance.

Moon, M. 2006. *Medicare: A policy primer.* Washington, DC: Urban Institute Press.

National Association of Insurance Commissioners. 2010. Questions and answers regarding implementation of Medicare supplement plan N copayment, deductible and coinsurance. Memo from commissioner Kevin McCarty, Chair, Senior Issues (B) Task Force. March 8.

National Association of Insurance Commissioners. 2011. Minutes from the Medigap PPACA Subgroup meeting in Austin, TX. March 28.

Peterson, C. L. 2009. *Setting and valuing health insurance benefits.* CRS report R40491. Washington, DC: Congressional Research Service.

Physician Payment Review Commission. 1997. *Annual report to Congress.* Washington, DC: PPRC.

RAND Corporation. 2006. *The Health Insurance Experiment: A classic study speaks to the current health care reform debate. Research highlight.* Santa Monica, CA: RAND.

Remler, D. K., and A. J. Atherly. 2003. Health status and heterogeneity of cost-sharing responsiveness: How do sick people respond to cost-sharing? *Health Economics* 12, no. 4 (April): 269–280.

Scanlon, W. J. 2002. Medigap: Current policies contain coverage gaps, undermine cost control incentives. Oral testimony before the Subcommittee on Health, Committee on Ways and Means, U.S. House of Representatives. 107th Cong., 2nd sess. March 14.

Swartz, K. 2010. *Cost-sharing: Effects on spending and outcomes.* Research synthesis report no. 20. Princeton, NJ: The Synthesis Project, Robert Wood Johnson Foundation.

Vesely, R. 2011. An ACE in the deck? Bundled-payment demo shows returns. *Modern Healthcare*, February 7.

Yamamoto, D., T. Neuman, and M. Kitchman-Strollo. 2008. *How does the benefit value of Medicare compare to the benefit value of typical large employer plans?* Medicare issue brief. Washington, DC: Kaiser Family Foundation.

ENHANCING MEDICARE'S TECHNICAL ASSISTANCE TO AND OVERSIGHT OF PROVIDERS

Recommendations

4-1 The Congress should redesign the current Quality Improvement Organization program to allow the Secretary to provide funding for time-limited technical assistance directly to providers and communities. The Congress should require the Secretary to develop an accountability structure to ensure these funds are used appropriately.

COMMISSIONER VOTES: YES 16 • NO 0 • NOT VOTING 0 • ABSENT 1

4-2 The Congress should authorize the Secretary to define criteria to qualify technical assistance agents so that a variety of entities can compete to assist providers and to provide community-level quality improvement. The Congress should remove requirements that the agents be physician sponsored, serve a specific state, and have regulatory responsibilities.

COMMISSIONER VOTES: YES 16 • NO 0 • NOT VOTING 0 • ABSENT 1

4-3 The Secretary should make low-performing providers and community-level initiatives a high priority in allocating resources for technical assistance for quality improvement.

COMMISSIONER VOTES: YES 16 • NO 0 • NOT VOTING 0 • ABSENT 1

4-4 The Secretary should regularly update the conditions of participation so that the requirements incorporate and emphasize evidence-based methods of improving quality of care.

COMMISSIONER VOTES: YES 16 • NO 0 • NOT VOTING 0 • ABSENT 1

4-5 The Congress should require the Secretary to expand interventions that promote systemic remediation of quality problems for persistently low-performing providers.

COMMISSIONER VOTES: YES 16 • NO 0 • NOT VOTING 0 • ABSENT 1

4-6 The Secretary should establish a public recognition program for high-performing providers that participate in collaboratives or learning networks, or otherwise act as mentors, to improve the quality of lower performing providers.

COMMISSIONER VOTES: YES 16 • NO 0 • NOT VOTING 0 • ABSENT 1

Summary

The Commission continues to be concerned about the slow pace of quality improvement and recognizes that Medicare has a responsibility to exercise its policy levers to accelerate improvement. The Commission has recommended numerous payment policy changes to encourage quality improvement.

These changes include pay for performance, medical homes, penalties for high rates of hospital readmissions, and bundled payment. In this chapter, the Commission concludes that other policy levers—technical assistance and conditions of participation—can better complement the intent of recent changes in payment policy and contribute to quality improvement. Specifically, the Commission's recommendations aim to:

- fundamentally restructure the quality improvement organization program to give providers and communities the choice of who assists them and flexibility in how they use the resources.
- increase the number and variety of technical assistance entities that can assist providers and communities and introduce greater competition in the market.
- make technical assistance to low-performing providers and community initiatives a high priority as a strategy to complement payment policy and address persistent health care disparities.
- update the conditions of participation so that the requirements incorporate and emphasize evidence-based methods of improving quality of care.
- increase accountability of providers by expanding CMS's use of interventions that promote system-wide remediation of quality problems among persistently low-performing providers.
- improve public recognition of high-performing providers that participate in learning networks to assist low-performing providers.

This package of recommendations seeks to address some of the problems that likely have constrained the effectiveness of Medicare's technical assistance and oversight efforts in the past. While CMS's management of the Quality Improvement Organization (QIO) program evolves to address past problems, the program has had difficulty in demonstrating its effectiveness; according to our recent interviews with various experts and stakeholders, the level of expertise of the current QIO contractors is perceived as uneven and, in some cases, unequal to the task. By reforming technical assistance while expanding the use of regulatory consequences for persistent low performance and creating a recognition program for high performers that help low performers, this package of changes could create a better balance in incentives and accountability for the whole spectrum of providers.

This package is also shaped by changes in the environment surrounding the QIO program. First, a growing number and type of organizations dedicated to supporting quality improvement have emerged and their expertise could benefit Medicare's technical assistance program. In addition, payment policies (e.g., penalties for high readmission rates, hospital-acquired complications, value-based purchasing) have recently been enacted that are intended to create the incentive for providers, particularly hospitals, to improve their quality. A concern with these policies is that low performers subject to payment penalties—some of which are serving a poor or minority population facing public health challenges—will find it more difficult to improve because of the penalties. By directing technical assistance resources to these providers, Medicare could, at least in part, allay concerns about holding providers accountable when they serve a challenging or disadvantaged patient population. The goal of improved care should exist for all patients, regardless of health status, income, and race, but the Commission recognizes that those expectations are more likely to be met if they are combined with additional resources to accelerate the provider's ability to address particularly challenging care delivery environments. Instead of lowering standards, the goal is to target assistance to those who need it most.

To be clear, this package of recommendations envisions fundamental changes to the current QIO program. No longer would there be a standing organization in every state financed by the federal government to ask providers to participate in quality improvement activities as QIOs do today. Instead, funding would be made available directly to providers and communities—with a focus on those that are low performing or that face a challenging environment—for them to purchase technical assistance in the market.

These recommendations reflect the Commission's judgment that it is time to try another approach to supporting quality improvement. There are reasons to believe the structure we outline will be effective, but success is not certain. For this reason, the grant program should be independently evaluated at a reasonable interval after inception to determine its efficacy. In addition, the Commission's recommendations are intended to be directional and do not address all implementation issues likely to arise. We recognize that administrative challenges may require that these changes be implemented in stages and expect that administrative feasibility will be taken into consideration in shaping implementation.

We pursue these ideas while noting that CMS continues to work to improve the QIO program. CMS is in the process of finalizing the 10th statement of work, the three-year contract that governs the work of the QIOs, that begins in August 2011. Concurrently, the fiscal year 2012 President's budget includes several legislative proposals to address problems the Commission and others have raised (Institute of Medicine 2006, Medicare Payment Advisory Commission 2010). They include changing the geographic scope of QIO contracts, eliminating the conflict of interest between beneficiary protection and quality improvement activities, and expanding the pool of contractors eligible for QIO work. However, the Commission's package of recommendations goes further than these proposals and initiatives, particularly as it would redirect funding for technical assistance to providers and communities and emphasize a strategy for focusing on and engaging low performers, improving accountability for low performance, and recognizing the role of high performers in helping low performers.

The Commission's June 2010 report highlighted the evidence of the slow pace of quality improvement in Medicare (Medicare Payment Advisory Commission 2010). More recently the Commission's analysis of overall inpatient hospital quality found that, from 2006 through

2009, risk-adjusted in-hospital and 30-day mortality rates declined for 5 major clinical conditions, but patient safety indicators for 7 monitored conditions did not improve significantly, and readmission rates remained unchanged (Medicare Payment Advisory Commission 2011). This research suggests there is considerable room for quality improvement in reducing readmissions and hospital-acquired infections as well as in eliminating errors in the delivery of care that result in harm to patients.

Other recent studies add to the sense of stagnancy in quality improvement. A study looking at 10 hospitals in North Carolina over 6 years found a common rate of harm to patients that remained unchanged over the period, despite extensive national efforts to improve patient safety (Landrigan et al. 2010). The Department of Health and Human Services Office of Inspector General examined a small nationally representative random sample of Medicare beneficiaries discharged from inpatient hospitals during October 2008 and estimated that 13.5 percent of hospitalized Medicare beneficiaries experienced serious adverse events during their hospital stays. An additional 13.5 percent of beneficiaries experienced events during their hospital stays that resulted in temporary harm. Physician reviewers determined that 44 percent of adverse and temporary harm events were clearly or likely preventable (Levinson 2010). Another study looking at three of the nation's large leading hospitals found similar rates of adverse events (Classen et al. 2011).

Medicare has a number of ways to encourage quality improvement. Among them are the technical assistance provided through the Quality Improvement Organization (QIO) program and Medicare's standards for providers' participation in the program, known as the conditions of participation (COPs). To understand these efforts in context, it is helpful to enumerate the other prominent levers Medicare has to influence quality:

- ***Payment policy***—The way Medicare pays for covered benefits influences how and what care is delivered, particularly because Medicare is the single largest purchaser in the market. Over the next few years, Medicare will begin to adjust for most health care services some portion of payment based on the quality of care. Hospital payment policies aimed at quality improvement include value-based purchasing, reduced payment for hospital-acquired conditions, and penalties for relatively high rates of readmissions. In addition, through its demonstration authority, Medicare is experimenting with payment policies aimed at quality (and efficiency) improvement, including additional payments for medical homes and shared savings programs such as disease management and the physician group practice demonstration. Recently, CMS announced a five-year demonstration project that will provide grants to hospitals working in tandem with community-based organizations or to community-based organizations directly to offset the costs associated with better managing care transitions.
- ***Public reporting***—Medicare's share of the market and volume of claims allows it to measure the relative performance of providers on a variety of quality metrics. Increasingly, Medicare is publicly reporting the results by provider on its website (e.g., Hospital Compare, Home Health Compare, Medicare Advantage Compare), allowing providers to see how they compare with their peers and allowing beneficiaries to make more informed choices about their care. Providers, often citing professional pride, note that this public display has motivated improvement. There is less evidence that beneficiaries are widely using the data. Public reporting is

evolving as consensus around new measures emerges and older measures that have exhausted their usefulness are retired.

- ***Medical education***—Medicare has a large role in financing the nation's medical education system (spending $9.5 billion in 2009); its policies can influence the number of physicians and nurses trained and the nature of their training. The Commission has noted that Medicare requires minimal accountability from the recipients of this funding and has recommended that a portion of the funding be allocated based on standards specifying ambitious goals for practice-based learning and improvement, interpersonal and communication skills, professionalism, and systems-based practice (Medicare Payment Advisory Commission 2010).
- ***Benefit design***—Several aspects of benefit design can be used to promote improved quality. For example, under a value-based insurance design, Medicare has eliminated cost sharing for preventive services (e.g., bone mass measurement, flu vaccinations) to encourage beneficiaries to use these services.
  Another approach that private insurers have taken is to rank providers in tiers based on their performance on quality metrics and to charge beneficiaries lower cost-sharing rates for seeking care from providers in the higher tiers. Another way to potentially improve quality is through coverage decisions so that Medicare covers only care known to be medically necessary and effective.

The federal government has agencies and programs other than Medicare designed to influence the quality of care provided nationally. They include the Office of the National Coordinator for Health Information Technology, the Federal Coordinating Council for Comparative Effectiveness Research, the Centers for Disease Control and Prevention, the Agency for Healthcare Research and Quality, the National Institutes of Health, the Health Resources and Services Administration, and the Institute of Medicine. In addition, the Medicaid program and the Department of Veterans Affairs have their own policies, which can influence providers' quality improvement activities.

In this environment, we examine how Medicare can better use the resources and leverage of its QIO program and conditions of participation, and we make several recommendations for improvement. This package of recommendations seeks to address some of the problems that likely have constrained the effectiveness of Medicare's technical assistance and oversight efforts in the past. While management of the QIO program evolves to address past problems, the program has a history of not demonstrating its effectiveness and even now, according to our interviews with experts and stakeholders, the expertise of its contractors is perceived as uneven and, in some cases, unequal to the task.

While some QIOs have certainly provided outstanding service, the growth over the past decade in the type and number of entities devoted to quality improvement combined with the emergence of new payment incentives presents an opportunity to improve the effectiveness of these resources. By reforming technical assistance while expanding the use of regulatory consequences for persistent low performance as well as a recognition program for high performers, this package of changes could create a better balance in incentives and accountability for the whole spectrum of providers.

These recommendations reflect the Commission's judgment that it is time to try another approach to supporting quality improvement. There are reasons to believe the new structure we outline might be effective, but success is not certain. For this reason, the grant program should be independently evaluated at a reasonable interval after inception to determine its efficacy. In addition, the Commission's recommendations are intended to be directional and do not address all the implementation issues that are likely to be implicated. To the extent that these recommendations are pursued, the Commission will have additional opportunities to address those issues.

Redesign Medicare's Technical Assistance Program for Quality Improvement

In the current three-year contract for QIOs known as the ninth statement of work (SOW), Medicare is spending $1.1 billion to support the QIO program. Most of that money goes to private QIOs, mostly not-for-profit organizations, to perform activities related to quality improvement in specific clinical areas (e.g., pressure ulcers, methicillin-resistant *Staphylococcus aureus* (an antibiotic-resistant bacterium), surgical infections, and care transitions) and beneficiary protection (e.g., handling beneficiary complaints and other review activities). Currently, 41 QIOs hold 53 contracts to provide services in every state as well as in Puerto Rico, the Virgin Islands, and the District of Columbia.

Technical assistance funds now go directly to the designated QIOs, and it is incumbent on them to reach out to providers and encourage improvement. However, if the funds instead went directly to the providers and communities, who in turn would use the grant money to purchase technical assistance from a qualified agent of their choice, providers and communities would be more constructively engaged in sustained quality improvement.

Under this approach, providers and communities would be empowered to select the technical assistance agent best suited to their needs. Accordingly, technical assistance agents working with their clients would conduct a needs assessment to determine their process and organizational defects and have the flexibility to determine how technical assistance would be best provided. The focus of the assistance could vary by provider and community. For some, quality problems stem from the challenges of meeting the needs of a poor population, a geographically isolated population, or a culturally diverse population. For example, providers may lack the cultural competency to communicate with patients in ways that overcome language barriers and take into consideration key factors, such as patients' perspectives, lifestyle, and preferences, all of which can influence outcomes. For other providers, problems stem from not understanding how to collect and manage their data to identify quality problems, from operating in a culture that does not promote safety, from having limited physician cooperation, or from experiencing high staff turnover so that the benefits of training efforts are quickly lost. Under the approach envisioned here, technical assistance would be tailored to the provider as it strives to meet the needs of the community.

In addition, because objectively measuring the effectiveness of quality improvement interventions is so challenging, introducing competition and provider choice could be an important force in promoting effective assistance. Providers and communities would be able to vote with their feet, ideally basing their choice on expertise and the experience of fellow consumers (i.e., other providers and communities).

To be clear, under this approach, there would no longer be a single organization designated to serve a state. Providers and communities receiving a grant could choose to work with organizations that previously served as QIOs and met CMS criteria for technical assistance agents, but, presumably, there would be other organizations to choose from as well. The beneficiary protection functions, such as receiving and investigating complaints, would be moved to another entity, which would avert the current conflict of interest concerns and ideally yield some efficiency gains.

There are numerous considerations in how the technical assistance grants would be allocated to providers and communities, a few of which we address here. First, some low performers might not know how poorly they are doing or might not be equipped to make an informed choice. They might need guidance, which could come in the form of oversight of compliance with the COPs, as discussed later in this chapter (see p. 109). Surveyors and accreditors could be responsible for helping providers assess their needs and for informing them of their choices. Alternatively, CMS, either directly or through a contracting entity, could be responsible for providing that direction, particularly if the provider is at risk of failing to meet the COPs. Poorly performing communities may be similarly unaware of their relative performance.

Therefore, CMS may also have a role in identifying these communities and suggesting that they avail themselves of technical assistance resources.

Second, CMS would need to establish criteria for how grant money will be allocated and how it can be used. One possibility is that the magnitude of the grant could vary depending on the relative needs of the grantee. For example, some could receive larger grants to be used for one-on-one assistance, while others could receive smaller amounts sufficient to offset the costs of participating in a learning collaborative being offered in the private sector. Helping to support provider participation in private learning collaboratives could be a cost-effective way to increase the number of providers who gain from this funding. Additional considerations in prioritizing who receives grants would be the provider's performance on quality measures (addressed later in this chapter, p. 106), the likelihood that significant improvement will result, and the financial resources of the provider. In addition, whether the grant money can be used for costs associated with quality improvement (such as health information technology or staff), rather than solely for technical assistance, will need to be determined. If flexibility is allowed, sustainability of those improvement activities when the technical assistance grant has ended should be planned for.

Third, the grant program would need to hold providers and communities accountable for use of the funds. The burden of accountability would be largely on the provider or community that receives the funds. Low performers must improve performance; if not, they will face payment penalties through new payment policies such as value-based purchasing, readmission penalties, and reduced payment for hospital-acquired conditions.

Further accountability could be imposed through oversight of compliance with the conditions of participation (see discussion, p.109). For example, very-low-performing providers who do not improve within a reasonable interval after having received assistance could be terminated from Medicare. The need for accountability also suggests that communities should be defined as provider-led coalitions or entities, as providers can ultimately be held accountable for poor performance. In addition, spending of this federal grant money (i.e., the current QIO funds) should be transparent and subject to audit.

For technical assistance agents, the quality of the assistance will, at least in part, be evident by their ability to improve the performance of their clients on the mix of measures discussed above. This assessment could be complemented by clients' qualitative reviews, so that even if the improvements in performance were not yet evident in the data, improvements in culture or processes (e.g., new procedures, management changes) that should soon lead to measurable improvements could be noted. Similarly, providers who thought their performance improved despite the role of the technical assistance agent could report that to CMS. The record of improvement as well as these reports could be made available to the marketplace, much as is done by Consumer Reports, Angie's List, and other websites that provide feedback from former customers to prospective customers.

Fourth, to create an effective market of technical assistance agents, CMS would need a structure conducive to producing good "consumer" information; relying on market forces can work well only if adequate information is available to consumers (i.e., providers and communities). For example, the agency could create an online marketplace, where providers would see their choices of technical assistance agents (those who have met the standards and agreed to the transparency requirements associated with the program that serve their geographic area). Each agent's record of improving performance would be posted along with qualitative reviews by previous clients. In addition, technical assistance agents would include marketing material that indicates their area of expertise. Being able to access this information in one place should facilitate the best match between providers and assistance agents.

In considering these changes, we are mindful of the budgetary impacts. This recommendation is designed to redirect current resources and not increase spending.

The Commission recognizes that quality improvement is important and some may believe it deserves significantly more federal resources than are currently available. However, quality improvement should be central to every provider's mission and should not be considered an extra function that needs separate funding on a routine basis. At the same time, some providers simply may not have the knowledge to undertake the breadth of initiatives required, or they may face a particularly challenging environment. Because the consequences of these challenges adversely affect the quality of care for beneficiaries, Medicare has a role in supporting providers' quality improvement efforts to the extent that its support is effective.

We recognize that changing the program as outlined here entails new administrative tasks for CMS to perform or oversee—for example, grant making, setting up a web-based marketplace, and approving assistance agents—but the current program requires substantial resources and staff to manage, and they can be redirected.

Recommendation 4 - 1

The Congress should redesign the current Quality Improvement Organization program to allow the Secretary to provide funding for time-limited technical assistance directly to providers and communities. The Congress should require the Secretary to develop an accountability structure to ensure these funds are used appropriately.

Rationale 4 - 1

Directing financial assistance to providers who in turn seek out technical assistance creates a more competitive marketplace, which could improve the quality of technical assistance offered. In addition, it could increase the likelihood that the provider and community receive assistance relevant to their quality improvement needs.

Implications 4 – 1

Spending

- Spending would be constrained to no more than the QIO program funding levels.

Beneficiary and provider

- To the extent that providers are responsive to the intent of technical assistance funding, beneficiaries should receive improved care. Providers would receive the technical assistance funds directly.

Stimulate the Quality and Value of Technical Assistance by Increasing Competition

In the last decade, an increasing number of organizations have gotten involved in spreading quality improvement, including national quality organizations, professional associations, providers (e.g., Geisinger Consulting Group was formed by the Geisinger Health System to advise other providers about innovative strategies to improve quality and transform the delivery system), consulting firms, and regional health improvement collaboratives. For example, more than 40 regional health improvement collaboratives around the country—many of which have recently formed—help improve quality by measuring performance, providing training and assistance to providers, and coordinating the health improvement activities in the community (Network for Regional Healthcare Improvement 2011). Ideally, Medicare-sponsored technical assistance would draw on the expertise of this diverse and growing set of organizations. Under the current QIO program, it does not. A variety of requirements serve as barriers to entry for other organizations. In the ninth SOW, CMS awarded a new QIO contract to only one new contractor (another QIO). Competition for new QIO contracts is usually from organizations serving as QIOs in other states.

One barrier is that QIOs must serve an entire state. Some entities may not be prepared to serve a whole state but might be particularly good at helping specific types of providers, such as those in a given region of the state or rural providers. The current requirement that each state have a QIO can result in money being directed to states where providers are generally good, leaving a smaller portion of funding for states with greater need.

Another well-noted barrier is that QIOs be either a "physician-sponsored" or a "physician-access" organization. These designations require specific thresholds for the number of physicians in the organization's ownership or membership and serve to limit competition for designation as QIOs.

A third barrier is the requirement that QIOs perform regulatory oversight as well as receive and investigate beneficiary complaints. Currently, QIOs have responsibility for addressing beneficiary complaints about quality-of-care concerns and conducting other reviews of the adequacy of care and billing, such as reviewing medical records to determine whether a hospital emergency department failed to provide federally mandated emergency medical care or whether a hospital request for a higher paying diagnosis related group is appropriate.

Aside from creating other problems, these requirements may preclude some good technical assistance agents from competing to participate as QIOs. First, organizations that specialize in technical assistance may not want to develop the expertise and infrastructure to perform the oversight functions. Second, a QIO's regulatory responsibilities can restrict its technical assistance activities because of concern about potential conflicts of interest. In general, QIOs are not permitted to accept payment from the same entities over which they have regulatory authority. This restriction can limit the ability of the technical assistance experts to develop and maintain other lines of business outside the QIO contract.

These restrictions must be lifted to expand the pool of expertise and the competitiveness of the program. Some requirements would be necessary to ensure that only legitimate organizations with experience are eligible to participate and that conflicts of interest are avoided; the Secretary would need to develop those criteria. Given those assurances, however, a diversity of technical assistance agents could be encouraged. In this way, organizations participating in the private sector on quality improvement could be available to work with the providers and communities in greatest need. In the absence of the restrictive provisions, technical assistance agents could be available, for example, to address rural problems or to focus on data management, inner city challenges, or management issues. Expanding the pool would not mean that organizations that currently function as QIOs would be excluded; given their experience with Medicare providers, they would be expected to meet the criteria for participation and compete successfully for business.

Recommendation 4 - 2

The Congress should authorize the Secretary to define criteria to qualify technical assistance agents so that a variety of entities can compete to assist providers and to provide community-level quality improvement. The Congress should remove requirements that the agents be physician sponsored, serve a specific state, and have regulatory responsibilities.

Rationale 4 - 2

Currently, multiple barriers exist to prevent a broader array of technical assistance agents from competing for Medicare funding to assist providers and communities in quality improvement. Increased competition should result in more effective technical assistance being available to providers and communities. An entity not engaged in technical assistance could assume the beneficiary protection and other regulatory responsibilities currently provided by QIOs.

Implications 4 – 2

Spending

- There are no direct spending implications.

Beneficiary and provider

- To the extent that providers are responsive to the intent of the incentive, beneficiaries should receive improved care. Some providers would receive technical assistance directly.

Target Quality Improvement Funds

The Commission is supportive of collaborative and learning networks, where providers share their experiences, benchmark their performance to others', and learn from their peers' successes and failures. Many in the field find that significant benefits can come from allowing peer-to-peer learning and mentoring relationships to develop. However, the Commission believes it is important to underscore the value of assisting low-performing providers. In addition, the Commission recognizes the value that can be gained from supporting community-wide quality improvement initiatives.

Low-Performing Providers

There are at least two advantages of targeting quality improvement funds to low performers. First, this approach can help providers respond to new payment policies that hold them accountable for poor quality of care. These policies include payment penalties for high readmission rates, hospital-acquired infections, and poor performance on quality measures as part of the value-based purchasing program for hospitals. A concern with these policies is that low performers subject to payment penalties—some of which are serving a poor population facing public health challenges—will find it more difficult to improve because of the penalties. By directing technical assistance resources to these providers, Medicare could, at least in part, allay concerns about holding providers accountable when they serve a challenging or disadvantaged patient population. The goal of improved care should exist for all patients, regardless of health status, income, and race, but the Commission recognizes that those expectations are more likely to be met if they are combined with additional resources to accelerate the provider's ability to address particularly challenging care delivery environments. Instead of lowering standards, the goal is to target assistance to those who need it most.

Second, focusing technical assistance on low performers could help address disparities in care. Where beneficiaries receive their care matters. Different facilities have dramatically different levels of success, and this difference matters especially for minorities because they tend to receive most of their care from physicians and hospitals that tend to have lower quality (Bach et al. 2004, Jha et al. 2007). For example, among African American beneficiaries in a market with high racial segregation, the risk of admission to a high-mortality hospital was 35 percent higher than for whites in the same market (Sarrazin et al. 2009). Another study found that risk-adjusted mortality after acute myocardial infarction was significantly higher in hospitals that disproportionately served African Americans (Skinner et al. 2005). Another study, which uses volume as a proxy for quality of care by looking at services where a volume–outcome relationship has been established, found that African American patients of all ages and insurance types in the New York metropolitan area from 2001 to 2002 were significantly less likely than white patients to use a high-volume hospital for all but one of the services examined; Hispanic patients were less likely than whites to use high-volume hospitals for 15 of the 17 services (Gray et al. 2009). The observed differences in the use of high-volume hospitals did not seem to be accounted for by proximity (minorities tended to live closer to the high-volume hospitals) or insurance status (differences persisted among patients with the same insurance coverage). Similarly, African American patients have been found to enter the worst-quality nursing homes (Angelelli et al. 2006).

The success of technical assistance targeted to low performers will depend on the metrics used to rate performance. Evaluation of a provider's performance should be based on outcome measures, which include measures of "systemness," select process measures, patient experience measures, functional status, and findings from survey and certification agencies. The mix and weighting of these components would evolve to allow for changes that reflect the latest findings in reliability and value in quality measurement. The process for their development should be evidence based and transparent.

A concern with focusing on low performers is that some are unlikely to improve even with assistance. When certain ingredients are absent—effective leadership, for example—culture change and quality improvement may be elusive, even with sound technical assistance (Curry et al. 2011). This possibility may be minimized by empowering the targeted providers with choice and flexibility about the type of technical assistance needed to help their institution. For providers resistant to improving quality, this package of recommendations seeks to expand oversight interventions that can further improve care. An example is system improvement agreements in which a provider makes a substantial investment in quality improvement as an alternative to termination from participation in Medicare (see p. 111). Combining assistance to low performers with the structure and accountability of these agreements may be critical to increasing the likelihood of improved quality. In addition, current law allows for termination without these agreements, and that may well be appropriate for providers who have poor quality and are functioning in a community where other providers can meet patients' needs.

While the reasons for focusing on low performers are compelling, the success of collaboratives that bring a variety of providers together warrants flexibility in allocation of technical assistance resources. Lessons can be learned and shared from helping midrange performers who face challenging environments. In addition, high performers can function as models and mentors and can help motivate struggling providers. For these reasons, some share of quality improvement resources could remain available for technical assistance to midrange and high performers.

Communities

Another consideration in targeting technical assistance resources is the need to address the fragmentation— or lack of "systemness"—in health care delivery, which can be particularly problematic for Medicare beneficiaries who are often dealing with multiple chronic conditions and declining functional status. Bringing all the resources together in a community—physicians, community health centers, and hospitals as well as local government agencies, nonprofit social services, and patient advocates—could be especially productive in developing more comprehensive care and strategies that can prevent readmissions, initial admissions, and emergency department visits. Therefore, assistance should also be available to communities so that a combination of providers and stakeholders can work together to address problems. Assistance could be restricted to those communities that face challenges as measured by Medicare data on cost and quality, or eligibility could be open to any community that demonstrates initiative and commitment to use the funds to improve the health of the community regardless of the challenges present.

QIOs, working on the Care Transitions project, under the ninth SOW, have worked with communities to reduce readmission rates and report success (Brock and Goroski 2010).

Communities could also be defined as a group of providers seeking to work together to address a common problem— one that they share but that is not necessarily related to local coordination of care. Accordingly, an additional approach may be to allow groups of a given provider type (e.g., hospitals, nursing homes), including those that are geographically disparate, to apply to use the funds to collectively improve a quality problem like hospitalacquired conditions or culture change.

Recommendation 4 - 3

The Secretary should make low-performing providers and community-level initiatives a high priority in allocating resources for technical assistance for quality improvement.

Rationale 4 - 3

Targeting Medicare's limited technical assistance resources to low performers would help to balance the intent of payment policies that financially penalize low performers, may reduce racial disparities in quality of care, and will minimize displacement of private resources. However, the Commission recognizes the value of engaging a spectrum of expertise in addressing quality problems and believes flexibility is warranted. Community-level initiatives should be a high priority because they can effectively address issues such as care transition and chronic disease management as well as issues that groups of providers collectively identify and commit to addressing.

Implications 4 – 3

Spending

- There are no direct spending implications.

Beneficiary and Provider

- To the extent that providers are responsive to the intent of the incentive, beneficiaries should receive improved care. Minority beneficiaries in particular should benefit from improved quality of care.

Update Conditions of Participation to Align Them with Current Quality Improvement Efforts

Another way Medicare can stimulate quality improvement is by reforming its COPs—the minimum standards that certain provider types are required to meet to participate in Medicare—and their enforcement. Providers, state governments, and the federal government collectively spend millions of dollars annually preparing for and conducting surveys to ensure compliance with these standards, yet it is unclear if and to what extent these efforts have accelerated the pace of change.

COPs are heavily structural requirements and have not been broadly updated, particularly for hospitals, in a long time. While the COPs require that facilities conduct "quality improvement activities" and processes like reporting drug administration errors, they do not broadly require that providers adopt processes that are known to improve quality. They also do not require that providers demonstrate improvement or efforts to improve their performance on publicly reported quality measures.

Yet, anecdotal evidence suggests that better performing facilities are adopting process improvements (e.g., checklists to prevent central line infections, medication reconciliation, adhering to hand-washing protocols) and are focused on measuring and improving their performance on widely accepted quality measures.

The COPs could be updated to build in and reinforce the importance of making the process changes that improve outcomes. At the same time, COPs could be changed to better reflect organizational structures that have evolved (e.g., vertically integrated entities that have streamlined management responsibilities) and reduce the perception that being surveyed for compliance with the COPs is like "death by a thousand duck bites" (as observed by Robert Wachter, a noted expert on patient safety and health care quality). CMS recognizes the need for revisions and has begun drafting a proposed rule updating the hospital COPs.

New requirements that could be included in the COPs to accelerate improvement in outcomes are discussed below:

- ***Improved performance on publicly reported measures***—For hospitals, the publicly reported measures could be those used for Hospital Compare. An advantage of this measure set is that they are widely accepted as valid indicators of quality and that specifics about reporting performance are well known. A disadvantage of focusing quality improvement efforts around these measures is that they focus on three conditions: acute myocardial infarction, pneumonia, and congestive heart failure. Facilities can respond by hiring nurses to work on quality for those conditions and make no other system-wide changes that improve quality. The Joint Commission is considering whether to require demonstrated improvement as part of its accreditation process and is seeking comment on the idea.
- ***Compliance with hand-washing protocols and discharge instructions***—At the November 2010 Commission meeting, Robert Wachter suggested using two measures that would reflect a greater commitment to quality improvement facility wide: compliance with hand-washing protocols and with getting discharge instructions to the appropriate community provider within 48 hours of discharge. Hand-washing has been shown to be a highly effective strategy in reducing hospital-acquired infections, while poor communication between the hospital and community physicians is associated with higher readmission rates. How compliance is defined, measured, and audited are significant issues to be addressed in pursuing this approach since a national consensus on these measures has not been achieved.
- ***Compliance with the Joint Commission's National Patient Safety Goals***—Currently, the Joint Commission has requirements called National Patient Safety Goals that are surveyed as part of its accreditation process. These requirements go beyond the COPs and include processes known to reduce central line infections, harm associated with anticoagulant therapy, and wrong-site surgery, for example.
- ***Participation by and accountability for physicians with respect to patient safety activities***—Physician leaders have called for more accountability and consequences for physicians, saying that "as long as transgressions carry no risk of penalty, some providers ignore the rules, believing that they are not at risk for the mistake the practices are designed to prevent, that they are too busy to bother, or that the practice

is ineffective" (Wachter and Pronovost 2009). To encourage hospitals to monitor physician actions in the hospital for appropriateness, the COPs could require hospitals to demonstrate that physicians individually and as medical staff share accountability for patient safety.

This type of requirement can vary in its stringency. At the least, the COPs could require that the hospital demonstrate that physicians participate in activities such as using checklists or team-based training (Livingston 2010). Increasing in rigor, the COPs could require that hospitals develop their own penalties for clinicians' failure to adhere to safe practices, such as failure to practice hand hygiene, mark the surgical site to prevent wrong-site surgery, or use a checklist when inserting central venous catheters (Wachter and Pronovost 2009).

Any changes to the COPs must be written in a way that allows for innovation and evolution that can lead to higher quality health care as well as new models of health care delivery.

Our recommendation focuses on the COPs specifically, but multiple levels of regulation govern how they are implemented, and the way that each is developed and pursued affects the ability of these standards to drive productive change. The COPs state requirements at the broadest level.[1] Interpretive guidance exists as well as state manuals. Currently, changes to the interpretive guidelines are made without formal public comment.

While this process improves the speed with which they are updated, the lack of formal input can potentially lead to counterproductive requirements. Updating the COPs more regularly should help address tensions that have recently arisen in the context of revisions to interpretive guidance.

Recommendation 4 - 4

The Secretary should regularly update the conditions of participation so that the requirements incorporate and emphasize evidence-based methods of improving quality of care.

Rationale 4 - 4

CMS has not regularly updated the COPs to include evidence-based processes that lead to high-quality care. By incorporating such processes, oversight of health care providers' compliance with the COPs could be more productive in driving quality improvement.

Implications 4 – 4

Spending

- There are no direct spending implications.

Beneficiary and Provider

- To the extent that providers are responsive to the intent of the incentive, beneficiaries should receive improved care. Providers may find the survey process more constructive.

Improve Provider Accountability and Oversight of COPs

Oversight of COPs is achieved through surveys by state agencies or by CMS-approved accrediting bodies. Some providers do not have a choice—for example, only state agencies survey nursing homes and dialysis facilities. In contrast, hospitals are given the option and about 80 percent of short-term, acute care hospitals are surveyed by CMS-approved accrediting bodies; however, state surveyors survey some accredited hospitals in response to complaints or as part of a "look behind" effort to verify the work of accreditors. If a state survey agency finds that a provider fails to meet the conditions, that provider can be terminated from the Medicare program. While potentially a very powerful tool given the large adverse financial effect it would have for the vast majority of providers, it is rarely used.

A problem with oversight of the current survey and accreditation process is the limited range and use of intermediate consequences for significant violations of the criteria, particularly for hospitals. The concern is that this limitation results in poorly performing providers continuing to provide care without taking steps to change the institution's culture and its commitment to quality care. The discussion below explores existing tools and, in some cases, the possibility of expanding their use to a broader set of providers. Ultimately, the Commission finds the greatest promise in requiring system-wide remediation.

Levels of Accreditation

In general, the accreditation process includes reviewing compliance with and encouraging improvement on the COPs. For example, the Joint Commission, the largest accrediting body, has different levels of accreditation that indicate the extent to which providers meet the COPs. In 2008, there were three levels: full, conditional, and preliminary denial of accreditation. In that year, 94.7 percent of hospitals that applied for accreditation received full accreditation and 4.6 percent received conditional accreditation (Tucker 2010). Under conditional accreditation, a facility is subject to more frequent surveys to check that problems have been addressed. Virtually no hospital is denied accreditation once an application is initiated, partly because providers who face the prospect of denial often withdraw from the process. In the past year, the Joint Commission revamped its levels of accreditation so that the designations are now: full accreditation, accreditation with follow-up survey, contingent accreditation, and preliminary denial of accreditation. At the moment, the Joint Commission staff is unsure whether all these various distinctions will be publicly available (Kurtz 2011).

Accreditors do not have enforcement authority. Even if they find a substantial violation of a condition or a situation that may pose immediate danger, they do not report it to the state agency. Instead, they issue requirements for improvement and conduct more frequent inspections; in very rare circumstances, they deny accreditation. In addition, accreditors have recently begun submitting their survey results to CMS on a regular basis.

Financial Penalties

When state surveyors find problems, depending on the type of facility, intermediate sanctions exist that impose financial penalties. For example, nursing homes and laboratories in violation of COPs can be subject to civil monetary penalties (CMPs). Nursing homes can be denied payment for new admissions. Hospitals are not subject to these types of penalties.

Expanding the use of financial penalties to other providers is an option but raises some issues. First, given recently enacted payment system penalties for poor quality (i.e., hospital value-based purchasing and high rates of readmissions), imposing additional penalties outside the payment system may penalize a provider twice for the same problem. To avert "double jeopardy" but still allow additional enforcement tools for failure to adequately meet the COPs, individual providers could be exempted from additional penalties, like CMPs, if they already incurred penalties under the payment system.

Second, financial penalties may undercut the ability of providers to improve quality since the penalty would drain needed resources. Third, to the extent that some providers view CMPs for quality problems as the "cost of doing business" and still not make needed improvements, their effectiveness is limited.

In this context it is worth noting an innovation the Congress recently adopted. With regard to nursing home CMPs, the Patient Protection and Affordable Care Act of 2010 provided CMS with the ability to reinvest Medicare CMP funds back into quality improvement activities for nursing homes. A subsequent CMS administrative rule provides that 90 percent of such funds will be reinvested. Funds may be reinvested in different nursing homes or in the same nursing home for which the CMP was applied, thereby allowing a facility's lack of resources to be less of a factor when quality improvements are to be made.

Public Disclosure

Low-performing providers can be identified publicly, either solely through their performance on process or outcome measures or in tandem with survey results. Under Medicare's Special Focus Facility (SFF) program, nursing homes designated as deficient are identified publicly (on Nursing Home Compare) and the board of each facility is informed of the designation. No such program applies to hospitals. While online sites such as Hospital Compare identify poor performance on specific measures, they do not inform consumers that a facility has systemic quality problems that were detected by surveys.

The SFF program was created in 1987 to decrease the number of persistently low-performing nursing homes by focusing attention on them, and it has been strengthened over time. CMS has historically created a list of the 15 worst performing nursing homes in each state based on the number and severity of deficiencies cited on standard surveys, and states have discretion about which of them to choose for the program. States are then instructed to increase scrutiny of SFFs with more frequent surveys and to impose sanctions (e.g., CMPs) that increase in severity when the SFF does not improve.

The Government Accountability Office (GAO) finds the SFF program to be "essential" to protecting highly vulnerable beneficiaries and identifies the recent requirements for public disclosure and communication with boards as positive additions to the program. Interestingly, GAO found that some SFF facilities improved even though they may not have been surveyed as frequently as required or subjected to more robust enforcement, as the program requires (Government Accountability Office 2010). In addition, while most SFFs improved their performance, some failed to sustain their improved performance after graduation. Some states have added more aggressive policies around the SFF program. For example, Michigan sends a notification letter to all SFF candidates explaining that they are at risk of being selected as an SFF if they fail to address performance problems (Government Accountability Office 2010). The GAO recommended this practice to CMS, and CMS has implemented it nationwide.

Another approach to publicly identifying both low and high performers is exemplified in Nursing Home Compare's five-star system. This system reflects overall nursing home performance across three domains: quality measures, staffing ratios, and survey findings.

Demonstrated Remediation of Violations

Another type of consequence for poor performance imposed by CMS (in coordination with state survey agencies and regional offices) requires remediation of the identified violations. Among the less stringent measures are corrective actions required to address specific deficiencies within 2 (for immediate jeopardy) to 90 days, depending on the scope and severity of the problems, to avoid termination from Medicare. This approach tends to result in quick fixes that are stopgap rather than transformative. Surveyors and facilities alike generally agree that they are not often triggering the kind of change needed, and one study found that enforcement of corrective action plans in nursing homes could be minimal (Louwe et al. 2007).

A more stringent measure before termination involves the temporary takeover of a facility's management. When a nursing home is cited with one or more deficiencies that constitute immediate jeopardy to resident health or safety, the law allows for federal temporary management. The temporary management appointed by CMS has full authority to hire, terminate, and reassign staff; spend nursing home funds; alter nursing home procedures; and otherwise manage a home to achieve its objectives. In reviewing the program, GAO found that most homes under temporary management (15 between 2003 and 2008) corrected deficiencies in the short term, although some continued to have compliance issues in the longer term. One limitation of this program is the lack of a cadre of temporary managers ready to step in. GAO has recommended that such a resource be developed to gain more from this authority. In addition, it recommends that CMS develop best practices for states and regional offices in implementing federal temporary management (Government Accountability Office 2009).

An approach that falls in the middle of the spectrum is to directly engage persistently poorly performing providers in system-wide, meaningful improvement. To demonstrate improvement, providers would need to perform a root cause analysis of their problems and demonstrate their efforts to ameliorate the situation. This effort could include being required to contract with a technical assistance agent or join a learning collaborative in clinical areas such as care transitions and reducing infections.

Another option would be to require low-performing providers to collect data on system-wide performance regularly and have a process for acting on it. In a recent study that looked at high- and low-performing hospitals on mortality rates from acute myocardial infarction, researchers found that high-performing hospitals viewed adverse events as opportunities to analyze root causes, learn from experience, and improve care. They reported incorporating data feedback into the organizational culture with a focus on learning rather than blaming.

In contrast, low-performing hospitals reported variable interest in data and minimal use of root-cause analysis (Curry et al. 2011).

Medicare has recently begun pursuing this type of approach with what it calls "system improvement agreements"(SIAs). Such agreements typically require an interrelated package of key actions within a defined period of time, such as:

- a root cause analysis of systemic issues through onsite peer review by individuals or by an entity that CMS selects or the facility selects subject to CMS approval,
- an action plan in consultation with a peer-review entity,
- funds placed in escrow to finance quality improvement,
- an independent quality monitor who can verify implementation of the plan,
- regular reports on improvements made, and
- waiver of appeal rights contesting termination.

CMS has used this tool with a select number of nursing homes and with seven transplant centers. These agreements accompany termination notices with delayed effective dates and are negotiated between CMS and the provider.

GAO finds that these agreements have the potential to improve the performance of nursing homes, even if the results to date are mixed. Four homes met the terms of their SIAs and graduated from the SFF program. As of August 2009, one of these homes was above average according to CMS's five-star system, and three were below or much below average. Two homes were terminated, and four others were continuing to struggle to improve. GAO notes that the program has had a slow rollout. As of March 2010, two years after the program started, CMS had not disseminated information to the regional offices describing elements that should be part of SIAs and had not catalogued lessons learned from their use. In addition, GAO found that as of May 2009, the central office was unaware of all the SIAs regional offices had in place and that one regional office had not heard of SIAs. GAO recommends that CMS provide its regional offices with a description of the elements that should be part of SIAs and catalogue any lessons learned (Government Accountability Office 2010).

CMS staff report a fair amount of success with SIAs with hospital transplant centers. Of the seven transplant centers targeted because they failed to meet minimum mortality rate standards, three improved performance to be within legal standards. Two others appear to be making progress. One or two others appear unable to improve their performance. In addition to care process reforms, often the problems center around changing leadership or key personnel in the program, adding specialized expertise, and improving internal quality improvement systems. The SIA process spotlights the problems and creates the imperative to make management changes that were previously allowed to continue (Hamilton 2011).

The Department of Health and Human Services Office of Inspector General has taken a similar approach to quality problems in nursing homes through its qualityof-care Corporate Integrity Agreements (CIAs). While similar to SFFs in the types of requirements, CIAs tend to focus more on the conduct of chain nursing homes than the SFF, have been in use longer (since 2000), and are generally in effect for longer periods. As of June 2008, 35 nursing home corporations had entered into these agreements. Under CIAs, nursing homes are required to seek outside technical assistance to identify changes that will help address quality problems. They may also require the establishment of corporate-level compliance officers, quality assurance monitoring committees, and the hiring of an independent monitor to see that the appropriate systems are in place. GAO notes there is little coordination between the SIA and CIA program, even though some facilities are in both programs (Government Accountability Office 2010).

These approaches offer a constructive way to improve care that facilities provide to beneficiaries and could be pursued more broadly if it were a formal program with adequate administrative resources. While the program is relatively labor intensive, efficiencies may be gained by establishing clear criteria for application as well as by standardizing terms.

In addition, there can be an important interplay between SIAs and the availability of technical assistance grants. The structure and oversight involved in executing an SIA could increase the likelihood that the grant would result in quality improvement. Having grant money available may also allow SIAs to be expanded to a larger number and more types of poorly performing providers. We see potential in this collaboration between the two programs despite the mixed experience CMS has had with the Nursing Home in Need (NHIN) program, which is part of the QIOs' ninth SOW. While the results of the program have not been released, we understand that it did not appear to be effective and was costly to implement.

A number of design flaws appear to have undermined the intent of the NHIN program. First, there was a mismatch between the QIO measures used to monitor the effect of QIO assistance and the measures CMS uses to evaluate the performance of nursing homes. Second, because each QIO worked with just one nursing home in each state, efficiencies may have been lost; some QIOs had minimal expertise in working with nursing homes and required more resources as part of the learning process, and they were not able to defray those costs over multiple facilities.

Recommendation 4 - 5

The Congress should require the Secretary to expand interventions that promote systemic remediation of quality problems for persistently low-performing providers.

Rationale 4 - 5

While CMS has experimented with strategies to engage failing providers in system-wide improvement, it has not pursued them broadly. A mandate from the Congress would create a better platform to require low performers to make a system-wide investment in quality improvement or face being terminated from the program. Persistently poor performance comes at too great a cost to beneficiaries and should not go unaddressed.

Implications 4 – 5

Spending

- There are no direct spending implications.

Beneficiary and Provider

- To the extent that providers are responsive to the intent of the interventions, beneficiaries should receive improved care. Certain providers will need to increase their investment in quality improvement.

Publicly Recognize High Performers

Although a focus on poor performers is essential to improving quality in Medicare, public recognition of high-performing providers, as measured across a broad range of metrics, is also important. These providers can shape expectations and standards for excellence in health care delivery, and they can help others achieve the same level of excellence.

Medicare Compare websites publicly report relative performance for several provider types. Some of Medicare's payment policies also give financial recognition based on performance. In addition, there are national quality award programs. For example, the National Quality Forum presents the National Quality Healthcare Award annually to an outstanding, quality-driven health care organization based on effective prioritization of performance improvement goals, a well-designed and deployed "dashboard" to measure and manage whole system performance, a commitment to transparency, data-driven improvement with an emphasis on care coordination and reducing disparities, and demonstrated results on publicly reported performance measures. The National Quality Forum, in partnership with the Joint Commission, also presents The John M. Eisenberg Patient Safety and Quality Awards annually, which recognize individuals and health care organizations that have made significant contributions to improving patient safety. In addition, the National Institute of Standards and Technology operates the Baldrige Award program, which makes awards for excellence in a number of areas, including health care. The award focuses on performance in six areas: product and service outcomes, customer-focused outcomes, financial and market outcomes, workforce-focused outcomes, process effectiveness outcomes, and leadership outcomes. In addition, private-sector organizations such as HealthGrades use hospitals' performance on the Agency for Healthcare Research and Quality Patient Safety Indicators for Medicare patients to distinguish high-performing facilities around the country.

These efforts could be complemented by a new recognition program that calls attention to high-performing providers that work to help their peers improve quality by participating in collaboratives or in direct mentor arrangements. Encouraging providers to assume these roles would likely accelerate improvements system wide. Recognition for taking on this role could be awarded by type of provider (e.g., hospital, nursing home, home health agency). In addition, there could be a further distinction so that, for example, high performance for hospitals could be recognized for rural hospitals, community hospitals, and academic medical centers separately.

Recommendation 4 - 6

The Secretary should establish a public recognition program for high-performing providers that participate in collaboratives or learning networks, or otherwise act as mentors, to improve the quality of lower performing providers.

Rationale 4 - 6

Public recognition of exceptional performance inspires other providers to improve their performance and continually redefine excellence. It helps avoid complacency among providers and beneficiaries alike.

Implications 4 – 6

Spending

- There are no direct spending implications.

Beneficiary and Provider

- To the extent that providers are responsive to the intent of the incentive, beneficiaries should receive improved care.

Endnotes

[1] Some aspects of the COPs are specified in statute and changes in them would require legislation.

References

Angelelli, J., D. C. Grabowski, and V. Mor. 2006. Effect of educational level and minority status on nursing home choice after hospital discharge. *American Journal of Public Health* 96, no. 7 (July): 1249–1253.

Brock, J., and A. Goroski. 2010. *The care transitions theme: Experiences from community-based hospital readmission reduction initiative.* Englewood, CO. The Colorado Foundation for Medicare Care. http://www.cfmc.org/caretransitions.

Bach, P. B., H. H. Pham, D. Schrag, et al. 2004. Primary care physicians who treat blacks and whites. *New England Journal of Medicine* 351, no. 6 (August 5): 575–584.

Classen, D.C., R. Resar, F. Grifin, et al. 2011. Global trigger tool shows that adverse events in hospitals may be ten times greater than previously measured. *Health Affairs* 30, no. 4: 581–589.

Curry, L. A., E. Spatz, E. Cherlin, et al. 2011. What distinguishes top-performing hospitals in acute myocardial infarction mortality rates? *Annals of Internal Medicine* 154, no. 6 (March 15): 384–391.

Government Accountability Office. 2009. Nursing homes: Opportunities exist to facilitate the use of the temporary management sanction. Letter to Congressional requestors. GAO–10–37R. November 20.

Government Accountability Office. 2010. *Poorly performing nursing homes: Special focus facilities are often improving, but CMS's program could be strengthened.* GAO–10–197. Washington, DC: GAO.

Gray, B. H., M. Schlesinger, S. M. Siegfried, et al. 2009. Racial and ethnic disparities in the use of high-volume hospitals. *Inquiry* 46, no. 3 (Fall): 322–338.

Hamilton, T., Centers for Medicare & Medicaid Services, Department of Health and Human Services. 2011. Personal communication with author, March 14.

Institute of Medicine. 2006. *Medicare's Quality Improvement Organization program: Maximizing potential.* Washington, DC: National Academies Press.

Jha, A. K., E. J. Orav, Z. Li, et al. 2007. Concentration and quality of hospitals that care for elderly black patients. *Archives of Internal Medicine* 167, no.11 (June11): 1177–1182.

Kurtz, P. 2011. E-mail to the author. March 10.

Landrigan, C. P., G. J. Parry, C. B. Bones et al. 2010. Temporal trends in rates of patient harm resulting from medical care. *New England Journal of Medicine* 363, no. 22 (November 25): 2124– 2134.

Levinson, D. R., Office of Inspector General, Department of Health and Human Services. 2010. *Adverse events in hospitals: National incidence among Medicare beneficiaries.* OEI–06–09– 000090. Washington, DC: OIG.

Livingston, E. H. 2010. Solutions for improving patient safety. *Journal of the American Medical Association* 303, no. 2 (January 13): 159–161.

Louwe, H, C. Parry, A. Kramer, et al. 2007. *Improving nursing home enforcement: Findings from enforcement case studies.* Report prepared for the Centers for Medicare & Medicaid Services. Contract number 500–00–0026 0003. Baltimore, MD: CMS.

Medicare Payment Advisory Commission. 2009. *Report to the Congress: Improving incentives in the Medicare program.* Washington, DC: MedPAC.

Medicare Payment Advisory Commission. 2010. *Report to the Congress: Aligning incentives in Medicare.* Washington, DC: MedPAC.

Medicare Payment Advisory Commission. 2011. *Report to the Congress: Medicare payment policy.* Washington, DC: MedPAC.

Network for Regional Healthcare Improvement. 2011. *Regional health improvement collaboratives.*

Pittsburgh, PA: NRHI. http://www.nrhi.org/downloads/RegionalHealthImprovement Collaboratives.pdf.

Sarrazin, M. V., M. Campbell, and G. E. Rosenthal. 2009. Racial differences in hospital use after acute myocardial infarction: Does residential segregation play a role? *Health Affairs* 28, no. 2 (March–April): w368–w378.

Skinner, J., A. Chandra, D. Staiger, et al. 2005. Mortality after acute myocardial infarction in hospitals that disproportionately treat black patients. *Circulation* 112, no. 17 (October 25): 2634–2641.

Tucker, D., The Joint Commission. 2010. E-mail to the author, January 13.

Wachter, R. 2010. Presentation to the Medicare Payment Advisory Commission. November.

Wachter, R. M., and P. J. Pronovost. 2009. Balancing "no blame" with accountability in patient safety. *New England Journal of Medicine* 361, no. 14 (October 1): 1401–1406.

Coordinating Care for Dual-Eligible Beneficiaries

Summary

Beneficiaries who qualify for Medicare and Medicaid often have complex care needs that result in high program spending, yet the care furnished to them is typically uncoordinated. In June 2010, the Commission reported that combined program spending on dual-eligible beneficiaries varied considerably by number of chronic conditions, whether the beneficiary had dementia, and whether the beneficiary received care in a nursing home. It noted that improving the care for dual-eligible beneficiaries ideally would require integration of the financing and service delivery and described a handful of integrated programs. Although some integrated programs coordinate the Medicare and Medicaid services furnished to dual-eligible beneficiaries, those programs are small in number and enrollment.

As part of our ongoing work considering how to improve the coordination of services furnished to dual-eligible beneficiaries, this year we report on programs with the potential to integrate and coordinate services provided to their enrollees. In integrated programs, either a managed care organization or a provider receives capitated payments from the Medicare and Medicaid programs and assumes risk for the full spectrum of the dual-eligible beneficiaries' care. Some states implement care coordination programs that retain the fee-for-service system (and are paid a small monthly amount). While these programs do not align the financial and care management incentives as the capitated programs do, they represent a step toward integration of Medicare and Medicaid benefits. Commission staff conducted interviews and site visits to understand how integrated programs coordinate care and what lessons can be learned for states and entities seeking to develop integrated programs. Another avenue for coordinating care is through dual-eligible special needs plans (D–SNPs). D–SNPs are Medicare Advantage (MA) plans that target their enrollment to dual-eligible beneficiaries and thus have the potential to integrate and coordinate the services covered by both Medicare and Medicaid. Staff also examined D–SNPs' model-of-care descriptions submitted to CMS to evaluate whether D–SNPs were adequately coordinating beneficiaries' care and were integrating beneficiaries' Medicaid benefits.

We found that integrated programs vary considerably in their design and in the scope of services they manage. No single approach seemed likely to fit in every state, and the lack of comparable outcomes research on most approaches leaves open the question of which models are more effective. Nevertheless, we found two constants. First, administrators of integrated programs told us that the flexibility of capitated payments allowed them to deliver the mix of medical and social services each patient needed. Second, all the programs were similar in a number of key care coordination activities, including care transitions, medication reconciliation, patient education, and patient assessment with respect to risk for hospitalization or nursing home placement.

Expanding enrollment was a challenge for many of the programs. Program officials had ideas about how to grow enrollment but acknowledged that these ideas were likely to result in only incremental expansion. Many interviewees told us that the requirement to recruit on a person-by-person basis was a key limitation to expansion. State officials also consistently commented on the lack of financial incentives for states to pursue integrated programs, most notably that states cannot share in Medicare savings.

CMS may want to modify its model-of-care requirements for two reasons. First, the information that SNPs have submitted was too general to evaluate the plans' care coordination activities, whether the D–SNPs integrate Medicare and Medicaid services, or whether the D–SNPs tailored care coordination activities to the enrolled population. Some key care coordination elements and the plan's integration with Medicaid are not required elements in the model of care, and, with a few exceptions, plans did not describe them. To meet the requirements of the Patient Protection and Affordable Care Act of 2010 that all SNPs be approved by the National Committee for Quality Assurance, CMS recently announced an approval process based on evaluation of the plans' models of care. While this approval process may improve the specificity of the model-of-care descriptions, it will not eliminate the gaps in the model of care requirements. Second, SNPs already report care coordination and integration activities in other reporting requirements, including quality measures to the National Committee for Quality Assurance and a detailed set of questions as part of the plan's MA application to CMS. CMS should target and streamline its model-of-care requirements to those key elements that are not otherwise available.

It is also not possible to evaluate the quality of care furnished by most D–SNPs. The star rating information for most SNPs is included in the overall reporting under a larger MA contract, which includes non-SNP plans. In addition, CMS has not routinely made available other quality information submitted by SNPs, including SNP-specific Healthcare Effectiveness Data and Information Set measures and structure and process measures developed by the National Committee for Quality Assurance. The Commission encourages

CMS to shift its quality focus to outcome measures such as patient satisfaction, quality of life, and rates of emergency room use; institutionalization for long-term care; hospital admission and readmission rates; and medication errors. Many of these measures would allow for comparisons across the programs, MA plans, SNPs, and fee-for-service Medicare. D–SNPs could also be required to report the degree of integration with Medicaid.

Over the coming year, the Commission plans to continue its work identifying key elements of care coordination that should be components of any integrated care program and exploring program designs that improve care for dual-eligible beneficiaries.

Many dual-eligible beneficiaries are frail, have disabilities, or have multiple chronic conditions, including some form of cognitive impairment. Their conditions often result in high program spending and many of these beneficiaries need coordinated care. Because dual-eligible beneficiaries qualify for benefits under Medicare and Medicaid, their care in particular needs to be coordinated so that their providers are aware of their acute and chronic medical, behavioral health, long-term care, and social service needs and the care they receive. Last year, the Commission reported that the combined program spending on dual-eligible beneficiaries varied considerably according to the number of a beneficiary's chronic conditions, whether the beneficiary had dementia, and whether the beneficiary received care in a nursing home. The Commission noted that improving care for dual-eligible beneficiaries would require the integration of Medicare and Medicaid financing and care delivery. In addition, the Commission reviewed the literature on integrated programs—programs that coordinate Medicare and Medicaid benefits for dual-eligible beneficiaries (Medicare Payment Advisory Commission 2010).

This year we report on our examination of the care coordination activities of integrated programs and dual-eligible special needs plans (D–SNPs). Staff conducted interviews and site visits to understand how integrated programs coordinate care and what lessons can be learned for states and entities seeking to develop integrated programs. We also examined D–SNPs' model-of-care descriptions submitted to CMS to evaluate whether D– SNPs were adequately coordinating beneficiaries' care and were integrating beneficiaries' Medicaid benefits. With both efforts, we wanted to identify core activities that programs use to coordinate care and whether the activities improved the care beneficiaries received.

Background

Dual-eligible beneficiaries make up 16 percent of Medicare enrollment but account for one-quarter of its spending. Compared with other beneficiaries, dual-eligible beneficiaries are sicker, frailer, less educated, and more likely to be a minority, live alone, and be mentally impaired. However, within the dual-eligible population, care needs vary considerably. While more than one-quarter have three or more limitations in the ability to perform activities of daily living, almost half of dual-eligible beneficiaries have no limitations. Eleven percent of dual-eligible beneficiaries have five or more chronic conditions and dementia, while 38 percent have one or no chronic conditions (Medicare Payment Advisory Commission 2010). Given these wide differences, the amount of care coordination individuals need varies considerably.

As a reflection of this range in care needs across the dual-eligible population, there is considerable variation in per capita spending based on a beneficiary's condition and whether the beneficiary is a long-term care resident. In 2005, average per capita Medicare and Medicaid spending was $26,185 for dual-eligible beneficiaries but averaged $50,278 for those with five or more chronic conditions; spending for beneficiaries with dementia was 30 percent to 90 percent higher than for those without it, depending on other comorbidities. Spending varied almost fourfold for beneficiaries with no nursing home spending compared with those with the highest nursing home spending (Medicare Payment Advisory Commission 2010). Given the range of spending, care coordination should vary in intensity, depending on the care needs of the individual.

Integrated Programs

Few programs coordinate all Medicare and Medicaid benefits for dual-eligible beneficiaries. Under these programs, either a managed care organization or a provider receives capitated payments from Medicare and Medicaid and assumes risk for the full spectrum of the dual-eligible beneficiaries' benefits. Examples of these programs are the managed-care-based Senior Care Options program in Massachusetts and the provider-based Program of All-Inclusive Care for the Elderly (PACE).[1] Under the managedcare-based programs, the managed care plan is typically both a Medicaid managed care plan and a SNP. Some of the managed-care-based programs place limits on the amount of long-term care services covered, such as the number of nursing home days. The PACE program, in contrast, is a provider-based program. Under capitation with Medicare and Medicaid, the PACE organization is responsible, and at full risk, for providing all medically necessary care and services, including all nursing home days.

Programs that integrate some, but not all, of the Medicare and Medicaid benefits for dual-eligible beneficiaries are more common. For example, New Mexico and Texas have programs operated by managed care organizations that integrate some of the Medicare and Medicaid benefits. Programs that integrate some or all Medicare and Medicaid services vary considerably in the population and the size of the area they serve and in the services they manage. Enrollment in integrated programs is generally low. Most beneficiaries who enroll in the Medicaid managed care plan side of the integrated program enroll in Medicare fee-for-service or a Medicare Advantage (MA) plan with a different company. Enrollment in PACE programs is also typically low, with individual PACE centers serving between 11 and 2,500 participants at each center (National PACE Association 2010). Fewer than 2 percent of all dual-eligible beneficiaries are enrolled in some type of integrated care program that coordinates some or all services (Center for Health Care Strategies 2010).

Some states pursue care coordination programs that are fee-for-service overlays—that is, providers continue to be paid under fee-for-service and receive an additional, small monthly payment to coordinate services for beneficiaries—rather than capitated, at-risk programs through managed care organizations or providers. These programs are not fully integrated because they do not cover all beneficiaries' Medicare and Medicaid benefits. An example of a fee-for-service overlay program is the North Carolina Community Care Networks. Under this program, networks of physicians receive per member per month payments from the state to coordinate dual-eligible beneficiaries' Medicare benefits. One reason states may pursue a fee-for-service overlay program is that few states manage Medicaid long-term care benefits through managed care. Although it is becoming increasingly more common, currently only 13 states enroll or intend to enroll dual-eligible beneficiaries in Medicaid managed care organizations to manage their long-term care (Smith et al. 2010). More commonly, many

Medicaid managed care programs exclude dual-eligible beneficiaries or, if they do include them, carve out long-term care and behavioral health from their programs.

Dual-Eligible Special Needs Plans

D–SNPs are MA plans that focus enrollment on beneficiaries who are eligible for both Medicare and Medicaid (see text box, pp. 128–129, on SNPs). Although D–SNPs by themselves are not integrated programs, they can be if a plan also has a contract with a state to provide Medicaid benefits. In these instances, dual-eligible beneficiaries can be enrolled in the same health plan (or plans offered by the same company) for their Medicare and Medicaid benefits and the plan coordinates services covered by both programs. D–SNPs that manage beneficiaries' Medicaid benefits, including long-term care, are referred to as fully integrated D–SNPs.[2]

Most D–SNPs are not integrated programs because they do not also receive a Medicaid payment to manage Medicaid benefits. Although D–SNPs are required to have contracts with states, they are not required to contract with states to manage the dual-eligible beneficiaries' Medicaid benefits, and most do not. The requirement for D–SNPs to have state contracts by 2013 is a step in the direction of more D–SNPs becoming integrated. A D–SNP that is not an integrated program may offer some degree of coordination with beneficiaries' Medicaid benefits, such as furnishing lists of providers that participate in the Medicaid program.

The SNP models of care can be one tool to evaluate whether D–SNPs are coordinating beneficiaries' Medicare benefits and whether the D–SNPs are moving toward becoming integrated programs. The Medicare Improvements for Patients and Providers Act of 2008 (MIPPA) requires SNPs to submit evidence-based models of care. Only SNPs that were new or expanding plans in 2010 were required to submit their models of care to CMS as part of the MA application process; however, beginning in 2012, all SNPs must submit their model-of-care descriptions to CMS. The descriptions must contain information on 11 elements, including the SNP's target population, the interdisciplinary care team, beneficiaries' individualized care plans, and care management for vulnerable populations (Table 5-1, pp. 126–127). In addition, SNPs are required to complete an attestation covering their model of care as part of the MA application (Centers for Medicare & Medicaid Services 2011a). The attestation requires yes or no responses to more than 250 questions about the model of care, such as the members of the SNP's interdisciplinary care team and the specific care coordination activities the plan conducts.

Methods for Gathering Information on Integrated Programs for Dual-Eligible Beneficiaries

We completed two analyses of integrated programs for dual-eligible beneficiaries. For the first, our goal was to learn about the characteristics of integrated programs that have been implemented, are in the planning phase, or failed to be implemented; the results of integrated programs on utilization and costs; and whether the programs could be readily expanded or replicated. We contracted with Mathematica Policy Research to conduct a series of interviews with nine state programs and site visits to three of the programs. In addition, Commission staff conducted site visits to two PACE providers and interviewed a third PACE provider and representatives from the Medicaid managed care and SNP industries, advocacy groups, and foundations (see text box, p. 130, on site visits and interviews).

The goal of our second analysis was to assess whether D–SNPs provide care coordination activities for dual-eligible beneficiaries consistent with those offered by the integrated programs (state programs and PACE) we researched. We developed an analytic framework based on the key care coordination elements provided by these integrated programs and then used this framework to assess the D–SNP model-of-care descriptions submitted to CMS. Our framework consisted of the following elements: description of the enrolled population, the risk assessment process, care during transitions, medication reconciliation, patient education, utilization management, and coordination with Medicaid benefits. An incomplete description of care coordination or Medicaid integration efforts could reflect that a D–SNP was not offering these activities or was offering them but did not describe them in the model of care.

Models of care were not submitted by every D–SNP because existing SNPs that were not expanding were not required to submit them. In addition, many SNPs with the same parent company (such as a parent company having SNPs in multiple states) submitted the same model-of-care description for all their D–SNPs, and some submitted the same description for all their SNPs (chronic, dual eligible, and institutional). We received about 140 models of care from CMS. After we removed those that described models of care for chronic or institutional SNPs as well as the duplicate models of care, there were approximately 40 distinct D–SNP models of care.

In addition to the D–SNP model-of-care analysis, we explored whether a relationship existed between the quality of the model-of-care descriptions and D–SNPs' performance on quality measures. We were interested to know whether D–SNPs with stronger descriptions performed better on outcome measures than the other D–SNPs. For this analysis, we identified stronger and weaker model-of-care descriptions based on our framework and reviewed the publicly available quality measures for those D–SNPs.

Integrated Programs Vary in Approach and Scope

Many states have become interested in integrated programs, in part as a way to control their spending on dual-eligible beneficiaries. Existing and planned programs vary considerably. For administration, some states use managed care organizations while others employ provider-based approaches; for financing, some states implement capitated, risk-based structures while others prefer fee-forservice overlays. No single approach seems likely to fit in every state and the lack of comparable outcomes research on most approaches leaves open the question of which models are more effective.

Program Characteristics Reflect States' Circumstances

Integrated programs take a variety of forms, reflecting the state's support for and experience with managed care, their approach to their Medicaid-only population (which they adapt to the dual-eligible population), and the level of support from providers and advocates. Interviewees told us that some states, such as Colorado, will not consider a managed care approach and some states are exploring or developing medical homes for the dual-eligible population.[3] Other states that have experience with managed care entities (such as Massachusetts) expand their managed care models to other populations. One state, Vermont, is exploring a design in which the state assumes the role of a managed care entity and manages the Medicare funds for dual-eligible beneficiaries. This model-of-care delivery is one of multiple approaches that the Center for Medicare and Medicaid Innovation may test (see text box, p. 131). Other states have expressed interest in this model in part because the state can retain any savings from reduced expenditures on Medicare services. Not all states pursue a single strategy. Massachusetts, for example, has managed care plans that operate both the state's Senior Care Options integrated care program and PACE programs.

Table 5-1. Reporting requirements for special needs plans

Instrument	Measure or domain
HEDIS® measures	• Colorectal cancer screening
	• Glaucoma screening in older adults
	• Use of spirometry testing in the assessment and diagnosis of COPD
	• Pharmacotherapy management of COPD exacerbation
	• Controlling high blood pressure
	• Persistence of beta-blocker treatment after a heart attack
	• Osteoporosis management in older women who had a fracture
	• Antidepressant medication management
	• Follow-up after hospitalization for mental illness
	• Annual monitoring for patients on persistent medications
	• Potentially harmful drug–disease interactions in the elderly
	• Use of high-risk medication in the elderly
	• Board certified physicians
	• Care for older adults
	• Medication reconciliation postdischarge
Structure and process measures	• Identifying members for complex case management: the number of different data sources used to identify
	enrollees for case management, how frequently identification is done, the ways members are referred for
	case management, the scope of the initial patient assessment, and whether the plan considers the members'
	cultural and linguistic needs and caregiver resources.
	• Care transitions: how SNPs manage transitions, identify unplanned transitions, and attempt to reduce them.
	• Medication management: does the plan document medication use by a member.
	• Patient education: whether the goals and preferences of members are considered in the development of the
	care plan, communication of self-management plans to a member, and patient notification of changes to the
	plan of care resulting from a care transition.
	• Real-time utilization management: the share of admissions to hospital and long-term care facilities reported
	within one business day of admission.
	• Coordination with Medicaid benefits: inform members about maintaining their Medicaid eligibility and
	the benefits they are eligible to receive under Medicare and Medicaid; help members understand their claims and correspondence from both programs and coordinate any adjudication of claims; and assist with

Table 5-1. Reporting

Instrument	Measure or domain
	accessing network providers including an assessment of the adequacy of the network.
Models of care	• Target population
	• Measurable goals
	• Interdisciplinary care team
	• Staff structure and care management roles
	• Model of care training for personnel and provider network health risk assessment
	• Individualized care plan
	• Communication network
	• Provider network having specialized expertise
	• Clinical practice guidelines and protocols
	• Care management for vulnerable subpopulations
	• Performance and health outcome measurement
MA application attestation	• Interdisciplinary care team members
	• Medication reviews
	• Telemedicine services
	• Home safety assessments
	• Tracking and analysis of transitions of care
	• Identification and facilitation of access to community resources and social services
	• Conducting risk assessment
	• Facilitation of the implementation of the individualized care plan
	• Coordination of care across settings and providers
	• Monitoring provision of services to ensure care is seamlessly transitioned across settings and providers
	• Conducting care coordination meetings annually

Note: HEDIS® (Healthcare Effectiveness Data and Information Set), COPD (chronic obstructive pulmonary disease), SNP (special needs plan), MA (Medicare Advantage).

Source: Centers for Medicare & Medicaid Services 2010, CMS model of care attestations, National Committee for Quality Assurance structure and process measures

One commonality among states that successfully implemented integrated programs is that each state had a champion—that is, an influential and effective leader—who steered the program through numerous administrative and financial barriers from development through implementation. The states also had stability in their leadership at the gubernatorial and agency levels to steer the programs' development through the design phase, engagement with providers and advocates, and implementation. Some states tried and failed to implement an integrated program or the program they implemented was narrower in scope than originally intended because of opposition from providers. In some states, advocates opposed integrated programs out of concern that restrictive provider networks would require beneficiaries to switch providers or that beneficiaries would lose their independence. The latter concern was more common among advocates for individuals with disabilities.

States that were planning programs agreed that they were motivated by a desire to control spending on dual-eligible beneficiaries. Although every state has a financial incentive to invest in care coordination that averts nursing home use, some states plan to start with managing only a portion of the dual-eligible beneficiaries' care, such as Medicare-covered primary care. In North Carolina, even this narrow scope reflects the state's belief that coordinating services it is not responsible for will eventually lower the state's spending on long-term care services. For example, the state pays its network of primary care practices a per member per month payment to coordinate Medicare services, provides the network with data on hospitalization rates from nursing homes, and works with the provider network to develop strategies to lower readmission rates. State officials recognize that changing practice patterns takes time. Officials in New Mexico told us that they hoped the state's managed longterm care program would lower the growth in long-term care spending over three to five years.

Programs Vary in the Scope of Services They Manage

Administrators of fully integrated, risk-based programs emphasized the flexibility capitated payments gave them to decide which clinical and nonclinical services to furnish. It was particularly true among administrators of the PACE program because PACE providers have more flexibility in how they spend Medicare funds than SNPs, which are not permitted to spend Medicare dollars on non-health-care-related services. Administrators of programs that are not fully integrated appreciated that to control their spending they needed to include a full range of long-term care and behavioral health services, but the administrators told us that providers blocked their efforts to include these services in the integrated program. Longterm care services are often left out of Medicaid managed care plans, leaving states with little experience managing these services. Behavioral health services are even more frequently carved out of programs. This omission leaves states and programs relatively inexperienced at managing services that shape total spending for dual-eligible beneficiaries.

Flexibility to Furnish Necessary Clinical and Nonclinical Services

Administrators of integrated programs told us that they needed the flexibility to deliver the services they thought mattered. Capitation, rather than fee-for-service payments for covered services, gave them this latitude. Examples of this flexibility from PACE providers include sending meals home and installing grab bars in a beneficiary's home when the care team believed the services would prevent more costly spending on medical services. In addition, PACE transportation van drivers were able to detect subtle changes in a participant's behavior or to notice uneaten meals when they picked up participants at the beginning of the day. The drivers alerted the care team for follow-up once the beneficiary checked in at the day care center. Further, one PACE program supplied some participants with air conditioners to prevent dehydration.

What are special needs plans?

Special needs plans (SNPs) were authorized by the Medicare Modernization Act of 2003. SNPs must meet Medicare Advantage (MA) requirements and are paid the same as any other MA plan. However, unlike other MA plans, they must limit enrollment to their targeted populations (dual-eligible beneficiaries, beneficiaries residing in institutions, and beneficiaries with chronic or disabling conditions). Dual-eligible beneficiaries can enroll each month, whereas other MA plans can enroll beneficiaries only during annual open enrollment and during defined special election periods. Like any MA plan, SNPs are required to go through an approval process with CMS.

Plans must submit materials such as proof of state licensure, names of key management staff, evidence of fiscal soundness, provider participation contracts, and a quality improvement program description.

Between July 2006 and January 2011, the number of SNPs grew rapidly (from 276 to 455), with beneficiary enrollment in these plans more than doubling during this period to almost 1.3 million (Table 5-2). Dual-eligible SNPs (D–SNPs) account for 71 percent of SNPs and enroll 81 percent of the Medicare beneficiaries enrolled in SNPs (data not shown). Currently, 11.4 percent of dual-eligible beneficiaries have enrolled in D–SNPs (data not shown). Most D–SNPs (80 percent) are parts of chains that enroll about three-quarters of all beneficiaries enrolled in D–SNPs. Among these chains, 1 company has 49 plans, while 3 run about 20 plans. Together, these four companies manage more than one-third of all SNPs.

There are 45 plans that are stand-alone D–SNPs. These plans are not part of larger parent organizations.

With the rapid growth in SNPs came concerns that Medicare's requirements did not ensure that SNPs were targeting populations with special care needs and tailoring their benefit plans to them. The Medicare, Medicaid, and SCHIP Extension Act of 2007 placed a moratorium on the approval of new SNPs and the expansion of existing ones. The Medicare Improvements for Patients and Providers Act of 2008 (MIPPA) converted the moratorium to a one-year freeze, allowing plans to begin submitting applications for new plans or expansions in 2009 for the 2010 SNP contract year. In 2010, CMS tightened the definitions for chronic or disabling condition SNPs.

In response to the concern that SNPs were not providing specialized care, the Commission recommended in 2008 that the Secretary establish performance measures tailored for SNPs, evaluate SNP performance on the measures, and make the information available to beneficiaries and their counselors. This recommendation has been partially addressed—SNPs are required to report two sets of information: Healthcare Effectiveness Data and Information Set (HEDIS®) measures and structure and process measures developed by the National Committee for Quality Assurance (NCQA). The 15 required HEDIS measures are a combination of a subset of the HEDIS measures that all MA plans must report and some SNPspecific measures (Table 5-1, pp. 126–127). Although SNPs have been required to report the 15 HEDIS measures since 2008, the results of these measures were published once (in 2008) and have not been published since then. The NCQA structure and process measures consist of six domains specific to SNPs: complex case management, improving member satisfaction, clinical quality improvements, care transitions, institutional SNPs' relationship with their facilities, and coordination of Medicare and Medicaid benefits (see http://www.ncq.org for a detailed list). Each measure consists of multiple elements that are individually scored. Plans began submitting these measures in 2009; however, the results are not publicly available. In addition, as part of their MA applications to CMS, plans describe 11 elements of the models of care used to coordinate the care for their enrollees.

Table 5-2. Enrollment by type of SNP as of February 2011

Type of SNP	Number of plans	Enrollment	Percent of all SNP enrollment
Chronic or disabling	92	162,207	13%
Institutional	65	80,508	6
Dual eligible	298	1,050,864	81
Total	455	1,293,579	100

Note: SNP (special needs plan).

Source: MedPAC analysis of February 2011 SNP Comprehensive Report, CMS (http://www.cms.gov/MCRAdvPartDEnrolData/SNP/list.asp#TopOfPage).

The Patient Protection and Affordable Care Act of 2010 (PPACA) requires all SNPs to be approved by NCQA by 2012. In April 2011, CMS provided guidance to plans about the NCQA scoring and approval process it will use (Centers for Medicare & Medicaid Services 2011b). NCQA will review and score the models of care based on the completeness, detail, and depth of the discussion of each of the 11 elements, with scores ranging from zero to four for each element. For each element, a plan that includes multiple specific examples or a case study may receive full points (four), while a plan's description that includes incomplete details or incorrect information may receive no points. Plans with higher total scores will receive approval for two or three years (depending on the total score); those with lower total scores will be approved for one year. As part of its approval, NCQA will not review a SNP's responses to the attestation questions or the plan's performance on the structure and process measures.

The Commission has raised concerns that, although D–SNPs manage the Medicare services for patients who qualify for Medicaid, the plans were not necessarily providing or coordinating the services covered by the states' Medicaid programs. To that end, the Commission recommended that the Congress require D–SNPs to contract with states in their service areas to coordinate Medicaid benefits (Medicare Payment Advisory Commission 2008). MIPPA required new D–SNPs and expansions of existing SNPs to have a contract with the state Medicaid agency by 2010. The contracts must explain details such as which (if any) Medicaid benefits the SNP will cover, the SNP's service area, the process for verifying Medicaid eligibility, and the process for the state to share information on Medicaid provider participation with the SNP. Existing SNPs that were not expanding were required to submit a signed state Medicaid contract to CMS by 2011. PPACA extended the deadline for state contracts for Medicaid services from December 31, 2010, to December 31, 2012. States are not required to contract with SNPs and plans could have difficulty establishing contracts with some states.

MIPPA also required that CMS provide technical assistance to states to encourage Medicare and Medicaid benefit integration for dual-eligible beneficiaries. CMS has implemented a resource center that helps states negotiate contracts with SNPs and has developed best practices for model contracts with states.

The resource center has also led training sessions and established a website to provide information on coordination issues (Centers for Medicare & Medicaid Services 2010).

States Vary in Including Long-Term Care and Behavioral Health in Integrated Programs

States and programs vary in whether they would consider including long-term care services in their integrated program. In some states, the nursing home and home health care industries opposed the development of integrated programs because they worried about the loss of volume and negotiating power for higher payments.

Site visits and interviews on integrated programs

To learn about a range of programs that coordinate the care for dual-eligible beneficiaries, we contracted with Mathematica Policy Research to conduct a series of interviews and site visits using structured interviews (Verdier et al. 2010). We selected programs to interview that represented a mix of well-established programs (Minnesota, Massachusetts, and Arizona), new approaches (Vermont, North Carolina, and New Mexico), and one state that currently excludes dualeligible beneficiaries from Medicaid enhanced primary care case management but may include them in the future (Oklahoma). We also spoke with two states (Maryland and Virginia) that tried to establish programs but were not successful, hoping to learn from their experiences. In selecting our site visits to Massachusetts, New Mexico, and North Carolina, we considered a mix of approaches to integrated programs and geographic diversity. During each site visit, we interviewed representatives from state agencies, health plans, providers, and beneficiary counselors.

We also spoke with representatives from the Association for Community Affiliated Plans, the SNP (Special Needs Plan) Alliance, the National Governors Association, the SCAN (Senior Care Action Network) Foundation, the Center for Medicare Advocacy, the Medicare Rights Center, CareOregon, the Office on Disability within the Department of Health and Human Services, the Kaiser Family Foundation, AARP (formerly, the American Association of Retired Persons), the National PACE (Program of All-Inclusive Care for the Elderly) Association, and the Independent Care System (a nonprofit managed long-term care plan in New York for adults with disabilities). In addition, we spoke with a PACE provider in Boston and visited two others (in Philadelphia, Pennsylvania, and Hampton, Virginia). Commission staff also participated in a roundtable discussion with Medicaid officials from 11 states at the Transforming the Care for Dual Eligibles conference hosted by the Center for Health Care Strategies.

In other states, provider support was won over with augmented payment rates or incentive payments to shorten stays. States also differ in their interest in and progress toward rebalancing their institutional and communitybased long-term care services, which influences whether a state includes long-term care services in its integrated care approach.

Even fewer states and programs consider including behavioral health services in their integrated programs. In New Mexico and Arizona, where behavioral health services are excluded from their integrated programs, health plan representatives said these exclusions resulted in poorly coordinated care. In some states, behavioral services were excluded from the integrated programs as a concession to mental health providers. In these states, behavioral health providers thought stand-alone behavioral health programs could offer better care.

In adapting a Medicaid program to the dual-eligible population, some states expanded their network of providers to include specialists and social and behavioral health services. For example, North Carolina's primary care network initially excluded pharmacists and behavioral health services but integrated these services after it had difficulty controlling expenditures and coordinating beneficiary care. When the mentally ill are included in the enrolled population, program administrators told us that a broad range of behavioral health providers are needed. They also said that primary care providers are often unaware of the range of behavioral health providers in their areas and do not coordinate services with them.

Integrated Programs Had Similar Key Care Coordination Elements and Challenges

Programs that coordinate the care for dual-eligible beneficiaries have many common care coordination elements. They typically enroll broadly defined populations, use similar care coordination activities, and are challenged to expand enrollment.

States as the entity to manage Medicare funds

At least five states (Vermont, Massachusetts, Tennessee, Texas, and California) expressed interest in directly receiving Medicare funding for their dual-eligible beneficiaries. Under this approach, a state would receive Medicare payments and either assume the financial risk for Medicare benefits itself or make a combined Medicare–Medicaid payment to an entity (e.g., a managed care organization or an accountable care organization) to manage the beneficiaries' acute and long-term care benefits. Savings achieved by lowering the use of all services (including those financed by Medicare) would accrue to the state, if the state is receiving Medicare and Medicaid payments. The Patient Protection and Affordable Care Act of 2010 gave the Center for Medicare and Medicaid Innovation in CMS the authority to test this model and permits the Secretary to waive any Medicare requirements during the testing of this model. Under CMS's State Demonstrations to Integrate Care for Dual Eligible Individuals initiative, 15 states received planning grants to design integrated programs for dual-eligible beneficiaries, and some of those states are designing programs in which the state would manage the Medicare funds.

This approach raises concerns about how Medicare funds would be used. States would have a financial incentive to use Medicare funds to reduce their own spending and Medicare would not receive any savings. There is a long history of states using financial strategies such as intergovernmental transfers to maximize federal support while minimizing the state's Medicaid contributions and increasing federal spending. If these types of programs are implemented, there will have to be carefully designed transparent accountability mechanisms to ensure program integrity.

Programs Enroll Broadly Defined Populations

None of the integrated program officials we spoke with targeted their programs at clinically defined groups of dual-eligible beneficiaries, such as those with specific chronic conditions. Program and state representatives we spoke with thought that selecting specific diseases tended to focus care on a narrow set of care needs, too often ignoring other care needs of the beneficiaries. Interviewees told us that while beneficiaries with different diseases require different mixes of services, the basic model of care coordination—regular risk assessment and development of a patient-specific care plan by a multidisciplinary team, tailored to each beneficiary's care needs and living situation—would be the same.

Interviewees thought the services to coordinate care for the dual-eligible population of individuals under age 65 with disabilities would need to be broader than those coordinated for the population age 65 or older but that the care model would be similar. Care coordination would still center on risk assessment, a patient-specific plan of care, regular monitoring, and transition care, but the mix of the services and providers would differ. Services for individuals with disabilities would emphasize supporting independence and would include behavioral health, social, fitness, and other community-based services—such as assisting with meal preparation, finding accessible transportation and housing, and repairing wheelchairs.

Core Care Coordination Activities Were Similar

According to officials of coordinated care programs for dual-eligible beneficiaries, all the programs use multidisciplinary teams and conduct similar activities:

- assess and assign each patient to a risk group,
- design and periodically update an individualized care plan,
- assist the beneficiary in negotiating the health care and community service system,
- manage service use (including averting hospitalizations, nursing home stays, and emergency room visits),
- reconcile medications prescribed and check they have been taken, and
- coordinate behavioral and primary care.

Table 5-3. Integrated programs had common care coordination activities but intensity varies by patient

Common core activities	Activities vary by enrollee's care needs
• Assess patient risk	• Frequency of contact
• Individualize care plan	• Mix of providers
• Reconcile medications	• Mix of medical and social services
• Transition care	• Coordinator-to-patient ratios vary by services that require coordination
• Medical advice available 24/7	
• Regular contact with enrollee	
• Centralized electronic health record	

Note: SNP (special needs plan).
Source: MedPAC review of SNP models of care submitted to CMS.

When we asked care teams at integrated programs what core elements of their care coordination activities would be essential to replicate in any integrated care program, they replied that having medical advice available 24/7, the financial flexibility to furnish any needed service, and a centralized medical record accessible to all caregivers were key features.

All the coordinated care programs in our study assess all patients for their relative risk for costly services— including hospitalization, emergency room use, and institutionalization— and use this assessment to assign the enrollee to a level of care coordination. Programs vary, though, in how they assess each patient's care needs and risk for high-cost services. The intensity of the core care coordination activities varies based on the risk each patient poses for hospitalization, nursing home institutionalization, and medical complexity requiring coordination of many services (Table 5-3). For those patients with the least risk, care coordination includes periodic risk assessment, regular but less frequent communication with the beneficiary, reminders to keep medical appointments, documentation of changes to the patient's care regimen in the patient's medical chart, and medication reconciliation. These activities are intended to prevent beneficiaries' health status from deteriorating.

For beneficiaries at greater risk for hospitalization or institutionalization, programs focus on averting hospitalizations and making smooth transitions between care settings and the beneficiaries' living situation. Some programs place nurses in the nursing homes where dual-eligible beneficiaries are residents or make additional payments to the homes as a way to raise the facilities' level of nurse staffing. Community-dwelling beneficiaries otherwise certifiable for nursing home care have frequent contact with the care manager, medication management, and coordination of multiple medical and social service needs to avert hospitalizations and institutionalization. Even subtle changes in a patient's general orientation— such as dehydration, lack of eating, and increased need for supportive services at home—are followed up to avert hospitalizations.

Some programs use nurses to monitor and manage their enrollees' care in hospitals and have nurses visit beneficiaries during the hospital stay to begin care coordination before discharge. Nurses inform the hospital of a beneficiary's care before hospitalization (such as medication use), ensure that the beneficiary understands and follows care instructions after discharge, and inform the beneficiary's primary care team of any information from the hospitalization that would change the beneficiary's care regimen. Medication reconciliation, home visits to high-risk beneficiaries, and reassessment of the beneficiary are key components of transitional care. Care managers often coordinate a beneficiary's medical appointments, follow up to make sure the appointments are kept, and identify social services in the community if needed.

Program officials commented that when their enrollees are a small share of a nursing facility's or hospital's volume, it is often difficult to focus attention on averting hospitalizations or managing care transitions. Some programs use a limited number of institutional providers to give them leverage to change provider behavior.

Lack of Real-Time Data Hinders Care Coordination

Lack of real-time data on dual-eligible beneficiaries' Medicare utilization was a challenge for many of the integrated care programs. Many of the entities we interviewed did not receive utilization data on Medicare-funded services—most importantly, on their use of prescription drugs, hospitalizations, and physician services. This lack of information makes it very difficult for them to manage beneficiaries' care and to realize the savings from better coordinated care.

To work around this lack of information, some entities have developed their own mechanisms to obtain patient data on hospitalizations but often receive this information after the patient is discharged. For example, one managed care entity in New Mexico estimated that it does not learn about one-quarter of hospitalizations until it reviews claims for payment. In contrast, PACE providers learn about hospitalizations immediately given their almost daily contact with participants and their families. The CMS physician group practice demonstration illustrated that Medicare data are unlikely to flow to providers on a real-time basis and that successful entities will develop their own systems for gathering the information they need to manage their populations, including phone calls from hospitals when patients are admitted or an accessible common electronic health record. The North Carolina network recently launched a web-based portal to facilitate providers' access to the health records for program enrollees.

Increasing Enrollment Is a Challenge for Many State Programs

Increasing the number of dual-eligible beneficiaries served by fully integrated plans that include long-term care will be a challenge for many states and plans. Except for PACE, few programs integrate acute care, long-term care, and behavioral health services. Only 13 states include or plan to include long-term care services in managed care (Smith et al. 2010). Most Medicaid managed care plans and MA plans exclude the dual-eligible population and, if they do include them, they do not cover long-term care services. Despite the success of the PACE program (evaluations show the program's lower hospitalizations and emergency room visits (Chatterji et al. 1998)), fewer than 1 percent of beneficiaries enroll in this provider-based program. Though existing programs may grow incrementally, large expansions in enrollment are unlikely without major changes in policy.

Interviewees' Ideas to Expand Growth Incrementally

Given the small scale of most existing programs and the limited results, increasing the number and size of programs is likely to happen incrementally. Interviewees in our study discussed ways for states and Medicare to increase voluntary enrollment. Some thought that information about integrated programs sent by the state or Medicare would be more likely to be read than materials sent directly from a program.

Interviewees also thought the MA marketing and membership materials (whose format and content are developed by CMS) could better explain the Medicare and Medicaid benefits enrollees receive through the integrated program (such as help managing their prescription drugs; furnishing transition care between settings; and covering podiatry, vision, dental, and personal care assistants at home) to make it easier for beneficiaries to appreciate the value of integrated programs.

Some SNP representatives thought the requirements for the SNP descriptions were not tailored to integrated programs and resulted in informational materials that were inaccurate and confusing. For example, fully integrated SNPs must describe Medicaid benefits in a section separate from the explanation of Medicare benefits, even though the beneficiary would receive both sets of benefits through the plan. Interviewees also noted that the materials need to be made easier to understand for dual-eligible beneficiaries whose education levels tend to be low or for whom the materials are not available in their primary language. CMS could approve a template for fully integrated SNPs that is tailored to the benefits dual-eligible beneficiaries would receive through the program.

Some Interviewees Perceived Voluntary Enrollment as Limiting the Number of Eligible Beneficiaries Enrolled in Integrated Programs

Many interviewees in our study told us that Medicare's requirement for voluntary enrollment in coordinated care programs was a key limitation to expansion. Some thought an opt-out approach, in which beneficiaries are assigned to an integrated program with the option to switch to another integrated program or to fee-for-service, was needed to substantially increase enrollment in integrated programs. Supporters thought an opt-out policy could be designed to allow beneficiaries to switch integrated programs or select fee-for-service with an easy disenrollment process. Others opposed an opt-out policy for three reasons. First, they disagreed with a policy that would interfere with beneficiary choice of provider or require beneficiaries to change providers. Second, they contended that the opt-out policy does not consider the importance of beneficiary "buy in" to the program's approach, and the adherence needed for the program to be successful. Third, opponents maintained that the programs could limit the independence of individuals with disabilities and their access to needed social and community services.

Sharing Medicare Savings Would Raise Interest in Integrated Programs

Officials we spoke with thought the lack of ability for states to share the Medicare savings and the slower rate of realizing state savings inhibited the development of new programs. State officials and program administrators told us they were reluctant to develop integrated programs that save Medicare money mostly by reducing hospitalizations and emergency room visits. They said the savings that result from lower nursing home use require costly state investments and take a longer time to realize, making it difficult for states to commit the necessary resources to start integrated programs in the current budget environment. Officials from states with integrated programs said they hope to realize Medicaid savings from better managed Medicare-covered services that may, in turn, lower spending on long-term care.

Key Information Is Often Missing from D–SNP Model-of-Care Descriptions but Is Available from Other Data Sources

The model-of-care descriptions submitted by D–SNPs to CMS vary considerably in content, with most lacking the detail needed to assess whether the plan offered coordinated and integrated services tailored to their enrolled populations. This finding is not surprising, as D– SNPs are not required to report on many of these elements. The lack of reporting does not necessarily indicate that D–SNPs are not conducting these key care coordination activities, only that the activities were not described. Other data were not available to determine whether the quality of the SNPs' model-of-care descriptions was related to the quality of care the plans delivered or whether the plans coordinated or integrated the care they furnished. Given the multiple requirements for SNPs to report their care coordination and integration activities, CMS may want to consider targeting and streamlining its model-of-care requirements.

Models of Care Generally Do Not Describe Their Enrolled Population

Most D–SNP models of care note "all duals" or "full duals" as their enrolled population, but they do not describe additional population characteristics—such as the percentage of the population that have disabilities, are under age 65, have dementia, are frail, are nursing home certifiable, or have multiple chronic conditions. In addition, most models of care did not specify whether the D–SNP limited enrollment to a group of dual-eligible beneficiaries. Two plans stated that they enrolled nursing home certifiable individuals, while another plan excluded individuals who were not full dual eligibles (individuals eligible for Medicare and all Medicaid benefits). Because the description of the enrolled population was not included in most of the models of care, in most cases, it is not possible to assess whether a model of care is appropriately tailored to the enrolled population. The descriptions of the populations may improve because the scoring method NCQA will use to rate a D–SNP's model of care considers information about characteristics of the Medicare and Medicaid populations served by the plan.

More frequently, plans described limiting their integrated programs to specific enrollees, such as beneficiaries with certain chronic conditions, or to those who elected to participate in care management. Participation in care coordination was voluntary in almost one-fifth of models of care we reviewed. One D–SNP required beneficiaries to mail back a survey or call member services or their primary care physician to participate. In D–SNPs with voluntary participation, some continued to monitor the utilization of beneficiaries who opted out and, if spending was high, they asked beneficiaries midyear to reconsider their decision.

A few D–SNPs submitted the same model of care for more than one type of SNP. For example, in some cases, the D– SNP's model-of-care description was the same as for the chronic care SNP, the institutional SNP, or both. In one instance, the model of care did not differentiate between the D–SNP and the chronic care SNP on any elements. While some care coordination activities and benefits could be expected to be the same across all SNP populations, the lack of differentiation in some of the models of care brings into question whether the care management activities were in fact tailored to meet the distinct needs of the different special needs populations.

Models of Care Do Not Discuss Key Elements of Care Coordination

The majority of the D–SNP models of care included very little discussion of the key elements of care coordination. Specifically, activities to ensure good transitions between sites of care, medication reconciliation, patient education, and real-time utilization management were typically not mentioned or only vaguely described. In contrast, most D– SNPs discussed how they assess patient risk. Plans are not required to include the key elements in their submissions and only a handful of plans clearly stated their specific care coordination activities (Table 5-4). The NCQA scoring of plans may improve some of these descriptions (see specifics below).

Table 5-4. Excerpt from a strong dual SNP's model-of-care description on transition care and patient education activities

	Description
Transition care	• During care transitions, SNP staff will make postdischarge calls to review discharge plans and medications, to make sure that members understand the discharge instructions, and to make sure that follow-up care is scheduled and appropriate. • The case manager is responsible for ensuring that all relevant clinical information is sent to the institution the member is transitioning to, performing postdischarge calls to ensure members understand discharge orders and have access to medications and services, and investigating adverse events such as medication errors and inappropriate discharges and providing feedback to providers and institutions regarding transitions.

Table 5-4. (Continued)

	Description
Patient education	• High-risk members receive a complete condition-specific assessment, review of the current treatment plan, health education, and calls from a nurse health coach to discuss the member's goals. • Low-risk members receive ongoing health education related to their chronic condition and they can contact a nurse health coach.

Note: SNP (special needs plan).
Source: MedPAC review of SNP models of care submitted to CMS.

Transition Care

About half of the D–SNPs did not mention how they managed beneficiaries' transitions between settings. Of the plans that discussed this element, the transitional care activities most frequently noted were coordinating with hospital discharge planners and ensuring that beneficiaries made the follow-up medical appointments listed in the discharge plan. The majority of plans that reported on care transitions began their discharge planning process once the patient was home. A handful of plans mentioned that transitional care included movement between multiple settings, not just between the hospital and home. This aspect of models of care may improve because NCQA will score each plan's narratives of how the plan will know whether it has achieved its goals to improve seamless transitions across settings.

Medication Reconciliation

Fewer than half of the D–SNP models of care described activities of medication reconciliation. For a majority of plans, we could not determine whether the plans reconciled medications at initial enrollment, after hospital stays, or on a regular basis. In contrast, one D–SNP described its efforts in detail. The plan described reviewing the lists of enrollees' medications, opening medication containers, and ensuring that beneficiaries understood how to store the medication. Only a handful of plans mentioned conducting a medication review in the beneficiary's home, which some integrated programs told us is the most effective way to see which medications a beneficiary takes.

Patient Education

Another area lacking in detail was how D–SNPs educate patients about their medical conditions and about how to seek care before a condition becomes acute. Although the majority of plans had a 24-hour nurse advice line, most plans did not describe whether patients were taught how to recognize signs of a worsening condition, who to call, and when to go to the emergency room. The models of care may become more specific in this aspect of care coordination. NCQA's scoring will evaluate a plan's description of the efforts the plan makes to educate beneficiaries and beneficiaries' access to the interdisciplinary care team.

Table 5-5. One D–SNP's description of efforts to coordinate with Medicaid

Description
• The SNP has a team that assists with the coordination of Medicare and Medicaid benefits and assists with directing members to community resources when needed. The SNPs' customer service department representatives are trained in coordination of benefits so that they can provide accurate information to members.
• SNP staff maintain a registry of service organizations and governmental agencies in the SNPs' service areas and direct members to housing assistance, legal and financial counseling, and community support groups.
• The members are provided with a provider directory that indicates which providers accept both Medicare and Medicaid. Also, the SNP's service representatives discuss Medicare and Medicaid benefit coordination with providers during in-person meetings and educational material.
• Care managers are able to view changes in members' Medicaid eligibility, access coverage, and contact information and assist members in the coordination of benefits.

Note: D–SNP (dual-eligible special needs plan).
Source: MedPAC review of D–SNP models of care submitted to CMS.

Real-Time Utilization Management

Most D–SNP models of care did not discuss real-time utilization management. While many plans tracked emergency room use, many models did not discuss how plans tracked other resource use, such as an admission, in real time so that care could be coordinated. Some plans noted that a requirement for prior authorization triggered care management. A handful of models of care focused less on care management than on describing prior authorization, bringing out-of-network use within the network, and identifying when services were no longer needed. NCQA will score each plan's narratives of how the plan will know whether it has achieved its goals to ensure appropriate service use.

Coordination with Medicaid Benefits

Despite the fact that dual-eligible beneficiaries, by definition, can receive benefits from both Medicare and Medicaid, D–SNP model-of-care descriptions are not required to report on their efforts to coordinate beneficiaries' Medicaid benefits. Most of the D–SNP models of care we reviewed did not describe efforts to coordinate dual-eligible beneficiaries' Medicaid benefits and did not discuss which, if any, Medicaid benefits the plan covered. D–SNPs are not required to report on their coordination with Medicaid and the majority of D–SNPs did not. Of the few plans that mentioned coordinating with Medicaid, the descriptions were vague. For example, most of the D–SNPs did not state which of the following activities they provided: covering Medicaid services in their benefit packages, finding providers that accept Medicaid, coordinating services covered by Medicaid, explaining Medicaid benefits to dual-eligible beneficiaries, and assisting with claims and coverage decisions. Even if the plans did not cover Medicaid benefits, coordination activities would facilitate dual-eligible beneficiaries' access to Medicaid services. Only a handful of plans noted that they helped inform beneficiaries about their Medicaid benefits or helped identify Medicaid providers (see Table 5-5 for one D–SNP's description).

Fewer than one-quarter of the plans we reviewed specified whether the D–SNP had a contract with the state and, if so, what the contract covered. The lack of reporting on Medicaid coordination did not appear to be related to whether a D–SNP had a contract with a state or was fully integrated. For example, one D–SNP stated that it was also a Medicaid managed care plan, but the model of care described only the members' Medicare benefits and not how coordination with Medicaid benefits would occur. The plan's patient questionnaire implied that the health plan coordinated Medicare and Medicaid benefits, but it was not clear whether dual-eligible members had the same case manager for their Medicare and Medicaid benefits or separate case managers.

Enrollee Risk Assessment

Assessing enrollees' risk for high use of costly services was the one key care coordination element in our framework that most D–SNP models of care described, which is not surprising given that detailing a plan's health risk assessment is one of the required elements in the model-of-care description. In general, D–SNP enrollees are initially surveyed, usually by paper survey or telephone, about their health, their ability to perform daily activities, their mental state, and, less frequently, their use of prescription medications and recent hospitalizations. This information is often combined with existing Medicare data on utilization and the beneficiary's risk score (the CMS–hierarchical condition categories (CMS–HCC) score) in assigning an enrollee to a risk group. For example, many plans use a predictive model that combines information on diagnoses (especially chronic conditions), severity, recent emergency room and hospital use, and CMS–HCC score. Less frequently, the stratification considers referrals from providers, the use of hospice/palliative care, an assessment of the enrollee's social isolation and risk for depression or falls, laboratory results indicating a worsening condition, pharmacy data indicating high-cost patients, diet and exercise, and whether the enrollee has received services from multiple specialists or lacks a primary care provider. A minority of plans mentioned conducting a home or in-person assessment for enrollees identified as high risk based on an initial assessment. Only one plan mentioned doing a cultural assessment. Enrollee risk groups are often disease specific, based on the enrollee's frailty and risk for hospitalization.

Most D–SNPs described reassessing the risk level assigned to enrollees at least annually. In these plans, certain service use—most often hospitalizations, emergency room or behavioral health service use, and specific patterns of prescription drug spending—prompts reevaluation. Without specific events that generally trigger a reassessment, plans' frequency of assessments varied by risk level and plan. For example, one plan reassessed its enrollees monthly, bimonthly, or every three months, depending on the risk group. Another plan offered case management to dual-eligible beneficiaries with specific chronic conditions and reassessed them every three months; all other enrollees were evaluated annually. A couple of plans contract out their periodic evaluations, with specific problems forwarded to them for follow-up.

Table 5-6. Publicly reported quality data on special needs plans are limited

	Star ratings	heDIS® measures	NCQa structure and process measures
Year data made available	Every year	2008	Not made available
Limitations	• SNP data are included under a broader contract with non-SNP plans. • Many SNPs have small enrollments— ratings are missing for many plans.	• No composite measure • Many SNPs have small enrollments—many plans have missing data.	• No composite score to summarize a plan's performance across the measures.

Note: HEDIS (Healthcare Effectiveness Data and Information Set), NCQA (National Committee for Quality Assurance), SNP (special needs plan).

Source: MedPAC analysis of the public reporting of Medicare Advantage star ratings, HEDIS® measures, and NCQA structure and process measures.

Additional Care Coordination Information Is Available from Unpublished Data Sources

Our analysis of whether D–SNPs with stronger model-ofcare descriptions performed better on outcome measures was limited by a lack of publicly available quality data for D–SNPs. There are three potential sources for D– SNP quality-of-care data: MA plan star ratings, SNP-specific HEDIS subset measures, and NCQA structure and process measures. Of these sources, only the SNP-specific HEDIS subset measures are publicly available, but this information has not been updated since 2008. CMS could publish SNP-specific data to facilitate the evaluation of plans and beneficiary choice among SNPs, MA plans, and fee-for-service. Making the SNP HEDIS and NCQA data publicly available and developing and reporting SNP star ratings could help the policy community compare the quality of care of D–SNPs and identify areas for improvement. In addition, publicly reporting SNP-specific quality data could help dual-eligible beneficiaries make informed decisions when choosing among a SNP, another MA plan, an integrated care program, or fee-for-service.

Star Ratings Are Not Separately Calculated for Most Snps

It was not possible to discern whether the quality of the model-of-care descriptions was related to the D–SNPs' MA plan star rating, because most SNPs do not have their own star ratings (Table 5-6). Star rating information for most SNPs is included in the overall reporting under a larger MA contract, which includes non-SNP plans. As a result, the data used to calculate MA star ratings are not currently submitted at the SNP level. The exception is a health plan that is exclusively a SNP and has an enrollment large enough to calculate a rating.

The Commission has discussed the need for SNPs to have their own star ratings so that CMS and beneficiaries can compare a SNP's performance with regular MA plans.

To rate them under the star system, SNPs would need to submit data in addition to what is currently required. CMS may need to address the issue of small sample sizes for some of the individual measures—for example, by pooling a plan's data over multiple years.

Publicly Reported SNP-Specific HEDIS Measures Are Not Regularly Available

CMS has not published the results for the 15 HEDIS measures that SNPs have been required to report since 2008. Because the models of care we reviewed were submitted only by new or expanding plans that were generally not in operation in 2008, we were missing measures for most of the plans for which we had models of care. In reviewing the SNP-specific HEDIS data that were publicly available, we found this information difficult to use, particularly from a beneficiary's perspective.

For one thing, data are reported for individual HEDIS measures, but there is not a composite measure reflecting the overall performance across all measures. In addition, many of the HEDIS results are blank because SNPs' sample sizes were too small for measures to be calculated. A strategy such as pooling data over multiple years may be needed to obtain sufficient sample sizes for the smaller plans. CMS is planning to make public the more recent SNP-specific HEDIS results but has not set a timetable to do so.

NCQA Structure and Process Measures Are Not Publicly Reported

A SNP's structure and process measures are not publicly available; therefore, we were not able to compare the model-of-care descriptions with these data. This information is collected by NCQA and forwarded to CMS. To date, NCQA has not developed a composite measure to aggregate a plan's performance across all six measures.

Information D–SNPs Report Needs to Be Targeted and Streamlined

On the basis of our review of the D–SNP models of care, we have concluded that the model-of-care descriptions as currently submitted cannot be used to evaluate the care coordination for dual-eligible beneficiaries. However, CMS is undertaking several activities aimed at improving the models of care submitted by SNPs. In 2011, CMS held a series of training sessions for plans to learn what CMS expects in the models of care. Plans have been told to give specific examples for each element in the model of care. CMS also audited a sample of models of care, including site visits to verify that the plan conducted its activities as reported. CMS will use this information to revise and improve the models of care. CMS also intends to provide feedback to those plans and share the results of this review as part of a "best practices" discussion with all plans.

Last, CMS may develop template models of care for each type of SNP so that the submissions more closely match the target populations. While these efforts are aimed at the shortcomings associated with the currently required elements, they will not address the problem of missing key elements of care coordination that are not required as part of the MA approval process.

The Commission questions whether the model-of-care descriptions are necessary to assess if plans coordinate care, given that SNPs already submit documents that are easier to review and include more of the key elements of care coordination of integrated programs (see Table 5-2, p. 128). One alternative to the model of care is the attestation submitted as part of the MA application. Currently, this information is not reviewed as part of the model-of-care evaluation even though it includes information relevant to care coordination activities, such as the plan's transition care activities and medication reconciliation. Compared with the models of care, the format of the attestation questions is much simpler for plans to submit and easier for CMS to review. The attestation does not include questions about the D–SNP's coordination with Medicaid services, however, and those questions would need to be added to the attestation to make that tool complete.

Other alternatives to the model-of-care descriptions are the NCQA structure and process measures that SNPs are required to report. CMS could use these measures as the basis for NCQA's approval of SNPs rather than the model-of-care descriptions. The structure and process measures include many of the key care coordination and Medicaid integration elements of the integrated programs we researched. SNPs are already required to report on these measures and the information is collected in a survey format. Additional elements would need to be added or existing elements expanded to gauge all key care coordination elements, such as patient education. Compared with the model-of-care descriptions, the structure and process measures would be less burdensome for SNPs to report and for CMS to review. In addition, NCQA and CMS could develop a composite score of the measures to make them easier for beneficiaries to understand.

Another option is for CMS to focus on measuring the impact of care coordination through outcome measures (see discussion, p. 140) rather than on the model-of-care descriptions. Outcome measures would gauge whether care coordination has improved patient satisfaction, enhanced quality of life, and averted hospitalizations and emergency room use. The outcome measures could be collected in addition to data on structures and processes. Continuing to collect structure and process measures would facilitate our understanding of which care coordination activities result in good performance. CMS should decide which key elements of care coordination and outcomes programs should be required to report on and streamline its reporting requirements to that limited set.

Conclusions and Next Steps

Programs that integrate Medicare and Medicaid financing and are responsible for all services are more likely to have the flexibility to meet beneficiary care needs. The variation in programs across states reflects individual state circumstances and preferences toward integrated programs, availability of state resources to implement integrated programs, and the ability of states to overcome or accommodate providers' and advocates' concerns. Capitated, risk-based programs that integrate financing and care delivery offer the most promise for improving care coordination. However, not all states can or want to implement such programs. Also, fee-for-service overlays can begin to coordinate services for these beneficiaries. Low enrollment in integrated programs is a barrier and a large expansion in enrollment in these programs is unlikely without major policy changes.

Full Integration of Finances and Services Offers the Best Opportunity for Care Coordination

Fully integrated managed care plans and PACE providers offer the best opportunity to improve care coordination for dual-eligible beneficiaries across Medicare and Medicaid services. In these programs, an entity receives capitated payments from Medicare and Medicaid to offer and assume risk for all services to dual-eligible beneficiaries. Under one plan type, a managed care entity receives the payments; under the other, a PACE provider does. Because either entity is at full risk, it has the financial incentive to furnish an efficient, effective mix of services that lower total costs while improving patient outcomes. The entities also have the flexibility to intervene with whichever medical and social services are covered by Medicare and Medicaid and are necessary to help beneficiaries avoid hospitalizations, nursing home placements, and deterioration. PACE providers also have the flexibility to intervene with noncovered, nonclinical services such as fixing the carpet in beneficiaries' homes to prevent falls or supplying bottled water to prevent dehydration. In contrast, fee-for-service payment systems lack such financial incentives and flexibility and instead encourage individual providers to deliver a high volume of care, regardless of its clinical value or connection to services furnished by the patient's other providers.

Care Coordination within Fee-for-Service Medicare

Care coordination can operate within fee-for-service Medicare but this approach has less promise than capitated, risk-based integrated programs for effectively coordinating services. The range of services covered under the integrated program could vary from acute care services (as in the North Carolina primary care network) to longterm care and behavioral health services. Accountable care organizations (ACOs)—which combine a fee-for-service payment structure with some financial risk incentives— are also of interest with regard to care coordination for dual-eligible beneficiaries. Although more limited than capitated, full risk-based programs in the alignment of financial incentives, ACOs and other fee-for-service overlays represent a stepping stone to fuller integration in states unlikely to adopt managed care or full risk-based integrated arrangements.

A Single Program Design Is Not Likely to Be Adopted in Every State

States develop integrated care program designs based on a state's unique characteristics, including its approach to managing the Medicaid-only population, experience with managed care, providers' and advocates' concerns, presence of provider networks and managed care organizations, and the support of a strong leader to champion integrated care. Given the variation across states, it would be unlikely for states to embrace the same program approach, scale, or scope. In addition, there is no clear evidence about which programs are most effective for every type of dual-eligible beneficiary.

Acknowledging that multiple designs might be needed to match the varying states' environments, the Federal Coordinated Health Care Office at CMS requested proposals from states to design and implement programs to coordinate the care for dual-eligible beneficiaries. CMS has funded 15 contracts to assist states in developing a range of integrated care program designs.

Increasing Differentiation among D–SNPs

Recognizing that D–SNPs need to coordinate Medicaid-financed services, CMS has begun to distinguish between fully integrated SNPs and other D–SNPs. PPACA defines a fully integrated D–SNP as a D–SNP with a capitated contract with a state to provide Medicaid benefits, including long-term care. SNPs that meet this definition and enroll patients with similar average frailty levels as PACE providers will receive a frailty adjustment.

CMS is also considering an initiative to promote enrollment in high-quality, fully integrated SNPs beginning in 2013. The fully integrated SNPs that qualify for this initiative may be eligible for flexibilities that would encourage care coordination and simplify administrative procedures. CMS has not determined how high quality will be defined, how enrollment in these plans will be promoted, or what types of flexibilities the qualifying SNPs will be eligible for. In our research on integrated programs, we found that PACE providers had more flexibility in how they used Medicare payments than SNPs because SNPs are not permitted to use Medicare dollars to cover non-health-care services and may be able to offer nonclinical services only if they are covered under Medicaid.

Consistent Set of Outcome Measures Is Needed to Evaluate Integrated Programs

Common performance measures are critical to evaluating alternative designs for integrated programs. The evaluation should include cost, administration, and quality measures. Cost measures should consider the total annual cost of all services to both programs. It is important to know, for example, if a program that is narrow in scope has lowered its own spending but has shifted costs to services and providers beyond its purview. Administrative measures could evaluate the efficiency of program administration (medical loss ratio), call waiting times for enrollees, and disenrollment rates. Outcome measures could include patient satisfaction, quality of life, hospital admission and readmission rates, rates of emergency room use, institutionalization for long-term care, and medication errors. In its 2012 call letter, CMS outlined plans to add several outcome measures to the MA plan star ratings, including all-cause admission rates, risk-adjusted mortality rates, preventable hospitalizations, and serious reportable adverse events including hospital-acquired conditions.

The collection and public reporting of these measures for integrated programs, MA plans, SNPs, and fee-for-service Medicare would allow for comparisons across programs. Beginning in 2012, all MA plans, including SNPs, have to submit encounter data that will allow some of these outcome measures to be calculated, including hospital admissions and readmissions and emergency room use.

In addition, MA plans will begin reporting all-cause readmission rates in 2011.

In addition to outcome measures, programs should report on a consistent set of measures focused on care coordination activities. This set would need to measure activities associated with care transitions, medication reconciliation, patient education, utilization management, and coordination with Medicaid benefits.

Next Steps

In the coming year, the Commission plans to continue its work identifying key elements of care coordination that should be components of any form of integrated care program. In addition, it plans to explore the key elements of provider-based models of integrated care. Last, the Commission will examine an opt-out policy to increase enrollment in integrated programs and whether one could be designed to minimize the risks for providers and beneficiaries, while ensuring beneficiary protections.

Endnotes

[1] PACE coordinates all services for dual-eligible beneficiaries who require the level of care furnished in a nursing home, referred to as nursing-home certifiable. Currently, there are 75 PACE providers around the country, enrolling more than 18,000 dual-eligible beneficiaries (National PACE Association 2010).

[2] The other two types of SNPs—institutional SNPs and chronic SNPs—may also enroll dual-eligible beneficiaries. Some individual institutional or chronic SNPs enroll mostly dual-eligible beneficiaries.

[3] In the medical home model, primary care practitioners are typically paid an extra fee on a per member per month basis to coordinate care for patients between visits and across providers.

References

Center for Health Care Strategies. 2010. *Dual eligibles: Opportunities to integrate care.* Hamilton, NJ: CHCS.

Centers for Medicare & Medicaid Services, Department of Health and Human Services. 2010. Announcement of calendar year 2011 Medicare Advantage capitation rates and Medicare Advantage and Part D payment policies and final call letter. http://www.cms.gov/MedicareAdvtgSpecRateStat/downloads/announcement2011.pdf.

Centers for Medicare & Medicaid Services, Department of Health and Human Services. 2011a. 2012 Part C MA cost plan application. http://www.cms.gov/MedicareAdvantageApps.

Centers for Medicare & Medicaid Services, Department of Health and Human Services. 2011b. Special needs plan approval process scoring criteria for contract year 2012. Memo from Danielle Moon, Director, Medicare Drug and Health Plan Contract Administration Group. April 5.

Chatterji, P., N. R. Burstein, D. Kidder, et al. 1998. *Evaluation of the Program of All-Inclusive Care for the Elderly (PACE) demonstration: The impact of PACE on participant outcomes.* HCFA contract 500–96–0003/TO4. Report prepared by Abt Associates for the Health Care Financing Administration. Baltimore, MD: HCFA.

Medicare Payment Advisory Commission. 2008. *Report to the Congress: Medicare payment policy.* Washington, DC: MedPAC.

Medicare Payment Advisory Commission. 2010. *Report to the Congress: Aligning incentives in Medicare.* Washington, DC: MedPAC.

National PACE Association. 2010. PACE in the States. October. http://www.npaonline.org/website/download.asp?id=1741.

Smith, V. K., K. Gifford, E. Ellis, et al. 2010. *Hoping for economic recovery, preparing for health reform: A look at Medicaid spending, coverage and policy trends. Results from a 50-state Medicaid budget survey for state fiscal years 2010 and 2011.* Prepared by staff from Health Management Associates and the Kaiser Commission on Medicaid and the Uninsured/Kaiser Family Foundation. Washington, DC: KCMU.

Verdier, J. M., M. Au, and J. Gillooly. 2010. *Managing the care of dual eligible beneficiaries: A review of selected state programs and special needs plans.* Report prepared by Mathematica Policy Research for MedPAC. Washington, DC: MedPAC.

Federally Qualified Health Centers

Summary

Federally qualified health centers (FQHCs) provide access to primary care in areas where primary care resources are constrained. In 2009, FQHCs that received federal grant funding (which comprise over 80 percent of all FQHCs) served 18.8 million people, including 1.4 million Medicare beneficiaries. Total operating revenue for these FQHCs in 2009 was $11.5 billion, with 6 percent from Medicare ($674 million).

FQHCs are required to be community-centered and either not-for-profit or public organizations that emphasize coordination of care. They make use of physician assistants, advanced practice nurses, and clinical nurse midwives where appropriate. Patients at FQHCs are predominantly low income and largely uninsured or covered by Medicaid.

The Medicare FQHC benefit provides primary and preventive care to Medicare beneficiaries. Historically, the Medicare program has reimbursed FQHCs according to an all-inclusive per visit payment rate based on the reasonable costs reported by the centers, subject to productivity targets for medical practitioners and a dollar limit on the per visit payment.

The Patient Protection and Affordable Care Act of 2010 establishes a Medicare prospective payment system (PPS) for FQHCs starting October 1, 2014. In the first year of the PPS, aggregate payments under the PPS must equal the estimated payments that would have occurred under the current reasonable cost payment system without regard to the productivity target or the per visit upper payment limit. The result will likely be higher total payments on average. A great deal of flexibility is afforded to the Secretary of the Department of Health and Human Services in the design of a Medicare FQHC PPS, including the ability to create a system with differentiation of payment rates by service and intensity.

This chapter focuses on FQHCs for three reasons. First, FQHCs are illustrative of a team-based approach to primary care, relying on advanced practice nurses, physician assistants, and other nonphysician practitioners as well as physicians. Second, FQHCs are required to provide care in medically underserved areas or to treat medically underserved populations and play a role in meeting primary care capacity challenges in low-density rural areas. Third, the change in Medicare's payment system from a per visit cost-based reimbursement to a PPS will likely result in higher payments to FQHCs, thus encouraging these providers to serve more Medicare beneficiaries.

Introduction

Federally qualified health centers (FQHCs) provide a resource for primary and preventive care outside the private practice physician's office. In meeting federal requirements for FQHCs, these clinics provide an integrated model of health care delivery emphasizing a team-based approach.

Community health centers started as locally run institutions providing care to indigent and underserved people in the early 1960s; in 1965, the federal government created a demonstration program that funded these community health centers as part of the Office of Economic Opportunity, which ran many of the War on Poverty programs. The current model of providing grants to FQHCs was established in 1975; in 1996, three different funding streams were merged to create the consolidated health center grant program under Section 330 of the Public Health Act. Currently, the Health Resources and Services Administration (HRSA) is responsible for distributing grants to FQHCs.

In 1990, the FQHC benefit under Medicare and the FQHC benefit under Medicaid were established (Taylor 2004). Most grant-funded health centers are classified as general community health centers that serve all populations; however, some centers target specific populations, such as residents of public housing and homeless and migrant farmworker communities.

Three types of entities are eligible to become FQHCs under Medicare and Medicaid: health centers that receive federal grant funds under Section 330 of the Public Health Service Act (PHSA), known as health center grantees; health centers that do not receive a federal grant but meet all the requirements of the grant program, known as lookalikes; and certain outpatient clinics operated by the Indian Health Service.[1] Health center grantees constitute the vast majority—over 80 percent—of all FQHCs. After receiving a grant under Section 330 or a designation as a look-alike, health centers must request that CMS designate them as an FQHC to receive payment for delivering Medicare and Medicaid benefits. The Medicare FQHC certification process requires each FQHC site to be separately approved for Medicare participation.

At present, 1,131 centers receive grants under Section 330 of the PHSA. These grantees deliver care at approximately 7,800 sites; in addition to the 1,131 central grantee locations, there are nearly 6,700 sites ranging from full clinics to satellite sites open a few days a week to mobile vans. In addition to the 1,131 grant-funded centers, 106 centers are certified as FQHC look-alikes. In comparison to the 7,800 federally funded health center sites, there are roughly 4,900 Medicare-participating FQHC sites as of April 2011. To be certified as an FQHC, each center location must be certified separately, whereas a grant-funded health center may operate multiple sites under the same program. We use the term FQHC in this chapter to refer to health centers that are certified by CMS to deliver the Medicare and Medicaid FQHC benefit.

FQHCs Are Federally Qualified Nonprofit Organizations Delivering Primary Care

FQHCs offer primary and preventive medical care and enabling services (such as translation, transportation, and care management) that help individuals access care (Government Accountability Office 2010). About three-quarters of FQHCs offer preventive dental and mental health treatment on site, while about half of FQHCs offer substance abuse treatment on site (Shi et al. 2010). Most FQHCs also have laboratory services on site or by arrangement and may also perform minor procedures. In a 2009 survey of FQHCs, 40 percent of centers indicated that they used electronic medical records (Commonwealth Fund 2010). This number is comparable to the adoption rate for physician offices (48 percent) and is significantly higher than the adoption rate in hospitals (12 percent) (Jha et al. 2010, National Center for Health Statistics 2010). FQHCs are not eligible for Medicare electronic health record (EHR) incentive payments, although the individual clinical professionals who practice in an FQHC may be eligible for either the Medicare or the Medicaid EHR payments if they meet certain eligibility criteria (Centers for Medicare & Medicaid Services 2011c).

Providers may deliver FQHC services at approved locations that are not health center sites, such as providing medical rounds at a hospital or visits at a patient's home. If an FQHC is in an area with a designated shortage of home health agencies, it may also provide visiting nurse services (Health Resources and Services Administration 2006).

FQHCs Receive Federal Benefits that Supplement Grants and Payments from Federal Health Programs

FQHCs are eligible for certain benefits beyond the federal grant. All FQHCs can participate in the Health Resources and Services Administration's 340B drug discount program, which can help centers save from 20 percent to 50 percent on the cost of pharmaceuticals (Health Resources and Services Administration 2011c). Grantees and their practitioners, staff, and board members can be covered under the Federal Tort Claims Act program, which eliminates the need for these individuals and the health center to obtain private malpractice insurance (Health Resources and Services Administration 2006). FQHC grantees are also eligible for federal loan guarantees for capital improvements.

FQHCs Deliver Accessible Care to Underserved Populations and Incorporate Community Representation

HRSA runs the FQHC grant program under Section 330 of the PHSA. An organization applying for an FQHC grant can deliver care at one or more service sites that are most appropriate for the center's target population. The Section 330 statute specifies the services that health center grantees are required to provide (for more detail, see the section on Medicare's FQHC benefit and payment mechanism). These requirements apply at the grantee level—not at the level of individual service sites. As a result, not all required services are provided at every grantee service site, and each service site does not necessarily have to provide care year-round or cover all working hours. The HRSA requirements for FQHCs state that the patient "must have reasonable access to the full complement of services offered by the center as a whole" (Health Resources and Services Administration 2007). This requirement could result in a site offering a limited set of services, provided that the main grantee location offers reasonable access to other services the FQHC is required to provide.

Service sites include permanent sites, which are open year-round in a defined location, seasonal sites, mobile van sites, and other intermittent sites. For example, an FQHC focusing on delivering care to the homeless could provide year-round care at a permanent site as well as operating a van at locations the homeless population uses during certain times of the year. FQHCs must also provide off-hours coverage (e.g., through providers on call) and have admitting privileges at local hospitals.

FQHCs Must Have a Board that Is Representative of the Population They Serve

Given their role as community-based safety net providers, FQHCs are subject to fairly extensive governance requirements. They are required to have a board of between 9 and 25 people, with a majority of the members being patients receiving services from the FQHC. The remaining members must be selected for their expertise in community affairs, local government, finance and banking, legal affairs, trade unions, commercial and industrial concerns, or social service agencies (Health Resources and Services Administration 2011a). The board is required to meet monthly and cannot have any members who are employed by the center. No more than half of the consumer board members can derive more than 10 percent of their income from the health care industry, and the center must have a conflict of interest policy for board members.

The board must have responsibility for setting personnel policies; overseeing the center's financial management and budget; ensuring compliance with state, federal, and local laws; approving the selection of the director or chief executive officer of the center; and defining the health benefits delivered by the center, including the scope of services, the location, and hours of service delivery (Centers for Medicare & Medicaid Services 2011a).

FQHCs Must Be Located in Medical Shortage Areas or Treat Medically Underserved Populations

Medically underserved areas (MUAs) and medically underserved populations (MUPs) are designations made by HRSA and identify areas or populations with insufficient access to primary care and a high infant mortality rate, a high poverty rate, or a high share of the population that is elderly (Health Resources and Services Administration 2011a). FQHCs must be located in MUAs or serve MUPs and document the needs of its target population (Health Resources and Services Administration 2011a).

MUAs and MUPs are similar but not identical to health professional shortage areas (HPSAs), which are areas that have a shortage of primary, dental, or mental health care. All FQHCs receive an automatic designation as an HPSA facility, which permits them to hire clinical staff through the National Health Service Corps (NHSC) program.

There Are Similarities between FQHCs and Rural Health Clinics, Although Differences Remain

Given the presence of FQHCs in rural areas, a brief discussion of rural health clinics (RHCs) is warranted. In 1977, the Congress created RHCs to deliver primary care in rural areas to Medicare and Medicaid beneficiaries. CMS approves RHCs as eligible for participation in the Medicare and Medicaid programs (Centers for Medicare & Medicaid Services 2010b). As of September 2010, there were 3,820 RHCs in 45 states. RHCs can be provider based or freestanding, and they can be nonprofit, for profit, or operated by a state or local government. RHCs can be established by physician offices that include specialty care as long as the physician office can establish that the goal of the practice is primary care (Health Resources and Services Administration 2006).

Section 1861(aa)(2) of the Social Security Act requires that, when applying for determination as an RHC for the purpose of Medicare payment, RHCs must be in a nonurbanized area. For the purposes of the RHC program, a nonurbanized area is an area outside of an urban area, which is defined as a densely settled area with at least 50,000 residents. Upon establishment, RHCs must also be located in an area that within the previous four years was designated as a shortage area. Under Section 1861(aa) (2), shortage areas for the purposes of RHC designation include MUAs, HPSAs, and a shortage area as designated by the state governor. The Secretary of the Department of Health and Human Services must certify the shortage designation.

The Medicare RHC benefit includes services delivered by physicians, nurse practitioners, physician assistants, and other medical professionals as well as services and supplies incident to such services, visiting nurse services, services of registered dieticians or nutritional professionals, and otherwise covered drugs furnished by physicians and other practitioners (Centers for Medicare & Medicaid Services 2009). Preventive care under the RHC benefit is limited to those services that otherwise would be covered under Medicare Part B, whereas the Medicare FQHC benefit includes the primary care services that FQHCs are required to provide under the conditions of their Section 330 grant (Centers for Medicare & Medicaid Services 2009).

Medicare's method of reimbursing RHCs is similar to the reimbursement method for FQHCs—an all-inclusive payment rate that incorporates per visit payment limits and provider productivity caps. The per visit payment limit for RHCs is $78.07 in 2011, and RHCs based in hospitals with fewer than 50 beds receive cost-based reimbursement without respect to the per visit payment limit (Centers for Medicare & Medicaid Services 2009, Centers for Medicare & Medicaid Services 2010a). The per visit payment amount for RHCs is less than the per visit payment amount for FQHCs—which is $109.24 for rural FQHCs and $126.22 for urban FQHCs in 2011 (Centers for Medicare & Medicaid Services 2010a). To receive payment from Medicare, RHCs and FQHCs file cost reports that indicate the type of visit and the cost of providing services. Starting in January 2011, FQHCs will report HCPCS codes for their patients to facilitate CMS's development of the new FQHC prospective payment system (PPS). However, RHCs will not report HCPCS codes for their patients, as they will continue to be paid based on an all-inclusive payment rate.

In considering the difference in the upper payment limit for FQHCs and RHCs, it is worth noting the differences between the services provided, and the population served, by FQHCs and RHCs. First, FQHCs must provide preventive primary health services as required by Section 330 of the PHSA, while the preventive health services provided by RHCs is limited to those who would otherwise be covered under the Medicare Part B benefit (discussed in more detail in the section on Medicare's FQHC benefit and payment mechanism). Second, FQHCs are required to accept patients without regard to their ability to pay. While some RHCs do offer a sliding scale of charges or accept patients without regard to their ability to pay, they are not required to do so. RHCs that establish a sliding scale of patient charges and accept all patients without regard to their ability to pay can be designated as an HPSA facility, which allows them to hire from the NHSC.

Given the differences in payments, services, and patient populations, it will be important to fully understand the complement of services provided by FQHCs and RHCs, as well as physician offices and other Medicare providers, particularly in anticipation of the upcoming changes in Medicare's reimbursement to FQHCs from a cost-based per visit payment amount to a PPS. This change could further widen the differences in reimbursement across settings, making it more critical that policymakers understand the differences in the benefit package, intensity, and patient mix across different primary care providers.

FQHCs Rely on a Range of Clinical Staff to Deliver Care

Among the 43,000 medical professionals employed at FQHCs, more than 9,100 are physicians; 5,800 are nurse practitioners, physician assistants, or clinical nurse midwives; and the balance are nurses and other medical personnel (Health Resources and Services Administration 2010). Medicare pays the same rate for an FQHC visit whether it is provided by a physician or an advanced practice nurse, physician assistant, or clinical nurse midwife.[2] This reliance on advanced practice nurses, physician assistants, and clinical nurse midwives to deliver care where appropriate is one of the original principles behind establishment of the FQHC Medicare benefit. An FQHC run by a physician assistant, nurse practitioner, or other health professional must have an arrangement with a physician to supervise these staff.[3] Work done by all practitioners at an FQHC must comply with state law regarding scope of practice (Centers for Medicare & Medicaid Services 2009).

FQHCs Face Challenges in Recruiting and Retaining Health Professionals and Obtaining Specialty Referrals

FQHCs experience some difficulty recruiting and retaining clinical staff, particularly specialty providers (mental health, dental, and obstetrician or gynecologist practitioners). A 2006 study by Rosenblatt and colleagues found that 13 percent of family physician or general practitioner slots at FQHCs were vacant, and certain specialties had even higher vacancy rates—21 percent of obstetrician or gynecologist slots were vacant and 23 percent of psychiatrist slots were vacant (Rosenblatt et al. 2006).

Federal Hiring and Loan Repayment Programs Help FQHCs Recruit Health Professionals

All FQHCs—because of their designation as health professional shortage facilities—are permitted to hire from the NHSC, which provides grants to students applying to medical or professional schools if they agree to work at FQHCs or other designated safety net providers.

The NHSC also runs a loan repayment program for practitioners who have already completed their training. FQHCs make up the largest single placement site for NHSC health professionals (Kaiser Commission on Medicaid and the Uninsured 2010). FQHCs also hire staff through the Conrad 30 (J-1 waiver) visa program for foreign medical graduates. Among a survey of FQHC grantees, 24 percent used the NHSC scholarship program, 36 percent used the NHSC loan repayment program, and 32 percent used the J-1 visa program to fill at least one physician position (Rosenblatt et al. 2006).

FQHCs Sometimes Face Difficulty in Securing Specialty Referrals, which Is Often Related to the Patient's Insurance Status

A successful referral from an FQHC to a specialist often depends on the insurance status of the patient and the patient's ability to absorb the cost of specialty care if the patient's insurance does not cover it (Gusmano et al. 2002, Shi et al. 2010). A study of the 2006 National Ambulatory Medical Care Survey (NAMCS) did not find a large difference in the rate of FQHCs (14 percent) and physician offices (10 percent) saying they had "a lot of difficulty" or "some difficulty" in referring Medicare patients to specialists. However, more FQHCs and physician offices reported "a lot of difficulty" referring Medicaid patients (16 percent for FQHCs, 22 percent for physician offices) and uninsured patients (46 percent for FQHCs, 24 percent for physician offices) to specialists (Shi et al. 2010). In a survey of 20 FQHC directors across the country, 35 percent of respondents said they often try to negotiate lower prices with specialists if the cost of specialty care would be prohibitive for the patient (Gusmano et al. 2002).

FQHCs May Play a Larger Role in Medical Education as a Result of Recent Legislative Changes

FQHCs offer an opportunity for medical residents to experience care delivery in an ambulatory setting. To facilitate these connections, two provisions in the Patient Protection and Affordable Care Act of 2010 (PPACA) establish funding sources for development of, and payment to, teaching health centers. Teaching health centers are community-based ambulatory care sites that operate a primary care residency program and can include FQHCs, RHCs, and other entities. PPACA authorized (but did not appropriate) HRSA grants to help eligible establishments start up teaching health center residency programs. Separately,

PPACA appropriated $230 million over the next five years to support the costs of operating residency programs in teaching health centers. HRSA will administer this funding process. On January 25, 2011, the Secretary of Health and Human Services announced that $1.9 million had been awarded to 11 teaching health centers under the Teaching Health Centers Graduate Medical Education Program (Health Resources and Services Administration 2011b).

Separate from these provisions, FQHCs are eligible to receive Medicare payments for graduate medical education, either directly from Medicare or more commonly through arrangements with teaching hospitals. Medicare can make direct graduate medical education payments for specified teaching-related expenses to FQHCs that sponsor their own accredited residency training program. Because very few FQHCs sponsor their own residency programs, these direct payments are relatively rare. It is more common, however, for FQHCs to receive payments through an arrangement to provide a rotation for a hospital-based residency program. Unlike teaching hospitals, FQHCs cannot receive Medicare indirect medical education payments for the higher costs associated with being a teaching institution. However, if an FQHC enters an arrangement with a hospital-based residency program to provide an ambulatory rotation, it may negotiate reimbursement from the hospital that could include the indirect costs of having the residents rotate through the FQHC. Although PPACA eliminated some regulatory burdens that discouraged residency rotation to these nonhospital settings, financial disincentives remain (Medicare Payment Advisory Commission 2010).

The Largest Source of FQHC Revenue Is Medicaid, with Federal Grants Contributing a Significant Share

Among all sources of revenue, Medicaid makes up 37 percent of total revenue and 63 percent of patient-related revenue for health center grantees (Figure 6-1). In 2009, Medicaid paid $4.25 billion to FQHCs. In contrast, Medicare paid $674 million to federally funded FQHCs, or 6 percent of their total revenue.

Medicaid Payments to FQHCs Are Made under a Prospective Payment System

The Benefits Improvement and Protection Act of 2000 established a PPS for Medicaid reimbursement, changing from a cost-based methodology. The law also allowed state Medicaid agencies to establish their own reimbursement rates for FQHCs provided that: (1) the reimbursement would not be less than the payment under the Medicaid PPS, and (2) the center agreed to it (referred to as an alternative payment methodology). In 2005, the Government Accountability Office (GAO) found that about half of states had established an alternative payment methodology for reimbursing FQHCs (Government Accountability Office 2005).[4] In 2009, 56 percent of Medicaid patients at FQHCs were covered by a Medicaid managed care organization (Health Resources and Services Administration 2010). In these situations, the managed care organization pays the FQHC an amount that the two parties negotiated, and the state Medicaid program pays the FQHC a wraparound payment equal to the difference, if any, between the PPS rate and the payment from the managed care organization.

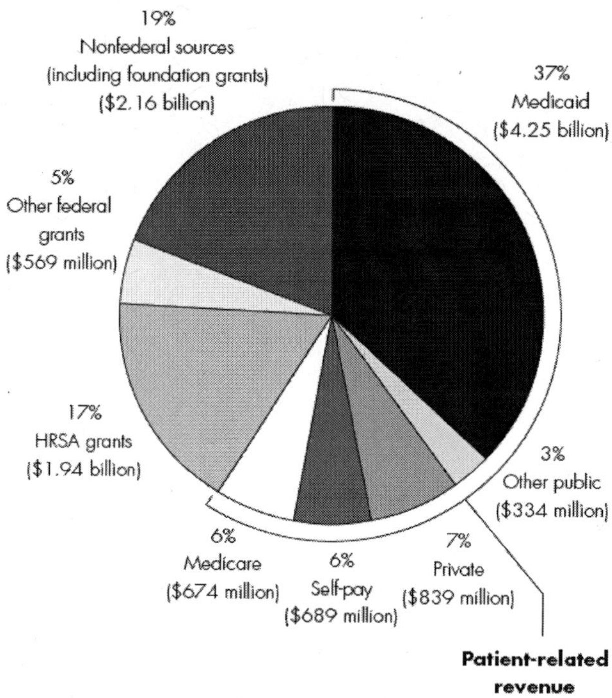

Note: FQHC (federally qualified health center), HRSA (Health Resources and Services Administration).

Source: 2009 data compiled by MedPAC from the HRSA data warehouse.

Figure 6-1. Of the more than $11 billion in revenue reported by FQHC grantees, Medicaid makes up the largest single share.

Grants to FQHCs Are Funded through the Annual Appropriations Process

The FQHC grant program is funded through the yearly appropriations process, although recent legislation has also provided mandatory grant funding for FQHCs. The American Recovery and Reinvestment Act appropriated $2 billion for construction, equipment, health information technology, and related improvements to existing FQHCs and establishment of new FQHC sites. Finally, PPACA appropriated $11 billion over the next five years (including $1.5 billion for construction) for FQHCs. In 2009, the average FQHC grant award was $1.7 million (Health Resources and Services Administration 2011d).

Medicare Reimburses FQHCs for Visits by Beneficiaries Using An All-Inclusive Payment

The FQHC benefit under Medicare became effective in October 1991 and was modeled after the Medicare RHC benefit (Government Accountability Office 2010). It generally covers primary and preventive care and related services provided to Medicare beneficiaries. The current Medicare reimbursement is a single payment per covered visit based on the

FQHC's costs and subject to a productivity assumption for clinical staff and an upper limit on the per visit payment.

Medicare FQHC Benefit Covers Comprehensive Primary and Preventive Care

The FQHC benefit under Medicare generally covers:

- ***Primary care:*** Treatment of acute or chronic medical problems furnished under the supervision of a physician, nurse practitioner, physician assistant, clinical psychologist, clinical nurse midwife, visiting nurse, or clinical social worker (Health Resources and Services Administration 2006).
- ***Preventive care:*** Screening services furnished under the supervision of a medical professional. Initially, these services included broad risk-targeted services such as physical exams, blood pressure management, and nutritional assessments. Over time, preventive services under the Medicare FQHC benefit have been expanded to include mammography, Pap tests and pelvic exams, prostate and colorectal cancer screening, diabetes self-management training, bone mass measurement, glaucoma screening, cardiovascular screening, medical nutrition therapy, and tobacco cessation.[5]

PPACA expanded the FQHC Medicare benefit by cross-referencing the Medicare preventive services established by the law. As shown in Figure 6-2, some services provided in FQHCs are separately billable under Part B because they are not covered in the Medicare all-inclusive payment rate. In addition, because an FQHC has to offer the same services to all patients, regardless of their insurance status, FQHCs may provide Medicare beneficiaries care such as preventive dental services that are not covered by Medicare under either the all-inclusive payment rate or the Part B fee schedule (Centers for Medicare & Medicaid Services 2010b).

Medicare Reimburses FQHCS Using a Cost-Based All-Inclusive Reimbursement Rate

Medicare pays for beneficiaries' visits to FQHCs using an all-inclusive rate per covered visit. Medicare's all-inclusive payment rate for FQHCs was generally modeled after the system in place for payment to RHCs, including productivity thresholds and per visit limits (Government Accountability Office 2010).

Medicare's FQHC Reimbursement Rate Is Based on the Center's Costs, Subject to Productivity Requirements and a Per Visit Payment Limit

Medicare payment to an FQHC is based on allowable visits and allowable costs. Allowable visits include an in-person encounter with a physician, physician assistant, nurse practitioner, clinical nurse midwife, clinical psychologist, clinical social worker, or visiting nurse for preventive or primary care. A visit for diabetes self-management training or medical nutrition therapy services can be counted as a visit, provided that it is not a group session (Centers for Medicare & Medicaid Services 2009).[6] FQHCs may bill for only one medical visit per patient per day. FQHCs may also bill for one mental health visit per patient per day and one diabetes self-management individual training visit per patient per day.

Allowable costs are those that are "reasonable in amount and necessary and proper to the efficient delivery of services," as described in the Medicare claims processing manual (Centers for Medicare & Medicaid Services 2010b). These costs include practitioner compensation, overhead, supplies, and other costs incident to delivery of the Medicare FQHC benefit. Costs for services provided that are not covered by Medicare (e.g., preventive dental care) must be excluded as well as costs associated with items outside the FQHC benefit, such as the technical component of labs (Centers for Medicare & Medicaid Services 2010b).

In general, the calculation of the FQHC per visit payment rate uses allowable costs divided by allowable visits. However, Medicare applies an adjustment for the productivity of FQHC medical staff, using a floor of 4,200 visits for each full-time physician and 2,100 visits for each full-time physician assistant, advanced practice nurse, or clinical nurse midwife in a year. FQHCs with total allowable visits below these thresholds must nevertheless use them to calculate the number of allowable visits. This requirement raises the number of visits in the calculation and thus reduces the per visit rate.

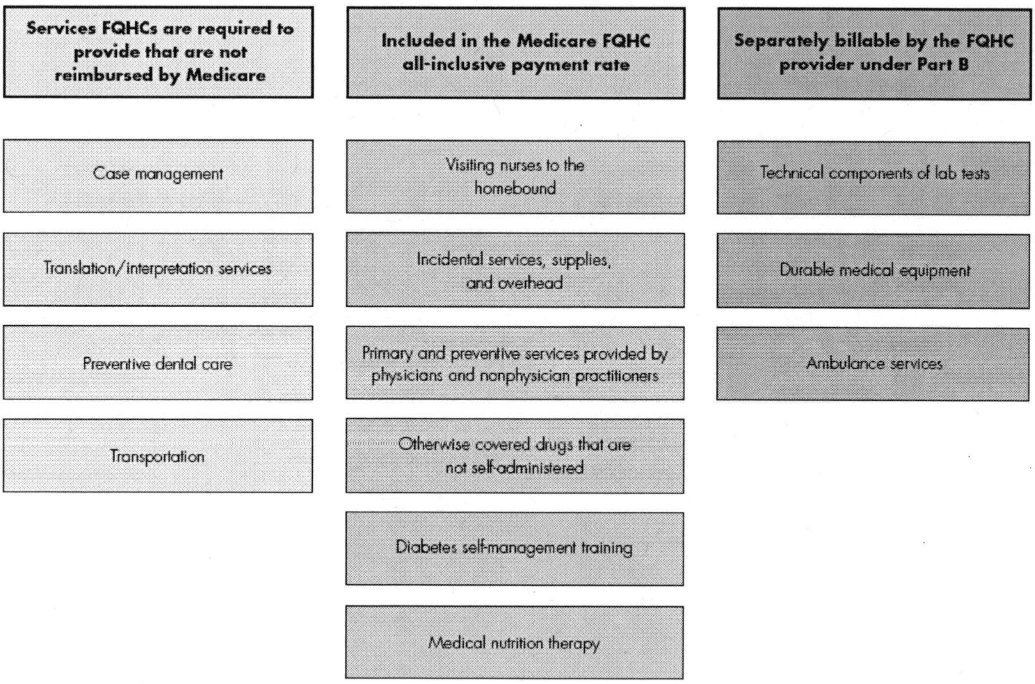

Note: FQHC (federally qualified health center).
Source: Compiled by MedPAC from the Medicare benefit policy manual.

Figure 6-2. Benefits provided at FQHCs.

An FQHC's reimbursement is the lower of its calculated per visit rate or the per visit payment limit. In 2011, the per visit payment limit is $109.24 for rural FQHCs and $126.22 for urban FQHCs. Urban FQHCs are those that are located in a metropolitan statistical area (Centers for Medicare & Medicaid Services 2010a).

Using 2007 cost reports, GAO estimated that 72 percent of FQHCs had costs for delivering the FQHC Medicare benefit that exceeded the Medicare per visit limit and that their costs exceeded Medicare reimbursement by approximately $72 million in total, or 17 percent of payments that year.[7]

In reviewing these findings, it is worth noting that CMS dissented with the findings as the data used in the report were not derived from "comprehensive, full scope audited Medicare FQHC cost reports." As CMS noted in its comments, the presence of the per visit payment limit reduces the need for a detailed audit of the FQHC cost reports (Government Accountability Office 2010). The use of unaudited cost reports for reimbursement may also have implications for the transition to the PPS.

Medicare Provides an Interim Payment to FQHCs that Is Later Reconciled with FQHC's Actual Spending

Medicare currently pays FQHCs using cost-based reimbursement. Under this arrangement, a Medicare contractor makes interim payments to an FQHC at the beginning of the reporting period based on either the FQHC's historic costs of providing services or the FQHC's budget for that year.[8] At the end of a period up to, but not exceeding, 12 months, the FQHC submits a cost report, which includes the detail needed for the Medicare contractor to determine the FQHC's final Medicare reimbursement. If interim payments to the FQHC exceed the final settlement amount, the FQHC must repay the excess amount. Similarly, if the interim payments are less than the final settlement amount, Medicare pays the FQHC the difference in a lump sum up to the per visit payment limit (Centers for Medicare & Medicaid Services 2010b).

Table 6-1. Comparing Medicare's FQHC and RHC payment limits with payment for a physician office visit and hospital outpatient department visit, 2011

	Medicare payment amount
payment limit	
FQHC, rural	$109.24
FQHC, urban	126.22
RHC	78.07
physician office	
Physician fee schedule,	
office visit by an established patient	68.97
hospital outpatient department	
Facility	75.13
Physician work	49.27
Total	124.40

Note: FQHC (federally qualified health center), RHC (rural health clinic). The physician fee schedule and outpatient department (OPD) figures are the national payment amount. Healthcare Common Procedure Coding System code 99213 is used for the physician fee schedule and OPD payment amounts. Medicare's payment rate for a physician office visit includes the practice expense (i.e., facility-level) payment. Please see text on this page for additional caveats to this comparison.

Source: Calendar year 2011 physician fee schedule, Hospital Outpatient Prospective Payment System Addendum A.

Medicare's Payments to FQHCs and Medicare's Payments for Office Visits in Other Ambulatory Care Settings

Table 6-1 shows the Medicare FQHC payment limit with Medicare's payment for a level three physician office visit and a level three hospital outpatient clinic visit. There are a number of important caveats to this comparison. First, Medicare's payment to FQHCs includes all services covered by the FQHC benefit. Thus, the FQHC payment includes the professional component of laboratory services or procedures, physician-administered medication, and some additional Medicare-covered services that FQHCs provide as a condition of their grant or look-alike designation, which could be billed separately in the case of a private physician practice or a hospital outpatient department. In other words, an apples-to-apples comparison would use Medicare's payment for a physician visit and outpatient visit (and other services that may be billed separately) that corresponds to a typical FQHC visit. However, our ability to define a typical visit to an FQHC for a Medicare beneficiary is not possible because FQHCs did not report Healthcare Common Procedure Coding System (HCPCS) codes until very recently. Beginning in January 2011, FQHCs are required to report HCPCS codes.

Second, the payment rate to FQHCs does not vary based on whether the visit is with a new or established patient or on the intensity of the visit.

Third, the payment limit for FQHCs is an upper payment limit—meaning that some FQHCs receive a per visit amount that is less than the amount shown in Table 6-1.

With these caveats, Table 6-1 shows Medicare's payment rate for a level three office visit with an established patient for the physician fee schedule rates and a level three outpatient department visit. We chose a level three visit because, as noted above, Medicare's FQHC payment limit covers all types of visits to the FQHC—including shorter or less complex visits with established patients as well as longer or more complex visits with new patients.

According to the Medicare physician fee schedule, for a level three office visit by an established patient, practitioners typically spend 15 minutes face to face with patients or their families, compared with 5 minutes of face-to-face time for a level one office visit and 40 minutes for a level five office visit.

FQHCs Can Reduce Cost Sharing for Low-Income Medicare Beneficiaries

Medicare's Part B deductible does not apply to FQHC visits. Patients at FQHCs pay a coinsurance of 20 percent of the center's reasonable customary charge for the service (Centers for Medicare & Medicaid Services 2011b).

The coinsurance percentage is applied to the FQHC's customary charges, even if this customary charge would exceed the Medicare FQHC payment limit. However, per the Section 330 PHSA grant requirements, the patient's coinsurance is also subject to a sliding scale reduction based on income. The coinsurance for patients with income below 200 percent of the federal poverty threshold is reduced and patients with incomes below 100 percent of the federal poverty threshold pay a nominal fee. If patients do not pay their coinsurance, Medicare reimburses 100 percent of the bad debts for the FQHC. Of the general population over age 65 years, 34 percent are below the 200 percent federal poverty threshold and so could receive some reduction in their coinsurance (Census Bureau 2010). This reduction in coinsurance may become less of a relative benefit of FQHCs as Medicare cost sharing for certain preventive services has been eliminated in all settings.[9]

Patients at FQHCs Are Predominantly Low Income and Minority

In 2009, 1.4 million Medicare beneficiaries received care at an FQHC—an increase of 20 percent from 2006 (Health Resources and Services Administration 2010). Despite this increase, over the same period, the share of the FQHC population who were Medicare beneficiaries fell slightly, as the overall FQHC patient population increased by 25 percent, to 18.8 million people (Figure 6-3) (Health Resources and Services Administration 2010).

More than 70 percent of grantee FQHCs' patients have income below 100 percent of the federal poverty threshold (Health Resources and Services Administration 2010). Patients at FQHCs are disproportionately minority and non-English speakers—in 2009, 63 percent were members of a racial or ethnic minority (predominantly Hispanic), and 25 percent were best served in a language other than English (Health Resources and Services Administration 2010).

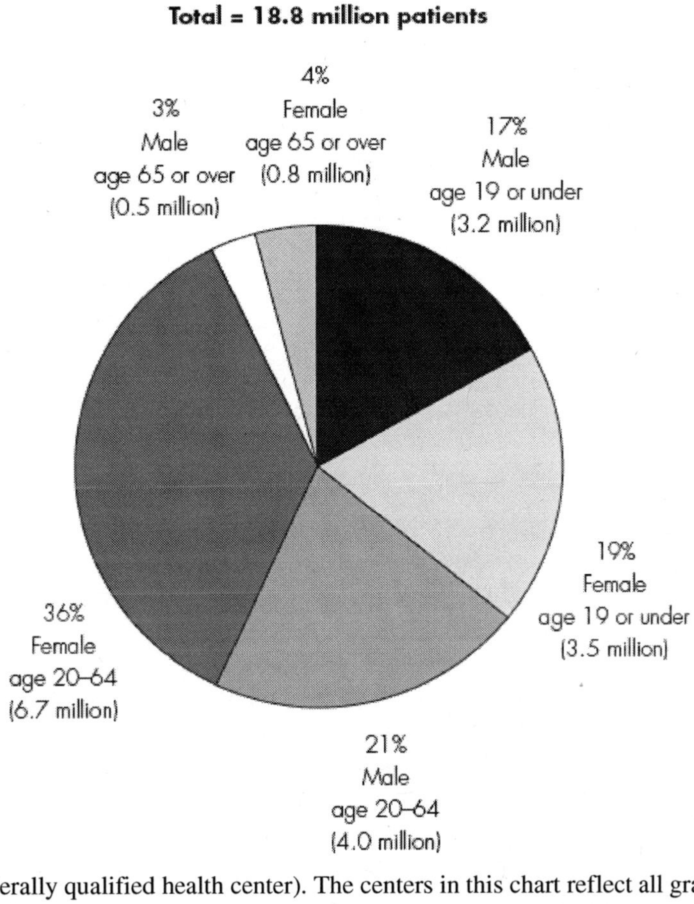

Note: FQHC (federally qualified health center). The centers in this chart reflect all grantees, but exclude look-alikes, and may include some centers that are not certified as FQHCs.

Source: Health Resources and Services Administration, Department of Health and Human Services. 2010. *2009 national summary report.* Rockville, MD: HRSA.

Figure 6-3. FQHC patients are predominantly young, 2009.

Chronic Disease Burden of Patients at FQHCs Appears to Be Higher than for Comparable Patients at Physician Offices

Studies over the years have assessed the chronic disease burden of patients visiting FQHCs, outpatient departments, and physician offices. One study using the 2006 NAMCS found that a higher percentage of community health centers' patients (13 percent) were more likely to have diabetes than physician offices' patients (9 percent). Significantly higher rates of patients at health centers were obese or suffering from depression compared with patients in physician offices (Shi et al. 2010). A study that updated these findings based on the 2008 NAMCS found that patients in FQHCs were more likely to have a chronic condition than patients in a physician office or outpatient department (Hing and Uddin 2010).

Patients with Chronic Conditions Make More Visits to FQHCs, and Frequent Visitors to FQHCs Are More Likely to Be Older

In 2009, FQHC patients with chronic conditions were more likely than other FQHC patients to make multiple visits to FQHCs in a year—three visits a year on average for those with diabetes, two and a half visits a year for those with heart disease, and just over two visits a year for those with hypertension (Health Resources and Services Administration 2010). In contrast, the number of visits for those with acute conditions ranged from 1.45 visits for patients with dehydration to 1.22 visits for patients with contact dermatitis.

One study of an FQHC in central Massachusetts that reviewed center records for 1999 found that among all patients, frequent visitors to the FQHC were more likely to be older. Patients aged 45 to 64 years made up a third of all established patients but half of frequent visitors. The share of the total patient population at the FQHC over age 65 was 7 percent, but it made up 13 percent of frequent visitors (Savageau et al. 2006).

FQHCs Report Chronic Care Outcomes for Their Patients

FQHCs track and report intermediate outcome measures to HRSA on an aggregate basis for their patients who have been diagnosed with certain common chronic diseases. Among patients between the ages of 18 and 85 who visited an FQHC in 2009 and who were diagnosed with hypertension, 63 percent had a reading on their last blood pressure measurement of 140/90 or below (Health Resources and Services Administration 2010).[10] Among FQHC patients with diabetes, 71 percent had a hemoglobin A1c (HbA1c) level below 9 percent—one measure of blood sugar control for diabetics. Overall, the literature of quality at FQHCs in comparison to other primary care sites is mixed, and the underlying health status of patients confounds these findings. One analysis of chronic care management at health centers found that the rates of blood pressure control were better than the documented rates for hospital-affiliated clinics or the Veterans Affairs health system; it also found that the quality of diabetes care was lower at health centers than for publicly reported rates for some managed care organizations, although this comparison does not adjust for patient status between those at FQHCs and in managed care organizations (Hicks et al. 2006). Another study that focused directly on glycemic control in FQHCs found that the rate of glycemic testing equaled or exceeded national figures for the total U.S. population as well as managed care plans participating in the Healthcare Effectiveness Data and Information Set reporting. This study also found that the percentage of patients with HbA1c levels below 9.5 percent was higher for the surveyed health centers than managed care plans (Maizlish et al. 2004).

Presence of an FQHC May Reduce Preventable Hospitalizations

One study conducted among publicly insured and uninsured residents noted that FQHCs reduced the rate of preventable hospitalizations (Epstein 2001). Using a database of hospital discharges in Virginia, Epstein found that the presence of an FQHC reduced the preventable hospitalization rate for those residing in an MUA. Over the three years covered in his study, the presence of an FQHC in an MUA was associated with 5.8 fewer preventable hospitalizations per 1,000 people, as compared with the rate of preventable hospitalizations in MUAs without an FQHC. The study did not disaggregate the findings among those with public insurance and those without insurance.

Other studies have found that the presence of an FQHC reduced the rate of ambulatory-care-sensitive conditions among the uninsured and that, even among the insured population, the presence of an FQHC decreased use of the emergency department for ambulatory-care-sensitive conditions (Falik et al. 2006, Rust et al. 2009).

Recent Legislation Directs Significant Increases in FQHC Capacity and Fundamental Changes in Medicare's Payment

PPACA establishes a new PPS for Medicare payment to FQHCs beginning on October 1, 2014. As noted earlier, current payments to FQHCs are constrained by both the productivity assumption and the per visit limit. Under the new payment system, payments in the first year of the PPS shall be set equal to the estimated payments that would have occurred under the current reasonable cost payments without respect to the productivity assumptions or the per visit payment limit. The payment rate shall be increased each year by either an FQHC-specific index or the Medicare Economic Index if an FQHC index is not available. There is not a specific statutory provision for an ongoing budget-neutrality factor after the first year of the PPS.

In preparation for the PPS, starting in 2011, FQHCs must report to CMS on the specific services they provide to Medicare beneficiaries using HCPCS codes (Centers for Medicare & Medicaid Services 2011d). The statutory language establishing the PPS also contemplates that payment rates could take into account the type, intensity, and duration of services and could incorporate geographic adjustments.

One concern in Medicare payment policy is that in transitioning from a cost-based reimbursement system to a PPS, there may be less of an incentive for providers to constrain their costs so that costs in a base year result in a higher payment amount under the PPS.[11]

FQHCs could have the same incentive to not constrain their costs in anticipation of the PPS. It is also important to note that CMS does not audit FQHC cost reports, and they note in their comments to the GAO report on Medicare's payment to FQHCs that the presence of the per visit payment limit constrains Medicare's overall payment to FQHCs without requiring a detailed audit (Government Accountability Office 2010). If these cost reports form the basis of the PPS along with the procedure and service codes reported, it will be important for CMS to audit the growth in costs for FQHCs in the years before the PPS is established and ensure that Medicare's payment rates reflect the efficient provision of services at FQHCs.

FQHC look-alike program

The federally qualified health center (FQHC) look-alike program was established in 1990 as a result of the demand for FQHC services by lowincome uninsured or Medicaid enrollees and limited Section 330 grant funding (Taylor 2010). The creation of this program enabled centers that complied with all the grant requirements to be reimbursed as FQHCs by Medicare and Medicaid, even if they were unable to receive grant funds. Many FQHC look-alikes compete for and obtain federal grant funding—between 2002 and 2007, 286 FQHC look-alikes applied for an FQHC grant, and 36 percent of them were successful (Health Resources and Services Administration 2008). FQHC look-alikes can also participate in the 340B program, although they are not covered under the Federal Tort Claims Act.

Considerations in Developing Medicare PPS for FQHCs

There are three general reasons to look at the relationship between FQHCs and Medicare. First, FQHCs are one model of team-based primary care delivery. FQHCs emphasize the use of physician assistants, nurse practitioners, clinical nurse midwives, and other practitioners for routine care, allowing physicians affiliated with FQHCs to focus their attention on more complex cases. They are required by their grants or look-alike designations to coordinate care by having off-hours coverage, having admitting privileges with facility-based providers, and locating their service sites to facilitate access to care.

Second, FQHCs can provide access for Medicare beneficiaries seeking routine and preventive care in areas where physician office capacity is limited. As a result of their grant requirements, FQHCs are located in underserved areas (such as rural areas where health care services are widely dispersed) or treat populations that have barriers to care (such as those whose members have difficulty obtaining transportation to a doctor's office).

Third, the conversion to a Medicare PPS could encourage FQHCs to serve more Medicare beneficiaries, as it is likely that Medicare payments to FQHCs will increase under the PPS. In designing the PPS, CMS will have to address questions about the most appropriate services for Medicare beneficiaries at FQHCs and the relative value of these services.

Several questions remain regarding FQHCs' delivery of care to Medicare beneficiaries. For example, do FQHCs have the expertise to handle multiple chronic conditions among the elderly? While FQHCs treat a significant number of patients with chronic and disabling conditions, the share of their patients who are over age 65 is relatively small. Next, is the care provided at FQHCs of comparable quality to other ambulatory care sites available to Medicare beneficiaries, and does Medicare's payment to FQHCs reflect the efficient delivery of care? These issues will be part of the discussion as CMS develops Medicare's PPS for FQHCs.

Endnotes

[1] Health centers classified as comprehensive federally funded health centers as of January 1, 1990, are also categorically eligible to be FQHCs.

[2] Outside an FQHC or RHC, nurse practitioners and physician assistants are paid at 85 percent of the physician fee schedule.

[3] CMS requires that physicians make at least one visit every two weeks to meet the physician supervision requirement.

[4] Since this report was issued, the Congress raised the Medicaid FQHC PPS by $5.

[5] Preventive care under the Medicare RHC benefit is limited to services that are covered under Medicare Part B.

[6] In general, group education sessions are not included in the FQHC Medicare benefit.

[7] GAO estimates that the productivity threshold had a smaller effect on Medicare spending—7 percent of FQHCs had their total reimbursement rate lowered because of the productivity threshold, reducing Medicare payment to FQHCs by $1.1 million.

[8] For example, if an FQHC is new, the Medicare administrative contractors may pay an interim rate based on a budget. If the FQHC is expanding the services it provides or expects a significant increase in costs (such as rent) it may request payment based on a budget.

[9] PPACA eliminates cost sharing for preventive services ranked as A or B by the Preventive Services Task Force.

[10] Lower blood pressure measurement and higher shares of patients with lower hemoglobin A1c levels suggest higher quality.

[11] For example, GAO found that "HCFA [Health Care Financing Administration] used 1995 reported SNF [skilled nursing facility] costs as the basis for the federal per diem rates under PPS. We believe these base-year costs are likely to be too high as a result of inefficient service provision, unnecessary care, and improper billing for services, which went undetected due to minimal program oversight." (Government Accountability Office 1999).

References

Census Bureau. 2010. 2010 Annual social and economic supplement: 2009. *Current population survey.* Table POV25.

Centers for Medicare & Medicaid Services, Department of Health and Human Services. 2009. *Chapter 13: Rural health clinic and federally qualified health center services. Medicare benefit policy manual.* Baltmore, MD: CMS.

Centers for Medicare & Medicaid Services, Department of Health and Human Services. 2010a. Announcement of Medicare rural health clinics and federally qualified health centers payment rate increases. Transmittal no. 2123.

Centers for Medicare & Medicaid Services, Department of Health and Human Services. 2010b. *Chapter 9: Rural health clinics/federally qualified health centers. Medicare claims processing manual.* Baltimore, MD: CMS.

Centers for Medicare & Medicaid Services, Department of Health and Human Services. 2011a. *Code of Federal Regulations.* 42 CFR 51c 304. Governing board.

Centers for Medicare & Medicaid Services, Department of Health and Human Services. 2011b. *Code of Federal Regulations.* 42 CFR 405.2410. Application of Part B deductible and coinsurance.

Centers for Medicare & Medicaid Services, Department of Health and Human Services. 2011c. Eligibility for EHR incentive programs. http://www.cms.gov/EHRIncentivePrograms/15_ Eligibility.asp#TopOfPage.

Centers for Medicare & Medicaid Services, Department of Health and Human Services. 2011d. Rural health clinics and federally qualified health centers billing guide. *MLN Matters®* no. SE1039.

Commonwealth Fund. 2010. *Enhancing the capacity of community health centers to achieve high performance*. New York, NY: The Commonwealth Fund.

Epstein, A. J. 2001. The role of public clinics in preventable hospitalizations among vulnerable populations. *Health Services Research* 36, no. 2 (June): 405–420.

Falik, M., J. Needleman, R. Herbert, et al. 2006. Comparative effectiveness of health centers as regular source of care: Application of sentinel ACSC events as performance measures. *Journal of Ambulatory Care Management* 29, no. 1 (January– March): 24–35.

Government Accountability Office. 1999. *Skilled nursing facilities: Medicare payment changes require provider adjustments but maintain access.* Washington, DC: GAO.

Government Accountability Office. 2005. *Health centers and rural clinics: state and federal implementation issues for Medicaid's new payment system.* GAO–05–452. Washington, DC: GAO.

Government Accountability Office. 2010. *Medicare payments to federally qualified health centers*. GAO–10–576R. Washington, DC: GAO.

Gusmano, M. K., G. Fairbrother, and H. Park. 2002. Exploring the limits of the safety net: Community health centers and care for the uninsured. *Health Affairs* 21, no. 6 (November–December): 188–194.

Health Resources and Services Administration, Department of Health and Human Services. 2006. *Comparison of the rural health clinic and federally qualified health center programs.* Rockville, MD: HRSA.

Health Resources and Services Administration, Department of Health and Human Services. 2007. *Defining scope of project and policy for requesting changes.* HRSA policy information notice. Document no. 2008–01. Rockville, MD: HRSA.

Health Resources and Services Administration, Department of Health and Human Services. 2008. *Health centers: America's primary care safety net, reflections on success, 2002–2007.* Rockville, MD: HRSA.

Health Resources and Services Administration, Department of Health and Human Services. 2010. *2009 national summary report*. Rockville, MD: HRSA.

Health Resources and Services Administration, Department of Health and Human Services. 2011a. *Health center program requirement slides*. http://bphc.hrsa.gov/about/.

Health Resources and Services Administration, Department of Health and Human Services. 2011b. HHS announces new

Teaching Health Centers Graduate Medical Education Program. Press release. January 25. http://www.hrsa.gov/about/news/pressr eleases/110125teachinghealthcenters.html.

Health Resources and Services Administration, Department of Health and Human Services. 2011c. Introduction to 340B Drug Pricing Program.
http://www.hrsa.gov/opa/introduction.htm.

Health Resources and Services Administration, Department of Health and Human Services. 2011d. *Justification of estimates for appropriations committees, fiscal year 2012.* Rockville, MD: HRSA.

Hicks, L. S., A. J. O'Malley, T. A. Lieu, et al. 2006. The quality of chronic disease care in U.S. community health centers. Health Affairs 25, no. 6 (November–December): 1712–1723.

Hing, E., and S. Uddin. 2010. *Visits to primary care delivery sites: United States, 2008.* National Center for Health Statistics data brief, no. 47. Hyattsville, MD: NCHS.

Jha, A. K., C. M. DesRoches, P. D. Kralovec, et al. 2010. A progress report on electronic health records in U.S. hospitals. *Health Affairs* 29, no. 10 (October): 1951–1957.

Kaiser Commission on Medicaid and the Uninsured. 2010. *Community health centers: Opportunities and challenges of health reform.* Issue paper. Washington, DC: KCMU.

Maizlish, N. A., B. Shaw, and K. Hendry. 2004. Glycemic control in diabetic patients served by community health centers. *American Journal of Medical Quality* 19, no. 4 (July–August): 172–179.

Medicare Payment Advisory Commission. 2010. *Report to the Congress: Aligning incentives in Medicare*. Washington, DC: MedPAC.

National Center for Health Statistics. 2010. *Electronic medical record/electronic health record systems of office-based physicians: United States, 2009 and preliminary 2010 state estimates*. Hyattsville, MD: NCHS.

Rust, G., P. Baltrus, J. Ye, et al. 2009. Presence of a community health center and uninsured emergency department visit rates in rural counties. *Journal of Rural Health* 25, no. 1 (Winter): 8–16.

Savageau, J. A., M. McLoughlin, A. Ursan, et al. 2006. Characteristics of frequent attenders at a community health center. *Journal of the American Board of Family Medicine* 19, no. 3 (May–June): 265–275.

Shi, L., L. A. Lebrun, J. Tsai, et al. 2010. Characteristics of ambulatory care patients and services: A comparison of community health centers and physicians' offices. *Journal of Health Care for the Poor and Underserved* 21, no. 4 (November): 1169–1183.

Taylor, J. 2004. *The fundamentals of community health centers.* National Health Policy Forum background paper. Washington, DC: NHPF.

Taylor, J. 2010. *The primary care safety net: Strained, transitioning, critical.* National Health Policy Forum background paper no. 79. Washington, DC: NHPF.

VARIATION IN PRIVATE-SECTOR PAYMENT RATES

Summary

In this chapter, we examine how payment rates in the private sector vary across and within geographic areas. There are a number of reasons for studying such variation as it relates to Medicare payment policy. A better understanding of the dynamics of private health care markets can inform the development of Medicare payment policies. Questions of particular interest are: to what extent do factors such as the market power of providers or insurers affect the variation in private-payment rates and, if those are major factors that explain the variation, what does that mean for Medicare payment policy and policies that are intended to promote greater integration among providers?

In a preliminary analysis of private-sector payment rates for hospital and physician services, we find wide variation in payment rates geographically for both types of services, with greater differences for hospital services. Payment rates for some physician services—certain imaging services, for example— vary more across areas than payment rates for office visits and obstetric care. In a given area, payment rates for some types of physician services have more variation than payment for other types of physician services. We also found no strong pattern of correlation between rates for physician services and those for hospital services; that is, areas with relatively high rates for physician services do not necessarily have high rates for hospital services and vice versa.

In future work, we plan to explore the reasons for variation in payment rates. Factors such as the health care market structure in a geographic area and relative power of providers or insurers are likely to affect the payment negotiation process and the resulting payment rates. The exact nature of the relationship between market characteristics and variation in rates is likely to be complex. We plan to continue our data analysis and undertake a more in-depth look at specific markets. We will also seek alternative ways to measure provider and insurer market power and market concentration to examine their effect on variation in private-payment rates.

Introduction

The Commission has examined payment rates for physician and hospital services by private payers in different contexts. Each year, the Commission analyzes private insurer fees for physician services in the context of evaluating the adequacy of Medicare payment rates. Our last reported ratio of Medicare rates to private-payer rates for physician services, based on 2009 data, was 0.80 (Medicare Payment Advisory Commission 2011a). That is, private payers were paying nationally an average of 25 percent more than Medicare for physician services in 2009. We did not find that the difference between Medicare and commercial payment rates appreciably affected access to physician services for Medicare beneficiaries. Overall, we found that most beneficiaries were able to get timely appointments.

Similarly, Medicare payments for hospital services in recent years have been below the levels paid by private payers, and hospitals' Medicare margins—their profitability expressed as the relationship between their payments and costs—have been lower than their private-sector margins. Some have argued that providers need higher payment rates from private payers to compensate for the differential between their costs and Medicare payment rates (i.e., "cost shifting" is necessary). However, the Commission's recent work suggests that the level of hospitals' Medicare margins is associated with the extent to which private payers' rates put financial pressure on hospitals to be efficient. Hospitals under financial pressure from private payers have lower costs and higher Medicare margins than hospitals with higher private-payer rates (Medicare Payment Advisory Commission 2010). If private-payer rates continue to increase, there is a risk that the widening differential between private and Medicare rates will be interpreted as a need for Medicare to increase its rates rather than as a reflection of private-sector market dynamics.

In one context, private-sector prices are directly relevant to the Medicare program. Under the Medicare Advantage program, plans pay for medical services on the basis of prices they negotiate with providers. Therefore, their payment rates for the same services can differ from one provider to another, in contrast to Medicare fee-for-service prices, which are set by formulas in law and regulation.

While the Commission's analyses to date have focused on how Medicare payment rates compare with private-payer rates, this analysis examines how payment rates in the private sector vary across and within geographic areas.

There are a number of reasons for studying such variation as it relates to Medicare payment policy. Questions of particular interest are: to what extent do factors such as the market power of providers or insurers affect the variation in private-payment rates and, if those are major factors that explain the variation, what does that mean for Medicare payment policy and policies that are intended to promote greater integration among providers?

Providers can exert market leverage in several ways when negotiating prices with insurers and health plans. They can consolidate through horizontal integration (e.g., two hospitals merging to create a single hospital system in a market) or through vertical integration (e.g., hospitals employing physicians). When such combinations achieve market power for the providers, insurers risk not having key providers in their networks if they do not accept the providers' contracting terms. Similarly, when insurers are dominant in the market, they can negotiate with providers and obtain favorable terms (i.e., lower prices for services). Such market dynamics between insurers and providers might contribute to the observed geographic variation in expenditures and will affect the differential between Medicare and private-payer rates.

The gap between Medicare and private-payment rates does not necessarily imply that Medicare rates are set incorrectly, especially when higher private-payer rates reflect market conditions rather than differences related to cost and quality. It is possible that some providers would stop seeing Medicare beneficiaries if private-sector rates were much higher than Medicare rates. However, the supply of privately insured patients is not unlimited, nor is the ability to negotiate even higher private-sector prices. Providers may find it financially advantageous to continue seeing Medicare patients despite a differential in payments.

Generally, we observe many different payment rates in the private sector for a given service in an area for various reasons. Consequently, it is difficult to know which payment rate may serve as a meaningful reference rate for Medicare payment adequacy. If high private-payment rates enable providers to be less efficient in the absence of financial pressure, then the comparison of Medicare and private-payer rates is not meaningful. Gaining a better understanding of how and why private-payment rates vary can inform the Commission's work on payment policy and issues related to the organization of health care delivery.

Provider integration not only leads to market power but can also promote more coordinated, efficient care. Vertical integration can lead to less fragmentation of care across different settings, and it allows for the effective alignment of financial incentives among diverse providers. Examples of this type of integration include the Kaiser and Geisinger models, among others. In this vein, Medicare policies that encourage greater integration of care—such as accountable care organizations—can also lead to greater market power and give providers the ability to negotiate higher payment rates from private payers. In the Commission's ongoing efforts to encourage delivery system reform, it is useful to understand the potential effects of Medicare payment policy on the health care market beyond the Medicare program.

Other Research on Geographic Variation in Payment Rates

In a 2005 report, the Government Accountability Office (GAO) found that preferred provider organization (PPO) plans in the Federal Employees Health Benefits (FEHB) Program had substantially different payment rates for hospital inpatient services and physician services across metropolitan statistical areas (MSAs) (Government Accountability Office 2005). Using claims data from several large national insurers participating in the FEHB Program in 2001, GAO found a twofold difference in physician payment rates across 319 MSAs and an almost fourfold difference in hospital payment rates across 232 MSAs. (This study's results were limited to MSAs for which there were sufficient claims data to evaluate relative payments.) In addition, the variation was affected by market characteristics: Higher payment rates were associated with a greater concentration in the hospital market and with smaller shares of primary care physicians paid on a capitated basis. GAO also found that physician payment rates were lower in areas with higher rates of the uninsured and lower Medicaid payments, but hospital payment rates did not show such a relationship. GAO did not find evidence of cost shifting, in which providers raise private-sector prices to compensate for lower Medicare or Medicaid payments.

Other research shows that even in a single geographic area, insurers' payments to providers for the same or similar services can vary widely. In a 2010 study, the Attorney General of the Commonwealth of Massachusetts investigated insurers' payments to hospitals and physician groups in Massachusetts (Attorney General of the Commonwealth of Massachusetts 2010). The variation in payments made by two major insurers to hospitals in 2008—after accounting for volume, product mix, service mix, and other factors—showed a 300 percent difference in payments between the lowest paid and the highest paid network hospitals. A similar analysis of payments made to physician groups showed a difference of up to 130 percent. The report concluded that payment variations were not correlated with quality of care, case mix, payer mix, or academic status. However, they were correlated with market leverage factors, such as provider size and the share of the insurer's revenues going to the provider group.

The payment variations found in Massachusetts can result from various contracting practices. The attorney general's report identified several practices that "exemplify a contracting dynamic that obscures transparency, perpetuates market leverage, and prioritizes competitive position (parity) over consumer value" (Attorney General of the Commonwealth of Massachusetts 2010).

Various strategies used by providers to negotiate higher payment rates from private insurers are documented in a recent study of six California markets (Berenson et al. 2010, California Healthcare Foundation 2009). In 2008, the Center for Studying Health System Change (HSC) conducted site visits to Fresno, Los Angeles, Oakland/San Francisco, Riverside/San Bernardino, Sacramento, and San Diego. The study reported the shift of negotiating power from insurers to hospitals and physicians, and it identified various ways market power is achieved and exercised. For instance, consolidation of hospitals into larger systems, especially those including "must-have" hospitals (e.g., prestigious hospitals that consumers want included in plan networks), and tighter relationships between hospitals and physicians have resulted in larger, more powerful negotiating entities and the growing clout of providers.

A more recent HSC publication shows wide variation in hospital and physician payments within and across markets (Ginsburg 2010). The study examined eight health care markets, using data from four national insurers who reported their payment rates as a percentage of Medicare rates. Average payment rates in relation to Medicare for outpatient hospital services were generally higher than those for inpatient services, but within-market variation for outpatient hospital services was similar to that of inpatient hospital services. Variation in physician payment rates was not as pronounced but was still notable across and within markets and by specialty.

A study by Laurence Baker and his colleagues analyzed private-payer payment rates using 2007 MarketScan data (i.e., the data source we used in our analysis but for a prior year) (Baker et al. 2010). The authors' preliminary findings reported variations in insurer payment rates across areas by type of service. There was less variation for office visits, for example, than for neck–spine–disk surgery (a frequent procedure in the study's commercial data). The surgery had about three times as much variation across areas as office visits. In examining several possible explanatory variables, the authors found that the MSA of the provider as a variable explained up to 42 percent of the variation (ranging from 18 percent to 42 percent for different codes). Among MSA-level factors that could explain the variation across areas, the authors found only one—the level of insurer competition in the market—to be significant. The MSA levels of education of the population, income, number of uninsured individuals in the area, and number of physicians per capita were not significant.

Methodology for and Limitations of Our Analysis

Data Sources for Our Analysis

Our preliminary analysis is based on commercial sector claims for 2008 from MarketScan (2008 Thomson Reuters MarketScan® Commercial Claims and Encounter Data, Copyright 2009 Thomson Reuters, formerly MedStat). The MarketScan data include primarily self-insured employer plans from across the country—including HMO, PPO, point-of-service (POS), and indemnity plans. Individual employers and health plans voluntarily contribute data to MarketScan, so the contribution rate varies by area and by plan type. The data do not identify the insurer or plan administrator, nor do they identify the provider or practitioner.

Overall, the 2008 MarketScan data are somewhat skewed by the greater contribution of data from the South. After trimming to remove extreme values at the high and low ends of the physician claims data—payments below one-third of the average or higher than three times the average for a specific payer type in each market—the MarketScan data contain more than 200 million claim line items for physician services, accounting for about $18 billion in physician payments. (Trimming removes about 2.2 percent of physician claims and 1.6 percent of total physician payments.) Trimming hospital claims at the low end reduces the number of stays by about 3 percent and payments by less than 1 percent, resulting in more than 780,000 hospital stays and $14 billion in hospital inpatient payments (Table 7-1, p. 168).[1]

Under the MarketScan licensing agreement, we are not permitted to report data for South Carolina except when they are aggregated to a larger geographic area. (For example, South Carolina data may be included in calculating a national average.) For some MSAs,

MarketScan has too few payers contributing data to allow public reporting by area. As a result, we are unable to report specific hospital and physician information on 57 MSAs, of which 12 are in California and 11 are in Texas. In such cases, we are permitted by the terms of the data use agreement to combine areas in certain ways to report data.

We define payment rate as the plan's allowed payment for a particular service. Our definition includes any cost sharing required of a health plan member but excludes balance billing, the amount beyond the insurer-allowed payment that a non-network or nonparticipating physician or other provider can charge.[2] To the extent that an insurer pays a non-network provider a higher rate (e.g., an HMO paying for out-of-network or out-of-area care in an emergency), those higher payments are included in our data. In the physician data, less than 10 percent of total payments is indicated as non-network services.

We define the market area as an MSA or each single-state portion of an MSA. For example, the Washington– Arlington–Alexandria, DC–VA–MD–WV, MSA includes the District of Columbia and three separate state portions.

This distinction is to allow for the state-based nature of the health insurance market, in which differences in insurers across states and differences in state regulations or rules applying to insurers and providers can affect payment rates. Given these parameters, our sample initially included 432 discrete metropolitan areas.

Calculation of Payment Rates for Hospital Services

We define the payment rate for hospital services as an average payment per hospital stay in a geographic area. From the 432 MSAs and MSA state areas in our sample, we exclude areas with fewer than 200 hospital stays in 2008. After applying the hospital stay minimum criterion and excluding Maryland as an all-payer rate-setting state, our sample is reduced to 344 areas.

Payment rates for hospital services are calculated in three steps. First, in each area, the payment for each stay is adjusted by the diagnosis related group (DRG) weight for the stay, using the Medicare severity–DRGs (MS–DRGs). Second, a portion of the payment (68 percent) is further adjusted for area-specific input prices, using the adjustment for the area wage index described in the Commission's June 2007 report, updated for 2008 prices (Medicare Payment Advisory Commission 2007). Finally, we calculate the relative payment rate for each area as the ratio of that area's adjusted average payment per hospital stay compared with the national adjusted average payment. (The national average payment rate is based on data from all areas, including areas with fewer than 200 stays and nonmetropolitan areas.)[3]

Calculation of Payment Rates for Physician Services

The set of physician services that we examine comprises items and services billed through the Health Care Common Procedure Coding System (HCPCS). HCPCS includes the American Medical Association's copyrighted Common Procedure Terminology (CPT–4) and additional codes developed by CMS. HCPCS is used by both Medicare and commercial insurers and health plans.

The largest share of the commercial sector payments for physician services is for office visits—at about 30 percent—followed by imaging services.

Because there are thousands of services and their payment rates can vary in different ways, we constructed a summary measure or price index that captures the overall payment rate for a given area. First, we defined a market basket of physician services, consisting of about 160 HCPCS codes that represent a little more than 60 percent of total dollars for physician-billed services. Because the full set of possible codes includes many infrequently billed services—for example, some codes have only one instance of being billed in a particular geographic area or not at all—selecting a subset presents a practical compromise. The set of 160 services contains both the most frequently billed services and some infrequent, often high-payment, services.[4]

Table 7-1. Descriptive statistics for MarketScan claims data

Statistic	Inpatient hospital services	physician services
Number	1.2 million discharges	210 million claim line items
Total payments	$14.4 billion	$18.2 billion
Number of areas for aggregate data	1,030 (416 metropolitan areas; 570 micropolitan areas; 44 states' other non-metro areas)	1,030 (416 metropolitan areas; 570 micropolitan areas; 44 states' other non-metro areas)
Number of areas for area-level analysis	344 metropolitan areas	432 metropolitan areas
Distribution of dollars by plan type HMOs (including EPOs) PPOs	20% 64	14% 72
POSs (capitated and noncapitated) Indemnity plans	13 3	11 3

Note: EPO (exclusive provider organization), PPO (preferred provider organization), POS (point of service).

Source: MedPAC analysis of 2008 Thomson Reuters MarketScan® Commercial Claims and Encounter Data.© Copyright 2009 Thomson Reuters.

Second, we adjusted the payment amounts in the private-payer data for differences in practice costs faced by physicians across areas. We used a set of geographic adjustment factors at the core-based statistical area (CBSA) level developed by CMS.[5] This approach adjusts payments for physicians' input costs and does not reflect other factors that may affect how insurers set or negotiate physician payment rates. When the Commission examines regional variation across areas in Medicare expenditures, we make similar adjustments for the varying costs of doing business across areas. Such geographic adjustment is intended to make prices comparable across areas and to control for factors that justifiably contribute to higher or lower prices.

Third, we weighted each service in the market basket by the share of national spending associated with each code and applied that weighting to the services in each area. This step was necessary to account for differences between a given area's distribution of services and the aggregate distribution of services nationwide.

We considered only HCPCS codes for which there are more than 30 claims in an area, although not all areas have more than 30 claims for each of the 160 codes in the market basket. Consequently, in many markets, payment data were missing for some of the codes in the market basket. In those cases, we imputed a relative price level by assigning a price ratio equal to the weighted average of the price ratios for the codes with more than 30 claims in the area.[6]

Discussion of Data and Methodology

The MarketScan data and the methodology described above provide a large and rich source for analyzing private-sector payments. The database includes 1.2 million total hospital discharges and 210 million claim line items for physician services, capturing $14 billion of hospital payments and $18 billion of physician payments in the private sector (Table 7-1). However, our analysis contains several sources of potential bias.

Selective contribution of data to MarketScan by employers and plans results in a database that may not be a representative sample of the commercial market. Comparing some statistics from our data with those from other data sources suggests that this issue might be important. For example, at an aggregate level, the distribution by plan types in the MarketScan data is consistent with the distribution reported in the Kaiser Family Foundation (KFF)/Health Research and Educational Trust (HRET) 2008 Survey of Employer Health Benefits (Kaiser Family Foundation/ Health Research and Educational Trust 2008). The KFF/ HRET survey reports that about two-thirds of covered lives in large plans are enrolled in PPO-type plans: 58 percent are in PPOs and 8 percent are in high-deductible plans, which are generally on a PPO "platform." Analogous statistics in our data (recognizing the difference between covered lives and payments) are roughly similar: 64 percent of hospital payments and 72 percent of physician payments are from PPO claims. The distribution of HMO and POS plans is similar in the two sources.

However, there are notable differences in the distribution of plan types at the state level. For example, in the MarketScan data, 53 percent of total HMO payments to inpatient hospitals come from three states: California (33 percent), Texas (12 percent), and Georgia (8 percent). While the top placement of California might not be surprising given its historically high HMO penetration rate, the inclusion of Texas and Georgia is unexpected. Moreover, some states with traditionally high HMO penetration show very low shares of HMO payments in the state. In Oregon and Washington, only 3 percent of the state's hospital payments are from HMO claims, compared with 57 percent in California. These statistics suggest that we might not have a representational sampling of the privately insured market, and factors such as variation in the number of insurers providing data to MarketScan in a given market could affect our findings on payment variation within and across markets.

Our analysis is also sensitive to various adjustments made in calculating payment rates. For example, geographic adjustments for input prices—the area wage index for hospital prices and the geographic adjustment factors for physician practice expense—are intended to remove factors that likely vary from area to area. But they also change the relative payment rates across areas. Although these adjustment factors represent commonly accepted methods of geographic adjustment for input prices, one can disagree on the exact value of adjustment factors used in the analysis. For example, although input prices vary from one area to another within a state, our analysis of the data suggests that private-payer rates do not necessarily incorporate a specific adjustment to account for differing input prices. A given service may have a uniform payment rate in a state even when input prices vary.

Variation in Private-Payment Rates by Metropolitan Area

Variation in Payment Rates for Hospital Services

The results of our analysis are preliminary and subject to change. We find wide variation in private-sector payment rates for inpatient hospital care across metropolitan areas (Figure 7-1, p. 170). For the 344 metropolitan areas where at least 200 hospital stays occurred in 2008, the area-level index values—that is, the area's adjusted per discharge payments divided by the national average payment—range from 0.46 to 2.62, or a nearly sixfold difference between the highest and the lowest values. In other words, the highest payment area has an average payment per stay that is six times higher than the lowest paid metropolitan area. However, the highest paid area is an outlier in that a large difference exists between its index value of 2.62 and the second-highest index value of 1.92. At the lower end of the distribution, the second-lowest index value (0.47) is relatively close to the lowest value (0.46). If we remove the highest and lowest area index values, the second-highest index value (1.92) is slightly more than four times greater than the second-lowest value (0.47). The ratio narrows to 1.9 when we compare the index value at the 90th percentile of values with the index value at the 10th percentile of values.

Among the 20 areas with the highest index values for inpatient hospital payments, 7 are in California and the rest are in 11 other states. Areas of Alabama, Illinois, and Michigan are among the 20 areas with the lowest index values.

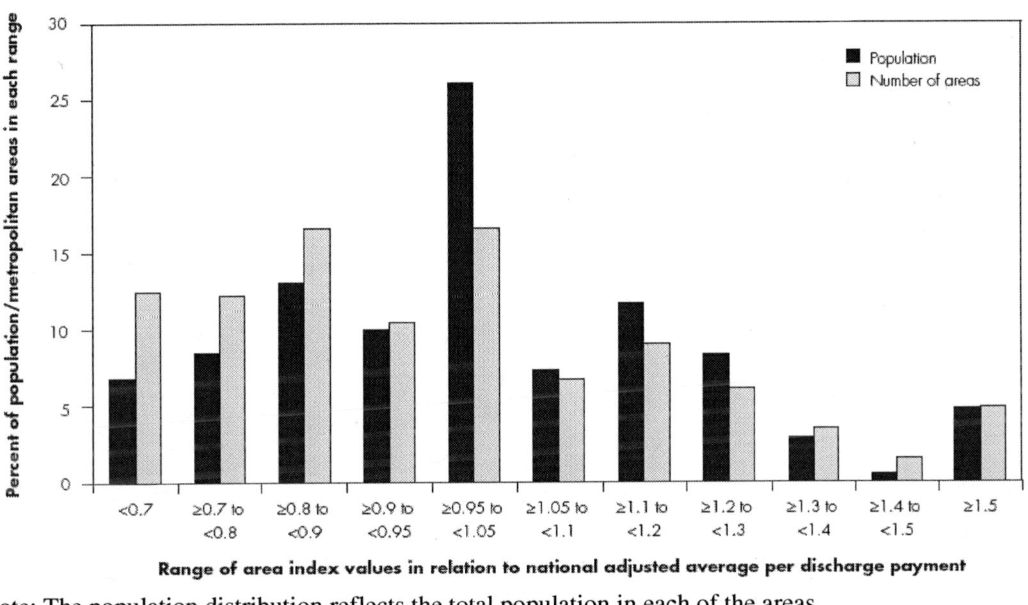

Note: The population distribution reflects the total population in each of the areas.
Source: MedPAC analysis of 2008 Thomson Reuters MarketScan® Commercial Claims and Encounter Data.© Copyright 2009 Thomson Reuters.

Figure 7-1. Average adjusted per stay hospital payments vary widely across 344 metropolitan areas.

Compared with the GAO study, which found an almost fourfold difference in hospital payment rates, our findings show higher variation in payment rates for hospital services. The ratio between the areas with the highest and the lowest relative payment rates in the

MarketScan data is 5.7 (compared with 3.6 in GAO's findings), and the ratio between the second-highest and the second-lowest relative payment rates is 4.1 (compared with 2.8 in GAO's findings). Comparing the 90th and the 10th percentile index values for hospitals, the GAO ratio is 1.6, compared with 1.9 for the MarketScan data. For some geographic areas, our results, based on 2008 data, varied widely from GAO's results, based on 2001 data. For example, in our analysis, all areas in California for which we had a sufficient number of hospital stays were higher in their relative payment rates than they were in the GAO study. (The two analyses are not entirely comparable: In addition to the difference in the time period analyzed—2001 data for the GAO study and 2008 for our analysis—the analyses also differ in data sources, the basis of the wage index for hospital services, the number of MSAs included the study sample, and the definition of MSAs, owing to the difference in years studied. The case-mix adjustment would also differ because we are using MS–DRGs while the GAO report would have used an earlier version of DRGs.)

Table 7-2. Metropolitan areas have slightly higher than average payments, but payments vary widely across states

	all areas	Metropolitan areas
Number of areas	1,030	416
Number of stays	1,209,275	1,093,781
Average adjusted per stay payment	$10,110	$10,250
Average adjusted per stay payment, excluding California	$9,730	$9,850
Average adjusted per stay payment, California Number of stays, California	$14,480 95,764	$14,490 93,851

Source: MedPAC analysis of 2008 Thomson Reuters MarketScan® Commercial Claims and Encounter Data.© Copyright 2009 Thomson Reuters.

We also see that many of the highest paid areas have a substantial level of out-of-area utilization. Because we are determining area-level payments based on the location of the provider, not the patient's residence, we define out-ofarea care as care provided to patients who reside outside the hospital's MSA or state area if the MSA crosses state borders. Out-of-area care may reflect border crossing from an immediately adjacent area, travel to a particular destination for specialized care or for care at an academic medical center, or travel to a prestigious institution.

We limited our area-specific analysis to metropolitan areas. Such areas have average payment levels that are higher than the national average across metropolitan and nonmetropolitan areas, as shown in Table 7-2. In the table, we use California data to show how payments can vary by state.

We have examined aggregate hospital payments in nonmetropolitan areas, defined as micropolitan areas, and other nonmetropolitan areas of each state. At the national level, our data show that nonmetropolitan areas have lower payment rates than metropolitan areas, but the relationship between nonmetropolitan and metropolitan payment levels varies across states. For example, in 11 states, average micropolitan area payments are higher than those in metropolitan areas. In four of those states, and in an additional seven states, nonmicropolitan rural area payments are higher than the average metropolitan payment rate.

Variation in Payment Rates for Physician Services

We find wide variation in private-sector payment rates for physician services across metropolitan areas, though not to the same degree as we find for hospital payments. The distribution of the physician payment index is shown in Figure 7-2 (p. 172). The input-price-adjusted index values range from 1.6 to 2.2 in areas with the highest index. At the other end of the distribution, the values range from 0.73 to 0.84. Comparing the index value at the 90th percentile with the index value at the 10th percentile, the ratio is 1.5 (lower than the hospital ratio of 1.9); 102 areas—nearly one-quarter of the areas and about 30 percent of the population—have an index value ranging from 0.95 to 1.05.

Among the 20 MSAs with the highest physician payment rates, 11 are in Wisconsin, 4 are in Oregon, and the remaining 5 are in various other states (including areas we cannot specify under the terms of the data use agreement). The 20 MSAs with the lowest payment rates are in Southern California, South Florida, the District of Columbia and surrounding areas, Maryland, New Jersey, Ohio, and Nassau–Suffolk, New York.

Across the 432 metropolitan areas in our sample, our preliminary estimate of the ratio of the highest to the lowest index value is 3.0 (2.2 divided by 0.73). This value is higher than the ratio of 2.0 reported in the GAO study based on 2001 claims data across 319 metropolitan areas (Government Accountability Office 2005). However, in most cases, the areas with high physician payment rates in the GAO study (e.g., Wisconsin) or with low payment rates (e.g., Maryland) continue to fall in the same relative grouping in our data.

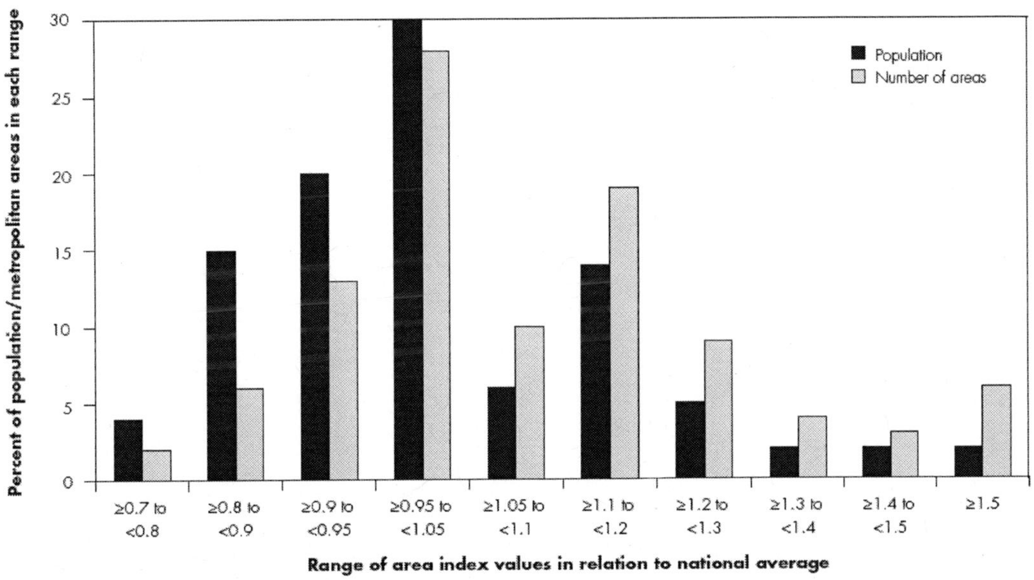

Note: There are no areas with an index below 0.7.

Source: MedPAC analysis of 2008 Thomson Reuters MarketScan® Commercial Claims and Encounter Data.© Copyright 2009 Thomson Reuters.

Figure 7-2. Private-payment rates for physician services also vary widely across 432 metropolitan areas.

Relationship between Hospital and Physician Payment Rates

For the 344 metropolitan areas for which we calculated hospital payment rates, we do not find a strong relationship between these areas' hospital rates and their physician payment rates. Areas with relatively high hospital rates can have relatively low physician payments, and vice versa. About 40 percent of the population resides in areas where the index value for hospital payments is relatively high but the index value for physician payments is relatively low. Also, about 10 percent of the population resides in areas where the relative index values for hospital and physician values are reversed (low hospital values and high physician values). The differences suggest that market conditions and dynamics between payers and providers for hospital care can be very different from those for physicians.

Examining Intramarket Variation

In some areas in our sample, we find evidence of considerable intramarket variation in physician payment rates. Intramarket variation has received more attention recently, in part because of the state attorney general's 2010 investigations in Massachusetts and recent HSC findings (Ginsburg 2010). Using the MarketScan physician data and other information about particular markets, we examined variation in physician payments within individual markets. Because the data do not provide the identity of insurers or administrators, or the identity of providers, the intramarket variation can be due to different insurers paying different amounts for the same service in an area, or it can be due to one insurer paying different providers different amounts for the same service. Other studies and other data we have examined suggest that the example we provide in Figure 7-3 does reflect payments that vary from one provider to another in the three markets with the widest variation (examples include the Massachusetts Attorney General's findings regarding the Boston market (Attorney General of the Commonwealth of Massachusetts 2010) and the GAO description of the Milwaukee market as one with significant provider leverage in negotiations with insurers, "which limited insurers' ability to control the prices they pay" in a geographic area with "highly consolidated provider networks ... that included both hospitals and physicians ... [with] established markets in separate geographic areas, each with loyal consumers" (Government Accountability Office 2004)).

Figure 7-3 shows the intermarket and intramarket variation across four metropolitan areas. The rates are geographically adjusted for a specific payer category (PPOs) for a specific service (a midlevel office visit, HCPCS code 99214—the second most frequently billed service in the private-payer data). The figure shows the median, the 10th percentile, and the 90th percentile of the payment rates for each area. In Miami, the median geographically adjusted payment rate is relatively low, and there is relatively less variation in the payment for this service. The three other markets shown have wider variation, and two markets have medians above the national average. In the San Jose market, for example, although half of the claims are paid at or below the national average, some claims are paid at more than twice the national average. In the Boston market, the median payment exceeds the national average, but some payments are below the national average. In Milwaukee, at least 90 percent of payments exceed the national average, and the median is well above the national average.

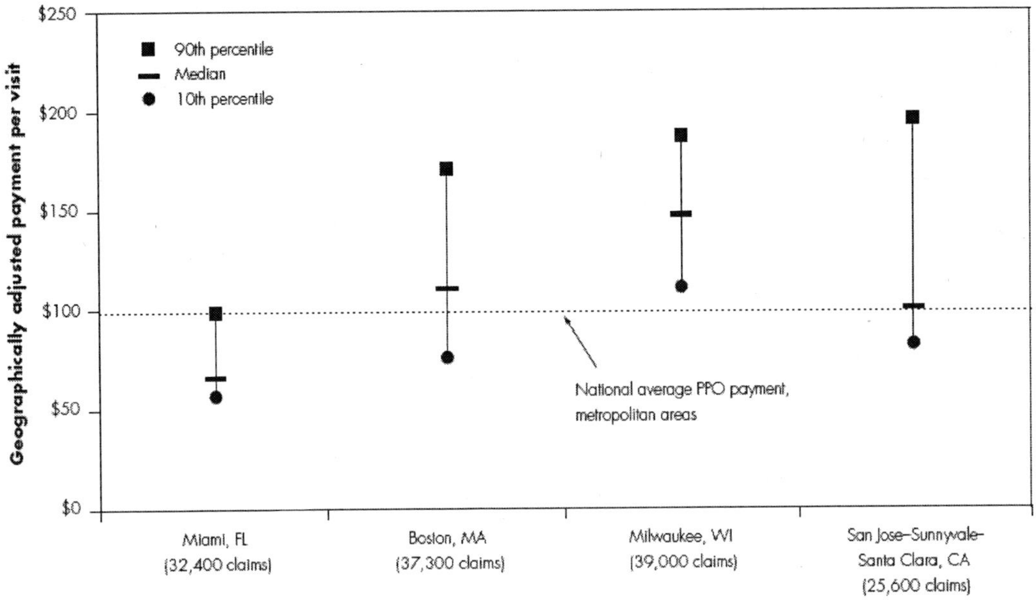

Note: PPO (preferred provider organization). Dollar amounts are geographically adjusted for area input prices. Payments are for PPO plans in each area.

Source: MedPAC analysis of 2008 Thomson Reuters MarketScan® Commercial Claims and Encounter Data.© Copyright 2009 Thomson Reuters.

Figure 7-3. PPO payment variation across and within areas for a midlevel physician office visit in 2008.

Physician Payment Variation by Type of Service

Additional analysis of the physician payment data shows different degrees of variation by type of service across areas. In general, on the basis of frequently billed HCPCS codes, we find that payment rates vary less for the following services:

- most categories of office visits,
- obstetric care and cesarean delivery,
- ophthalmology,
- chiropractic care, and
- some minor skin procedures.

In contrast, we observe large variation in payment rates across many lab test codes, heart echography, and other imaging related to heart procedures.

For each of the 74 service groupings in the midlevel Berenson–Eggers Type of Service (BETOS) classification system, we calculated a ratio of payment levels in each metropolitan area compared with the national average payment. We then calculated the 90th percentile and the 10th percentile of those ratios for each BETOS category. Table 7-3 shows the 10 sets of services with the greatest and the least variation across metropolitan areas.[7]

Table 7-3. Ratio of 90th to10th percentile of payment across metropolitan areas

10 service categories with greatest variation across MSAs			10 service categories with least variation across MSAs		
BETOS category		Ratio of 90th to 10th percentile	BETOS category		Ratio of 90th to 10th percentile
P8F	Endoscopy—bronchoscopy	3.97	P0	Anesthesia	1.69
M5D Specialist—other		3.60	M2B Hospital visit—subsequent		1.64
T1B	Lab tests—automated general profiles	3.47	M6	Consultations	1.64
I4A	Imaging/procedure—heart including cardiac catheter	3.11	M5B	Specialist—psychiatry	1.59
P5D	Ambulatory procedures—lithotripsy	2.96	P6C	Minor procedures—other (Medicare fee schedule)	1.59
T1D	Lab tests—blood counts	2.96	M1A	Office visits—new	1.55
T1A	Lab tests—routine venipuncture (non-Medicare fee schedule)	2.82	M1B	Office visits—established	1.53
I1D	Standard imaging—contrast gastrointestinal	2.63	P1G	Major procedure—other	1.51
T1C	Lab tests—urinalysis	2.52	O1B	Chiropractic	1.46
P1A	Major procedure—breast	2.48	O1G	Influenza immunization	1.42

Note: BETOS (Berenson–Eggers Type of Service).
Source: MedPAC analysis of 2008 Thomson Reuters MarketScan® Commercial Claims and Encounter Data.© Copyright 2009 Thomson Reuters.

There may be many reasons for the variation, or lack of variation, by type of service. For example, a flu vaccination is a standardized service and one might expect relatively small differences in payment rates. Table 7-3 shows little variation for the service, as expected. In contrast, lab tests are also standardized services, yet they show wide variation across markets. The nature of the service, the underlying economics of providing the service, and the manner in which providers are organized can affect the degree of variation in payment rates. In certain markets, single-specialty groups may be able to negotiate higher payments for services such as imaging and certain procedures, whereas in other markets those services may be provided in a more decentralized manner. We will continue to examine the variation by service category.

Not surprisingly, areas with high payment rates for the basket of physician services frequently have high payment rates for each service category. Table 7-4 reports how many of the 74 BETOS categories are at or above the 90th percentile, or at or below the 10th percentile, for a given area. For example, Eau Claire and Madison, Wisconsin, have high payment rates for the physician market basket, and each area has high payment rates for 70 of the 74 BETOS categories. Conversely, areas with lower payment rates for the basket of physician services—such as Florida, Maryland, and New Jersey—also are areas with lower payment rates across service categories. For example, Bethesda, Maryland, has relatively low payment rates for 58 of 74 service categories.

Table 7-4. Many areas show either generally high or generally low payment levels across a wide range of BETOS service categories

MSA	Of 74 service categories, number where payment is at or above 90th	MSA	Of 74 service categories, number where payment is at or below 10th percentile
Eau Claire, WI	70	Bethesda–Frederick–Rockville, MD	58
Madison, WI	70	MD:Wilmington, DE–MD–NJ	57
(unnamed metro area: DUA)	66	MD:Washington–Arlington–Alexandria, DC–VA–MD–WV	56
WI: La Crosse, WI–MN	65	West Palm Beach–Boca Raton–Boynton Beach, FL	53
Green Bay, WI	64	Baltimore–Towson, MD	53
Appleton, WI	63	Akron, OH	47
Oshkosh–Neenah, WI	63	VA:Washington–Arlington–Alexandria, DC–VA–MD–WV	47
Janesville, WI	62	Fort Lauderdale–Pompano Beach–Deerfield Beach, FL	45
Rochester, MN	60	OH:Youngstown–Warren–Boardman, OH–PA	45
Wausau, WI	59	Canton–Massillon, OH	43
Sheboygan, WI	57	DC:Washington–Arlington–Alexandria, DC–VA–MD–WV	41
(unnamed metro area: DUA)	56	Edison–New Brunswick, NJ	39
Sioux Falls, SD	56	Vineland–Millville–Bridgeton, NJ	39
Milwaukee–Waukesha–West Allis, WI	55	Nassau–Suffolk, NY	38
Fond du Lac, WI	54	Oxnard–Thousand Oaks–Ventura, CA	35

Note: BETOS (Berenson–Eggers Type of Service), DUA (data use agreement).

Source: MedPAC analysis of 2008 Thomson Reuters MarketScan® Commercial Claims and Encounter Data.© Copyright 2009 Thomson Reuters.

Table 7-5 (p. 176) shows how the relationship among physician payments for particular types of services varies from one market to another by using the five major BETOS categories. Nationally, across the markets for which we have data, imaging accounts for 15 percent of physician payments. In Rochester, Minnesota, however, imaging accounts for 33 percent of total payments in the area (not shown in table). After substituting the national average payment rate for the local rate for each HCPCS code, the share of payments for imaging services remains much higher than the national share, at 28 percent of total payments in Rochester. A possible explanation is that in Rochester, more than 90 percent of the payments for physician care in our data are for patients from areas outside the Rochester MSA. Those out-of-area patients may be more likely to receive diagnostic imaging and testing.

In the Miami market, the distribution of dollars by service category is about the same as the national distribution. Although payment rates are lower than the national average payment rates for all types of services, the relative payment rates across types of services are similar to those nationally. Therefore, the distribution across types of services remains similar despite the difference in the level of payment rates. (Given what we know about Medicare utilization in Miami, if it is a higher utilizing area for private payers, these data would suggest that high utilization of physician services is not limited to specific service categories but instead occurs across the board. The Miami data illustrate that Table 7-5 does not necessarily show the extent of service utilization in an area, nor does it necessarily show the intensity of services.)

Table 7-5. The share of payments for different service categories can vary widely across markets, even after adjusting for payment differences across types of services

Major BETOS category	National share of payments	Adjusted shares of payment in each area				
		Rochester, MN	Miami, FL	Grand Junction, CO	Portland, OR	Santa Cruz, CA
I (imaging)	15%	28%	16%	9%	10%	15%
M (visits)	47	30	49	47	45	45
P (procedures)	26	30	25	32	34	28
T (tests)	7	11	5	4	5	5
O (other)	5	1	4	8	6	7

Note: BETOS (Berenson–Eggers Type of Service). For each BETOS category, a market's proportion of dollars is adjusted by the price index to determine the ratios that would exist if services were paid at the national average level. "O" (other) category is chiropractic care and flu vaccine administration. Figures may not sum to 100 percent due to rounding.

Source: MedPAC analysis of 2008 Thomson Reuters MarketScan® Commercial Claims and Encounter Data.© Copyright 2009 Thomson Reuters.

Notable about the Grand Junction, Colorado, and Portland, Oregon, markets is that imaging as a share of dollars in these two areas is one-third less than the national average, while procedures make up a larger share than the national average. These two areas have low

Medicare service use rates, at 84 percent and 85 percent of the national average, respectively (Medicare Payment Advisory Commission 2011b). If service use is similarly low among private payers, the data in Table 7-5 may indicate that imaging and testing services are used judiciously in these areas, and the smaller share of the dollars for these services explains how procedures can make up a larger share of payments in these markets. Because we are looking at adjusted payments (payments as though they were made at national average levels), the lower share for imaging in these two markets indicates either that fewer imaging services are used, in general, or that the mix of imaging services tends toward lower priced services compared with the national distribution in this BETOS category.[8]

In Santa Cruz, California, the unadjusted share of dollars spent on imaging is 19 percent of the total dollars (not shown in table). Imaging payments in Santa Cruz average 1.66 times the national average, while payments for procedures in Santa Cruz average 1.19 times the national average (not shown in table). Adjusting the relatively high prices for imaging in Santa Cruz by computing the amount that would have been paid using national average rates (and similarly adjusting all other BETOS categories), the adjusted share of imaging in Santa Cruz equals the national average, at 15 percent. The Santa Cruz data illustrate that a market's higher payments for a given category of services cause a larger share of dollars to be spent on those services, and in some cases (as in Santa Cruz) the higher share is primarily, if not entirely, due to the higher payments made for this category of services.

Next Steps

Our preliminary analysis of private-payer payments for physician services across metropolitan areas shows that there is noticeable variation in payment rates and that there may be even wider variation across areas for some types of services.

We will continue our analysis of physician and hospital payment rates in the private sector. We plan to examine particular markets in depth. Areas that have been studied by others (such as the communities studied by HSC) provide a valuable opportunity to test the validity and enhance our understanding of the analysis. We also plan to study areas that have not been examined extensively.

Although we have noted several potential limitations of the data set, a systematic, quantitative approach to the private payer claims data is useful. It allows for a consistent analytic approach across areas. Overall trends and patterns inferred from the data might not be clear, but our analysis can provide a broader context for understanding specific markets. Consequently, it would be an important companion piece to case studies of individual market areas.

Another component of our future work would be to examine alternative ways to measure market concentration or provider market power. Market concentration involving horizontal mergers traditionally has been measured with the Herfindahl–Hirschman index (HHI), and antitrust guidelines establish relative levels of concentration based on that index.[9] Some of the literature suggests that the HHI cannot be relied on exclusively as the measure of the effect on prices of a horizontal merger. It may be appropriate to use alternatives to the HHI, or some modification of the HHI, to measure concentration in health care markets.

In addition, while the HHI measures concentration in horizontal mergers, we are not aware of a similar measure for vertical consolidation and its market effect (though there is some literature on this topic), nor does there appear to be a measure or index that considers horizontal and vertical integration together in determining market power.

The Commission views the analysis of private-payer payment rates as important. As policymakers look for market-based solutions to the issues the Medicare program faces, it is important to understand the mechanisms at play in the private sector, including reasons for the variation in payments that we see across and within markets. Our work examining the variation in private-payer rates also informs our ongoing analysis of Medicare payment adequacy and our understanding of the factors that need to be considered in determining payment rates, such as input prices and the relative quality of providers as a source of variation in payments.

Endnotes

[1] Trimming the physician claims is the same trimming we traditionally perform when we do the annual computation of Medicare–private-payment rates for physician services. MarketScan data are trimmed according to payer type (HMO, PPO) and geographic area. We believe this method is appropriate because we are trimming payments for specific Health Care Common Procedure Coding System (HCPCS) codes at a relatively small geographic level. We have also done spot checks using other data on private-sector physician payments to determine whether we see any pattern of payments falling outside the ranges that remain after trimming (e.g., ensuring that the highest payment for a particular HCPCS code that recurs in a different data set is not trimmed out in the MarketScan data). For the hospital data—for which we have far fewer claims per area than for many of the HCPCS codes—we trimmed only at the low end ($500 or less) because it appears that some of the low-payment claims in the data may be for providers other than acute care hospitals. At the high end of hospital claims we decided not to trim because, unlike the physician claims, we are dealing with various methods of payment (diagnosis related groups, per diems, discounted charges) that make it difficult to determine a unit of payment to which trimming could be applied. In addition, the hospital data contain claims from all provider types, including those that can have very high payments (often reflecting long lengths of stay), such as children's hospitals and hospitals specializing in cancer care. Aside from the trimming, we also removed claims for which there was coordination of benefits (e.g., another insurer) or for which the geographic area of the provider could not be identified. In the case of hospital claims, we removed claims for the state of Maryland, where payment is established under an all-payer rate system.

[2] We do not know the balance billed amount for a claim. The MarketScan data do not contain information on the billed charge, and therefore we do not know the difference between the billed amount and the paid amount. Even when the difference between the billed amount and the insurer-paid amount is known, it is not always the case that the provider receives the full difference from the patient. Some or all of the amount may be written off as bad debt, or a patient could negotiate a reduction in liability.

[3] For hospital services and physician services, to the extent that there are any capitated payments, we exclude such payments from our analysis, even when a fee-for-service equivalent is provided.

[4] There can be a "site of service differential." Often, but not always, the private-payer data show a different payment amount for the same service depending on whether it was provided in certain types of facilities rather than in a physician's office. For example, we treat a facility-based service as a separate service from a non-facility-based service in our analysis of payment rates by service (the equivalent of viewing each as having a different HCPCS code). We do not include the separate payment to the facility in the payment total.

[5] By coincidence, the CBSA factors applied to the private pay claims data for metropolitan areas are budget neutral. That is, across all areas the total of geographically adjusted dollars in the MarketScan data equals the total of unadjusted dollars paid by private payers. This result would be expected for Medicare payments, for which the adjuster was developed, but not necessarily for private-payer data. To use a simple example, payments made in areas with a geographic adjuster of 0.9 are evened out by payments made in areas with a geographic adjuster of 1.1, because the adjuster is based on relative cost factors in relation to the total expenditures, which is the national figure for expenditures (1.0).

[6] Because payment rates for certain services are imputed, some of the variation that we see across markets may be due to our inability to price particular services. Our imputation assigns the average price ratio of services

present in the market, but the actual price ratio of the missing services could be quite different from the average.

[7] Because we are examining groups of services by area, rather than individual services (specific unique HCPCS codes), some of the differences across areas can reflect the different mix of services included in the groupings in different areas if the pricing of particular services (specific HCPCS codes) differs from the pricing of a different service (a specific HCPCS code) that falls within the same BETOS category.

[8] It may also be the case that the lower share for imaging in Portland and Grand Junction is a function of procedures making up such a high share of payments in the area.

[9] The HHI is calculated by squaring the market share of each entity competing in a market and summing the result. The index "approaches zero when a market consists of a large number of firms of relatively equal size. The HHI increases both as the number of firms in the market decreases and as the disparity in size between those firms increases. Markets in which the HHI is between 1,000 and 1,800 points are considered to be moderately concentrated, and those in which the HHI is in excess of 1,800 points are considered to be concentrated. Transactions that increase the HHI by more than 100 points in concentrated markets presumptively raise antitrust concerns under the Horizontal Merger Guidelines issued by the U.S. Department of Justice and the Federal Trade Commission." (Department of Justice 2009).

References

Attorney General of the Commonwealth of Massachusetts. 2010. Examination of health care cost trends and cost drivers pursuant to G.L. c. 118G, § 61/2(b). Report for Annual Public Hearing. March. http://www.mass.gov/Cago/docs/healthcare/ final_report_w_cover_ appendices_glossary.pdf.

Baker, Laurence, A. Royalty, and K. Bundorf. *Variations in prices for physician services.* Slides from presentation at the June 2010 meeting of Academy Health.

Berenson, Robert, P. Ginsburg, and N. Kemper. 2010. Unchecked provider clout in California foreshadows challenges to health reform. *Health Affairs* 29, no. 4, web first (April). http://www. healthaffairs.org.

California Healthcare Foundation. 2009. Issues and trends from a six-region study of California health systems. http://www.chcf. org/publications/2009/12/issues-and-trends-from-a-sixregionstudy-of-california-health-systems.

Department of Justice. 2009. The Herfindahl–Hirschman Index. http://www.usdoj.gov/ atr/public/testimony/hhi.htm.

Ginsburg, P. B. 2010. *Wide variation in hospital and physician payment rates evidence of provider market power.* Research brief no. 16. Washington, DC: HSC.

Government Accountability Office. 2004. *Milwaukee health care spending compared to other metropolitan areas: Geographic variation in spending for enrollees in the Federal Employees Health Benefits Program.* GAO–04–1000R. Washington, DC: GAO.

Government Accountability Office. 2005. *Federal Employees Health Benefits Program: Competition and other factors linked to wide variation in prices.* GAO–05–856. Washington, DC: GAO.

Kaiser Family Foundation/Health Research and Educational Trust. 2008. *Employer health benefits: 2008 annual survey.* Menlo Park, CA: KFF/HRET.

Medicare Payment Advisory Commission. 2007. *Report to the Congress: Promoting greater efficiency in Medicare.* Washington, DC: MedPAC.

Medicare Payment Advisory Commission. 2010. *Report to the Congress: Medicare payment policy.* Washington, DC: MedPAC.

Medicare Payment Advisory Commission. 2011a. *Report to the Congress: Medicare payment policy*. Washington, DC: MedPAC.

Medicare Payment Advisory Commission. 2011b. *Report to the Congress: Regional variation in Medicare service use.* Online appendixes. Washington, DC: MedPAC.

APPENDIX A. REVIEW OF CMS'S PRELIMINARY ESTIMATE OF THE 2012 UPDATE FOR PHYSICIAN AND OTHER PROFESSIONAL SERVICES

In CMS's annual letter to the Commission on the update for physician and other professional services, the agency's preliminary estimate of the 2012 payment update is –29.5 percent (Blum 2011). Most of the prescribed reduction is due to a series of temporary increases enacted over several years that—under current law—expire at the end of 2011. Those increases prevented a series of negative updates under the sustainable growth rate (SGR) formula—the statutory formula for annually updating Medicare's payment rates for physician and other professional services. If the temporary increases expire, the physician fee schedule's conversion factor must decrease by 25.0 percent. The remainder of the reduction would be the formula's update—specific to 2012—of −6.1 percent. This further reduction would be applied to the conversion factor after it had been reduced by 25.0 percent.[1]

This appendix provides the Commission's mandated technical review of CMS's estimate. We find that CMS's calculations are correct and that—absent a change in law—the expiration of the temporary increases and the formula's update for 2012 are very unlikely to produce an update that differs substantially from –29.5 percent. The temporary increases—by far, the largest factor influencing the payment reduction—were specified in law. The estimate of an SGR formula's update of −6.1 percent for 2012 could change between now and when CMS would implement the update in January, but any such changes are likely to be small compared with the total reduction prescribed.

While this appendix is limited to technical issues, the Commission has concerns about the SGR formula as a payment policy. Those concerns are discussed in Chapter 1 of this report.

How Temporary Increases and Other Legislative Provisions Have Affected Payments for Physician and Other Professional Services

The SGR formula is intended to limit growth in Medicare spending for physician and other professional services. If aggregate spending—accumulated since 1996—exceeds the specified target spending accumulated in the same time period, the formula calls for a downward adjustment in the physician fee schedule's conversion factor.

In recent years, spending has exceeded the target, and updates calculated with the formula would have been negative. However, except for the negative update implemented in 2002, the Congress has passed specific legislation overriding the negative updates called for by the SGR formula.

Initially, the legislative overrides prescribed a positive update for a given year—resulting in higher spending—but did not allow the corresponding spending target to rise. The result was a growing gap between spending and the target. The formula could have recouped the difference, but the process would have required many years of negative updates. In response, the Congress instituted a new method. Starting with the update for 2007, legislation prescribed temporary increases. When the increases expire, updates are calculated—with the formula—as if the increases had never been applied.

From 2007 through 2011, the temporary increases totaled a cumulative increase in payment rates of 3.8 percent (Figure A-1).2 Meanwhile, the accumulated updates— called for by the formula but legislatively overridden— totaled –22.2 percent. The difference is a 25.0 percent reduction in payment rates required when the temporary increases expire.

In addition to the temporary increases, recent legislation has made further changes in payments for services furnished by physicians and other health professionals. Some provisions lowered payments. As an example, the Patient Protection and Affordable Care Act of 2010 (PPACA) changed the reduction for imaging procedures conducted on contiguous body parts, increasing it from 25 percent to 50 percent. Beginning in 2012, PPACA establishes a penalty for professionals who are not successful electronic prescribers.3 Other legislative provisions raised payments. For instance, beginning in 2011, PPACA established a 10 percent bonus payment for eligible practitioners who furnish two types of services: primary care services and major surgical procedures. Further, PPACA extended Physician Quality Reporting System bonuses through 2014.4 PPACA also established an incentive payment for eligible professionals who meet the requirements of a Maintenance of Certification program. And the law required the Secretary—when determining the physician fee schedule's geographic practice cost index (GPCI) for practice expense—to recognize only one-half of the geographic variation in practice expenses. Because this provision of the law included a hold-harmless requirement, it did not lower payments in any geographic area but it raised payments in a number of areas. Other legislation—the Medicare and Medicaid Extenders Act of 2010—extended through 2011 the floor on the GPCI for physician work.

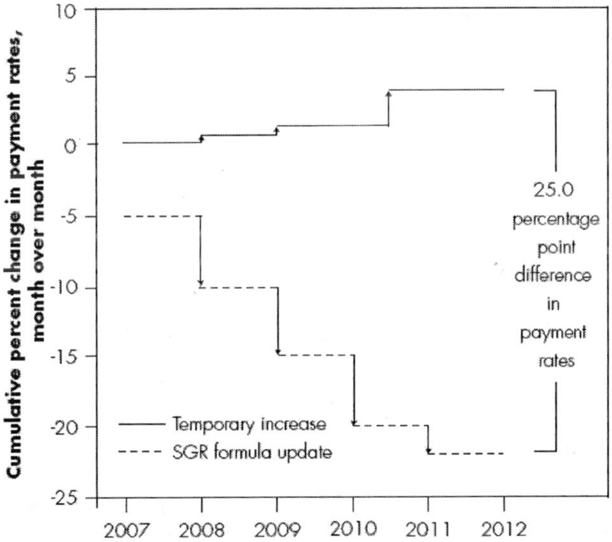

Note: SGR (sustainable growth rate). The 25.0 percentage point difference is the ratio of the cumulative SGR formula updates to the cumulative temporary bonuses (0.778/1.038 = 0.750 or –25.0 percent).
Source: Blum 2011 and Office of the Actuary 2011.

Figure A-1. Temporary increases prevented the SGR formula's negative updates.

How CMS Estimated the SGR Formula's Update for 2012

Calculating the update for practitioner services is a twostep process. CMS first estimates the SGR—the target growth rate for spending on these services—for the coming year. The agency then computes the update using that SGR and historical information on actual and target spending.

SGR for 2012

The SGR is a function of projected changes in:

- input prices for practitioner services—an allowance for inflation,5
- real gross domestic product (GDP) per capita—an allowance for growth in the volume and intensity of services,6
- enrollment in fee-for-service (FFS) Medicare—an allowance for fluctuations in the number of FFS beneficiaries, and
- spending attributable to changes in law and regulation—an allowance for policy changes that affect spending on practitioner services.

Allowing for these four factors, CMS's preliminary estimate of the SGR for 2012 is –17.2 percent (Table A-1). The first of these factors—the estimated change in input prices of 0.1 percent—is lower than the figure for previous years. Given economic conditions, CMS projects relatively modest increases in practitioner compensation, staff earnings, rent, and the prices of other inputs.

The next factor in the 2012 SGR—growth in real GDP per capita—is a 10-year moving average. It includes estimates of economic growth for 2003 through 2010 and projections for 2011 and 2012. CMS's estimate of 0.9 percent for this factor is just 0.1 percentage point less than the estimate we calculate when we use Congressional Budget Office projections for 2011 and 2012 to compute a 10-year moving average of growth in real GDP per capita (Congressional Budget Office 2011).

For the factor on the change in FFS enrollment, CMS is not projecting a change in FFS enrollment because of increases or decreases in enrollment in Medicare Advantage. Instead, the agency projects an increase in FFS enrollment of 3.3 percent, which is the same as the projected growth in Medicare enrollment overall (FFS plus Medicare Advantage).

The remaining factor in the 2012 SGR is a –20.6 percent change in spending due to law and regulation. For this factor, expiration of the temporary increases is the primary source of CMS's estimate of the 20.6 percent decrease in spending. Other changes in spending due to law and regulation—such as expiration of the floor on the work GPCI and expiration of the provision limiting variation in the practice expense GPCI—would be relatively small.

Why is the change in spending due to law and regulation a smaller reduction than the 25.0 percent reduction in payments that would occur when the temporary increases expire? There are two reasons for the difference. First, if the temporary increases expire, payment rates in the physician fee schedule would go down. However, payment rates in the laboratory fee schedule would not be affected. The law and regulation factor in the SGR accounts for changes in spending under both of these payment systems.7 Second, the law and regulation factor is not an estimate of a change in payment rates; it is an estimate of a change in spending. A change in payment rates would not necessarily equal a change in spending if the change in payment rates were accompanied by a change in the volume of services. Indeed, when projecting a decrease in payment rates, CMS offsets the decrease by almost a third to account for a volume increase, consistent with the agency's research (Codespote et al. 1998).[8]

Table A-1. Preliminary estimate of the sustainable growth rate, 2012

Factor	Percent
2012 change in:	
Input prices*	0.1%
Real GDP per capita	0.9
Fee-for-service enrollment	3.3
Change due to law or regulation	–20.6
Sustainable growth rate	–17.2

Note: GDP (gross domestic product). Percentages are converted to ratios and multiplied, not added, to produce the sustainable growth rate. Estimates shown are preliminary. *The change in input prices includes inflation measures for services furnished by a physician or other health professional or furnished in the office of a physician or other health professional. As defined for the sustainable growth rate, those services include services billable under the physician fee schedule and laboratory services.

Source: Blum 2011.

Calculating the SGR Formula's Update Specific to 2012

After estimating the SGR, CMS calculates the SGR formula's annual update specific to the given year. It is a function of:

- the change in productivity-adjusted input prices for physician and other professional services, as measured by the Medicare Economic Index (MEI);9 and
- an update adjustment factor (UAF) that increases or decreases the update as needed to align actual spending, cumulated over time, with target spending determined by the SGR.

The estimate of the change in input prices for use in the 2012 update is 0.3 percent (Table A-2, p. 186). This factor could change by November 2011 when CMS finalizes the update for 2012. By then, the MEI could be somewhat higher or lower than 0.3 percent as further data become available on changes in input prices for physician and other professional services.

The UAF is projected to have a larger effect on the update calculation. For 2012, CMS estimates a UAF of –6.4 percent. Combining this adjustment with the estimated change in input prices results in an update estimate of –6.1 percent. The UAF is negative because from 2001 to 2009 actual spending for physician and other professional services exceeded the target (Figure A-2).[10] Like the MEI, the UAF could change by November. The UAF is partly a function of actual spending for physician and other professional services. When calculating the preliminary estimate of the 2012 update, CMS had data on actual spending that were nearly complete for the first three quarters of 2010 but less so for the last quarter of that year. As more data become available, the estimate of actual spending in 2010 may change somewhat before CMS issues a final rule on the update in November. The estimates of actual spending for 2011 could also change.

Nonetheless, changes in the UAF are not likely to have a large impact on the update calculations. By law, the update adjustment is limited to a maximum reduction of –7.0 percent, so it can go no lower even if spending goes up faster than projected by CMS. Alternatively, the update adjustment could lead to a somewhat smaller reduction in payment rates if spending increases at a slower rate than CMS anticipates. For instance, if spending in 2011 were 1 percent lower than CMS projects, the update adjustment for 2012 would be −5.3 percent instead of −6.4 percent.

In turn, the SGR formula's update specific to 2012 would go from −6.1 percent to −5.0 percent. Such changes do not appear large compared with an overall reduction in payment rates—due to expiring temporary increases and the formula's update specific to 2012—of 29.5 percent.

Table A-2. Preliminary estimate of the SGR formula's update specific to 2012

Factor	Percent
Change in MEI*	0.3%
Update adjustment factor	–6.4
Update	–6.1

Note: SGR (sustainable growth rate), MEI (Medicare Economic Index).

Percentages are converted to ratios and multiplied, not added, to produce the update. Estimates shown are preliminary. *For the SGR formula update, physician services include only those services billable under the physician fee schedule.

Source: Blum 2011.

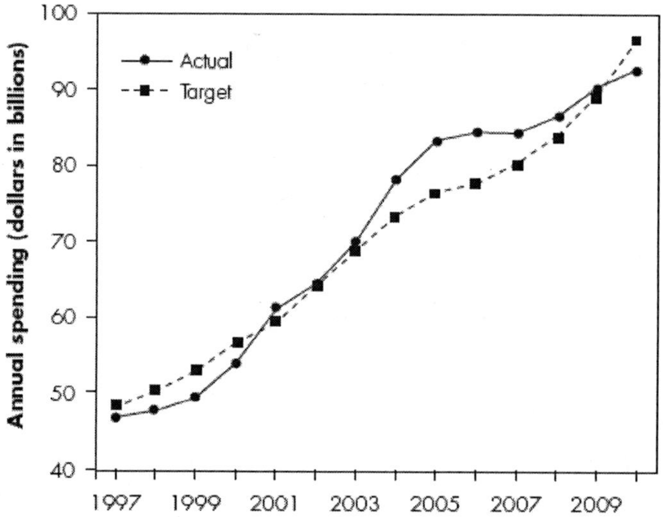

Note: Estimates shown are preliminary. Data for 1997 and 1998 are for the last three quarters of each of those years and the first quarter of the following year.

Source: Final rule on the physician fee schedule for 2011.

Figure A-2. From 2001 to 2009, actual spending for physician services exceeded the target.

End Notes

[1] For the update calculations discussed in this appendix, percentages are not added. Instead, they are converted to ratios and multiplied. For instance, the decrease in payment rates of 29.5 percent is the arithmetic product of the 2012 update (–6.1 percent, or 0.9388) and the expiration of the temporary increases (–25.0 percent, or 0.7505). The multiplication is 0.9388 Ч 0.7505 = 0.7046, or –29.5 percent.

[2] For 2007, the Tax Relief and Health Care Act of 2006 maintained payment rates at 2006 levels. For the first six months of 2008, the Medicare, Medicaid, and SCHIP Extension Act of 2007 raised payment rates by 0.5 percent. For the second six months of 2008, the Medicare Improvements for Patients and Providers Act of 2008 (MIPPA) maintained payment rates at the levels for the first six months of that year. For 2009, MIPPA raised payment rates by 1.1 percent. For January and February of 2010, the Department of Defense Appropriations Act of 2010 maintained payment rates at their 2009 levels. For March 2010, the Temporary Extension Act of 2010 maintained payment rates at the levels for the first two months of the year. For April and May of 2010, the Continuing Extension Act maintained payment rates at the levels for the first three months of the year. For June through November of 2010, the Preservation of Access to Care for Medicare Beneficiaries and Pension Relief Act of 2010 raised payment rates by 2.2 percent. For December 2010, the Physician Payment and Therapy Relief Act of 2010 maintained payment rates at the levels for June through November of 2010. For all of 2011, the Medicare and Medicaid Extenders Act of 2010 maintained payment rates at the levels for June through December of 2010.

[3] To determine who is a successful electronic prescriber, the Secretary is authorized to use one of two possible criteria. First, eligible professionals must meet a threshold for reporting on quality measures for electronic prescribing. Second, eligible professionals must submit electronically a sufficient number of prescriptions under Medicare Part D.

[4] Beginning in 2015, PPACA establishes a penalty for professionals who do not report on quality measures.

[5] For calculating the SGR, practitioner services are services commonly performed by a physician or in a physician's office. In addition to services in the physician fee schedule, these services include diagnostic laboratory tests.

[6] As required by the Medicare Prescription Drug, Improvement, and Modernization Act of 2003, the real GDP per capita factor in the SGR is a 10-year moving average.

[7] For the SGR, practitioner services are defined as services furnished by a physician or other health professional or furnished in the office of a physician or other health professional.

[8] The maximum volume offset is 4.5 percent (a 30 percent offset of a payment reduction of up to 15 percent). The 15 percent limit was established because that was the largest reduction seen in CMS's volume offset study.

[9] For the update, practitioner services include only those services billable under the physician fee schedule.

[10] Starting with the update for 2010, CMS removed physicianadministered drugs from the SGR definition of practitioner services. This change narrowed the gap between actual spending and the target.

References

Blum, Jonathan D., Centers for Medicare & Medicaid Services, Department of Health and Human Services. 2011. Letter to Glenn M. Hackbarth, Medicare Payment Advisory Commission. March 7. http://www.cms.hhs.gov/SustainableGRatesConFact.

Codespote, S. M., W. J. London, and J. D. Shatto. 1998. Physician volume and intensity response. Baltimore, MD: CMS. http://www.cms.hhs.gov/ActuarialStudies/downloads/PhysicianResponse.pdf.

Congressional Budget Office. 2011. *The budget and economic outlook: Fiscal years 2011 to 2021*. Washington, DC: CBO. http://www.cbo.gov/doc.cfm?index=12039.

Office of the Actuary, Centers for Medicare & Medicaid Services, Department of Health and Human Services. 2011. *Estimated sustainable growth rate and conversion factor, for Medicare payments to physicians in 2012*. Baltimore, MD: CMS. http://www.cms.gov/SustainableGRatesConFact/Downloads/sgr2012p.pdf.

Appendix B. Commissioners' Voting on Recommendations

In the Medicare, Medicaid and SCHIP Benefits Improvement and Protection Act of 2000, the Congress required MedPAC to call for individual Commissioner votes on each recommendation and to document the voting record in its report. The information below satisfies that mandate.

The sustainable growth rate system: Policy considerations for adjustments and alternatives

No recommendations

Improving payment accuracy and appropriate use of ancillary services

2-1 The Secretary should accelerate and expand efforts to package discrete services in the physician fee schedule into larger units for payment.

Yes: Armstrong, Baicker, Behroozi, Berenson, Borman, Butler, Castellanos, Chernew, Dean, Hackbarth, Hansen, Kane, Kuhn, Miller, Stuart, Uccello

Absent: Naylor

2-2 The Congress should direct the Secretary to apply a multiple procedure payment reduction to the professional component of diagnostic imaging services provided by the same practitioner in the same session.

Yes: Armstrong, Baicker, Behroozi, Berenson, Borman, Butler, Castellanos, Chernew, Dean, Hackbarth, Hansen, Kane, Kuhn, Miller, Stuart, Uccello

Absent: Naylor

2-3 The Congress should direct the Secretary to reduce the physician work component of imaging and other diagnostic tests that are ordered and performed by the same practitioner.

Yes: Armstrong, Baicker, Behroozi, Berenson, Borman, Butler, Castellanos, Chernew, Dean, Hackbarth, Hansen, Kane, Kuhn, Miller, Stuart, Uccello

Absent: Naylor

2-4 The Congress should direct the Secretary to establish a prior authorization program for practitioners who order substantially more advanced diagnostic imaging services than their peers.

Yes: Armstrong, Baicker, Behroozi, Berenson, Borman, Butler, Chernew, Dean, Hackbarth, Hansen, Kane, Kuhn, Miller, Stuart, Uccello

No: Castellanos

Absent: Naylor

Medicare's fee-for-service benefit design

No recommendations

Enhancing Medicare's technical assistance to and oversight of providers

4-1 The Congress should redesign the current Quality Improvement Organization program to allow the Secretary to provide funding for time-limited technical assistance directly to providers and communities. The Congress should require the Secretary to develop an accountability structure to ensure these funds are used appropriately.

Yes: Armstrong, Baicker, Behroozi, Berenson, Borman, Butler, Castellanos, Chernew, Dean, Hackbarth, Hansen, Kane, Kuhn, Miller, Stuart, Uccello

Absent: Naylor

4-2 The Congress should authorize the Secretary to define criteria to qualify technical assistance agents so that a variety of entities can compete to assist providers and to provide community-level quality improvement. The Congress should remove requirements that the agents be physician sponsored, serve a specific state, and have regulatory responsibilities.

Yes: Armstrong, Baicker, Behroozi, Berenson, Borman, Butler, Castellanos, Chernew, Dean, Hackbarth, Hansen, Kane, Kuhn, Miller, Stuart, Uccello

Absent: Naylor

4-3 The Secretary should make low-performing providers and community-level initiatives a high priority in allocating resources for technical assistance for quality improvement.

Yes: Armstrong, Baicker, Behroozi, Berenson, Borman, Butler, Castellanos, Chernew, Dean, Hackbarth, Hansen, Kane, Kuhn, Miller, Stuart, Uccello

Absent: Naylor

4-4 The Secretary should regularly update the conditions of participation so that the requirements incorporate and emphasize evidence-based methods of improving quality of care.

Yes: Armstrong, Baicker, Behroozi, Berenson, Borman, Butler, Castellanos, Chernew, Dean, Hackbarth, Hansen, Kane, Kuhn, Miller, Stuart, Uccello

Absent: Naylor

4-5 The Congress should require the Secretary to expand interventions that promote systemic remediation of quality problems for persistently low-performing providers.

Yes: Armstrong, Baicker, Behroozi, Berenson, Borman, Butler, Castellanos, Chernew, Dean, Hackbarth, Hansen, Kane, Kuhn, Miller, Stuart, Uccello

Absent: Naylor

4-6 The Secretary should establish a public recognition program for high-performing providers that participate in collaboratives or learning networks, or otherwise act as mentors, to improve the quality of lower performing providers.

Yes: Armstrong, Baicker, Behroozi, Berenson, Borman, Butler, Castellanos, Chernew, Dean, Hackbarth, Hansen, Kane, Kuhn, Miller, Stuart, Uccello

Absent: Naylor

Coordinating care for dual-eligible beneficiaries

No recommendations

Federally qualified health centers

No recommendations

Variation in private-sector payment rates

No recommendations

Appendix A: Review of CMS's preliminary estimate of the 2012 update for physician and other professional services

No recommendations

ACRONYMS

AARP	(formerly) American Association of Retired Persons
ACCF	American College of Cardiology Foundation
ACO	accountable care organization
ACR	American College of Radiology
AHIP	America's Health Insurance Plans
AMA	American Medical Association
BETOS	Berenson–Eggers Type of Service
CABG	coronary artery bypass graft
CBO	Congressional Budget Office
CBSA	core-based statistical area
CDRH	Center for Devices and Radiological Health
CEO	chief executive officer
CIA	corporate integrity agreement
CMP	civil monetary penalty
CMS	Centers for Medicare & Medicaid Services
CMS–HCC	CMS–hierarchical condition category
COP	condition of participation
COPD	chronic obstructive pulmonary disease
CPT	Current Procedural Terminology
CRS	Congressional Research Service
CT	computed tomography
DHHS	Department of Health and Human Services
DHS	designated health services
DME	durable medical equipment
DRG	diagnosis related group
D–SNP	dual-eligible special needs plan
DSS	decision support systems
DUA	data use agreement
E&M	evaluation and management
EBRI	Employee Benefit Research Institute
EHR	electronic health record
EPO	exclusive provider organization
ER	emergency room
FEHB	Federal Employees Health Benefits [Program]
FFS	fee-for-service
FIDE–SNP	fully integrated dual-eligible special needs plan
FQHC	federally qualified health center
GAO	Government Accountability Office
GDP	gross domestic product
GE	General Electric
GPCI	geographic practice cost index
HbA1c	hemoglobin A1c
HCC	hierarchical condition category

HCFA	Health Care Financing Administration
HCPCS	Healthcare Common Procedure Coding System
HEDIS®	Healthcare Effectiveness Data and Information Set
HHI	Herfindahl–Hirschman index
HIE	health insurance experiment
HMO	health maintenance organization
HPSA	health professional shortage area
HRET	Health Research and Educational Trust
HRSA	Health Resources and Services Administration
HSA	health savings account
HSC	Center for Studying Health System Change
ICSI	Institute for Clinical Systems Improvement
IDTF	independent diagnostic testing facility
IOAS	in-office ancillary services
IOM	Institute of Medicine
KCMU	Kaiser Commission on Medicaid and the Uninsured
KFF	Kaiser Family Foundation
LIS	low-income [drug] subsidy
MA	Medicare Advantage
MAC	Medicare administrative contractor
MedPAC	Medicare Payment Advisory Commission
MEI	Medicare Economic Index
MIP	minimally invasive procedure
MIPPA	Medicare Improvements for Patients and Providers Act of 2008
MPC	multispecialty points of comparison
MPPR	multiple procedure payment reduction
MRI	magnetic resonance imaging
MSA	metropolitan statistical area
MS–DRG	Medicare severity–diagnosis related group
MSP	Medicare Savings Program
MUA	medically underserved area
MUP	medically underserved population
NAIC	National Association of Insurance Commissioners
NAMCS	National Ambulatory Medical Care Survey
NCHS	National Center for Health Statistics
NCQA	National Committee for Quality Assurance
NHIN	Nursing Home in Need
NHPF	National Health Policy Forum
NHSC	National Health Service Corps
NPI	National Provider Identifier
NSQIP	National Surgical Quality Improvement Program
OEBB	Oregon Educators' Benefit Board
OHLC	Oregon Health Leadership Council
OMB	Office of Management and Budget
OOP	out-of-pocket
OPD	outpatient department

PACE	Program of All-Inclusive Care for the Elderly
PEBB	Public Employees' Benefit Board
PHSA	Public Health Service Act
PLI	professional liability insurance
POS	point-of-service (plan)
PPACA	Patient Protection and Affordable Care Act of 2010
PPIS	Physician Practice Information Survey
PPRC	Physician Payment Review Commission
PPO	preferred provider organization
PPS	prospective payment system
QI	qualified individual
QIO	Quality Improvement Organization [Medicare]
QMB	qualified Medicare beneficiary
RBM	radiology benefit manager
RHC	rural health clinic
RUC	Relative Value Scale Update Committee
RVU	relative value unit
SCAN	Senior Care Action Network
SCHIP	State Children's Health Insurance Program
SFF	Special Focus Facility [program]
SGR	sustainable growth rate
SIA	system improvement agreement
SLMB	specified low-income Medicare beneficiary
SNF	skilled nursing facility
SNP	special needs plan
SOW	statement of work
S–PAYGO	Statutory Pay-As-You-Go Act of 2010
SSA	Social Security Administration
UAF	update adjustment factor
U.S.	United States
VBID	value-based insurance design

More about MedPAC

Commission Members

Glenn M. Hackbarth, J.D., chairman
Bend, OR

Robert Berenson, M.D., F.A.C.P., vice chairman
Urban Institute
Washington, DC

Term Expires April 2011

Peter W. Butler, M.H.S.A.
Rush University
Chicago, IL

Michael Chernew, Ph.D.
Harvard Medical School
Boston, MA

Jennie Chin Hansen, R.N., M.S.N., F.A.A.N.
American Geriatrics Society

New York, NY

Nancy M. Kane, D.B.A.
Harvard School of Public Health
Boston, MA

George N. Miller, Jr., M.H.S.A.
First Diversity Healthcare Group
Springfield, OH

Term Expires April 2012

Mitra Behroozi, J.D.
1199SEIU Benefit and Pension Funds
New York, NY

Robert Berenson, M.D., F.A.C.P.

Karen R. Borman, M.D., F.A.C.S.
Abington Memorial Hospital
Abington, PA

Ronald D. Castellanos, M.D.
Southwest Florida Urologic Associates
Ft. Myers, FL

Glenn M. Hackbarth, J.D.

Bruce Stuart, Ph.D.
The Peter Lamy Center on Drug Therapy and Aging at the University of Maryland Baltimore
Baltimore, MD

Term Expires April 2013

Scott Armstrong, M.B.A., F.A.C.H.E
Group Health Cooperative
Seattle, WA

Katherine Baicker, Ph.D.
Harvard School of Public Health
Boston, MA

Thomas M. Dean, M.D.
Horizon Health Care, Inc.
Wessington Springs, SD

Herb Kuhn
Missouri Hospital Association
Jefferson City, MO

Mary Naylor, Ph.D., R.N., F.A.A.N.
University of Pennsylvania, School of Nursing
Philadelphia, PA

Cori Uccello, F.S.A., M.A.A.A., M.P.P.
American Academy of Actuaries
Washington, DC

COMMISSIONERS' BIOGRAPHIES

Commissioners' Biographies

Scott Armstrong, M.B.A., F.A.C.H.E., is the president and chief executive officer of Group Health Cooperative, a consumer-governed health system serving 650,000 enrollees through coordinated care plans for groups and individuals and for Medicare, Medicaid, and SCHIP beneficiaries. He has worked at Group Health since 1986, serving in positions ranging from assistant hospital administrator to chief operating officer; he became president and CEO in 2005. Before joining Group Health, Mr. Armstrong was the assistant vice president for hospital operations at Miami Valley Hospital in Dayton, Ohio. Mr. Armstrong is chair of the board of the Alliance of Community Health Plans and board member of America's Health Insurance Plans and the Seattle Chamber of Commerce. He is also immediate past-chair of the Board of the Pacific Science Center and a fellow of the American College of Healthcare Executives. He received his bachelor's degree from Hamilton College in New York and a master's degree in business with a concentration in hospital administration from the University of Wisconsin– Madison.

Katherine Baicker, Ph.D., is Professor of Health Economics in the Department of Health Policy and Management at the Harvard School of Public Health, where her research focuses on health insurance finance and the effect of reforms on the distribution and quality of care. Dr. Baicker has served on the faculty of the Department of Public Policy in the School of Public Affairs at the University of California, Los Angeles, the Economics Department at Dartmouth College, and the Center for the Evaluative Clinical Sciences and the Department of Community and Family Medicine at Dartmouth Medical School. From 2005 to 2007, Professor Baicker served as a Senate-confirmed member of the President's Council of Economic Advisers. She is a research associate at the National Bureau of Economic Research and is on the Congressional Budget Office's Panel of Health Advisers. She also served as a commissioner of the Robert Wood Johnson Foundation's Commission to Build a Healthier America and was a member of the Institute of Medicine's Committee on Health Insurance Status and its Consequences. She received her B.A. in economics from Yale University and her Ph.D. in economics from Harvard University.

Mitra Behroozi, J.D., is the executive director of the 1199SEIU Benefit and Pension Funds. Ms. Behroozi oversees eight major health and pension funds for health care workers. Collectively, these self-administered and self-insured health funds are among the largest in the nation. Under her leadership, the Funds have implemented a series of plan design and innovative cost containment programs, which are protecting benefits for members and retirees. Previously, Ms. Behroozi was a partner with Levy, Ratner & Behroozi, PC, representing New York City unions in collective bargaining negotiations and proceedings. While at the law firm, she also served as union counsel to Taft-Hartley benefit and pension funds. She serves on the board of the Brooklyn Health Information Exchange (BHIX), the steering committee of the Campaign for Better Care, and the New York State Health Care Reform Advisory Committee. Ms. Behroozi has a law degree from New York University and an undergraduate degree in sociology from Brown University.

Robert A. Berenson, M.D., F.A.C.P., is an Institute Fellow at the Urban Institute. From 1998 to 2000 he served as Director of the Center for Health Plans and Providers in the Centers for Medicare & Medicaid Services overseeing provider payment policy and managed care contracting. Dr. Berenson was founder and medical director of the National Capital Preferred Provider Organization from 1986 to 1996. He served as an Assistant Director of the White House Domestic Policy staff in the Carter Administration. Dr. Berenson has authored many articles in nationally recognized journals and several books, and he most recently co-authored *Medicare Payment Policy and the Shaping of U.S. Health Care*. Dr. Berenson is a board-certified internist who practiced for twenty years. He received his B.A. from Brandeis University and his M.D. from the Mount Sinai School of Medicine.

Karen R. Borman, M.D., F.A.C.S., is the Senior Associate Program Director of the General Surgery Residency Program and an attending physician at Abington Memorial Hospital, Abington, Pennsylvania. She holds clinical faculty appointments at Temple University and Drexel University Schools of Medicine. She is board certified in surgery and in surgical critical care. Her clinical focus is on endocrine surgery and her research focus is on surgical education. She is a member of General Surgery CPT/RUC Committee of the American College of Surgeons. She is a director and an executive committee member of the American Board of Surgery. She is the immediate past-president of the Association of

Program Directors in Surgery. She has worked with the Centers for Medicare & Medicaid Services on issues related to physician payment and service coverage. Dr. Borman was a member of the executive committee and vice-chair of the American Medical Association's Current Procedural Terminology Editorial Panel. She also served on the AMA Diagnostic and Therapeutic Technology Assessment Panel. Dr. Borman earned her medical degree from Tulane University. Her undergraduate degree in chemistry is from the Georgia Institute of Technology.

Peter W. Butler, M.H.S.A., is a nationally recognized health care executive with more than 30 years of experience in academic medical centers and health care systems. In addition to being president and chief operating officer of Rush University Medical Center in Chicago, Illinois, Mr. Butler is an associate professor and chairman of the Department of Health Systems Management at Rush University. Before joining Rush, he served in senior positions at The Methodist Hospital System in Houston and the Henry Ford Health System in Detroit. He currently serves as chairman of the Board of University HealthSystem Consortium. Mr. Butler holds an undergraduate degree in psychology from Amherst College and a master's degree in health services administration from the University of Michigan.

Ronald D. Castellanos, M.D., has practiced urology for more than 30 years. For the past four years Dr. Castellanos has been a member, and for the last year the chair, of the Practicing Physicians Advisory Council on issues related to physician payment. Dr. Castellanos was president of the Florida Urologic Society and has worked with several other organizations on health policy, including the American Urologic Association and the American Lithotripsy Society. Dr. Castellanos earned his medical degree from Hahnemann Medical College. His undergraduate degree is from Pennsylvania State University.

Michael Chernew, Ph.D., is a professor in the Department of Health Care Policy at Harvard Medical School. Dr. Chernew's research activities focus on several areas, most notably the causes and consequences of growth in health care expenditures, geographic variation in medical spending and use, and value-based insurance design (VBID). He is also a member of the Congressional Budget Office's Panel of Health Advisors and Commonwealth Foundation's Commission on a High Performance Health System. In 2000 and 2004, he served on technical advisory panels for the Centers for Medicare & Medicaid Services (CMS) that reviewed the assumptions used by the Medicare actuaries to assess the financial status of the Medicare trust funds. Dr. Chernew is a Faculty Research Fellow of the National Bureau of Economic Research. He co-edits the *American Journal of Managed Care* and is a Senior Associate Editor of *Health Services Research*. In 2010, Dr. Chernew was elected to the Institute of Medicine (IOM) of the National Academy of Sciences. Dr. Chernew earned his undergraduate degree from the University of Pennsylvania and a doctorate in economics from Stanford University.

Thomas M. Dean, M.D., is a board-certified family physician who has practiced in Wessington Springs, South Dakota, since 1978. He is chief of staff at Avera Weskota Memorial Medical Center. Dr. Dean is on the board of directors of Avera Health Plan, and is President-elect of the South Dakota Academy of Family Physicians. He was president of the National Rural Health Association, and he published articles and presented on health care in rural areas. Dr. Dean received the Dr. Robert Hayes Memorial Award for outstanding rural health provider, received the Pioneer Award from the South Dakota Perinatal Association, and was awarded a Bush Foundation Medical Fellowship to study leadership and health policy. Dr. Dean earned his medical degree from the University of Rochester School of Medicine and Dentistry. His undergraduate degree is from Carleton College.

Glenn M. Hackbarth, J.D., M.A., chairman of the Commission, lives in Bend, OR. He was chief executive officer and one of the founders of Harvard Vanguard Medical Associates, a multispecialty group practice in Boston that serves as a major teaching affiliate of Harvard Medical School. Mr. Hackbarth previously served as senior vice president of Harvard Community Health Plan and president of its Health Centers Division, as well as Washington counsel of Intermountain Health Care. He has held various positions at the U.S. Department of Health and Human Services, including deputy administrator of the Health Care Financing Administration (now known as CMS). He currently serves as chairman of the board of the Foundation of the American Board of Internal Medicine. He is also a board member at the Commonwealth Fund and a member of the Commonwealth Fund's Commission on a High Performance Health System. Mr. Hackbarth received his B.A. from Pennsylvania State University and his J.D. and M.A. from Duke University.

Jennie Chin Hansen, R.N., M.S.N., F.A.A.N., is currently CEO of the American Geriatrics Society, and previously she was president of AARP and a senior fellow at University of California's Center for the Health Professions. Ms. Hansen was executive director of On Lok Senior Health Services, the prototype for the Program of All-Inclusive Care for the Elderly (PACE), a capitated program for frail elders that integrates Medicare and Medicaid finances and care delivery and was signed into federal legislation as a provider type in the Balanced Budget Act of 1997. PACE now operates in over 30 states. She has practiced and taught nursing in both urban and rural settings. She currently serves as a board member of the National Academy of Social Insurance and the SCAN Foundation. Ms. Hansen consults with other foundations and programs on leadership development and independent reviews. She is a Fellow in the American Academy of Nursing. Ms. Hansen received her B.S. from Boston College and her M.S.N. from the University of California, San Francisco.

Nancy M. Kane, D.B.A., is professor of management in the Department of Health Policy and Management and associate dean of education at the Harvard School of Public Health. Dr. Kane directs the Masters in Healthcare Management Program, an executive leadership program for mid-career physicians leading health care organizations. She has taught health care accounting, payment systems, financial analysis, and competitive strategy. Her research interests include measuring hospital financial performance, quantifying community benefits and the value of tax exemption, the competitive structure and performance of hospital and insurance industries, and nonprofit hospital governance. Professor Kane consults with federal and state agencies involved in health system design, oversight, and payment. She is an outside director of Press Ganey, which provides patient satisfaction surveys and comparative performance reports to health care providers. Prior to obtaining her business training, she practiced as a hospital-based physical therapist. Dr. Kane earned her master's and doctoral degrees in business administration from Harvard Business School.

Herb B. Kuhn is the current president and CEO of the Missouri Hospital Association (MHA), the trade association serving the state's 176 hospitals and health systems. Prior to joining MHA, Mr. Kuhn served in multiple roles at the Centers for Medicare & Medicaid Services, including as Deputy Administrator from 2006 to 2009 and as Director of the Center for Medicare Management from 2004 to 2006. From 2000 to 2004, Mr. Kuhn served as corporate vice president for the Premier Hospital Alliance, serving 1,600 institutional members. From 1987 through 2000, Mr. Kuhn worked in federal relations with the American

Hospital Association. Mr. Kuhn received his bachelor of science in business from Emporia State University.

George N. Miller, Jr., M.H.S.A., has, over the last two decades, managed a series of hospitals, leading financial turnarounds at four of them. Since 2008, Mr. Miller has been the President and Chief Financial Officer of First Diversity Healthcare Group, a national healthcare consulting firm helping healthcare organizations improve their operations. He was the Regional President and CEO of Community Mercy Health Partners and senior vice president of Catholic Health Partners, a hospital chain in the Springfield, Ohio, area. Previously, he ran hospitals in Illinois, Texas, and Virginia and is the immediate past president of the National Rural Health Association. Mr. Miller has been an adjunct professor in health services administration at Central Michigan University since 1998. He has an undergraduate degree in business administration from Bowling Green State University and a master of science in health services administration from Central Michigan University.

Mary Naylor, Ph.D., R.N., F.A.A.N., is the Marian S. Ware Professor in Gerontology and Director of the NewCourtland Center for Transitions and Health at the University of Pennsylvania School of Nursing. Since 1989, Dr. Naylor has led an interdisciplinary program of research designed to improve the quality of care, decrease unnecessary hospitalizations, and reduce health care costs for vulnerable community-based elders. Dr. Naylor is also the National Program Director for the Robert Wood Johnson Foundation program, Interdisciplinary Nursing Quality Research Initiative, aimed at generating, disseminating, and translating research to understand how nurses contribute to quality patient care. She was elected to the National Academy of Sciences, Institute of Medicine in 2005. She also is a member of the RAND Health Board and the National Quality Forum Board of Directors and chairs the Board of the Long Term Quality Alliance. Dr. Naylor received her M.S.N. and Ph.D. from the University of Pennsylvania and her B.S. in Nursing from Villanova University.

Bruce Stuart, Ph.D., is a professor and executive director of the Peter Lamy Center on Drug Therapy and Aging at the University of Maryland in Baltimore. An experienced research investigator, Mr. Stuart has directed grants and contracts with various federal agencies, private foundations, state governments, and corporations. Mr. Stuart joined the faculty of the University of Maryland's School of Pharmacy in 1997 as the Parke-Davis endowed chair in geriatric pharmacy. Previously, he taught health economics, finance, and research methods at the University of Massachusetts and the Pennsylvania State University. Earlier, Mr. Stuart was director of the health research division in the Michigan Medicaid program. Mr. Stuart was designated a Maryland eminent scholar for his work in geriatric drug use. His current research focuses on the policy implications of the Medicare prescription drug benefit. Mr. Stuart received his economics training at Whitman College and Washington State University.

Cori E. Uccello, F.S.A., M.A.A.A., M.P.P., is Senior Health Fellow of the American Academy of Actuaries, serving as the actuarial profession's chief public policy liaison on health issues. Before joining the Academy in 2001, Ms. Uccello was a senior research associate at the Urban Institute where she focused on health insurance and retirement policy issues. She previously held the position of actuarial fellow at the John Hancock Life Insurance Company. Ms. Uccello has written extensively on the health insurance market and the Medicare program, including pieces on Medicare's financial condition and the Medicare prescription drug program. She serves as a member of the Technical Review Panel on the

Medicare Trustees' Report. Ms. Uccello is a fellow of the Society of Actuaries and a member of the American Academy of Actuaries. She received her B.S. from Boston College and her M.P.P. from Georgetown University.

Commission Staff

Mark E. Miller, Ph.D.
Executive director

James E. Mathews, Ph.D.
Deputy director

Analytic Staff

Christine Aguiar, M.P.H.
Adaeze Akamigbo, Ph.D.
Catherine Bloniarz, M.S.
Cristina Boccuti, M.P.P.
Carol Carter, Ph.D.
Evan Christman, M.P.Aff.
Zachary Gaumer, M.P.S.
David V. Glass, M.S.
Scott Harrison, Ph.D.
Kevin Hayes, Ph.D.
Dana Kelley, M.P.A.
Julie Lee, Ph.D.
Craig K. Lisk, M.S.
Anne Mutti, M.P.A.
Kim Neuman, M.A.
Nancy Ray, M.S.
John Richardson, M.P.P.
Joan Sokolovsky, Ph.D.
Jeffrey Stensland, Ph.D.
Shinobu Suzuki, M.A.
Ariel Winter, M.P.P.
Daniel Zabinski, Ph.D.

Research Assistants

Matlin Gilman
Kelly Miller

Assistant Director

Arielle Mir, M.P.A.
Communications and policy assistant
Kahlie Dufresne

Administrative Staff

Reda H. Broadnax, B.S.,
Executive officer
Wylene Carlyle
Paula Crowell
Tina Jennings, MTESL
Rachel Macias
Cynthia Wilson

Staff Consultants

Julian Pettengill
Carlos Zarabozo, A.B.

In: Medicare, Health Care Delivery and Payment Reform … ISBN: 978-1-62100-050-1
Editors: Leonore Gati and Travis Padilla

Chapter 2

MEDICARE PHYSICIAN PAYMENT UPDATES AND THE SUSTAINABLE GROWTH RATE (SGR) SYSTEM*

Jim Hahn

SUMMARY

Each year since 2002, the statutory method for determining the annual updates to the Medicare physician fee schedule, known as the sustainable growth rate (SGR) system, has resulted in a reduction in the reimbursement rates (or a "negative update"). With the exception of 2002, when a 4.8% decrease was applied, Congress has passed a series of bills to override the reductions. The SGR system was established because of the concern that the Medicare fee schedule itself would not adequately constrain overall increases in spending for physicians' services. While the fee schedule limits the amount that Medicare will pay for each service, there are no limits on the volume or mix of services. The SGR system was intended to serve as a restraint on aggregate spending. If expenditures over a period are less than the cumulative spending target for the period, the update is increased. However, if spending exceeds the cumulative spending target over a certain period, future updates are reduced to bring spending back in line with the target.

In the first few years of the SGR system, the actual expenditures did not exceed the targets and the updates to the physician fee schedule were close to the Medicare economic index (MEI, a price index of inputs required to produce physician services) in the first two years (2.3% in 1998 and 1999, compared with a MEI of 2.2% in 1998 and 2.3% in 1999). For the next two years, in 2000 and 2001, the actual physician fee schedule update was more than twice the MEI for those years (5.5% update vs. MEI of 2.4% in 2000, 5.0% update vs. MEI of 2.1% in 2001). However, beginning in 2002, the actual expenditure exceeded allowed targets and the discrepancy has grown with each year, resulting in a series of ever-larger cuts under the formula.

Some criticisms of the SGR system point to purported flaws in the technical details behind the formula, while others have just expressed displeasure with the resultant outcome. Although modifications have been proposed to replace the SGR system, no

---

* This is an edited, reformatted and augmented version of a Congressional Research Service publication, CRS Report for Congress R40907, from www.crs.gov, dated April 7, 2011.

proposal has garnered sufficient support and almost all proposals would be expensive to implement compared against the current baseline, which necessarily assumes that significant cuts to the fee schedule will occur.

Legislative activity in the 111th Congress included several bills that addressed the SGR system. The FY2010 Defense Appropriations Act delayed the implementation of the reductions for two months, from January 1 through February 28, 2010. The Statutory Pay-As-You-Go Act of 2010 (P.L. 111-139) exempts the amount it would cost to freeze payments for five years from PAYGO rules. H.R. 4691, which became law on March 2, 2010, delayed the payment cuts through March 31, 2010. On April 15, the Senate passed an amended version of H.R. 4851 that extended the payment cut delay through May 31, 2010. The House passed the amended bill, and the President signed P.L. 111-157 into law that day. On June 25, 2010, several weeks after the expiration of the extension created by the Continuing Extension Act, an amended version of H.R. 3962 was signed into law that increases fee schedule payments 2.2% retroactive to June 1 and continuing through November 30, 2010. On November 30, 2010, the President signed the Physician Payment and Therapy Relief Act of 2010 into law (P.L. 111-286), which extended the 2.2% increase for an additional month through December 31, 2010. The Medicare and Medicaid Extenders Act of 2010 (P.L. 111-309) preserves the payments at this level through December 31, 2011.

Introduction

Each year since 2002, the statutory method for determining the annual updates to the Medicare physician fee schedule, known as the sustainable growth rate (SGR) system, has resulted in a reduction in the reimbursement rates (or a "negative update").[1] With the exception of 2002, when a 4.8% decrease was applied, Congress has passed a series of bills to override the reductions. However, these actions have required almost yearly attention from the Congress. This report provides a background on the Medicare fee schedule, the SGR system and the annual updates, and discusses recent proposals to address this issue.

Background on the Medicare Fee Schedule Updates

Medicare payments for Part B services[2] provided by physicians and certain non-physician practitioners are made on the basis of a fee schedule, a list of over 7,000 tasks and services for which physicians bill Medicare.[3] From the inception of the program until 1992 and the introduction of the resource-based relative value scale (RB-RVS) fee schedule, Medicare paid physicians based on "usual, customary, and reasonable" charges.[4]

The Omnibus Budget Reconciliation Act (OBRA 89, P.L. 101-239) created the RB-RVS-based Medicare fee schedule, which went into effect January 1, 1992. Under the RB-RVS fee schedule, the Center for Medicare and Medicaid Services (CMS) assigns relative values that reflect physician work (i.e., time, skill, and intensity it takes to provide the service), practice expenses, and malpractice costs.[5] The adjusted relative values are then multiplied by a conversion factor to derive the actual payment amount in dollars. Medicare pays providers the lesser of the actual charge for the service or the allowed amount under the fee schedule.

Updates and the Sustainable Growth Rate (SGR) System

The SGR system was established because of the concern that the Medicare fee schedule itself would not adequately constrain overall increases in spending for physicians' services. While the fee schedule limits the amount that Medicare will pay for each service, there are no limits on the volume or mix of services. The SGR system was intended to serve as a restraint on aggregate spending. While the SGR targets are not limits on expenditures, they represent a "sustainable" trajectory for cumulative spending on Medicare physician services from April 1996 forward. The annual fee schedule update thus reflects the success or failure in meeting the goal. If expenditures over a period are less than the cumulative spending target for the period, the update is increased. However, if spending exceeds the cumulative spending target over a certain period, the update for a future year is reduced, with the goal to bring spending back in line with the target.

Expenditure targets have been a factor in the calculation of Medicare physician payment updates since the current fee schedule was first implemented in 1992. In the first year, one overall conversion factor was used to calculated the update. Then, two (surgical and non-surgical services) and eventually three conversion factors were used for different categories of services (surgical, primary care, and other nonsurgical services). However, under the Medicare Volume Performance Standard (MVPS) method, targets were set (and typically exceeded) each year; there was no cumulative goal and no significant consequence to exceeding the expenditure target. The current SGR method for calculating annual updates was created partly in response to the shortcomings of the prior method.

The Balanced Budget Act of 1997 (BBA97, P.L. 105-33) replaced the MVPS with the SGR, with the objective of creating a *sustainable* growth path for Part B expenditures. First, BBA97 added a cumulative spending criteria that resulted in actual consequences for failing to meet expenditure targets; beginning with April 1, 1996, as the starting point, actual program expenditures are compared to growth targets to determine annual updates. Second, BBA 97 introduced the rate of growth in the per capita amount of the gross domestic product (GDP) into the SGR calculation and also provided for the use of a single conversion factor instead of three.[6] By tying the expenditure targets to the growth in GDP per capita, this system attempted to hold Medicare physician expenditures to a level that would not consume an ever-increasing share of national income.

Since the conversion factor applies to all services, the update to the conversion factor is the key component for determining how reimbursements change from year to year.

Conversion Factor Calculation

The annual update to the conversion factor calculation is based on (1) the Medicare Economic Index (MEI), which measures the weighted average annual price changes in the inputs needed to produce physician services;[7] (2) the Update Adjustment Factor (UAF), used to equate actual and target (allowed) expenditures; and (3) allowed expenditures, equal to the actual expenditures updated by the SGR.

Sustainable Growth Rate (SGR)

The SGR sets both the cumulative and allowed expenditures under the UAF formula and consists of the following components:

- the estimated percentage changes in physicians fees,
- the estimated percentage changes in the number of fee-for-service beneficiaries,
- the estimated percentage growth in real gross domestic product (GDP) per capita (10-year moving average), and
- the estimated percentage changes resulting from changes in laws and regulations.

One important implication of the way this formula was constructed is that sustainable growth in Medicare physician expenditures should be equivalent to the rate of growth in the economy (i.e., the growth in GDP per capita). In addition, the formula implies that increases in managed care enrollment relative to fee-for-service Medicare would result in a slightly lower SGR.

Update Adjustment Factor

The update adjustment sets the conversion factor at a level so that projected spending for the year will meet allowed spending by the end of the year. The adjustment factor is the sum of (1) the prior year adjustment component; and (2) the cumulative adjustment component. Use of both the prior year adjustment component and the cumulative adjustment component allows any deviation between cumulative actual expenditures and cumulative allowed expenditures to be corrected over several years rather than a single year. As originally established, the adjustment factor can not be less than minus 7% or more than plus 3%. Thus, despite calculations which would have led to larger reductions, the UAF adjustment has been minus 7% for the last several years. The caps on the adjustment limit the annual reduction or increase. Thus, the gap between cumulative actual spending and cumulative allowed spending grows larger each year and is exacerbated whenever Congress overrides the reductions, since the targets are never modified under current law.

HISTORICAL UPDATES AND LEGISLATIVE OVERRIDES

Under the update formula, if actual expenditures do not exceed target expenditures, the update generally would be positive and payments would increase for all services under the fee schedule subject to the single conversion factor. In the first few years of the SGR system, the actual expenditures did not exceed the targets. (See Figure 1.) As a consequence, the updates to the physician fee schedule were close to the MEI in the first two years (2.3% in 1998 and 1999, compared with MEI of 2.2% in 1998 and 2.3% in 1999).[8] For the next two years, in 2000 and 2001, the actual physician fee schedule update was more than twice the MEI for those years (5.5% update vs. MEI of 2.4% in 2000, 5.0% update vs. MEI of 2.1% in 2001). However, beginning in 2002, the actual expenditure exceeded allowed targets and the discrepancy has grown with each year.

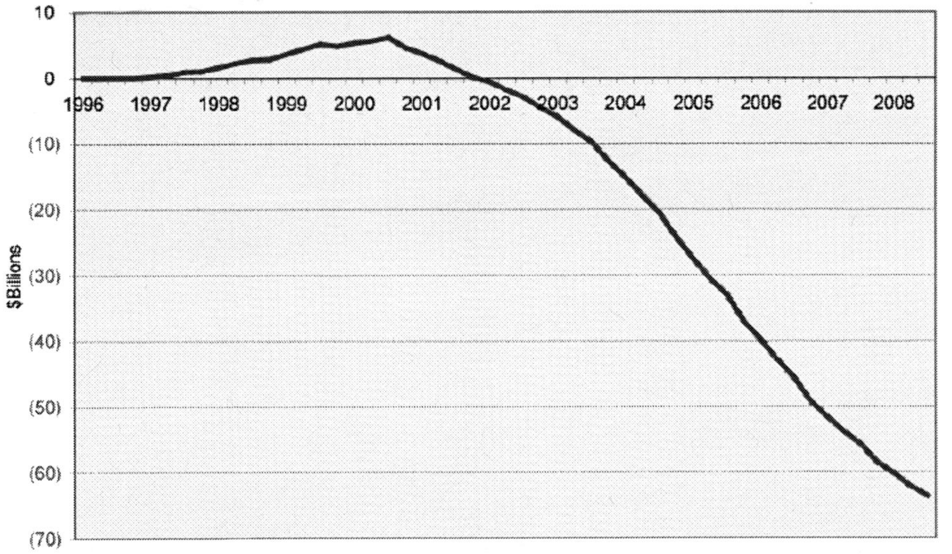

Source: CRS figure from CMS data contained in "Estimated Sustainable Growth Rate and Conversion Factor, for Medicare Payments to Physicians in 2010." Available at http://www.cms.hhs.gov/ SustainableGRatesConFact/ Downloads/sgr2010p.pdf

Notes: This graph shows the difference between *cumulative* allowed expenditures and actual expenditures for physician services. The 2008 figures for both allowed and actual expenditures are CMS estimates.

Figure 1. Difference Between Cumulative Allowed and Actual Expenditures for Physician Services Under the SGR System, 1996-2008.

As a consequence of exceeding the target, the formula dictated a reduction in the fee schedule in 2002. Although reductions have been called for every year since, Congress has passed legislation that has overridden the cuts each year since. (See Table 1.)

Table 1. Summary of Updates and Legislative Activity 2002-2009

Year	Formula update	Actual update	Legislation	Notes
2002	−4.8%	−4.8%		
2003	−4.4%	1.4%	Consolidated Appropriations Resolution of 2003 (CAR)	The update was 1.7% but was effective on March 1, 2003, so the average update for the year was 1.4%.
2004	−4.5%	1.5%	Medicare Modernization Act of 2003 (MMA, P.L. 108-173)	
2005	−3.3%	1.5%	MMA	

Table 1. (Continued)

Year	Formula update	Actual update	Legislation	Notes
2006	−4.4%	0.2%	Deficit Reduction Act of 2005 (DRA, P.L. 109-171)	Although the DRA froze the conversion factor update, refinements to the RVUs resulted in a 0.2% update for the year.
2007	−5.0%	0%	Tax Relief and Health Care Act of 2006 (TRHCA, P.L. 109-432)	
Jan–Jun 2008	−10.1%	0.5%	Medicare, Medicaid, and SCHIP Extension Act of 2007 (MMSEA, P.L. 110-173)	Physicians who voluntarily reported on certain quality measures during July 1, 2007-December 31, 2007, were eligible for a bonus payment of 1.5% in 2008 per TRHCA.
Jul–Dec 2008	−10.6% reduction from June 2008 level	0% (0.5% from 2007 level)	Medicare Improvement for Patients and Providers Act of 2008 (MIPPA, P.L. 110-275)	See above.
2009		1.1%	MIPPA	Physicians who voluntarily reported on certain quality measures during 2008 were eligible for a bonus payment of 1.5% in 2009 per MMSEA.
Jan 1–Feb 28, 2010	−21.3%	0%	Department of Defense Appropriations Act (P.L. 111-118)	
Mar 1–Mar 31, 2010		0%	Temporary Extension Act (P.L. 111-144)	Signed into law on Mar 2,
Apr 1–May 31, 2010		0%	Continuing Extension Act (P.L. 111-157)	Signed into law on Apr 15, 2010.
June 1–November 30, 2010		2.2%	Preservation of Access to Care for Medicare Beneficiaries and Pension Relief Act of 2010 (P.L. 111-192)	Signed into law on June 25, 2010. (increase was retroactive to June 1.)

Year	Formula update	Actual update	Legislation	Notes
December 1 – 31, 2010.		0% (2.2% from Jan – May, 2010 level)	Physician Payment and Therapy Relief Act of 2010 (P.L. 111-286P.L. 111-286)	
2011		0%	Medicare and Medicaid Extenders Act (P.L. 111-309)	

Source: 2010 Annual Report of the Boards of Trustees of the Federal Hospital Insurance And Federal Supplementary Medical Insurance Trust Funds, http://www.cms.hhs.gov/ReportsTrustFunds/downloads/tr2010.pdf, and CMS, Estimated Sustainable Growth Rate and Conversion Factor, for Medicare Payments to Physicians in 2011, http://www.cms.hhs.gov/SustainableGRatesConFact/Downloads/sgr2011f.pdf.

In addition to overriding the payment reductions, Congress has also included provisions in several of the laws to increase Medicare physician payments in other ways. For example, the Congress has altered the geographic adjustment factor for physician work, one component used in making regional adjustments to payments under the physician fee schedule. MMA set a floor on the work geographic adjustment index at 1.0 for 2004-2006, thereby slightly increasing the payment amounts in some areas. TRHCA extended this provision through 2007, MMSEA extended it through June 30, 2008, and MIPPA extends it through December 2009. In addition, beginning January 1, 2009, MIPPA also raised the work geographic adjustment in Alaska to 1.5.

Some of the bills also modified the cap on the conversion factor, which has led to the current situation where the consequence of not overriding the reduction would lead to cuts in excess of the 7% cap. TRHCA specified that the override of the reduction that would have been implemented under the statutory formula was to be treated as if it did not occur. Therefore, the starting base for the 2008 calculation was 5% below the actual 2007 conversion factor. MMSEA overrode the reduction for the first six months of 2008 and provided for a 0.5% increase for that period. However, the legislation again specified that the override of the statutory formula was to be treated as if it did not occur. MIPPA again specified that the override of the statutory formula was to be treated as if it did not occur. As a result, CMS estimates that a reduction of 21.2% will be necessary in 2010 unless Congress acts again to override the current situation.[9]

Analysis and Criticisms of SGR System

The experience in recent years has been that the volume and the intensity of physician services provided to Medicare beneficiaries are growing at more than double the rate allowed under the SGR system.[10] Payment reductions as called for under the update formula have required almost annual interventions by Congress and the SGR system has been criticized (and defended) amid calls for its repeal. While some of the criticisms of the SGR system point to purported flaws in the technical details behind the formula, others have just expressed general displeasure with the outcome.

General and Conceptual Concerns

One commonly asserted criticism is that the SGR system treats all services and physicians equally in the calculation of the annual payment update to the detriment of physicians who are "unduly" penalized. The expenditure target is a nationwide aggregate and the annual updates are applied uniformly; there is no direct link between individual behavior and the subsequent update. Thus, actions might be individually rational (physicians provide and bill for additional services and collect greater reimbursement) yet collectively detrimental (the annual update is reduced).[11] An individual physician who controls or reduces volume does not see a resulting increase in payments.

Others point out that there is no ability to distinguish between appropriate volume increases (for instance, due to changes in disease conditions that increase demand) and inappropriate volume increases (for instance, when tests or procedures are provided that are not necessary).

Technical Concerns

The inclusion of some items and services in the expenditure targets has also been called into question. Specifically, physicians have argued that Part B drug spending should be excluded from the calculation because physicians have no control or influence on the price of these drugs, although CMS is preparing to address this in its implementation of the 2010 proposed rule changes.[12]

Additionally, the targets may not be not adequately modified to reflect scientific and technological innovations or site-of-service shifts, and providers have often stated that actual increases in practice costs exceed those allowed under the system. The impact of legislative and regulatory changes also may not be fully reflected in the SGR calculation.

Per Capita Gross Domestic Product (GDP) and the Annual Update

The SGR is based on a number of factors, including the changes in the price of inputs required to produce physician services (such as rent, staff and supplies), the change in the number of Medicare fee-for-service beneficiaries, the effect of laws and regulations on part B expenditures, and the rate of growth in the per capita gross domestic product, calculated as a 10-year moving average.

The rate of growth in per capita GDP has a significant impact on the determination of the annual update. As can be seen in Figure 2, from 1997 through 2000, per capita GDP grew faster than part B expenditures, at more than 4% annually; part B expenditures were relatively stable from 1996 to 1998 and then started to increase in 1999 and 2000. However, economic growth slowed at the turn of the century (as can be seen in the flatter slope in the growth of per capita GDP during the period from 2000-2003), while part B expenditures grew at a faster rate from 2000 on. Because the comparison of actual to target expenditures includes a significant component that is cumulative (rather than just a comparison of the current period), the updates were positive during the early years of the SGR system but then became negative as a result of this imbalance. (See Figure 3.)

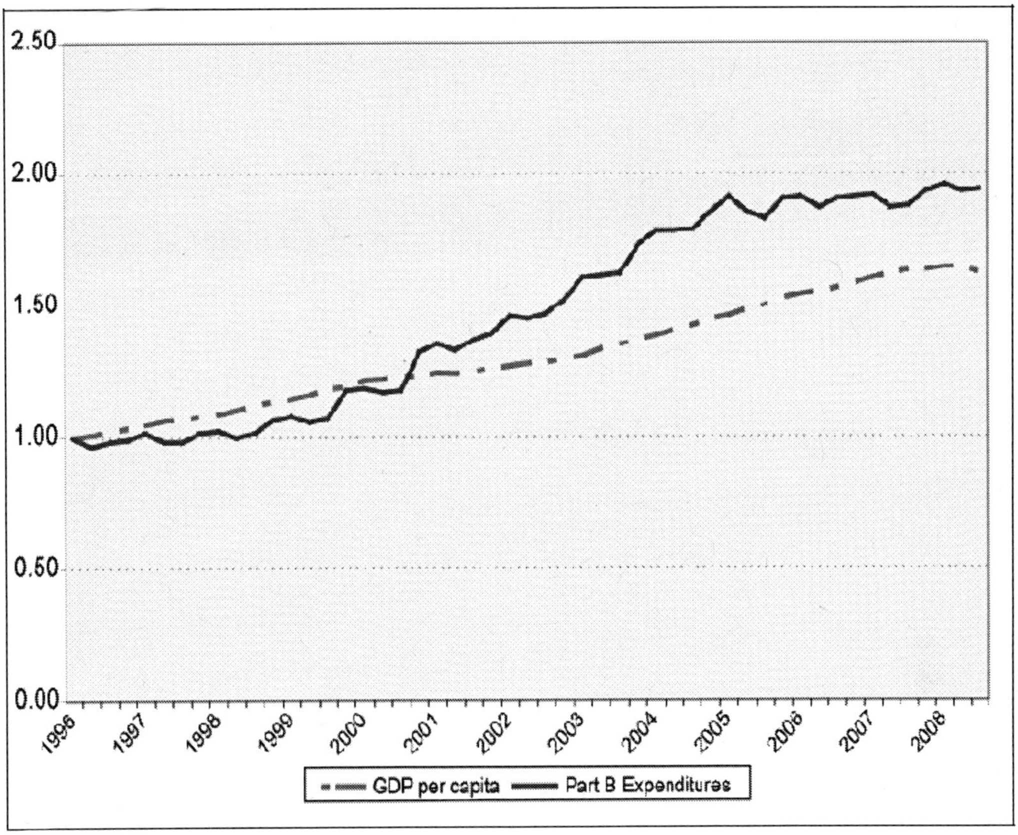

Source: CMS, "Estimated Sustainable Growth Rate and Conversion Factor for Medicare Payments to Physicians in 2010" http://www.cms.hhs.gov/SustainableGRatesConFact/Downloads/sgr2010p.pdf and U.S. Department of Commerce, Bureau of Economic Analysis, *National Income and Product Accounts*, Table 7.1. "Selected Per Capita Product and Income Series in Current and Chained Dollars" (http://www.bea.gov/national/nipaweb/ IndexP.htm#P).

Notes: The lines are based on quarterly data that are not seasonally adjusted. The uneven pattern of Medicare Part B expenditures reflects typical seasonal variation in health care use, which tends to increase with colder temperatures.

Figure 2. Relative Increase in Part B Expenditures vs. per Capita GDP, 1996-2008.

Thus, the relative health of the economy effectively masked the increases in total part B expenditures for the first few years under the SGR system, but as the economy slowed and expenditures continued to increase, the updates as determined under the SGR system have turned negative in order to bring projected actual expenditures back in line with target expenditures.

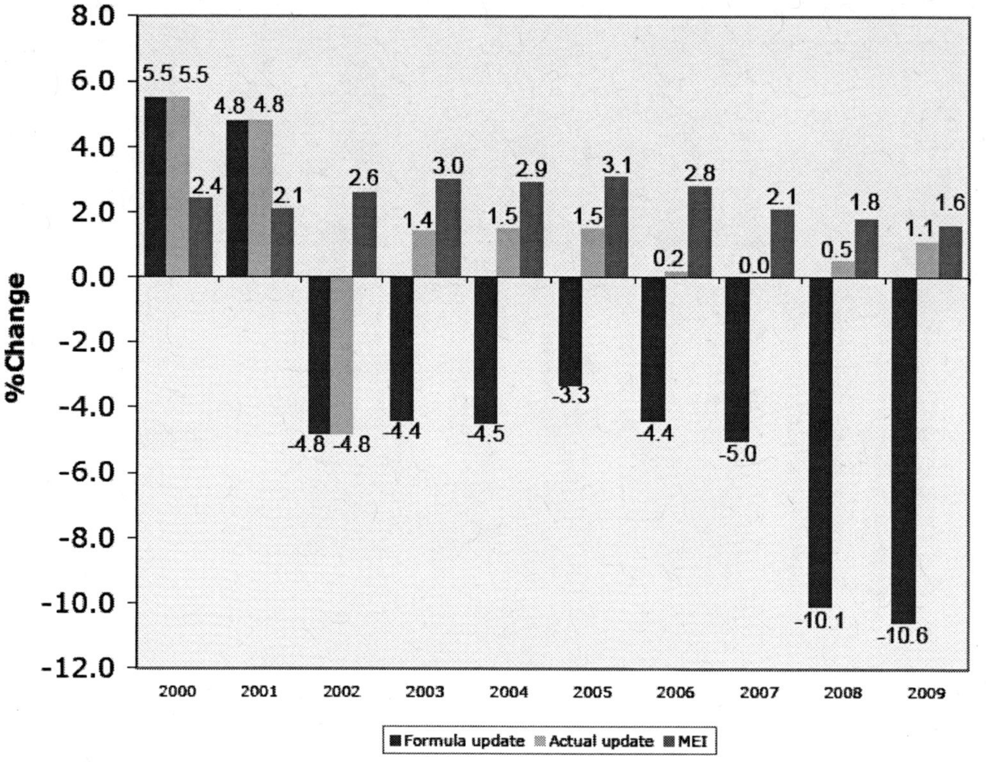

Source: 2009 Annual Report of the Boards of Trustees of the Federal Hospital Insurance And Federal Supplementary Medical Insurance Trust Funds, p. 22. http://www.cms.hhs.gov/ReportsTrustFunds/downloads/tr2009.pdf, and CMS, Estimated Sustainable Growth Rate and Conversion Factor, for Medicare Payments to Physicians in 2010, http://www.cms.hhs.gov/SustainableGRatesConFact/Downloads/sgr2010p.pdf.

Notes: MMSEA included a six-month override of the SGR update (−10.1%) for the first half of 2008. MIPPA provided for an 18-month override of the SGR update that would have taken effect on July 1, 2008 (−10.6%) that included the second half of 2008 and all of 2009. See also Table 1.

Figure 3. Formula Updates, Actual Updates, and the Medicare Economic Index, 2000-2009.

POTENTIAL MODIFICATIONS AND ALTERNATIVES

Although a number of modifications to the SGR system have been proposed, there is no consensus around a long-run alternative. In addition, any permanent change would likely be quite costly because the Congressional Budget Office (CBO) baseline must assume that a reduction in the conversion factor will occur for the next several years as required under current law. In addition to the impact on federal outlays, any change in the update formula will also have implications for beneficiaries; because Part B beneficiary premiums must cover 25% of Part B program costs, any overall increase in spending results in a proportional increase in premiums.[13]

Suggested modifications have ranged from modifying the current formula to replacing the formula and linking updates to payment adequacy and/or quality measures. While a change in the formula would require legislation, some observers have suggested that there are things CMS could do administratively to ease the impact of the current formula. Proponents argue that these changes, such as removing Part B drugs from the calculation, could somewhat moderate the negative updates that are predicted.

The Medicare Modernization Act of 2003 (MMA) required that GAO study "the appropriateness of the sustainable growth rate formula" and "the stability and predictability of such updates and rate and alternatives."[14] In a 2005 report, the GAO categorized options for alternatives around two themes: (1) proposals that end the use of spending targets and separate fee updates from explicit efforts to moderate spending growth; and (2) proposals that retain spending targets but modify the current SGR system to address perceived shortcomings.[15] The first approach emphasizes stable fee updates, while the second automatically adjusts fee updates if spending growth deviates from a predetermined target. GAO stated that "the choice between the two approaches may hinge on whether primary consideration should be given to stable fee increases or to the need for fiscal discipline within the Medicare program." The second approach would end targets as an explicit measure for moderating spending growth. Updates would be based on cost increases with the possibility of specifically addressing high volume service categories such as medical imaging.

The Deficit Reduction Act of 2005 (DRA) required MedPAC to submit a report to Congress on mechanisms that could be used to replace the SGR system, including "such recommendations on alternative mechanisms to replace the sustainable growth rate system as the Medicare Payment Advisory Commission determines appropriate."[16] In its March 2007 report, MedPAC described two possible paths: one path would eliminate the SGR and emphasize the development and adoption of approaches for improving incentives for physicians and other providers to furnish lower cost and higher quality care, while the second path would add a new system of expenditure targets in addition to these approaches.[17] However, MedPAC did not make any recommendations in favor of any single alternative to the SGR, citing "significant disagreement ... within the Commission about the utility of expenditure targets" and stating that the complexity of the issues made it difficult to recommend any option with confidence. MedPAC did stress in the report that "a major investment should be made in Medicare's capability to develop, implement, and refine payment systems to reward quality and efficient use of resources while improving payment equity." Examples cited by MedPAC include pay-for-performance programs for quality, improving payment accuracy, and bundling payments to reduce overutilization.

MedPAC has also recommended updating payments for physicians' services based on the estimated change in input prices for the coming year less an adjustment for savings attributable to increased productivity. Specifically, input prices would be measured using the MEI (without regard to the CMS adjustment for productivity increases). The recommended productivity adjustment would be that used across all provider services.[18]

In March 2008, CBO issued cost estimates for a variety of approaches for dealing with the physician payment issue.[19] Proposals with modest costs assumed a freeze for the second half of 2008 (as opposed to a 10.6% reduction), with reductions in future years to hold future rates at current law levels. More costly alternatives would freeze or increase payments over the 10-year budget window. For example, increasing payments by the MEI each year through 2018 would increase federal spending by $288.1 billion for the FY2008-FY2018 period. Coupling this with a provision excluding this change from beneficiary premium calculations ("premium hold-harmless") would increase federal spending by $364.3 billion over the same period.

Figure 3 shows that in each year since 2002, the MEI has been greater than the update as determined under the SGR formula and the actual update that physicians have received as a result of congressional intervention.

RECENT LEGISLATIVE ACTIVITY: NOT PASSED

H.R. 3162 (110th Congress)

Summary

The Children's Health and Medicare Protection Act of 2007 (CHAMP, H.R. 3162) was introduced on July 24, 2007. Section 301 of Title III would have modified the SGR system by eliminating the single conversion factor currently applied to all physician services and would have established separate target growth rates and conversion factors for each of six newly created service categories.[20] The six categories of physician services would have been the following: evaluation and management services for primary care and for preventive services; other evaluation and management services; imaging services and diagnostic tests; major procedures; anesthesia services; and minor procedures and other services.

The provision would have replaced the single SGR computation with separate target growth rates for each of the service categories created above. Beginning with 2008, the target growth rate for each service category would have been computed and applied separately using the same method for computing the sustainable growth rate under current law except that (1) "physicians' services" would refer to the physicians' services included in the appropriate service category, (2) the estimate of the annual average percentage growth in real gross domestic product per capita for the applicable period would have been increased by 0.03, and (3) a national coverage determination would be treated as a change in regulation and thus incorporated into the Secretary's estimate of the percentage change in expenditures for all physicians' services in the fiscal year (compared with the previous fiscal year) resulting from changes in law and regulations.

Beginning with 2008, the conversion factors would be computed and updated separately for each service category. In 2008, the conversion factors would have been based on the single 2007 conversion factor multiplied by the appropriate update for the category. In subsequent years, the conversion factor for each category would have been based on the conversion factor for the service category adjusted by the appropriate update. The provision would have established a floor for updates so that the conversion factors for each service category would be no less than 0.5% for 2008 and 2009.

The Committee on Ways and Means amended and reported the bill on August 1, 2007, and the House passed the bill the same day by a vote of 225-204.[21] The bill was never taken up by the Senate.

Brief Analysis

The approach to modifying the SGR as proposed in H.R. 3162 attempted to address, among other things, the criticism that the current update calculation penalized (or rewarded) all physicians identically regardless of the individual's or the specialty's contribution towards meeting or exceeding the aggregate expenditure target. Thus, even though imaging services have grown faster than other types of physician services (including evaluation and management services, tests, major procedures, and other procedures) the resulting impact on the annual update factor applies to all services across all specialties. However, others have countered that this delineation may not be appropriate and the CHAMP approach went too far. For example, some of the increase in imaging services may have allowed for the earlier detection of disease conditions such as cancer, which may have produced savings for other services and specialties (e.g., nuclear medicine and oncology services).

H.R. 3961 (111th Congress)

Summary

H.R. 3961, the Medicare Physician Payment Reform Act of 2009 was introduced on October 20, 2009. The proposals in this bill share some of the same approaches and objectives as Section 301 of the CHAMP Act, but also differ significantly in a few important ways. First, rather than creating six different categories of physician services, the bill would create two categories of service beginning in 2011, each with its own separate target growth rate and conversion factor update. The two categories of service would be (1) evaluation, management, and preventive services, and (2) all other services. Target expenditures for the E&M and preventive services category would be allowed to grow at the rate of growth of per capita GDP plus 2%, while the target expenditures for the all other category would be allowed to grow at the rate of growth of per capita GDP plus 1%. Second, the year 2009 would be established as the new baseline year for calculating expenditure targets (rather than 1996 under current law) for each of the two categories of services. Third, only physician services would be included in the calculation of actual and target growth expenditures; services provided incident to the physician visit (such as laboratory services), would not be included. Fourth, during the transition to the calculations required for the new method of calculating targets and updates, the 2010 update would be the percentage increase in the Medicare economic index (MEI). In its final rule for 2010 Medicare physician payments, CMS specified that the MEI will be 1.2%.[22]

On November 19, 2009, the House passed H.R. 3961 by a vote of 243-183.[23] However, on February 24, 2010, the Senate amended the bill by replacing everything after the enacting clause and renamed the bill "An Act to extend expiring provisions of the USA PATRIOT Improvement and Reauthorization Act of 2005 and Intelligence Reform and Terrorism Prevention Act of 2004 until February 28, 2011."[24]

Brief Analysis

The impact of this bill would be felt not only by physicians but also by other parts of the Medicare program, the Department of Defense TRICARE program, and beneficiaries under Medicare Part B. CBO estimates that enacting H.R. 3961 would increase direct spending by about $210 billion over the 2010-2019 period.[25] Not only would physician reimbursements under the Medicare physician fee schedule increase, but expenditures under the Medicare Advantage (MA) program would increase because per beneficiary spending for fee-for-service beneficiaries would increase as a result of the bill, raising the "benchmarks" that Medicare uses to determine the capitation payments for beneficiaries enrolled in Medicare Advantage plans. TRICARE expenditures would rise because its physician reimbursements are based on Medicare's physician fee schedule. Furthermore, since Medicare Part B beneficiary premiums are required to cover 25% of total Part B expenditures, the increases in physician reimbursements as a result of changing the update calculation would put pressure on future Part B premiums to rise.

The proposed modification might reduce the likelihood that future expenditures exceed the target expenditures, since the growth rates would be more generous under this bill than under current law, but this might lead to an increase in the total expenditures of the Medicare Part B program. While the SGR has been heavily criticized, a fundamental assumption was that tying physician expenditure growth to the rate of growth in GDP per capita could lead to a sustainable growth path. By allowing the two categories to grow at GDP per capita plus 1% or 2%, this bill would appear to allow for a situation where physician expenditures grow and consume a greater percentage of the national income.

A Senate Amendment in the Form of a Substitute to H.R. 3590 (111th Congress)

Summary

Section 3101 of the Senate health care reform bill, an amendment in the form of a substitute to H.R. 3590, would have overridden the reduction in the annual update to the conversion factor used in the determination of the Medicare fee schedule and provided an increase of 0.5% in 2010. The conversion factor for 2011 and for subsequent years would have been computed as if the increase in 2010 had never applied. CBO estimates that this provision would have cost $7.2 billion in 2010 and $4.1 billion in 2011, with no other budgetary impact in subsequent years. However, the manager's amendment contained several additions and modifications to the bill, including Section 10310, which repealed Section 3101. On December 24, 2009, the Senate passed the amended bill by a vote of 60-39.[26]

Brief Analysis

Much as other recent overrides have done, the original provision (Section 3101) would have increased Medicare physician payments slightly in the short term while increasing the cost of addressing this problem in the future because another year's worth of actual expenditures that exceed target expenditures would have contributed to the total amounts that would have to be recouped under the current SGR system. However, the manager's amendment struck this section, and thus the health care reform bill as passed by the Senate does not include any provisions that address the SGR situation.

RECENT LEGISLATIVE ACTIVITY: ENACTED INTO LAW

Department of Defense Appropriations Act, 2010 (P.L. 111-118)

Summary

On December 16, 2009, the House passed H.R. 3326, the FY2010 Defense Appropriations bill. One of the provisions in Section 1011 of the bill delayed the application of the update to the conversion factor until February 28, 2010.[27] Another provision in the same section reduced the amount of monies available in the Medicare Improvement Fund by $1.55 billion.[28] The Senate passed the bill on December 19, 2009,[29] and the bill was signed into law[30] that day.

Brief Analysis

The bill delayed the payment reductions from taking effect for two months while maintaining fee schedule reimbursements at 2009 levels.

Increasing the Statutory Limit on the Public Debt (P.L. 111-139)

Summary

Section 7 of Title I of this bill (H.J.Res. 45, the Statutory Pay-As-You-Go Act of 2010), which was signed into law on February 12, 2010 (P.L. 111-139), provides a limited exception to the "pay-as-you-go (PAYGO)" rules for addressing the Medicare physician payment situation as a result of the SGR system (as well as additional exceptions). The maximum amount of the exception is to be the difference between estimated net outlays if 2009 Medicare fee schedule payment rates were to be in effect for the next five years (i.e., a "freeze" through December 31, 2014) and what the payments would have been had fees reverted to levels as dictated under the SGR system. Furthermore, any future legislation that reforms or replaces the SGR system would be scored for PAYGO purposes only if the modification were to cost more than the cost of the five-year freeze at 2009 levels. If legislation changing the SGR system were to be enacted that costs less than the five-year freeze through 2014, any remaining amount in the adjustment could be used to offset costs after 2014 as a result of the change, but the total adjustment could not exceed the maximum adjustment amount.

Brief Analysis

The provision exempts the equivalent of a five-year freeze of Medicare reimbursement at 2009 levels from PAYGO—an amount the CBO estimates to be $88.5 billion.[31] Congress would still have to pass legislation that would override the cuts as directed by the SGR system.

Temporary Extension Act of 2010 (P.L. 111-144)

Summary

On February 25, 2010, the House passed H.R. 4691, the Temporary Extension Act of 2010, by voice vote. This bill extended a number of expiring programs, including unemployment insurance benefits, premium assistance for COBRA benefits, and the Medicare therapy caps, in addition to forestalling the Medicare physician payment cuts. Section 5 modified the Defense Appropriations Act, 2010, by delaying the payment reduction for another month, through March 31, 2010. The CBO score for this section is $ 1.04 billion in additional outlays.[32] Although a motion to pass the bill by unanimous consent failed in the

Senate that evening,[33] the bill eventually passed the Senate by a vote of 78-19[34] and was signed into law (P.L. 111-144) on March 2, 2010.

Brief Analysis

This bill delayed the payment reductions from taking effect until April 1, 2010, while maintaining fee schedule reimbursements at 2009 levels through March 31, 2010.

Continuing Extension Act of 2010 (P.L. 111-157)

Summary

On March 17, 2010, by voice vote, the House passed H.R. 4851, as amended (striking all after the enacting clause and inserting new text). The bill includes extensions for several programs, including certain unemployment insurance provisions, premium assistance for COBRA benefits, and the Medicare therapy caps exceptions process in addition to forestalling the SGR payment reductions for another month, until May 1, 2010. The Senate amended Section 4 of the bill by lengthening the Medicare physician payment cut extension until May 31, 2010, and both houses of Congress passed the bill on April 15, 2010. The President signed the bill into law (P.L. 111- 157) that day.

Brief Analysis

The bill delayed the physician payment reductions from taking effect until June 1, 2010, while maintaining fee schedule reimbursements at 2009 levels through May 31, 2010.

Preservation of Access to Care for Medicare Beneficiaries and Pension Relief Act (P.L. 111-192)

Summary

On June 18, 2010, more than two weeks after the May 31, 2010, expiration of the extension under the Continuing Extension Act of 2010,[35] the Senate passed an amended version of H.R. 3962 by voice vote that would avert the SGR-determined payment reduction and increase the conversion factor by 2.2% retroactive to June 1, 2010, and continuing through November 30, 2010. CBO scored this provision as adding $6.3 billion to direct spending over the 5- and 10-year budget window, with all spending occurring in fiscal years 2010 and 2011. The cost is offset (1) by imposing a three-day prohibition on hospital provision that would bar Medicare contractors from reopening or adjusting claims by hospitals during the three days preceding a patient's inpatient admission, and (2) from savings resulting from modifications that allow firms to spread out their pension fund obligations over a longer period, resulting in fewer tax-preferred contributions to pension plans and creating more taxable income for the firms.

The House passed the Senate-amended bill on June 24, 2010.[36] The President signed the bill into law (P.L. 111-192) the next day.

Brief Analysis

The act increases the Medicare physician fee schedule payments by 2.2% for six months. A substantial payment reduction (about 23%) would have been required beginning December 1, 2010, and an additional reduction (about 6%) would have been applied beginning January 1, 2011, in the absence of further congressional action.

The Physician Payment and Therapy Relief Act of 2010 (P.L. 111- 286)

Summary

On November 18, 2010, by unanimous consent, the Senate passed H.R. 5712,[37] which extended the 2.2% increase established by H.R. 3962 for an additional month through December 31, 2010. The House passed the amended bill on November 29, 2010, by voice vote, and the President signed the bill into law (P.L. 111-286) on November 30, 2010.

The cost of the override was to be offset by reductions to payments to providers for the second and for additional services when multiple therapy procedures are performed on the same patient on the same day.[38]

Brief Analysis

While this extension maintained provider payments at the existing level, additional legislative action was required to forestall the reduction to payments under the Medicare fee schedule that would have taken effect beginning January 1, 2011.

Medicare and Medicaid Extenders Act of 2010 (P.L. 111-309)

Summary

The Medicare and Medicaid Extenders Act of 2010 (H.R. 4994) extended many Medicare provisions that were due to expire on December 31, 2010, and made other changes to the Medicare and Medicaid program, including a one-year override of the payment reductions required under the SGR system. This act provided for a 0% update adjustment factor in 2011 compared to the (end-of-year) 2010 payments. These provisions were fully offset.[39]

Brief Analysis

Following the one-year override, the legislation states that "the conversion factor ... shall be computed ... for 2012 and subsequent years as if [the override] had never applied." CMS's March 2011 estimate of the 2012 SGR[40] is that a 29.5% reduction will be required beginning January 1, 2012, in the absence of further legislative action.[41] In its March 2011 report, MedPAC recommended a 1% update to the Medicare physician fee schedule for 2012.[42]

End Notes

[1] 2009 Annual Report of the Boards of Trustees of the Federal Hospital Insurance And Federal Supplementary Medical Insurance Trust Funds, p. 22. http://www.cms.hhs.gov/ReportsTrustFunds/downloads/tr2009.pdf.

[2] For detail on fee-for-service Medicare and other Medicare background information, see CRS Report R40425, *Medicare Primer*.

[3] Social Security Act, Sec. 1848. [42 U.S.C. 1395w–4]. In some instances, special rules apply to the calculation of Medicare fees for some services, including anesthesia, radiology, and nuclear medicine.

[4] Also called "customary, prevailing and reasonable charges," this method based physician payments on charges commonly used by physicians in a local community. The payment for a service was the lowest of (1) the physician's billed charge for the service, (2) the physician's customary charge for the service, or (3) the prevailing charge for that service in the community. For further discussion, see Physician Payment Review Commission, "Annual Report to Congress, 1997."

[5] The determination of the relative value units affects all payments under the fee schedule. Refinements in existing values and establishment of values for new services have been included in the annual fee schedule updates. This refinement and update process is based in part on recommendations made by the American Medical Association's Specialty Society Relative Value Update Committee (RUC) which receives input from approximately 100 specialty societies. The law requires a review every five years.

[6] The Balanced Budget Refinement Act of 1999 (BBRA 99, P.L. P.L. 106-113) incorporated an adjustment for the prior year into the UAF update calculation; it also moved from a fiscal year to a calendar year system.

[7] For more information on the components used to calculate the MEI and quarterly historical data, see http://www.cms.hhs.gov/MedicareProgramRatesStats/downloads/mktbskt-economic-index.pdf.

[8] See Table 6, Actual Past Medicare Economic Index Increases and Physician Updates for 1992–2009, and Estimated Values for 2010, in CMS publication, "Estimated Sustainable Growth Rate and Conversion Factor, for Medicare Payments to Physicians in 2010."

[9] CMS press release, "CMS Announces Payment, Policy Changes For Physicians Services To Medicare Beneficiaries In 2010," October 30, 2009. http://www.cms.hhs.gov/apps/media/press/release.asp?Counter=3539&intNumPerPage=10&checkDate=&checkKey=&srchType=1&numDays=3500&srchOpt=0&srchData=&keywordType=All&chkNewsType=1%2C+2%2C+3%2C+4%2C+5&intPage=&showAll=&pYear=&year=&desc=&cboOrder=date.

[10] U.S. Government Accountability Office (GAO), *Medicare Physician Payments: Trends in Utilization, Spending and Fees Prompt Consideration of Alternative Payment Approaches*, testimony of Bruce Steinwald before House Energy and Commerce Committee, July 25, 2006.

[11] Often referred to as the tragedy of the commons: while it may be individually rational for each herder to let livestock graze on the common field (to preserve his own), the collective consequence of many such individual decisions is that the common fields are overgrazed and all herders suffer from the degradation or depletion of the common good.

[12] See CMS Final Rule, *Medicare Program; Payment Policies Under the Physician Fee Schedule and Other Revisions to Part B for CY 2010*, to be published in the *Federal Register* on November 25, 2009.

[13] For details on Medicare Part B premiums see CRS Report R40082, *Medicare: Part B Premiums*, by Jim Hahn.

[14] P.L. 108-173, Section 953(a).

[15] U.S. Government Accountability Office, Medicare Physician Payments: Concerns about Spending Target System Prompt Interest in Considering Reforms, GAO-05-85, October 8, 2004.

[16] P.L. 109-171, Section 5104(c).

[17] Medicare Payment Advisory Commission, Assessing Alternatives to the Sustainable Growth Rate System, March 2007.

[18] MedPAC, Report to the Congress, Medicare Payment Policy, March 2008.

[19] http://www.cbo.gov/ftpdocs/90xx/doc9055/03-14-SGR_Options.pdf.

[20] This summary and discussion includes only the proposed modifications to the Medicare physician update methodology in the CHAMP Act relevant to the ongoing discussions regarding proposed solutions.

[21] http://clerk.house.gov/cgi-bin/vote.asp?year=2007&rollnumber=787.

[22] The MEI measures the weighted-average annual price change for various inputs needed to produce physicians' services. The calculation of the 2010 MEI is given in Table 33 of the final 2010 Medicare physician payment rule issued by CMS. http://www.federalregister.gov/OFRUpload/OFRData/2009-26502_PI.pdf.

[23] http://clerk.house.gov/evs/2009/roll909.xml.

[24] The Senate passed the amended bill by voice vote on February 24, 2010. The House passed the Senate-amended version on February 25, 2010, by 315-97 and the bill became P.L. 111-141.

[25] CBO Cost Estimate, "H.R. 3961—Medicare Physician Payment Reform Act of 2009," November 4, 2009, http://www.cbo.gov/ftpdocs/107xx/doc10704/hr3961.pdf.

[26] http://www.senate.gov/legislative/LIS/roll_call_lists/roll_call_vote_cfm.cfm?congress=111&session=1&vote=00396.

[27] For roll call details, see http://clerk.house.gov/cgi-bin/vote.asp?year=2009&rollnumber=985.

[28] Section 188 of MIPPA established the Medicare Improvement Fund (MIF), available to the Secretary to make improvements under the original fee-for-service program under Parts A and B for Medicare beneficiaries.

[29] For roll call details, see http://www.senate.gov/legislative/LIS/roll_call_lists/roll_call_vote_cfm.cfm?congress=111&session=1&vote=00384.

[30] P.L. 111-118.

[31] http://www.cbo.gov/budget/factsheets/2010b/SGR-menu.pdf.

[32] CBO score available at http://www.cq.com/displayfile.do?docid=3299370.

[33] See the Congressional Record at http://www.congress.gov/cgi-lis/query/D?r111:2:./temp/~r111LpI3Lx.

[34] http://www.senate.gov/legislative/LIS/roll_call_lists/roll_call_vote_cfm.cfm?congress=111&session=2&vote=00032.

[35] CMS issued two instructions to its contractors regarding claims affected by the expiration. The first, on May 27, instructed contractors to hold claims for services dated June 1 and later and paid under the Medicare physician fee schedule for the first 10 business days of June (i.e., through June 14, 2010). The second, on June 18, 2010, instructed contractors to begin lifting the hold and to begin processing June 1 and later Medicare physician fee schedule claims under the law's negative update requirement on a first-in/first-out basis.

[36] The vote was 417-1, with 14 members not voting. See http://clerk.house.gov/evs/2010/roll393.xml.

[37] Originally introduced in the House in July, 2010 as the Veterans', Seniors', and Children's Health Technical Corrections Act of 2010, the version passed by the Senate struck and substituted everything after the enacting clause. in addition to the physician payment modification, the bill also modified the discount applied to payments for therapy services when multiple procedures are performed on a beneficiary on the same day.

[38] See Congressional Budget Office, Estimate of the Statutory Pay-As-You-Go Effects for the Physician Payment and Therapy Relief Act of 2010, November 18, 2010, http://cbo.gov/ftpdocs/119xx/doc11969/PhysicianPaymentandTherapyReliefAct.pdf.

[39] The one-year override was offset by increasing the penalties collected from individuals who improperly receive health insurance tax credits (under health care reform), replacing the two fixed penalty amounts ($250 for individuals and $400 for families at or below 400% of the federal poverty level) with a scaled penalty related to income. The CBO score is available at http://cbo.gov/ftpdocs/120xx/doc12008/hr4994.pdf

[40] The Secretary is required (Section 1848(d)(1)(E) of the Social Security Act) to make public an estimate of the Sustainable Growth Rate (SGR) and the conversion factor applicable to Medicare payments for physicians' services for the following year by March 1 of each year.

[41] See CMS, "Estimated Sustainable Growth Rate and Conversion Factor, for Medicare Payments to Physicians in 2012" available at https://www.cms.gov/SustainableGRatesConFact/Downloads/sgr2012p.pdf.

[42] MedPAC, *Report to the Congress: Medicare Payment Policy*, MedPAC, Washington, DC, March 2011, http://www.medpac.gov/documents/mar11_entirereport.pdf.http://www.medpac.gov/documents/mar11_entirereport.pdf

INDEX

A

B

C

D

E

I

J

K

L

M

N

O

P

U

V

W

Y